RAYMOND WILLIAMS

RAYMOND WILLIAMS

Fred Inglis

London and New York

First published 1995
by Routledge
11 New Fetter Lane, London EC4P 4EE

Simultaneously published in the USA and Canada
by Routledge
29 West 35th Street, New York, NY 10001

First published in paperback 1998

Typeset in Times by
Florencetype Limited, Stoodleigh, Devon
Printed in Great Britain by
Biddles Ltd, Guildford
Bound in Great Britain by
Print Correct Ltd, Newquay, Cornwall

British Library Cataloguing in Publication Data
A catalogue record for this book is available from the British Library

Library of Congress Cataloguing in Publication Data
Inglis, Fred.
Raymond Williams / Fred Inglis.
p. cm.
Includes bibliographical references and index.
1. Williams, Raymond – Biography. 2. Authors. Welsh – 20th century –
Biography. 3. Critics – Great Britain – Biography. I. Title.
PR6073.I4329Z695 1995
828´.91409–dc20 95–19338
[B]

ISBN 0–415–18716–8

WHAT THEN?

His chosen comrades thought at school
He must grow a famous man;
He thought the same and lived by rule,
All his twenties crammed with toil;
'What then?' sang Plato's ghost. 'What then?'

Everything he wrote was read,
After certain years he won
Sufficient money for his need,
Friends that have been friends indeed;
'What then?' sang Plato's ghost. 'What then?'

All his happier dreams came true –
A small old house, wife, daughter, son,
Grounds where plum and cabbage grew,
Poets and Wits about him drew;
'What then?' sang Plato's ghost. 'What then?'

'The work is done,' grown old he thought,
'According to my boyish plan;
Let the fools rage, I swerved in naught,
Something to perfection brought';
But louder sang that ghost, 'What then?'

W.B. Yeats, 1937

To five friends and comrades:

Jim Hunter
Krishan Kumar
David McLellan
Michael Rae
Phillip Whitehead

CONTENTS

ACKNOWLEDGEMENTS

More than any other kind of writing in the human sciences, a biography is a collective piece of work. Indeed, as I suggest in the short discourse on biographical method which follows, a biography just is that collective creation; each of our lives is given value, shape and meaning by what others make of it, as much as by what we do ourselves.

This being so, acknowledgements need to be literal as well as courteous and conventional: I acknowledge the knowledge so many people have generously, unhesitatingly, precisely, given me. A great many of these people are included in the *dramatis personae* which opens the book.

Over a period of about twelve months I spoke at length with most of the names listed there, and by listening to and recording what they said, began to shape the story of the life of Raymond Williams as I tell it here. In many cases, when I wrote sending them the first draft of those pages in which they appeared as themselves, they wrote back, carefully amplifying and correcting what I had set down.

I believe I have written personally to nearly all of them to thank them for this kindly and unselfinterested help; to any that I haven't, I hereby apologise; but in any case I now offer them all my gratitude, and earnestly hope that they will be able to take a pride in what I have made out of our collective labours.

In a few cases, the contact has only been by letters, but I am, naturally, no less grateful for those, and in particular for the extensive correspondence initiated by John McIlroy of the University of Manchester with large numbers of the men and women who worked with Raymond Williams in Adult Education between 1945 and 1961. With immediate and entirely open-handed generosity, John McIlroy turned over this treasure trove for my use; since he knew so very much more than I did about the whole history as well as the actors in its drama, the pages I have written on those years are every bit as much his work as mine. While I cannot repay his kindness, I can salute in him a rare magnanimity and a commitment to scholarly and political comradeship of a quite exceptional kind.

Whenever I used his correspondence I wrote subsequently to the authors of the letters concerned and obtained, where I could, their permission to quote them, often receiving in return useful elaborations of their original memoir. In some sad cases, I was sent by surviving relatives news of the individual's recent death, at the same time as the heirs gave their permission for me to use the quotations, so I thank these people also.

Where so much has been given to me so handsomely, particular expressions of gratitude cannot be offered to everyone who helped. But some individuals did more than any honest biographer could hope for; one or two of these have become cherished friends as a direct consequence of the work. It is right to pick them out.

Merryn Williams has been my constant help and delicate-handed critic. Even where the matter of the biography touched her nearly, she always gave me a prompt and candid response, let alone effecting a dozen introductions and tolerating a dozen more phone calls, without which I could not have proceeded.

Stephen Heath, staunch friend of Raymond and Joy Williams, who knew, of course, both of them far better than I did, was unfailingly ready with reminiscences from his extraordinary memory, scrupulous in his handling of confidences, quick, searching and specific in the extended criticism he offered of the pages with which I burdened him.

Graham Martin, a new friend, and Dennis Butts, an old one, were alike in the encouragement as well as the careful corrections they made in what they saw of work in progress. Mari Shullaw proved the best of editors; astute, cordial, hard, and right. Michael Walzer urged me to start the thing when I first conceived it, Charles Swann was a delight to talk to, Bernard Sharratt another, Terry Eagleton approved the use of his hilarious parody, Perry Anderson passed on his grave, impressive correspondence, Michael Orrom and Mike Dibb their movies.

This must stop. But not until I have thanked another old friend – one, I'm daunted to realise, of almost forty years' standing – Jim Hunter, a proper novelist rather than somebody hiding a novel in a biography, as well as a better writer than I'll ever be. He read the manuscript, as he has read several predecessors, and gave, as before, exactly the right mixture of friendly criticism and critical friendship.

I suppose that, as so often, friendship is really the theme of my book; in token of which I have dedicated it to those staunch friends.

I would also like to praise Dai Smith for his forbearance while I wrote. He too is writing a biography of Raymond Williams, now delayed by the weight of his duties at the BBC in Wales. When it comes, it will surely show a much firmer grasp on historical method as well as a clearer view of Welsh purpose than my own cheerful encomium.

It is timely to thank the University of Warwick for the dispatch with which it granted me two terms of study leave in these difficult days in order to get on with the job; by the same token, I pay my tribute to the British Academy for its substantial bursary without which I simply could not have afforded the heavy travelling schedule which I set myself. Then, when I began writing, I was granted, by the good offices of Steven Lukes, access for a while to the quiet and beauty of the European University Institute in Fiesole in which to do so.

Lastly, I would very much like to acknowledge the generous help of Robin Gable with the photographs.

Formal acknowledgement is due to Faber and Faber for the lines quoted from Philip Larkin's *Collected Poems* and *The Collected Poems and Plays of T.S. Eliot*, for the poem from W.B. Yeats's *Collected Poems,* and to Oxford University Press for the verses from Henry Reed's *Collected Poems*.

A NOTE ON BIOGRAPHY

The present surge in biography writing signifies something cheering as well as fundamental in cultural life. With the going-down of some of the big stories of everyday history (meta-narratives in the jargon) people look for another way of telling the time of day. The cold war, which allotted everybody a part in the dramatic tableau of Us against Them, Left against Right, Good against Bad (whichever side you were on), suddenly dropped the curtain upon itself and the epoch. The old story of progress and emancipation has taken a heavy battering from the return of bloodthirsty nationalism and the unexpected and hate-filled refusal of modernity by religious fundamentalists. The revolting sanctimony of liberal capitalism at the cold war victory quickly disappeared behind the statistical mountains of unemployment, crime and poverty figures. If you seek a larger understanding of the day, it seems best to say that political theory begins at home.

This being so, biography – that happy conjunction of literary form and historical factuality – seems as ready a way as can be found of catching and holding a small arc on the long revolution of fortune's wheel. If the life itself signifies something, and if its story is well told, then the tale will comprehend more than a life-story; it will enclose history herself and make her intelligible. I like to think that this is one heartening reason for the brimming stacks of biography visible in the big bookshops. When we wish to understand a moment or an era, we take a man or woman from the day and tell their story as fully, as sympathetically as we can, balancing imagination against the compelling absoluteness of establishable facts as best we may in order to tell the truth.

Facts and truth have, however, undergone serious erosion in the heavy weather of a post-modern, relativising world. Oral history has its day, but one's presence-at-what-really-happened and one's unfaithful servant, memory, have come to be taken on very partial trust when bearing their witness to what really happened. Even archives, documents from the day it all happened, official records, have had their objectivity interrogated and their claims to matter-of-factness subjected to forensic challenge.

In such circumstances, a biography is hard put to it even to be a believable chronicle of one damn thing after another. Insofar as we trust the teller, most people believe the dates in the tale, and what may be rather straightforwardly framed as its key events. Raymond Williams, for instance, was, like Solomon Grundy, born on his birthday, went to first one school and then another in two Septembers, to Cambridge in an October, to war one June, published thirty-odd books, became a husband, father, grandparent, and died on dates fixed by time and chance, for the benefit of biographers.

Those same events in their turn partook of larger events, events so large they become tropes rather than truths, concepts scooping up lives and deaths by way of making them stand still. The rise of Fascism, the victory of Labour, the cold war, are each of them ways of inventing truisms rather than fixing the facts. But they have to be there if the single life and general times are to connect with and illuminate each other in a common circuitry.

Such phrases effect the literary turn as, I hope, do other, newer-minted and more vivid figures. A biography, like any other essay in narrative history, ought to be a good read. As in history on one side, however, and in the history of a different form of news from the past, the novel on the other, the point of view of the narrator has been broken up into countless refractions by all those doubts about truth, factuality and objectivity. The twin subjects of narrator and hero have been displaced from the transparent relationship they once enjoyed, according to which narrators looked down on heroes and heroines as they went about their lives, and reported what there was to see, even if it all took place generations ago. The authority of both agents has been deprived of such dependable centres of action and observation. Postmodernism, another name for relativism and all its exhilarating and misleading licence, teaches that individual people, whatever passionate identity of self they celebrate, are a tissue of many selves with no single centre, each constructed out of the innumerable roles and signs of being which the times provide.

Now this biography is not so much in thrall to these doctrines that it renounces the concept of character. 'Character' has been much bullied by fashionable criticism, and mocked by the *bien-pensants* for its alleged essentialism, nineteenth-century fixity, and other offences against modishness. For myself, I don't believe that we can even move provisionally through the world without the concept of character. It is certain that judgements as to the consistency, dependability and staunchness of others are the grounds of that trust without which there would be no society at all.

In any case, Raymond Williams most decidedly had a character, and this book is one version of its formation. That version includes my effort to explain both its integrity and its contradictions, the unity he made of it, and the divisions and darknesses he so much kept to himself. I don't think it's ever much help, let alone truthful, to accept the common-sense picture of the self as divided between an outer, sociable being and an inner, true self. People are as they appear and what they do. Our knowledge of them depends on being able to attend to this evidence, to see it straight, to feel it sensitively.

My knowledge of Raymond Williams came from twenty years of comradely but occasional collaboration; I was never a close friend. Accordingly, I have solved the problem of my authorial authority by telling the story of Williams's life as I knew it at first hand, and as I have found it out, from as close a position and in as personal an idiom as I can write. To bring this off, the biographer must be always present and audible in the biography. This prevents any implication of old-style authorial omniscience. It also brings the valuation of Williams's life, and the honour in which this author holds him, hard up against the effort of so many like-minded people to live Williams's kind of life, to fight his fights and think further about his preoccupations. The book then becomes an attempt at a novel of manners, with a great hero, about 'the condition of England', Wales, Scotland – to remain on one island – and what the intellectual Left and their allies did about it for the long era of war and cold war.

This being so, the author must tune into his story many more voices than his own ('heteroglossia', as you might say). The main narration is no doubt my responsibility. But if the social construction of reality is really how things happen and reality is made, then included among the things that get made are our very selves. We then must understand that what others make of us, makes us. This is a truth brought out by television biography. The standard form of these is a narration with old footage, punctuated by live personal reminiscence. So this biography is regularly interspersed by the direct, living reminiscences of Williams spoken or written by a large number of people who knew and worked with him, scattered over time from Pandy village school in 1926 to his all-too-brief retirement in Saffron Walden until he died in 1988.

Those voices contradict each other, as one would expect. They embody the vivid stuff of the lives of those who speak them, as well as Williams's life. What they (and I) say constitutes his life, as much as he made it for himself and whether or not they (and I) are right or wrong (this is 'structuration theory'). The play of our voices marks the meaning in history and the space in social structure assigned to the life of Raymond Williams.

DRAMATIS PERSONAE

The following is a list of all the speaking parts in this biography, giving the present appointments of the people listed, and the capacity in which they knew Raymond Williams best. Their words as quoted in the text were either spoken directly to me during my research or written in personal letters and cited as such in the notes, except in one or two instances referenced accordingly. In every case, whether direct speech or written recollection, the individual's permission to be quoted has been sought by me; in a handful of cases the persons did not or could not reply, so if I have in any way misrepresented them, I hereby apologise.

The date of every conversation is given in brackets.

Perry Anderson   Professor of History, UCLA, formerly editor *New Left Review*, friend and fellow-socialist (6 January 1994).

Anthony Barnett   General Secretary *Charter 88*, formerly editorial board *New Left Review*, friend and fellow-socialist (9 November 1993 and 1 December 1993).

Eric Bellchambers   (deceased): formerly District Secretary of the WEA, South East England.

Bernard Bergonzi   retired, formerly Professor of English Literature, the University of Warwick, fellow-academic.

Robin Blackburn   editor *New Left Review*, managing director Verso Books, friend and fellow-socialist (10 November 1993).

Marilyn Butler   Warden, Exeter College Oxford, formerly King Edward VII Professor of English Literature,

University of Cambridge, colleague (11 January 1994).

Dennis Butts   Lecturer, in English, University of Reading, formerly tutor in the Oxford Delegacy of Extra-Mural Studies (several conversations, particularly 18 November 1993).

Peter Carrington   Chair of Christie's, formerly Secretary-General of NATO, brother-officer (February 1991).

Colin Crouch   Professor of Politics, European University Institute, Florence, editor and fellow-academic (23 September 1994).

James Curran   Professor of Mass Communications, Goldsmiths' College, journalist, fellow-socialist (10 November 1993).

Fred Dalling   retired, brother-in-law (1 November 1993).

Mike Dibb   television producer and film-maker, TV collaborator (25 January 1994).

John Dunn   Professor of Politics, the University of Cambridge, colleague (25 November 1993).

Terry Eagleton   Warton Professor of English Literature, University of Oxford, student, friend, fellow-socialist (11 January 1994).

Dafydd Elis-Thomas   Party leader Plaid Cymru, member of the House of Lords, political ally (6 December 1993).

Martyn Everett   assistant librarian, Saffron Walden (22 June 1994).

Jim Fyrth   retired, formerly tutor in the Oxford Delegacy of Extra-Mural Studies.

Nicholas Garnham   Professor of Media Studies, formerly BBC producer, television and editorial collaborator (many conversations over the period 1990 to 1994).

Anthony Giddens	Professor of Sociology, the University of Cambridge, colleague (24 November 1993).
Maurice Glasman	Research Fellow, European University Institute, Florence, student (28 April 1994).
Heather Glen	Lecturer in English Literature, University of Cambridge (25 November 1993).
Andor Gomme	Professor of English Literature, University of Keele, extra-mural tutor (31 January 1994)
Peter Griffith	Open University Lecturer, producer of OU television programmes (15 November 1993).
Joe Griffiths	musician, neighbour in Pandy (14 October 1993).
Stuart Hall	Professor of Sociology, the Open University, friend, co-editor, fellow-socialist (11 February 1994).
David Hamilton Eddy	writer, student (8 November 1993).
David Hare	playwright, student (13 October 1994).
Stephen Heath	Fellow and Lecturer in English, Jesus College, Cambridge, friend, student and colleague (several conversations, particularly 25 November 1993 and 20 January 1994).
Douglas Hewitt	Fellow of Pembroke College, Oxford, tutor in the Oxford Delegacy of Extra-Mural Studies, colleague (13 December 1993).
Violet Higgs	(née James): retired, formerly Lecturer at Usk College, fellow-pupil at Pandy village school and neighbour (10 January 1994).
Eric Hobsbawm	retired, formerly Professor of History, University of London, fellow-socialist and contemporary at Cambridge (4 February 1994).
Thomas Hodgkin	(deceased): formerly Secretary to the University of Oxford Delegacy of Extra-Mural Studies, boss.

Richard Hoggart retired, formerly Assistant Director-General UNESCO, intellectual associate (23 April 1995)

David Holbrook retired, Fellow in English, Downing College, Cambridge, formerly tutor in the WEA, friend and colleague (23 November 1993).

Irving Howe deceased: editor *Dissent*, New York, fellow-radical (24 July 1992).

Lisa Jardine Professor of English Literature, University of London, formerly Fellow of Jesus College, Cambridge, colleague (14 February 1994).

Clarissa Kaldor (deceased): formerly vice-Chair, Cambridge constituency Labour Party (22 June 1994).

Frank Kermode retired, formerly King Edward VII Professor of English Literature, University of Cambridge, colleague (22 June 1994).

Lionel Knights retired, formerly King Edward VII Professor of English Literature, University of Cambridge, colleague (15 April 1993).

F.R. Leavis (deceased): formerly Reader in English Literature, the University of Cambridge, colleague.

Annette Lees retired, living in Abergavenny, lifelong friend of Joy Williams and her fellow-student at LSE (14 October 1993).

John Levitt tutor at the Oxford Delegacy of Extra-Mural Studies, colleague.

Colin MacCabe Director of Research, British Film Institute, formerly Assistant Lecturer in English, University of Cambridge, colleague (13 October 1994).

John McIlroy Reader in Industrial Relations, University of Manchester, historian of Adult Education (1 February 1994).

Graham Martin retired, formerly Professor of English, the Open University, friend and collaborator (10 November 1993).

John Maynard Smith Emeritus Professor of Biology, University of Sussex, contemporary socialist at Cambridge (May 1995).

Ruth Middlemiss (deceased): WEA student.

Francis Mulhern Senior Lecturer in English Literature, Middlesex University, formerly editor at Verso Books, editor and collaborator (1 December 1993).

Michael Orrom film-maker, contemporary and friend at Cambridge, collaborator on a book and film (8 December 1994).

Patrick Parrinder Professor of English Literature, University of Reading, student and colleague (18 November 1993).

John Rex retired, formerly Professor of Sociology, University of Warwick, co-editor and fellow-socialist (14 July 1994).

Christopher Ricks Professor of English Literature, Boston University, formerly King Edward VII Professor of English Literature, University of Cambridge, colleague (22 July 1993).

Bob Rowthorn Professor of Economics, the University of Cambridge, collaborator and fellow-socialist (22 June 1994).

Edward Said Professor of Comparative Literature, Columbia University, New York, fellow-theorist and -socialist (29 July 1992).

Raphael Samuel historian and tutor, Ruskin College, Oxford, formerly editor *New Left Review*, friend and fellow-socialist (15 December 1993).

Cecil Scrimgeour (deceased): formerly District Secretary of the WEA in North Staffordshire, and Oxford Delegacy tutor in English, colleague.

Bernard Sharratt Reader in Cultural Studies, the University of Kent, friend, student and fellow-socialist (24 January 1994).

Morag Shiach Reader in English Literature, University of London, student (19 January 1994).

Quentin Skinner Professor of Political Science, University of Cambridge, colleague (too many conversations to list).

Dai Smith BBC Wales programme-director, formerly Professor of History, University of Wales, fellow-socialist and biographer (28 April 1995).

Gladys Smith retired, formerly postwoman at Pandy (3 November 1993).

Gareth Stedman-Jones Reader in History, the University of Cambridge, formerly editorial board *New Left Review*, collaborator and fellow-socialist (18 January 1994).

Phil Stevens Head of Community Education, Estover Community College, Plymouth, doctoral subject (28 January 1994).

Joan Stratford-Leach retired, formerly district nurse and neighbour in Pandy (3 November 1993).

Charles Swann Senior Lecturer in American Literature, University of Keele, student and collaborator (15 November 1993).

Julia Swindells Lecturer in English, Homerton College, Cambridge, student and friend (26 November 1993 and 20 January 1994).

Derek Tatton Principal, Wedgwood College, student (15 November 1993).

Graham Taylor	(deceased): formerly tutor in the Oxford Delegacy of Extra-Mural Studies.
Dorothy Thompson	historian, fellow-socialist (several conversations, particularly one on 13 June 1994).
Edward Thompson	(deceased): historian, fellow-socialist, co-editor (several conversations over the years 1987 to 1993).
Boyd Tonkin	Literary editor *New Statesman and Society*, student (23 February 1995).
Albert Trevett	retired, formerly railwayman at Pandy and Llanvihangel Crucorney (17 November 1993).
Violet Trevett	retired, fellow-pupil at Pandy village school (17 November 1993).
Michael Walzer	Professor of Politics, Institute for Advanced Study, Princeton, fellow-socialist (July 1992).
Bill Webb	formerly literary editor of the *Guardian* for thirty years, editor and commissioner of reviews (6 December 1993).
Harold West	retired, formerly stationmaster at Pandy station (17 November 1993).
Ederyn Williams	eldest son (26 February 1994).
Edward Williams	composer, friend and student contemporary at university (21 April 1995).
Madawc Williams	second son (29 March 1995).
Merryn Williams	only daughter (many conversations and letters, particularly 16 November 1993 and 23 February 1994).
Jack Woolford	tutor at the Oxford Delegacy of Extra-Mural Studies, colleague.

1

PROLOGUE
In Memoriam

The death of Raymond Williams was a fearful shock. Only six or seven months before, the British Tory party led with radiant self-confidence and unreflecting arrogance by Margaret Thatcher, had won its third consecutive term of office. President Reagan was just about to be replaced by his own Vice-President. European politics were dominated by a mountainous Christian Democrat in Bonn. The domestic leaders of a once stouthearted and truculent trade union movement in Britain had been roundly defeated by the class enemy in the steelyards and the coalpits. The USSR with its surprising and gentlemanly new leader was making no progress towards an armistice in the cold war. Political radicalism at home and abroad had gone dismayingly quiet.

In a dark time, those substantial numbers of worthy men and women who wanted to keep faith with the great promises of happiness, mutuality, equality held out in socialism's large, rambling and disorderly church were hard put to it to keep their spirits up. Their organisations were always scrappy and impoverished, their efforts at political hospitality intended to keep the light of a few noble ideals shining in the murk always sporadic and often ill-attended. So it mattered like mad that there were still a few people capable of a calm courage when a country's best values were down and out, and defeat so familiar an experience. As long as Raymond Williams and Edward Thompson were still there, still speaking and writing in the splendid rhythms and time-honoured litany of the Labour movement, of common hopes and purposes, of the visible and monstrous injustice and indifference, the cruelty and wrong so apparent in all that mere power and ruling class did, then we could keep up a good heart. If you knew they were still there, even if the knowledge depended only on a newspaper article or two, the odd essay, the books still coming out, maybe a lecture if you were lucky, then you could hang on to hopefulness and spiritedness. You could still fight a bit of a fight locally, at the school, at the hospital, at the factory gates.

Idealism, political energy, hopefulness, they need something to live off, these qualities. They need solidarity and comradeship; they need plausible

1

action, some believable picture of efficacity. They need embodiment in leaders. They need, at the present time as never before, they need *celebrity*. Celebrity represents. Fame lends authority. Raymond Williams in 1988 was famous for his absolute probity, for the unshakeably principled way in which he, scholar, thinker, writer, citizen, liver of an ordinary life in the middle decades of the twentieth century, upheld principles and values then so publicly denigrated by the world's rulers. By his celebrity, he was able to celebrate some of those excellently civic virtues traduced and wounded in the political action of the day. His writing performed this necessary rite of celebration and his life, more than his books, enacted it.

Like Williams, like Thompson. For tens of thousands of men and women in England, Wales, Scotland, Ireland, North America, Australia, across the vast English-speaking imperium, Williams stood for a continuity of belief in internationalism and socialism, and in a Britishness with its decided and unmilitary picture of patriotism, for domestic settlement and a quiet, unglamorous local courtesy, a thing freeborn and strongly independent. Williams was 66, a bit tired no doubt, touched rather early by the ailments of the elderly; but still there, solidly up there as he had been since he took up the crown of left-wing dissent – when? After Suez? At the start of CND? With his first great books or the founding of *New Left Review*?

And then he died, a hard, sudden death, at a quarter to nine on a fine frosty morning. On 26 January 1988, his aorta ruptured and his heart stopped before anything could be done. Two generations of the most ideal-istic, the most generous-hearted and public-spirited citizens were each stopped by a sympathetic jolt to their own hearts when they heard the news.

I heard it in the bath, reported by the BBC *Today* programme the next morning, and jumped out, dripping, in sheer distress. Not many intellec-tuals in Britain have their deaths announced on the *Today* programme, and not many of them are held in such wide esteem, let alone being so well loved, as Raymond Williams. And love, love now, love is what counts in this story.

The funeral was at Clodock Church, a plain little building whose vener-able origins – most of the construction is late Norman – and remote situ-ation halfway up Williams's beloved Black Mountains make it a beautiful place to be buried, and a seemly spot for remembering him. The new road from Abergavenny to Hereford slices brutally through Williams's home village of Pandy, turning it into a few, separated clutches of buildings along the tatters of the old, winding hill road, and two main encampments, one around the new school and the other up the hill, at Llanvihangel Crucorney. Clodock is tucked into the flank of Black Mountain, on the narrow road to Hay on Wye, in the valley a few hundred yards below old Offa's Dyke path, which then continues south and east, and two or three miles later passes the front door of Harry and Gwen Williams's house.

2

Williams had been a serenely indifferent agnostic since he joined the army, though the custom of the border country was to fall into the rhythms of Church or Chapel, and the Williamses had been Church, much as other people were, say, down as Liberal voters. Raymond had gone to Sunday School for the poetry and for the friendship, and so had his two elder children in Hastings. Joy's family had been solid churchgoers in Barnstaple, and her brother a minister too, but student life at the London School of Economics was, in 1938, multicultural and atheistic, and she had followed her natural bent and Raymond also into religious indifference and theological uncommitment.

But now Raymond was dead and the world was stopped. The light fell crooked and the roads ran wrong. For forty-five years and more, Joy Williams had got up knowing which way things went because Raymond was there, and each could depend absolutely on one or the other doing what needed to be done. Even in the frightful anxiety of his absence in France after D-Day 1944, she never really doubted – who did so doubt until the worst happened? – that Raymond would come safely home. As to what Raymond Williams himself did or did not doubt inside his tank with the lid down and shrapnel bursting overhead, he kept it all to himself, as he did so much else.

So in the blankness and numbness, through which the outside world went unrepentantly on, and milk was delivered and cars lumbered over the sleepers on Common Hill, Joy arranged a funeral in the little Norman – *Norman* – church on the hill. She wanted to do the right thing, she said, and you couldn't say goodbye to Raymond in a crematorium. No history, for sure; no belonging, to the place or to each other; only the punctual coffins every half-hour, and the industrial column of smoke with its soft soot rising from the tall chimney.

So, on a bitter cold day in early February 1988, with the rooks cawing speculatively through vicious showers of sleet and snow on the hills, a little congregation set out variously, but on the whole along the M11 and down to the M4, taking the road back from eastern England which Raymond had so painfully taken the summer before when the prostatitis took hold.

They came, Joy and the Williams children, the Dalling family, and a scattering of the Left intelligentsia for whom Williams, as several of them were to say, was a kind of father. As one wrote, in one of the little torrent of obituaries which were scattered on either side of the funeral,

To be suddenly and unexpectedly without Williams is for any serious socialist today and in Britain like losing a father. I mean this, I realise, at once vehemently and with unbelieving anguish. In what Williams himself noted as the cold rudeness and sheer bloody-mindedness of British academic life, it is rare to find generous (or even any)

3

acknowledgement of intellectual indebtedness in the community of scholars. But in Williams's case, the tributes are paid not only in comradeship but also, it seems, in honest attempts to stand solid with his inspiring sense of the common endeavour and human mutuality which constitutes politics, if that dishonoured name is to mean anything more than murderous competition for the unequal allocation of the great finites of life: earth, air; fuel, food; capital.[1]

So they came, the family and a few of what Joy had always called 'Raymond's young men', though most of them were turning 45 by then, and paying the full price of experience, thinning and unkempt hair, eyesight going back as fast as hairline, a bad back here, a heavy paunch there, awful old grey suits and worse black ties fished out for the funeral; or else the drab uniform of the Left on parade: a dark old coat left open to the weather, a darker jersey with the points of the shirt collar neatly pulled out, corduroy trousers and Tuf boots.

Stephen Heath, dark, suspicious, edgy, closest to Raymond of the lot, had to miss the day; Terry Eagleton was there, the true jackanapes of the intelligentsia, small, solid, mischievous; Charles Swann, enormously tall and stooped, genial, as funny as Eagleton, and kinder too, wheezing with his awful respiration; Patrick Parrinder, silent, smiling, ironic, oblique, best dressed of the party; Tariq Ali, self-styled street fighter, lustrous brown eyes, a bit out of it all; Robin Blackburn, thick hair gone bright white but still an extremely good-looking, shy boy; they shook hands, professors, editors, producers, fellows, quondam revolutionaries, and shuffling uneasily at being in church at all, sat and stood and awkwardly kneeled, and then listened to Roger Dalling, Raymond's priestly brother-in-law, as he spoke, with a decent heartiness, the funeral address.

Then they came out from the dark church, its yellow lights flaring, and into a cold and darkening day, talked awhile amidst the quiet graves, and went, most of them, down the old winding hill road below the Williams's cottage at Craswall, the English-named village on the very edge of England, dug into the scarp of the Black Hill, the river Monnow, full in February, clattering below it, the forest of Mynydd Du tenebral over the horizon, the ghost of Offa faithfully patrolling his path a couple of miles away. They went down to funeral sandwiches and a cup of tea at the Angel in Abergavenny, shook hands again and kissed Joy goodbye.

So the funeral ended. Merryn, fearful for her mother's still delayed grief, stayed beside her for the whole time, daunted a little as well as impressed by her mother's impersonal brightness, the remorselessly cheerful beam of her features turned to each departing guest. The little caravan of cars parked in the market place behind the pub coughed one by one into life, as their long headlights lifted and lit the start of the long road out of Y Fenny, to Monmouth, the London road, east to England.

4

There were many farewells both blurred and sharpened by the suddenness of the death, by the fact that the Williamses had taken themselves off to Saffron Walden at Raymond's retirement in 1983 and not many people had even got as far as the new front door. Not that Raymond had helped very much: they didn't even have his home phone number at his college. But he had gone off to write the pile of books there still was to finish, and the demanding world could wait.

By the same token, there were farewells from all those who had thought to themselves that they'd leave old Raymond to settle down a bit, and then get in touch. There were agonised farewells from political allies who hardly knew him, who just didn't believe it, and for whom the bitter loss meant that now there was only Edward Thompson and he not well, to turn to, to look towards for an example of how to keep up a principled intellectual opposition in the wastelands of British academic life. Civic Britain in 1988, as in 1995, was enough to break your heart; it had just and most prematurely broken one of the biggest.

Finally, there were more compromised farewells, from those who, as always in the status-hungry, bitterly competitive and bellicose state of warfare in British intellectual life, looked for the thin edge of advantage from untimely death in the struggle.

He had, after all, worked for twenty-odd years in the Faculty of English at the University of Cambridge. So Frank Kermode, sometime colleague, an exemplary scholar later knighted, good heavens, for services to literature, wrote in one obituary,

> He was Chairman at a time when meetings were usually scenes of ignoble strife, almost endlessly prolonged. Given his powerful sense of real work to be done in the development of his own thought, it must have been painful to preside over that tedious and vainglorious brawling; but he watched it all through hooded eyes, patient and conciliatory . . .[2]

Kermode recalled, as so many did, Williams's strenuously ecumenical disposition, his calmly good-humoured determination to talk past the point of conflict to some further intersection of human encounter at which comradeship would be possible.

For the 'vainglorious brawling' of a mere University department at its meetings was a perverse creation not of an unhappy conjunction of individual egotisms, but of the culture and politics which brought those men and a very few women into the same room. 'Cambridge English' is more than a congeries of courses taught to the radically gilded youth of England, Ivy League, and a mixture of the privileged from the old dominions and the new Europe. Rather, it is one shining peak of a social order whose reproductions depend upon the obedience and assent given to the selec-

5

tion of young men and women who troop up to that bright eminence and kneel there.

A less appealing figure, one redolent of this same old England, chimed in after the early obsequies. This was George Watson, who contributed a memoir to the sort of seedy right-wing journal buoyed along by the cultural effluent of Reagan's America.

> By mid-career in Cambridge ... [Williams] was to become the proud owner of two country houses – one in England and one in his native mid-Wales – and the talk was much of hi-fi, wall-to-wall carpets, swimming pools, and color TV ...[3]

One house was the ordinary four-bedroomed family house Williams lived in four miles from Cambridge; the other was the derelict cottage he bought for £1,000 in Herefordshire, and restored after 1970.

> He was so utterly open about being rich, as academics go, and about wanting to be richer ... Williams' influence, before it faded, was not vicious. It even stretched to the United States where he publicly declined a rich post at an eastern university – I remember his eyes watering with desire as he spoke of the salary and free secretarial help that might have been his ...

Nastiness at this flyblown level is so obviously nasty even to the John Birch Society. Watson sprinkles his piece with salivatory keywords like 'Marxist' and 'socialist' and generalised animus is no doubt the large motive for his little act of indecency. But there is something else afoot as well, understanding which touches nearly upon what the worst as well as the best of intellectual life in Cambridge and, come to that, political life in Britain, is really like.

Watson's poison and envy are what they are: '[Williams] seldom, if ever, stooped to read or mark a student paper ... popularity, even sainthood was plainly the goal of his professional life.' But they are also actions which maintain a social structure, and that structure strengthens itself with this kind of thing. The British state could not continue to be the monster that it is without enough people at the élite universities which bring the next generation to power continuing to peddle lies about their critics, malice about better people than they are, hatred and rage about those who disagree or disobey the silent canons of class docility.

Stephen Heath had become Williams's collegiate son, as Terry Eagleton had been another, though Eagleton was the one who left home and, as sons will if success comes as full of fireworks as Eagleton's did, one who became a bit estranged from his academic father. But Heath came to Jesus College, Cambridge as a student not long after Williams came as a teacher. He was – is – a slight, taciturn, contained man with thick dark hair and

6

a dark, inward manner, apt at the touch of a tightly coiled spring to burst into low, voluble and urgent speech, as ready in French as English. He was quickly master of the full, difficult range of the Parisian *maîtres à penser* whom his own master read scarcely at all. He was entirely accomplished in an idiom of film analysis far removed from Williams's elementary and early textbook in the field, *Preface to Film.*

But when he spoke at a memorial service for Williams held in the Jesus College chapel on 21 May 1988, Heath turned the oration not only into a performance of suppressed, oblique passion, but into an act of defiance, of Watson and the works of all like him, the life and books of the dead man flung in accusation at the college as a measure of all that it had left undone which, according to its own best lights, it ought to have done.

> To remember Raymond Williams here today is to pay tribute to a major figure in a socialist tradition that he continued, questioned and renewed; to pay tribute to a thinker whose work transformed our understanding of society and culture, of the realities those terms offer to describe ... to pay tribute to a teacher whose teaching, directly or indirectly, was so profound and decisive an experience for so many of us here ... in Cambridge and in this college. It is quite simply to pay tribute to his life, the lived unity of all those of Raymond's activities as a coherent and fully engaged and richly generous project.[4]

That is the full *vox humana* stop on a powerful organ; some of the notes fairly resound in the smallish compass of a pretty chapel: 'socialist', 'a writer', 'fully engaged', and then, openly siding with Williams's scandalous project to vindicate 'culture as ordinary', in order to stand out plainly against the definition of 'minority culture' as a standard against what can then only be seen and dismissed as 'mass civilisation'. He ribs the college for its blank incomprehension of the titles of Williams's books when Williams was interviewed for the job ('which *was* the long revolution?'), and ruffles not a few decent old buffers then in their pews by reminding them, first, of the Coleridge whose rooms Williams ultimately inherited 'particularly distinguishing himself during a demonstration in the Senate House', and then of the way Williams put himself studiously out

> to explain the gestures of those who painted slogans demanding that Nelson Mandela be freed or who demonstrated against the Greek dictators at the Garden House Hotel, to explain and to indicate the reality and extent of the violence against which such gestures were being made.

Heath went on to sketch the form and line of the life work. He praised Williams's great effort to grasp the whole process of the stories of a society, of the forms of its writing as these change in response to history. And he followed his master into the conventions of reading, hearing, and valuing those stories. At first this project issued in works classified readily according to the way in which English literature was taught, and above all, examined in Cambridge – on the English novel, on European tragedy, on drama since 1880 or so, and on that local and domestic method of linguistic analysis which came to have such international and ethnographic force known as 'practical criticism'. Then Heath celebrated the books which, going beyond the official frontiers of an academic discipline, remind his congregation as well as declaring to the next generation the truth that all academic inquiry is an attempt to make human sense of what really happened. History was once life-in-earnest, and all intellectual endeavour, whether worked upon human experience or on the oddities of the physical and non-human world, is no more and no less than the effort to wrest what is interesting or useful from the facts of life, and turn it to benign account.

This innocent bromide, as Heath admonished Cambridge *in memoriam*, led Williams to such profane actions as writing books about television, as well as writing about truth and lies in the way people had of describing rural and city life, to say nothing of novels; to say not much – but Heath tells it right – of Williams's 'deep sense of sustained purpose throughout', that, 'and his utter lack of cynicism', the standard vice of political reaction, and of academic life.

Heath's is the cry of grief, one might presume to say, of the weaned child; not Freud, this, just the second generation praising the father's good life and his hard, heroic death, asking, as it must, what the heirs must do to live as well in such unalike circumstances.

At about the same time in the warm late spring of 1988, a more diffuse congregation gathered from different corners of the South of England, the tilted golden triangle of Oxford, Cambridge and London, to a shabby little public building built in the mid-nineteenth century as a kind of secular chapel in which British radicalism could conduct its godless worship. The building is Conway Hall, and when the Left doesn't meet there for its quarrelsome matins, it goes to St Pancras Town Hall, which is about the same age, and just as dark and dusty and smelling of floorboards.

This too was a commemoration of the life of Raymond Williams, but without the liturgy and forms which gave the Anglican funeral and the college service their shape and significance. Joy had said that 'she wanted to do what was right', and the only right forms to hand for an atheist's funeral were the wrongly fitting ones of the Church neither of them belonged to. Even a dead God has his linguistic immortality, however:

There was no need for a voice to speak these words which were already deep in memory. A time to cast away stone, and a time to

8

gather stones together; a time to embrace, and a time to refrain from embracing; a time to get and a time to lose; a time to keep, and a time to cast away; a time to rend, and a time to sew; a time to keep silence and a time to speak.[5]

The great words embody no superstition; they do no more and no less than give gravity and occasion to the hard, commonplace iterations of life. Williams saw that, at the death of his father, and wept brokenly, as he ought. When the unofficial British Left, and not a few European and North American leftists also came to mourn the death of its father, they had few words and no rhythms in which to do so. All that they had was the coin of friendship and admiration; but this was up for grabbing in the raucous counting-house of inter-Left rivalry. Every bid for Williams's name was made upon the ground of that colourful and ragged market.

It wasn't the fault of those who spoke. When Nick Garnham, elegant, intelligent, disdainful Wykehamist, who had helped out with the technology in Williams's television book, producer of the first BBC programme about Williams's work, spoke with his usual *hauteur* of Williams's faith in the canons of 'scientific rationalism' and of Williams's horror at 'the Lacanian madness', he was admonishing the many in the audience whose politics and livelihood alike were committed to the barmy irrationalism and elaborate sophistries according to which psychoanalysis and correctly arcane film criticism would together usher in the socialist paradise. And when Heather Glen, cheerful Australian-at-Cambridge character in Howard Jacobson's scatological novel *Coming from Behind*, startlingly decked out in a smart grey suit and beautifully coiffed hair, spoke warmly of working with Williams, her remarks were instantly checked for suitability by the gender police numerous in the audience. Feminism was on its long march through the Left, and about time, too; the remembrance of Raymond Williams was a key opportunity for a minor skirmish on the way to a better position. If Williams wasn't quite sound on feminism – and he wasn't – that must be said and heard.

The two men at the centre of the occasion – Stuart Hall and Terry Eagleton – were both entirely sincere in their grief, while both knew, none better, how what they said could not be theirs to say, but would at once dissolve unpredictably into the field of bombarding forces which is the natural wakeful physics of those to whom life is all politics, and never more so than when there is struggle for possession of the death of a socialist.

In this odd world, to whose valuation Williams gave his life, Hall and Eagleton are widely admired and also invisibly fought over. Stuart Hall is a leading character in this novel of political manners, and will be given his narrative due. At Williams's commemoration, however, he appeared as a vastly simplified hero. He is a black West Indian, good-looking, distractingly charming, very clever, a lifelong associate of the dead man. His words belonged to the blacks first, the multiculturalists second, and the motley sectarians of the Left groups third. The enormous respect in which he was and is held also means that the scuffle to lay first claim to his words would be a seemly one. So the words of Stuart Hall were ecumenical, general as to intellectual application, particular as to his love of Williams, unplaceable as to political action.

Terry Eagleton was – had to be – a different case. He had broken with Williams in a celebrated critique published twelve years earlier; he had once declared himself robustly for a heedlessly hard version of doctrinal Marxism and the critique of ideology. He was easily the brightest star in the faded galaxy of the Oxford English Faculty, soon after to be promoted to one of the two most senior professorships of the subject in the English-speaking and 'English'-teaching world (a striking case, as many people noticed, of the home of lost causes honouring Marxism at the historical moment at which it really did get put in the attic). He was – is – a dazzling expositor of some of the most fashionably difficult thinkers of the day – too difficult for Williams, as Williams said himself. He is terribly funny; protean in his quicksilver adoption of a dozen incompatible intellectual frameworks say his hosts of admirers; irresponsible, vain, shifty, say his detractors.

Whatever else, he was anguished at Williams's death, shaken to his heart by the suddenness of the loss and distressed to the limit also by an anxiety that he and his admired mentor had never quite made up, that someone whose regard mattered to him so much through his brilliantly egotistical rise to fame and fortune might have put him irrevocably to one side of his life. Eagleton wished earnestly to make amends. And he also wished, in his fiercely competitive way, to assume the position of Williams's heir. He was and is a prodigal writer, ridiculously gifted – a torrent of books, a novel, several plays, and his mordant ballad–satires all deservedly acclaimed. Hall, by contrast authoritative, charming, fluent, but much shorter-winded; grand, of course, but less interested in stardom. Eagleton was a star; the Left needed a star as does any political group in the star-studded firmament of contemporary debate. No star, no audience. Eagleton wanted to ride Williams's star. Nothing wrong with that.

So his oration was a bid to stand at Williams's shoulder. It wasn't easy in the first place to say because Eagleton, though thick-chested and bulky, is short; Williams was a bit gaunt and cadaverous, and quite a lot taller. As Eagleton put it:

> I found myself marooned within a student body where everyone seemed to be well over six foot and brayed rather than spoke ... Williams looked and spoke more like a countryman than a don, and had a warmth and simplicity of manner which contrasted sharply

10

with the suave, offhand style of the upper middle-class establishment
... It was a toss-up which of us was going to make it.[6]

Cambridge was always more mixed than that (and anyway Eagleton's
audience at the memorial wasn't so very lower middle class itself); this,
however, was a brutal way of laying claim to an inheritance. Besides which,
Eagleton meant it, and sincerity and modesty are not yet so completely
deconstructed by ideology-critique that nobody wants them any more.
Eagleton went on to praise Williams's way of speaking up for those values
which, once let loose, might undo some of the more horrible aspects of
bloody old England upon which Eagleton, just arrived from Salford and
not yet having reckoned up the Irish blood in the heart he later borrowed
to wear on his sleeve, had declared class war.

Anyway, in the gloaming which passes for ordinary daylight at Conway
Hall, Eagleton said this – and it is all vastly to his credit as well as being
true about Raymond Williams:

> Hearing him lecture was an extraordinary personal liberation: it was
> like seeing someone stand up in the most improbable place, formal
> and begowned, and articulate with enviable ease and eloquence all
> . the struggling and smouldering political feelings you had yourself,
> but which were not so to speak official or academic, and which one
> had simply not expected to hear given voice in such an environ-
> ment.[7]

Yes, of course, one says – as any admirer of Williams must say – that's
it. That's what he most characteristically did: he broke with the established, calmly superior assumptions and way of talking in England, but
did so with a manner, an idiom and diction themselves so unassailably
assured that those on the wrong side of the break couldn't see how to
stop him. And then, into the space made by the break, he dropped his
own, calm commonplaces about human connection, about solidarity and
equality, about those things we had been most fired by as young idealists,
and that he – and Leavis before him, in his queer, fierce, intimidating,
contradictory way – had best given voice to as an academic, as an educational project: all this at a time when education and teaching were still
good, powerful words, and hadn't been put down by snobbery from above
and timidity from below.

So when Eagleton spoke as he did, generous and calculating, incorri-
gibly self-referential and both big- and open-hearted, there was plenty
there for tears, and gratitude also.

> Williams was a man of remarkable grace and dignity; and through
> the medium of this authority I felt somehow authorised to speak
> myself, and through me all those relatives and friends who could

11

never speak properly, who had never been given the means to say what they meant, whom nobody ever bothered to ask what they meant . . .[8]

The theme recurs again and again in these valedictions, the poet's theme which is at the centre of Williams's work, that there are writers who give voice to what many others feel and think of as their deepest allegiances but for which they do not have a common speech. It transpires as theme and apothegm first in Wordsworth's stirring Preface to *The Lyrical Ballads* which he wrote for the second edition in 1800, when the fresh images of revolution and romanticism promised to unite the Parisian slogans of general freedom and equality with all that Wordsworth and his contemporaries found words and pictures for by way of individual passion and its fulfilment.

> What is a poet? To whom does he address himself? And what language is to be expected from him? He is a man speaking to men: a man, it is true, endued with more lively sensibility, more enthusiasm and tenderness, who has a greater knowledge of human nature and a more comprehensive soul than are supposed to be common among mankind . . .[9]

In each valediction, even, perhaps most of all in the ones intended to diminish or wound Williams, his opponents recognised the issue of speech itself as central, and of the representativeness and authority of that speech. Williams spoke for the speechless, and found in other voices, who had not always been heard on such terms, a prior speech. He spoke thus in places in which such a way of speaking had rarely won a hearing for itself, even though the argument had been going on for so long.

To do this, or anything like it, he had to have what Eagleton describes so affectingly:

> I think everyone who met Williams was struck by what I can only call his deep inward ease of being, the sense of a man somehow centred and rooted and secure in himself at a level far beyond simple egoism. I wondered then where this truer balance and resilience came from, and how I might get hold of a bit.[10]

It seemed a bit rich in Conway Hall at the time, this new youngish leader of the academic Left talking of a central and rooted man at a time when the *haut ton* in his audience spent much *hauteur* on the absurdity of supposing there to be such a thing as a subjectivity, and much heavy-handed processing of words went into deriding the very notion of a 'centred self' as terrible bourgeois nonsense. Eagleton himself is not untainted by these little ways and he has plenty of cheek; but he spoke for what was best in him as well as in Williams when he praised his hero's 'formative early experience of working-class solidarity and mutual support which had left him unusually trusting and fearless'.

This is right and, as we shall see, this is wrong. There was much in Williams as in everybody that was murky and muffled, obscure to himself; certainly there was fearfulness at what was fearful, but also at what was radically unfamiliar; and as for trust, his strong reclusiveness and exclusiveness together meant that trust rarely came up – he had entrusted himself to a tiny number of people, and they would do.

In any intellectual life worth praising and emulating, the pull is between the passionate excitement of immersion in the stuff of study, and the absolutely necessary detachment of the observer, keeping the proper balance between judgement and analysis. The hell and heaven of each is that you may go so mad with ecstasy, or you may go so ice-cold with dissociation, that either way you end up deranged.

Eagleton proposes as his Williams an oracular solitary, defined by membership of a lost and wholly enviable community, advocating at a calm distance the serenity and steadiness he had won by choosing that distance. And he readily takes any chance to represent all Williams's university colleagues either as timeservers or as class-warriors. Stephen Heath spoke to the college against the Cambridge which included the college; Eagleton speaks to the ragged elect in Red Lion Square, where old dissent has been honoured in London since Conway himself and Stanton Coir spoke there,[11] and charges them to honour dissent again against the toadies and cowards, the vicious snobs and the traitors who throng the roads leading to all places of learning.

There aren't many scholars and intellectuals who have been held in common public esteem in Britain; fewer still for whom the farewells summoned them to preside over such varied, though always small constituencies. Williams pretty well always remained beyond the limits of the official Labour Party in Britain, but spoke of it often and directly to those of its members and supporters despairing of its deep philistinism, its obdurate conservatism, its failure of nerve, in such a way as to revive their spirits and cause them once again to insist to the only major party in the country capable of spelling the words on questions of conscience, duty, value and virtue. Even so, only Williams's lifelong associate, the great historian Edward Thompson, might have received a tribute from an ex-Cabinet minister, and in the event it was Tony Benn, the only Labour figure of any seniority who even knew that there was an active intelligentsia in Britain still arguing the form and content of the good society, who offered his fraternal valuation.

It was, as they say, no accident that it was Benn who wrote the obituary in the house daily of the old CP and Tony Benn who praised Williams,[12] correctly and in good prose, for keeping alive a speakable moral idiom of the old Left, a language capable of naming life and death rather than the unspeakable, much spoken diction of crisis and capital management, the ethics-denying, death-dealing lies of weapons accumulation, power-fiddling, ordinary life-neglect. There is a wide gap between policy and a moral politics, and those who speak for the latter rarely know or do much about the former. But policy without a morality is power without value, a synonym for tyranny.

A death signifies, or it does not. 'Our best man,' Edward Thompson once said, and at his death, not in good health himself, writing for the United States, he marked down Williams 'as a point on the border country between the academy and the activist movement'.[13] Williams's best-known image, of life in the border country from which he took his famous title, called so clearly to so many, and made his never-stated claim to representativeness so potent. All of us live both here and there, wishing things were otherwise but living where they are as best we can. That is the border, between actuality and desire, the longed-for and the lived-in, the loved and the lost.

So it was well that so many little memberships could call to him after he had gone. Immediately after Thompson, also in *The Nation*, Edward Said spoke in an admirably generous, full-hearted way of Williams as being 'optimistic, charitable, gentle and large', and it was so.[14] Writing in his corner at the intersection of so many borders – Palestine, Columbia University New York, wealth and poverty, man of the idealistic Left in a country where Leftism is intolerable – Said saluted the thought, the breadth of Williams's writing, the lifelong effort to understand and describe the powerful flow of our deepest and most life-shaping feelings. Against what Said casually describes as 'the dreadful politics of his country and ours',[15] Williams persistently inquired into and lived within the very making of feeling, of those feelings of resistance as well as communality, which would conduce to better lives in the future.

Said makes no claim on Williams; he lets him go as equal, as comrade, as teacher, and formally, as someone he didn't know well but whose books, the endeavour of whose thought mattered much more than the lost chance of friendship. And even Merryn, his eldest child and only daughter, in writing her own homage, spoke not of a loved domestic presence but of a revered authority, less father than father-figure, a man who linked past and future with the force not of a mind and a life, more of nature itself. She claimed him, not quite unexpectedly, for green politics, for ecology; for Gaia.

It is of course right that a noble, even a grand life should be acknowledged at death in these august, sometimes breathy accents. Each speaker and writer sought to pull Williams's great authority a little his or her way, to this group or party or church or person; or else one sought to do him down, to screw a bit of advantage out of his now final silence. Countryman,

14

worker; socialist, intellectual; writer, critic; radical, democrat; railwayman's son, plain father; passionate advocate, dispassionate judge; cordial friend, remote teacher; sexist, egalitarian; Welsh European, Cambridge don; solitary, *communard*; voluble friend, gracious silence ...

The cacophony fades into the crackling photocopies in front of me. I look up, and putting my hands behind my head, stare unseeingly out of the window. I remember so much of Raymond from so little. A couple of dozen postcards, with that oddly formal superscription of his name and address; a couple of dozen encounters, this one about a book, those at odd meetings of Left political Saturdays in London; a meal or two at his house, a few half-pints of beer, a reference for a job when the University was agog to close my department, another half-dozen lectures, scattered over the country. But his life? His life, now that it has been gathered into the dread solemnity of the sages and patriarchs, leaving us still bereft and grieving?

This is the story of his life; as I knew of it, and then, as its meaning began after his death and me well into my middle age to press curiously upon me, there pressed upon me questions about what he was up to; and therefore what I, a much less gifted worker in the same sort of field, was up to; and then what all kinds of other people, many of whom I also admired and learned from, were up to. You ask, what was this man's life worth? You go on, who are you to say? There is always an implied comparison: what is my life worth, beside his, or just anyway? And these other lives, so caught up with Raymond's, what of them?

A biography, insofar as it is both truthful and serious, is only a record of what other people can tell you of the life and death in question. If the subject is long dead, what they tell you, also being dead, is all down on paper. But Raymond Williams has only been dead since 26 January 1988, and very many people live to talk about him as they knew him every day.

This is the story of what they told me, as well as what I found out from a collection of the books and archives, which also constituted his life. It is the story of what I knew directly for myself. It is also, as a biography must be, a story of the times, the times of world war and cold war, and of the small passage worked by a single individual through those immense seas.

That epoch – the epoch of world war, cold war, of the hideous night-clash of Stalinism, Fascism, and Liberalism – is over, thank goodness. Stripped of those large and deadly narratives, the best way we have to hand of grasping times past is a few decently told life histories. This is my attempt to tell one. This is the way it came.

2

UNDER THE MOUNTAIN
Railway House

There was always the mountain. The path led past the house up to the field gate. Just inside the field was the old iron trough for the cattle, brown and dark with heavy rust, the hedge running away south along the flat of the field until the steep rise started at the foot of the mountain.

The first stretch was always heavy and swampy. The water poured straight down the steep, wedge-shaped bulk of the mountain, hit the little bowl of the field, and then seeped slowly into the drains and ditches dug in long parallels east–west across the bottom of the valley. When he was a bit older and heavier, the boy would stamp hard beside the path a few yards beyond the black trough, and the surface of the field muttered and slobbered for yards around.

For much of the year, whenever he walked over the field, the ground tugged and sucked at his boots as he walked, even if he aimed to walk only on the thickest tussocks of grass; and at the wettest times, which was often, the water stood level with the grass and the only way on to the mountain was to take the main road and then cut across.

Once you hit the rise, the path dried out immediately, the grass thickened into sweet turf, and the bracken began to put out its tightly curled fronds. In after years, Raymond Williams used to say that he never dreamed of any other landscape than this one, and it is true that the sudden, honey-strong tang of bracken smelled anywhere would set him down instantly on the side of the Holy Mountain, which had been so variously a sacred burial ground, a chapel, a fortress and a battlefield, a vantage point and a beacon, a farm, a home and a picnic spot, ever since human beings first came up there to live, when the ice grudgingly unclenched its terrible grip 23,000 years ago.

> It seemed from this height that the whole south of the valley was drawn up from the road towards the peak of the Holy Mountain. Fields that down there were single and isolated were now only chequered pieces of that great movement of the land ... The mountain had this power, to abstract and to clarify, but in the end he

16

could not stay here; he must go back down where he lived.[1]

This was the power which made it holy. The bigger the mountain the more it commands the world below it, so that those who stand up there can see and prophesy, taking the magic of the mountain for their own. Mountains are hermaphrodite, he and she. For this solitary, only child, whose memories of the mountain were, as he later said, always of being alone up there, the mountain was home and parent, and not just parent: father. Time was, even when he was very small, that the mountain moved after him, like Wordsworth's mountain moved after him, 300 miles due north and a mere 150 years earlier.

> I heard among the solitary hills
> Low breathings coming after me, and sounds
> Of undistinguishable motion, steps
> Almost as silent as the turf they trod.[2]

He learned to feel on the mountain and then, as he grew strong and thin and ranged wider, to take in the other mountains of the range, Holy Mountain first, almost at the door of the house, and across the valley, the Kestrel,

> the guardian, the silent watcher over the meeting of the valleys, and beyond the Kestrel, the broken line of the Black Mountains themselves, marking the limits of the Old Marches, the power of the Old Lords and the new, Lords of the sword and the ruined castles, Lords of the coalpits and the black steel mills of the south.[3]

Fifty-odd years after the little boy trotted behind his father and mother on a Sunday when they walked over the boggy field and turned up on to the dry path, the alter ego Williams invented for himself in two novels says to his difficult, spikey disciple,

> It only comes occasionally. Some particular shape: the line of a hedge, the turn of a path around a wood, or in movement sometimes, the shadow of a cloud that bends in a watercourse ... What I really seem to feel is these things as my body. As my own physical existence ... As if I was feeling through them, not feeling about them.[4]

The mountain became a father, with a father's mysterious and arbitrary moods, his final authority; his expansive familiarity, such that he provided the grand, varied spaces of work and play, and his abrupt darkening and dismissals, which enjoined absolute obedience and an anxious, silent, guilty self-questioning about unacknowledged transgression.

As you climb the mountain and the valley recedes, the turf path with its satisfyingly short, thick grass and small outcrops of pink sandstone,

17

enters the waist-high, sweet–fresh-smelling forest of the bracken with the tough thongs of its stems fastened to the mountain's bones; at the age of 6 or 7, the bracken still made, at its highest points, a pale-green canopy overhead, safe as houses; at 11 or 12 Raymond could pelt down through it, running headlong and wild with the steep pitch of the hill, the bracken bending and breaking as he ran, as though he could destroy a jungle in the thunder of his downhill running.

Beyond the bracken line, heather and whin and stone, and the patient, scattered sheep with the big blotch of the James family's mark on their matted sides. Up there, the stony path curved slowly to the peak where the tip had, millennia ago, toppled off and lay in scattered piles of black rock. The path deceived you, so that every few hundred yards resembled a summit and then opened on to another rim of the horizon which still concealed the very top.

As mountains go, it wasn't much; none of them were. The queer wedge of brown and purple stone with its skin of turf, bracken and heather is no more than 1600 hundred feet high, an awkward triangle poking up at a pronounced tilt into the Welsh and English sky. But it was the margin where old agriculture and even older nature fought things out. The farmers, especially the Jameses, battled on behalf of sheep and cows to hold back the steady, invisible advance of the leathery bracken stems; the roadmen had blasted and levered the stones from the quarries smashed in long scars across the face of the heather; and far below Kestrel and Holy Mountain, the boy could watch from their shoulders the tough little trains go chuffing and tugging up the incline of the country towards Hereford, carrying stone or sheep, loins of beef and saddles of lamb, eggs, cans of raspberry and jars of honey from the few, high-flying bees even then at work on the flowers of the heather, harebell, scabious, pimpernel.

The baby Raymond was born to Harry and Gwen Williams on 31 August 1921 in an ugly, unfinished-looking blackstone house a yard or two from Offa's Dyke path as it turned southwards from the little villages of Pandy and Crucorney towards the Holy Mountain. The midwife said it had been a difficult and protracted birth, because he was a big lad, but one of the neighbours had really done all that could be done. He wasn't Gwen Williams's first baby, though few people – one of them, Harry, her husband – knew it at the time. Before marrying Harry nearly three years earlier, she had had a child, christened Herbert, brought up by her parents as their own belated child; nobody spoke of the father, and no one, any longer, even knows his name.

A child outside marriage, now, that was really difficult even during a world war which shook to their roots the old rules about sex and marriage. It wasn't just a matter of the proprieties amongst the respectable working and small farm-holding classes along the Monmouthshire borders at that date; it was also a matter of duty, in particular the hard responsibility of money at a time when the office of railway signalman, which Harry Williams assumed in Pandy when he came back from the war, paid £1 10s a week. But there was little fuss and no disgrace. Gwen's parents raised the baby as theirs, and when Harry came to marry her, he wasn't the man to turn away from her because of what was still known in England until the day before yesterday as an illegitimate child.

In later years, Raymond himself returned time and again in his novels to this peculiar title of legitimacy; he always translated it, as he did so much else, into a struggle over the meaning of loyalty. The uncertain conclusions to which he came, in *Second Generation*, in *Loyalties* and in *People of the Black Mountains*, were deliberatately more blurred than those allowed him by the confident church of his admirers.

In Brecht's great pantomime, *The Caucasian Chalk Circle*, the story-teller admonishes us that the princeling child, abandoned by his mother, is most truly the servant girl Grusha's child, who picked it up and cared for it, unable to ignore 'the soft breathing, the little fists'.

Williams battled with the queasy structure of loyalty in relation to class and family and political commitment throughout his life, coming down with a pretty heavy hand here and at home, but a much less convinced step over there: in the university, the regiment, or the imagination. Loyalty, you could say, is the elusive theme of this biography.

It was as elusive for him as much as it was his heart's desire. How much did the son belong to the father, to all the father stood for, and to his comrades behind him, stretching far away up and down the railway lines? Yet his father urged him to go away, to leave the railway and the small orchard and the black house, to go to Cambridge and be famous, and be lonely, and keep himself to himself and the four other members of the one household and its small democracy. Loyalty to that childhood and that valley always claimed him; but he had gone away. His life was to be a story of going away, and of trying to find the way back, to the right and not to the wrong place and people.

When he was 4, the family moved to the house next door, a few paces up the lane, paying a rent half as much again as the four shillings for the cramped one-down and two-up of the first house. 'Gwynnant' (now 'Llwynon') was semi-detached, as the English say, much larger, solider, with a stout bay window to one side of the front door and a low wall marking off the house from the path. Like all the vernacular building of south and east Wales, this was a stout, ugly, rectilinear house as black and grim as the chapel and school to which it was so clearly sibling. It had been built sometime in the 1870s when the railway arrived in the valley, and whatever light and decorative touch came to the trim, solid little stations of the Great Western Railway going north from the pits and steel-yards up to Birmingham was missed by the houses. Something a bit harsh

19

and grim in Harry Williams perhaps responded to this plain, upright example of railway valley architecture. But if he was a fanciful man, nobody knew much about it; he took the house because it had that much more space, three bedrooms above the narrow entrance corridor, and a long parlour before the squareish kitchen at the back.

The story of Raymond's christening has become a minor token of the man's life, and that life as projected by his parents: two names, one for each side of the border. 'Raymond' was his father's flat choice, no one knew why, it wasn't in the family. 'James' was his mother's preference, after her own father but in any case; and then Henry, of course, either way. His father went off to the Registry in Abergavenny immediately after his birth, with his mother still lying tiredly in bed, and put his names down as Raymond Henry in that set, fixed, unarguing way he had, and came back to say what had been done, was done.

So Raymond became the professor, and Jim was the cheerful little fair-haired lad trundling out to his father in the long vegetable garden across the path. Like so much of what Williams reports of his family's life, transmuted into the autobiography of *Border Country*, the disagreement about his name goes much deeper than what can be said. It marks a shadow thrown by a deep, wordless disjunction between the father and the mother, settling into a profound lack, unspoken because unspeakable. Nothing whatever could have been done to prevent it. It was written; written by the history of class and of gender.

'What did you put down then?'
The children below were quarrelling over the use of a stick. Harry watched them, prepared to shout.
'Matthew Henry Price.'
There was a silence. The stale heat of the room hung heavily between them. Harry caught for a moment the bitter scent of the elderflower that was spread to dry in the unused middle bedroom. He looked round, confused.
'You never went against me.'
'I put that down.'
'How could you? After how hard it was.'
'Keep quiet down there, you young shavers,' Harry got up and shouted, leaning from the window as the quarrel broke out again.
The children looked up at him and moved away.
'I'd said Matthew.'
Ellen did not answer.
'Anyway, now it's down, girl, no use us quarrelling.' Ellen smiled, and turned her face so that her cheek rested along the baby's head. 'What do it matter it's down?' she said as if to herself. 'He is Will whatever.'[5]

20

So Raymond grew up Jim to everybody, and as Jim followed his father out to the garden, fifteen yards by ten, heavy with flowers just across the path from the house: daffodils and wallflowers in the spring, purple and white stock, some of it the heavy night-scented kind, and sweet william a bit later, sweet rocket in white and lilac, a riot of tangerine nasturtium at the further end by the compost, and then in midsummer the brilliant yellow and carmine of the snapdragons, matching the show of the same flower up the road at the station, overshadowed by the great heavy-headed double dahlias in dark wine-red, yellow again, and ochre.

As soon as the baby was born, Harry Williams had applied himself to his second employment. The shifts at the signal box by the railway were long – twelve hours at a time – and sixty or seventy trains came through each day. But the work wasn't physically hard and it was gregarious: there was a porter and ticket clerk as well as the stationmaster at the station itself; there were the other two regular signalmen as well as those just down the line towards Abergavenny at the tiny halt of Llanvihangel Crucorney where the church stood at the top of the hill; there were the gangers and platelayers who maintained the line; there were the drivers, firemen and railway guards, who came through regularly on the same train services, each to his days of the week.

Nearly all of them ran their own gardens with an eye on what could be sold, locally or in the market, as well as eaten by their families, and in Harry Williams's case, the market gardening was much more than a help to the weekly wage and the grocery bill; it was integral to a way of life always more than just making a living. It was a livelihood. Like countless households then living on the shifting borders between an agricultural and an industrial order, they lived off and for both. Neither would pay enough by itself even to feed and clothe a family decently; together, they settled people, alongside a railway which had become as much a place of work and exchange and encounter as the two previous thoroughfares, the river and the road. Only when the massive new roads, reaching far beyond these small local markets, replaced the trains in the 1970s and 1980s with their vast container trucks hurtling 500 miles in nine hours, were these livings and livelihoods cut off and killed. Whether they can be reinvented was one of the major questions which Williams addressed to the future in the last decade of his life.

So Harry Williams planted a clutch of fruit trees among the cabbages and flowers, apple, pear and plum. He rented another length of garden, across the main road, for £1 a year, and mixed more fruit trees with redcurrant and gooseberry bushes, both so difficult to pick what with the sharp thorns on the gooseberries and the little bright currants only coming away in a tangle of stem and leaf, but both making good, strong, bitter-sweet jam which sold well in Abergavenny market.

As he became known and familiar, one of the unchanging team at the two stations, Pandy and Crucorney Halt barely a mile and a half down the line, he took another long piece of ground, thirty-odd yards of it, behind the cattle, coal and timber yards of Pandy station. Allotments, they call these bits of detached market garden in England;[6] they have a century-old pattern of social and productive life, especially in cities and at that date, for the men only. After formal work the men would take their walk in a stately way down to the allotment and there they would certainly labour hard – allotments were and are essential to many a household economy – but would also sit and smoke and chat, calling across the narrow strips of intensely cultivated land to their neighbours, sitting in an ancient kitchen chair, pipe clenched in their teeth.

Harry Williams rarely joined such easy-going conversations. He had ground the size of half a football field growing for him, and he was rarely at rest. In the intervals between trains at the box, he could nip down to the vegetables – potatoes, peas, leeks – growing behind the yards. And in time, he built up a stock of beehives, four across the path in front of the house, four more down at the station, more up at the James's; when each had a swarm, they would yield anything between 100 and 200 lbs of honey each.

The Beekeepers Society met regularly, and there was no shortage of tuition. Harry Williams had never kept bees before, nor his father, but he was a remarkably resourceful man, and learned fast. He bought a centrifugal strainer after the first year of beekeeping, and at the age of 6 Raymond was watching him cram the thick honeycomb, honey pouring from the punctured cells, and crank the handle round until the hub picked up speed and the honey poured thickly out into the outside channel, expelled by the spinning drum.

Lastly, Harry built a stout enclosure for hens at the end of the vegetable garden in front of the house. It had a wire-mesh run a few feet high with a plank henhouse at the end, and four nesting-boxes at the side. Looking after the hens was the only woman's work in all this busyness, apart from some tending of the flowers, and Raymond as a very little boy would trot with his mother to the henhouse in order to pick up the warm brown eggs as soon as he heard the raucous cackle of a bird proud of its product. There had to be a fierce cockerel or two, if chicks were to be raised or indeed any-way, to keep the hens in order, and everybody but Harry was afraid of the furious, brilliant, colourful creatures, and the frenzied clatter of wings and beak and talons which faced whoever came near, apart from their master.

As he always said, and as all his writings bring out so forcefully, his silent father dominated Raymond Williams's imagination. Harry Williams had gone to war in September 1915, although he never spoke of it; early in the same year, to his utter shock, a woman he hardly knew had presented him with a white feather in the main street of Pontypool, where he was then working as a boy porter. He came back from the front with a dose of chlorine gas. His life-experience, his soldiering and his railway work (both in signalling) came together in an absolute commitment to what he saw as the best values of the British Labour Party.

Albert Trevett was, much later, the porter at Pandy, a cheerful, friendly, round-faced, solidly built man in the informal uniform of the job when off-duty: navy-blue jersey, heavy black shoes, a well-cut cloth cap, a full-length raincoat.

Albert Trevett

Cyril Keddle, Frank Jenkins and Harry were the signalmen at Pandy. I was porter. Then a bit later, 1947 say, I went up to the box at Llanvihangel. We'd have sixty to seventy trains a day including the bankers. There'd be pitwood freight going south to the mines, then cattle, sheep, horses going north to Hereford, Worcester. I used to talk to Harry out of the signal box window; oh, about bees, about the drama society, about the neighbours, see, I liked gossip and so did he. He used to row with one of the gangers over politics. The ganger would say 'politics, mind, that's just trying to get other people down, you got to get them down', and Harry would go red and shout. Harry was always trying to push politics into you. In 1948 now there was talk of a rail-strike, and Harry said to me, wagging his finger, mind, 'You've got to stick by your rights – no one else will. If there's a vote for it, I want you out.' Well, there was one one-day strike. It was the only time I ever went on strike.

Williams's novel *Border Country* is centred on his father. It splendidly brings out the energy, the drivenness of the man in the steady rhythm of work and livelihood. In the 1920s, twelve hours on, twelve hours off at the box; sometimes nights, of course. Then a break, while the third signalman took over your shift. Besides the railway work, spring sowing, summer beekeeping, the heavy labour of the autumn harvest, fruit-picking, honey-bottling, lifting the potatoes and onions, Gwen Williams canning and bottling the berries, pears, plums; honey, a thousand jars at a time filling the kitchen and flowing out the door; they bought their own canning machine. Then in winter the heavy digging of sodden ground, turning it up for the frosts to break and air it until the waters receded, and then the endless, fastidious tilling and raking of the soil, so that sowing could begin once more.

The sharing out of work in such homes was as fixed as the rhythm of the work. To Gwen Williams, the hens, the canning and bottling of fruit. Bottling, a process now superannuated by deep-freezing, was no more than it said: preserving fruit in jars after boiling and vacuum-sealing them with a heavy glass top and a red rubber gasket. To the woman also, curing the big hams, bought as the money got better from the produce, from the James's farm up the hill; the laundry, boiled on Thursdays in the big copper in the kitchen with a square of Reckett's Blue to whiten the sheets, then possed with the heavy copper posser, its wooden handle softened and bleached by use, and finally all drawn through the mangle, two hands to turn it, the water cascading out of the heavy flannel sheets and shirts into the big enamel bowl beneath; the careful unremitting house-cleaning, Gwen Williams polishing the milk bottles until they shone.

To the man, in the house, almost nothing. His work was outside. He wrung the chickens' necks; his wife drew and plucked them, scorching off the feather roots in an acrid aroma. His domestic chore was to go out the back every third day to the tall, narrow wooden box which held the toilet frame above the heavy cauldron-shaped tin with the handle below its rim in which each family dumped its daily defecations. Each day a thick, petrol-based solvent was poured upon its load to hold down the stench and dissolve the solids. When the time came to empty it, Harry went to drag the bin grindingly out into the yard, holding his breath against the throat-gagging odour, then carrying it in front of him with two hands at his chest to the patch of sunken ground about 200 yards away where it was word-lessly agreed that the group of four or so houses should empty their sewage.

They weren't a sociable pair, Harry and Gwen Williams, or not together, at least; everyone seems agreed about that. Old Gladys Smith, well over 90 now, tiny, shrivelled, a bit mad-looking in her man's cap, and sounding it too with her piping, wandering voice, was postwoman in Pandy for nearly fifty years.

Gladys Smith

Harry kept to himself, like; *she* would mix with anybody by herself. But she was stern, like, stern with Jim, wouldn't let him go anywhere for years. He never mixed with anyone, Jim didn't, not until he went away to school in Abergavenny, then he left school and I don't know where he went ... course, Harry was a strong Union man, and *Labour!* Well, always for Labour, and round here like, we don't talk politics much. Course, I'm English, not that anyone round here talks about that, like, English, Welsh. England, Wales, and Monmouthshire, they used to say for the weather forecast, on the wireless.

Gwen Williams was a stern mother with Raymond, hard with him, they said. Harry, at home certainly, and more often than not at work, was silent and withdrawn, his eyes 'clouded and unfocused' as his son so often said, so that he rarely looked directly at anybody, but set his gaze on a line of trees, the flight of a bird, the Holy Mountain. He spoke most through his prodigious energy and the physical labour upon which it was spent. Yet Joe Griffiths, a little boy in Pandy long after Raymond left home, remembers him as jolly and joking, stopping Joe in the lane with a riddle and a joke. Violet James, as she was then, from the farm recalls Harry as 'a very well-educated man, I don't know how'.

Violet Higgs

He spoke at the village celebration for victory in Europe in 1945 – I made a celebration fruit cake for the WI, I had been a Domestic Science student–teacher, you see – and Harry spoke at the village party. He was very funny and genial, and rather good.

But together, they spoke little and showed each other few endearments. Time and again, in his novels and in his other writings (I think of the first paragraph of *Modern Tragedy* with what it says about his father driven into silence not by life so much, as by old History itself), Williams draws back at the gap between what can be said and what is felt. It is hard to doubt that although it was a completely solid and settled marriage, it was not a happy one. Harry was hard enough, when things called for it, but more than that, it seems that he would brook nothing which went against his deepest feelings. In *Border Country*, this is a quality for quite unadulterated praise, from his lifelong and close friend, Morgan Rosser, spoken while Harry is dying of a coronary: 'He couldn't see life as chances. Everything with him was to settle. He took his own feelings and he built things from them. He lived direct, never by any other standard at all.'[7] and he goes on ('Will' is Jim's name in the novel):

> What we talk about, Will, he's lived. It all depends on a mind to it, a society or anything else. And the mind we're making isn't the society we want, though we still say we want it. The mind he's got is to the things that we say really matter. We say it, and run off in the opposite direction ... That's what I say, what I always have said, and why Harry's different. He changes a thing because he wants the new thing, and he settles to it because he wants it right through, not because the rejection is driving him.[8]

It's a moving speech, but it has to be spoken for Harry because although, quite plainly, he has the words and the wit, he won't, can't speak, except on his deathbed, of what really counts. Then, agonisingly, he speaks out of his delirium and to his son, of marriage and, also quite plainly, of what he has never known. We do not know, either, thank goodness, whether Williams really heard his father say this; but the novel, and the recollections of those who knew Williams's parents, make it wholly true to the tale.

> 'You get these connections,' said Harry urgently. 'Like one way all into filth, and there's filth enough when you're ill. Only one way all into mental filth. Of course not only that.'
> 'Yes, take it easy.'
> 'Only the one trade to get into and that's a wife to love you. The only trade, sweetheart. A loving wife. The only trade to get into.'[9]

But the man we see never called his wife sweetheart, and there seemed little love, yet long experience, between them. As death approaches Harry is gentler with his fictional wife than anywhere else in the novel. After Harry Williams's death, as several people said, old Mrs Williams

Joan Stratford-Leach

a tartar, mind you – took on new life, became much more talkative and sociable, fell to gardening as never before, kept everything going, fruit trees, bees, vegetables, everything. And her wallflowers were *wonderful*.

Perhaps it was often the way at that time, in all social classes. Marriages, the poet says, 'lasting a little while longer' and, he goes on, 'Never such innocence again'. Rock solid the marriages were, but the partners were different people inside them to outside them. Both the Williams parents were vigorous local leaders, she in the Women's Institute, he at work and in the village. At home, it seems, they spoke of practical and domestic matters, and of Jim; or not at all. At work or in local life, each of them was much more animated, argumentative, garrulous, and they adored their grandchildren, 'spoiling me rotten', Merryn said.

But Harry lived a deep contradiction between gregariousness and withdrawal which he taught his son. He clenched his spirit upon what he wanted, both in speech and silence, but constantly he drew back into himself, and set his gaze upon the distance, where he could see but not reach the life that might be led.

Harry Williams made his living into his livelihood. But the cost of that living was high. It broke his heart. His son followed in that avocation. Either way, you could call it selfishness. 'Wanting it right enough', 'settling to it' may be good names for an absolutely fixed and, as in the case of Raymond-for-Jim, gigantic self-assertion. But then the way fictional Harry and true Harry lived was in terms of what we say really matters, half of it at least.

The word 'community' is either so threadbare that we see straight through it, or on the tongues of our public spokespeople it smells foul with dishonest use. But it is certainly a name for something we badly want, and Harry Williams both lived and did not live it, bequeathing exactly that ambiguity to his son. He turned the rhythm of very varied and creative work, desperately hard and necessary labour much of it, together with the steady, responsible companionability and deep mutual dependence of the railway into the self-explanatory and natural rhythm of a life. He was a strong and unusual man – everybody who recollects him agrees with his son about that – eager for ideas, spirited in his class loyalty and its fine independence, and of a marked reflexivity. Yet the thoughts he had, coming from his deep capacity for feeling, could find no words with which he could teach his devoted son. His actions had to embody his traditions, and when the son came to live his adult life, his actions and his reflection upon those actions could only sometimes be grounded in what he had learned as a boy. So there was a gap, as there is for everybody, between what he hoped and what he knew which, his work being words, could only be crossed on thin abstractions.

26

As the strong community of labour has broken up since 1960 or so, together with the working relations in which hardship, danger and inter-dependence made for such an excellent solidarity, people have sought to replace these strengths with the closeness of the single and self-chosen fulfilment of marriage, and if not marriage, of one other person and their sexuality as the ground of a fulfilled life confirmed by 1.8 children. It hasn't worked for lots of people; the weight is simply too much for love and sex to carry, when Party, neighbourhood, Church and history all prove unable to weave the bonds which will tie us to people and work and home.

Marriage simply mattered less to a man like Harry Williams. Or if it didn't – 'A loving wife. The only trade to get into' – and he didn't know what to do about it so that it died, there was everything to live in and for as given by market garden and by railway. He drew all the life in his home to him, and his wife was by turns severe and subordinated; she knew her space, as they say, and defended it against Harry, at times with bitter anger and resentment. But Harry it was who did things, and his son followed him in faithful and loving admiration.

Above all he followed his father to the railway. It was quite a step. Nowadays, since the much-needed, fast new road slashed Pandy in two in 1963, you could hardly walk it. In 1928 or so, when the 7-year-old Jim was first sent with messages or sandwiches to his father across the fields and under the little railway arch, it was a good mile walk, along the empty, dusty, curling country lane, past the pub and the two chapels, one Baptist, one Methodist, and then turn off towards the embankment, under the line and scramble up the bank to walk carefully beside the rails themselves, looking back to make sure that the huge, hurtling steam trains with their slicing, towering iron wheels were nowhere behind. Once a year at least *The Abergavenny Chronicle* of the week carried a report of ganger or platelayer killed somewhere on the dense network leading from the pit valleys north towards the industrial midlands. The men had heavy, noisy work to do; the line was busy; accidents happened.

Once, when Raymond was 11, a platelayer working some little distance from his gang was killed just below Pandy Station. The practice was for the men at the station to bring the body back on a hurdle, a springy portable mesh made of young larch or hazel, used to improvise sheep pens at the railway yards or to block a gap in the fence. The dead man had been hit from behind by forty tons of cast iron hurtling blindly forward at fifty miles an hour. The body would have been dreadfully broken, a limb perhaps amputated by the sharp and terrible wheels. Nobody in the hamlet could have been unaware of such a thing.

The railwaymen, like their brother miners, accepted the danger as part of the work. Not that they accepted it with docility. One of the most obvious achievements of the trade union movement, in Britain as else-where – that movement which Williams himself was the first man to salute as a great cultural creation – was the victory won over employers for greater safety at work. That employers always opposed such moves goes without saying, except that it needs saying again, now more than ever after so long a time during which trade unions have been so vilified and eroded. The employers refused protection and safety, as they do everywhere, in the name of profit, the threat of higher costs and therefore less employment, and in defence of their own mere power.

But danger remained, and had to be lived with. The work of the line was built round long and careful procedures for the guardianship of safety. The signal box was the embodiment of this vigilance, and each box stood as one link in an enormous network of communication, active on behalf of the traffic of commerce, certainly, but also keeping watch on the maintenance of human care and connection, on mutual safety, on the recognition, daily pledged to one another in formal procedures and ritual jokes, of what the trade union themselves coined as 'solidarity'. To be solidly together, as well as solidly against arbitrary power, injustice, cruelty, grew out of the form of the life, and the exchanges of country life along the railway line, the trading of honey, jam and ham, went to confirm that solidarity.

Life on the border marked by the railway was not like working-class life in the mining valleys or the dockyards and steel towns of South Wales. It was more like the part industrial, mostly agricultural life of the Yorkshire Dales, where the rail traffic also swept north from Leeds and Bradford to Thirsk and Darlington, where farmers voted Liberal and railwaymen voted Labour, and where there were few visible representatives either of the big landowning or the ruling industrialist class.

It was a picture of class accommodation and coexistence, of overlapping relations of work and production, which has long beguiled the English. The real enemy – Them – is London, what They tell you to do, and what They take away from you.

The men who lived and made this life were, as Williams later and almost grudgingly acknowledged, 'absolutely confident ... as an adolescent I remember looking at these men even with a certain resentment ... I have never seen such self-confident people since'.[10] (But then he sought to be one such himself.) Their clothes, class clothes, spoke for that confidence: the thick collarless shirts over the flannel vest and open at the neck – collars were only for best and rarely felt comfortable – a waistcoat with a family watch in the waist pocket or a dark woollen jersey, an open serge jacket and trousers, braces and a dark leather belt, and in the winter a heavy overcoat, also open like the doors of a wardrobe. Vest, shirt, jersey, jacket, overcoat: five good layers made the man, made him as solid and contained at work as at home; gave him authority, membership; declared a proud class.

To the railwaymen, in steady, decently paid work, the railway belonged to them and they to it. The owners never showed up, and their peers were not people to be afraid of. Harold West, now a keen-faced, sharp-eyed 90-year-old, came to Pandy as stationmaster in 1946.

Harold West

> We never had much to do with the bosses. It's not like that round here. No one's afraid of anybody else. I remember the Colonel who lived in the big house on the hill, a cousin of Lord Raglan. Well! They weren't liked. His wife was charged with shoplifting, and the Colonel wanted the railway rules bending. He got tickets, first-class ones of course, on credit from Frostie, the booking clerk. I had to go and ask him for the money at his house! Mind, they're one as bad as another. The old boy up at the other big house had a dog ate a whole box of sausages in the guards van one time, so we insisted it had to travel in a muzzle after that. Then he refused to pay his £2 as vice-president of Pandy Football Club! They were petty and high-handed; but there, it's of little relevance now.

The signal box and the station were a single social organism, but linked all the way up and down the line to all the other such organisms. They were neat, attractive products of railway architecture, itself such an agreeable even, at times, noble addition to the much-made landscape of Britain. Like all of them, the Pandy box, long since demolished, presented a perfectly square face to the passing trains, with a shallow pitched roof on top. A solid flight of well-banistered wooden stairs led up to the high-roofed, wide and rather handsome control room, with sliding windows on all the sides commanding the line to north and south. At the top of the steps were two doors into the control box with a stout printed notice board setting out the strict rules about when to come in, and when you must leave the duty signalman, checking in each direction the heavy steel signals high up on their iron stands, undisturbed and concentrated. In front of the high windows, with their perfect view of the long sweep of the Black Mountains, stood at an angle to the floor the rows of brass-handled, chest-high points controls, stiff and straight, which shifted the steel arm of the signals to stop or go, and inflected by the necessary few degrees the long articulations of the rails themselves, so that the trains ran truly on to a clear line. A signalman put his back into moving the long handles, grasping with both hands the winkingly polished two-tongued brass handle in a checked duster so as not to slip nor to disfigure it with fingerprints, closing the tongues and, pulling strongly back to disengage the ratchet, let the weight of signal or rail pull him gently forwards until the junction clicked and was made good. No electricity; no electronic pulse; handle and rail, handle and signal were simply joined together by strong wire hawsers. If they froze, or stuck, or broke, all traffic in the relevant section of line stopped until things were clear.

At the blind back wall of the box were four telephones, lines permanently open, two up and two down, but open beyond the next boxes down in Crucorney and Abergavenny, up to Pontrilas and Wormbridge, open west as far as Swindon, the huge railway marshalling yards of the Great Western, and north to New Street Birmingham, where GWR shared its fiefdom with London and North Eastern. In the long shifts at night, when traffic was light but watchfulness as necessary as on the bridge of a ship, the men talked across half the breadth of the country.

> See, a signalman's real mates aren't in his own box. They get on all right, I'm not saying that, but it's only the bit each day. Your real mates are in the box each side. It is with your Dad, it's been years with them.[11]

Above the telephone were ranged on a mahogany board the six brass bells, each saucer-sized and spherical, highly polished naturally, and attached to a stout brass sounding pin. One beat from the down box called the signalman to attention; one beat in reply.[12]

Harold West, eyes bright with recollection:

They're asking from Llanvihangel if the line is clear; four beats and it's the express, pull the home signal and she drops to 'go'; two beats and a train is entering the section …

Harry was *very* efficient. If there was *any* accident when Harry was on duty, a minor derailment for example – which doesn't mean an engine on its side and carriages turned over like in the pictures, only that the grooves of the engine wheels have slipped the track – if it was a derailment he'd get the message to the engineers, arrange for single line working and call me out. Of course it was 'Mr West' if people were about, otherwise 'Harold'. Well, anyway, Harry got it all organised, made me pilotman which meant I had to travel in every train, with a red arm badge, until the single line working was over, and both lines clear. All the points were clipped as 'trailing' or 'facing' – one man on that full time, while the accident lasted. In December 1946 when the bad winter started we had two foot of snow on the line all the way up, and three trains stuck, one at Pontrilas, one at Pandy, one at Llanvihangel. But Harry was a grand railwayman, the other chaps just called me out, expected me to take over, he'd been an NCO, he knew what had to be done.

The comparison of the inside of a signal box with a captain's cabin and his bridge comes naturally. There are still plenty of them working in Britain and Ireland, uncomputerised, brass-and-iron technology, solid plank floor. Williams paid tribute to much more than his father in the novel, and in his second television play, *Public Inquiry*. He celebrated the long line of tradition and duty well done which held each signalman in a minor dynasty with the lineaments of Joseph Conrad's ship's captain:

> Deep within the tarnished ormolu frame, in the hot half-light sifted through the awning, I saw my own face propped between my hands.

And I stared back at myself with the perfect detachment of distance, rather with curiosity than with any other feeling, except of some sympathy of what for all intents and purposes was a dynasty; continuous not in blood indeed, but in its experience, in its training, in its conception of duty, and in the blessed simplicity of its traditional view on life.[13]

The neatness and order of the box enforce the comparison. The gleaming brass, the polished windows, the rows of handles, the clever accommodation of the men's lockers below the telephones, the cleared wooden floor space, all speak of the compactness and discipline due to ordered procedures of work which must deal matter-of-factly with life and death, as well as racks of a few thousand eggs or ten tons of pit props or the GWR school trip to Paddington.

That order, like the maritime one, had its rich folklore and its history of disaster, festival, revenants, and battle honours. These latter, like most battles, were largely skirmishes, with the railway owners, with the road competition (that battle was finally and comprehensively lost; it was fixed, anyway), with other lines. But there was one battle which took its place on all trade union ensigns for decades, and marked the imagination of Raymond Williams just as he got to the gates of the elementary school in Pandy.

When Harry Williams came back from the First World War into which he had been conscripted and which he vigorously opposed, he had been, his son said, 'totally radicalised' like so many other soldiers by his experience of the war's hideous efficiency in presenting millions of targets to the certain death dealt out by industrialised machine-gun fire. Harry had gone to railway work in the Welsh mining valleys, which had reached back the other side of the war, to the memory of striking miners shot at Winston Churchill's behest in Tonypandy in 1912 and to the incipient revolution so many people had feared at that date. Since then, revolution had really happened: in Moscow in 1917, and then in Germany immediately after the armistice, where the Left had failed to win power and where, as Max Weber thinly said of its dead leaders, Rosa Luxemburg and Karl Kautsky, 'They summoned up the street. The street has dispatched them.'

In Britain, preparations by an apprehensive ruling class to make it 'a country fit for heroes to live in' had rather lapsed in the face of the necessities of profits and status, and the old, justified resentments began to boil back up again, in the docks, in the steelyards, and especially in the coal mines.

The miners, somebody once said, are the Brigade of Guards of the Labour movement, its most élite regiment. As is now well known though still hardly credible, the regiment has been disbanded by its class enemy exactly because of that distinction. In 1948, when the British pits were nationalised by a Labour government and all the pithead sirens sounded together in triumph – 'Now they're ours, bonny lad, now they're ours' – there were a million men working in nearly a thousand pits, all over Eastern Scotland, South Wales, Durham, Northumberland, South Yorkshire, South Derbyshire, Lancashire, Nottinghamshire, Leicestershire, Kent. As I write, forty-six years later, there are sixteen pits still worked by British Coal.

That history touches Williams's life several times more, especially during the year-long strike of 1984–85 which finally caused a virulently class-warfaring right-wing government to dedicate itself to finish off the miners as a political force for ever. But the history is not much helped by the regimental analogy. The Brigade of Guards has never been to war with itself. The minefields veered always between solidarity – 'One for all, and all for one' – and civil war. The Nottinghamshire fields and many of the Derbyshire ones were richer mines, with better coal and easier digging than elsewhere. They earned more money than down the sulphurous shafts of Wales or the fearful depths of Fife. There were secessions from the National Union.

So when Britain experienced her only General Strike ever, in the warm Maytime of 1926, there was no general readiness for revolution, not even a mood of nationally high tension. There was hatred, class vengeance, rancour in plenty, and those with power paid off the scores they insisted upon without much mercy. But no one was killed, and as the trains and buses stopped, the county cricket went on, and the executive committee of the Trades Union Congress went about its usual business of fixing and compromising and coming off worst.

As John Maynard Keynes was the first to understand,[14] world war had taught capitalism much. It had taught that huge, enforced Government investment not only reorganises and accelerates production, but (the multiplier) enlarges the circulation of money, quickens consumer spending, and conduces (controllably) to prosperity.

But he was up against the habits of old obduracy and stupidity on the part of the custodians of capital. They believed – they still do – that the injection of capital by Government was a work of charity, like giving the dole to undeserving workers who were simply out of work because they wouldn't try hard enough to find it. They believed that markets financed themselves according to the laws of supply and demand, and that it was the first business of Government not to 'interfere' (that uniquely powerful English word) in natural money processes. Finance must have the power over production.

Consequently, as the vast disorganisation of the coal industry reasserted itself after the concerted effort of the war, and the multiple tensions of a mass union against countless owners from all over the country but bound strongly together by class in the Coal Owners' Association became intolerable, the Government, with really fatuous timing, stopped the coal subsidy just at the moment when exports fell steeply in 1924.

There had been sporadic strikes in all industries since 1918, when even the British police came out. But the miners and the pitowners were always at loggerheads, the miners striking, the owners locking the gates against the workforce when stocks were high and demand poor. Coal was paying rotten dividends to shareholders, the owners hated the union and would relinquish nothing of their power. They offered a pay cut to the miners. The miners bitterly refused. The owners shut the mines and locked the gates. The miners appealed through their union to the hardy motto of the Congress of all Unions, 'United we stand, divided we fall'. The Congress in its executive committee voted to support the miners, to make their dispute a national dispute, and to force the owners to accept the union terms. The General Strike was called.

It was obeyed. The conditions put before the miners were clearly unjust; they offended the ordinary sense of fairness – 'a fair day's work for a fair day's pay' – which was the best principle at the heart of the Labour movement. So the heavy metal industries, coal, iron and steel, buses and railways, gas, came out. In *Border Country* Harry says 'I'll stand by the miners, if it comes to it',[15] and that was the point. His closest friend in the novel is Morgan Rosser, who had no direct equivalent in Pandy but was an interesting compound of Harry and Raymond Williams on their entrepreneurial side, Violet James's father, and the sometime mayor of Abergavenny in the late thirties, who was actually called Rosser and was Headmaster [sic] of the boys' elementary school. Morgan sees the General Strike as a decisive moment in the coming-to-power of the British working class. He is very intelligent, and passionately committed to the cause of socialism. But Harry warns him not to go on at the third signalman in those terms.

> 'Aye, only Jack's a funny chap, mind. Don't go talking to him about the working class and power and that.'
> 'Why not?' Morgan asked. 'He's a worker, isn't he?'
> Harry hesitated, and looked slowly round the box. 'Aye, only it's not the way we talk, so watch him'.[16]

On the whole, it *was* the way Harry Williams talked; he stood for the Parish Council alongside Harold West, but he didn't get in (though Harold West did), and he was secretary, organiser and everything else to the tiny Labour Party branch in Pandy and Crucorney. The railwaymen all voted Labour, but out in the country they didn't actually join very often, never have. It was too uncomfortably explicit a thing to do, what with the small farmers voting Liberal and the posh families being Tory (not that such considerations inhibited *them*).

Williams later reported that the account of the General Strike which he gave in *Border Country* is pretty faithful to the facts. Branches were kept in touch from union headquarters by telegram. On the evening of Friday 30 April 1926 a telegram was pinned up on the noticeboard in the signal box, the telex message pasted in thin strips on the blue flimsy. 'Executive instructs all members not to take duty after Monday next. Arrangements to be made locally so that all men will finish turn of duty at their home station Tuesday morning.'

The arguments were all in London – Eccleston Square for the TUC; along the railway lines they just awaited the next telegram. In London the chief union brokers were Ernie Bevin, Arthur Pugh and Walter Citrine, who together roughed out a scheme actually to reduce wages in view of the possibility of a future bargain between the coal industry, the owners and the unions.

All the Government's public presentation was in terms of its determination to smash 'extremism', and to this end the Special Branch was used, as it had been under Labour in 1921, to spy on communists and open their letters. (Twelve were actually convicted under an antique mutiny act.) The Cabinet was not displeased by the prospect of a strike, and put in train a special Supply and Transport Committee. The idea was to set the Trades Union Congress itself against the 'factional' miners, without too obviously being on the side of capital against labour. This dispute threatened that old chestnut, the national interest.

The TUC agreed on very little, and wavered over joint action right up to the start of the strike. Although all unions then owed allegiance to the TUC, its authority held only by custom, not by law. The miners were its members but not its subjects, and the Executive of the TUC, made up of the leading tough eggs of the most powerful unions, ruled only by vote, and assumed their power and status by virtue of the sheer numbers of men whom they represented.

But various of their number fancied themselves as dealers in a more national and political kind of power. They had the ear of Government and they hadn't really got the stomach for as big a fight as the miners had picked. So, while Herbert Smith and Arthur Cook, the miners' leaders, kept steady nerves and innocent faith with their members, Pugh and Baldwin negotiated together secretly at Chequers, and at the same time the print unions refused to set a *Daily Mail* leader describing all strikers as revolutionaries.

The strike began on 3 May. The coal owners refused mediation and encouraged new breakaway miners' unions.[17] Baldwin was successfully to turn public opinion in favour of what he called his constitutionalism, circulated by means of seven million anti-union pamphlets. But to begin with discipline held. Public transport stopped. Newspapers were pretty well silent, so much so that Winston Churchill brought out a pro-Government broadsheet, the *British Gazette*. There were troops everywhere, but they did little apart from shift perishable goods.

The TUC, through the devious hands of one Jimmy Thomas, kept up negotiations of which the miners knew nothing. The Government by way of Sir Herbert Samuel produced a memorandum proposing new national negotiations, and the always craven TUC caved in. The strike was called off unanimously, without even telling the miners. Government and owners moved in for the kill.

In Pandy, at the other end of the wire, the telegram which arrived on Monday 3 May read as follows: 'No trains of any kind must be worked by our members. Acting in full agreement with Associated and Railway Clerks Unions.' Harold West was a booking clerk in those days.

Harold West

> ... you got £80 a year at the age of 18, which went up £10 a year to a maximum of 200. Mr West, you were, though I was only a boy. I was 21 at the General Strike. The RCA came out – to make the miners' cause their own – the only time I've *ever* been on strike ...

At Pandy station, just as the strike began Williams describes a touching little scene, true to the facts he said, when all the men turned up in order to plant out the station's show of antirrhinums which used to make brilliant with yellow, white, carmine and shocking pink the flowerbeds of every local station in the country. They were planted out in the big, sloping, stone-edged beds giving on to the line; after that tiny dent in their refusal to handle goods or company business of any kind, Harry Williams and his friends closed the signal box, the stationmaster locked the station and, as an RCA member, joined the strike.

He was a commanding figure in his officer-style cap with gold braid on the peak and his uniform topcoat, and the men hadn't quite expected him to be with them. He posted a large, poster-sized appeal-with-threats from the Chairman of the company, which accused the men, as *always* happens in Britain when people go on strike, of breaking their contracts, let alone ruining the company and bringing civilisation as we know it to its knees.

Discipline held right across the country for nine days. It was enough of an achievement. The Trades Union Congress was wholly inexperienced in such collective and military strategy, and it was only the experience of the war which had really brought home to such an inchoate and fissiparous organisation the quite terrific strength which its leaders had not the least intention of using. They had no revolutionary ambitions and no great confidence that even the solidarity of the miners would hold, let alone that of the whole army of the working class. The men had learned from the army both the incompetence as well as the untrustworthiness of many of their own leaders, but the systems, structures and culture of the

35

society at war had never split open. An always docile political nation and its habits of awkward and protracted compromise, for better and for worse, parleyed with itself as well as between its ruling élites, through the warm days of May blossoms, and muddled together a sufficient deal.

At Pandy, to a man like Harry Williams, the deal looked like treachery. He was only a bit over 30 at the time, and this was before he became branch secretary of the National Union of Railwaymen. But he was a man with a much larger political grasp and commitment than was usual in the always quiet conduct of railway life. He had learned a sharper, harsher language of politics in the war and in the valleys. Nor was it easy to keep going on twenty-four shillings a week strike pay. His son describes in *Border Country* an incident which actually took place a year or two after the strike when Raymond was 8 and it was thought he had lost a whole pound note on the way to the shops. Back in 1926 the pound note was all but a week's wages, and Williams brings out vividly that what was always judged to be 'steady, well-paid work' was hard to hold back from sliding over the edge into poverty.

The nine days' strike had not been without their moments of tension, especially in a year when, as Trotsky famously wrote, the spectre of revolution was haunting Europe. In London the class villains had been the sort of absurd undergraduates mocked (but joined) by Evelyn Waugh's hero in *Brideshead Revisited*, who volunteered to deliver the fruit and vegetables, and biff a few of the Bolshie costermongers in Covent Garden on the way. Along the main road beside the GWR line the truckloads of soldiers passed, their rifles slung, to camps and cluster-points where they could be used to do some of the work of moving goods if it came to it. Guns and khaki and the whine of Bedford engines familiar to a nation since 1914 had their symbolic force, as well. 'Comrades, the struggle has begun' said the front page of *The British Worker*, but after a few days of lovely, sunny weather the agreement was come to, the thing was over, and the King appealed on the BBC, itself only a few months old, to the great myth of national unity and peacefulness which has held a believing country for so long, and today is once again under breaking strain.

There was, however, reparation to be made. The GWR began with its reprisals as soon as the strike was called off. Men were to go back to work unconditionally, some men would be, in a delicate turn of phrase, 'selected for dismissal', others would forego privileges and could be moved from place to place as the company chose.

It was a crude assertion of employer power, and angrily rejected. Even now, seventy years later, it's impossible not to feel bitter anger as one reads the conditions. (You would think such insolence had gone for good, until you consider the trade union history of the 1980s.) The telegrams came and went in a flurry of contradictions, but the main thing was to prevent the self-styled owners wreaking simple vengeance.

It didn't work. In a hateful statement, the company forced the union under threat of punitive and bankrupting legal action to admit that the strike was wrongfully called. The union, under the always duplicitous leadership of one Jimmy Thomas, further agreed never to strike without negotiation and not to suborn anybody further up the hierarchical ladder (in this case, suited clerks and stationmasters and suchlike, wearing shoes and shiny-peaked hats with gold on them) into enlisting on the wrong side. So the company would have its revenge, and 'certain persons' would be transferred with right of appeal to a general manager, who would ignore it. These certain persons included the stationmaster at Pandy, who took his humiliation hard, as well he might.

Finally, there were selective punishments, whereby former staff were only taken on again gradually. Without explanation, only two signalmen were re-engaged at the Pontrilas, Pandy and Crucorney boxes: they would work twelve hours each. Harry, as the most junior signalman, lost his job. He only got it back when the third man, who truculently refused to join the strike until the circumstances forced him out, stuck so rigidly to correct procedure that, for safety's sake, the company was forced to re-engage another signalman, and five weeks later, Harry was taken back.

The miners stayed out in most places for nine months, although the Nottinghamshire field went back, and seceded from the union, just as in 1984. The strike became the most important historical enigma and emblem for the British Labour movement from that day to this. For Raymond Williams, listening to his father and his friends at work – 'those absolutely self-confident men' – talk over and round the subject for years, it marked the point at which union leaders and the men they represented – 'their own people' – were drawn so far away from one another that solidarity dissolved, and the leaders became part of that fatal, resolution-melting myth of old class compromise and friendly accommodation. All his life, Williams simply hated that softening, even tone of the English ruling class even when it was truly well meant, perhaps most exactly then, because in meaning well, that class drew the best people of the opponent class away from the strong, living webs of connection, and located them at an unbridgeable remove from the places and the people to whom they belonged.

Yet Williams himself answered to those voices when they called, and went willingly, his father urging him on. At the age of not-quite-5 he began to act in the two contradictory narratives which constituted his life.

A biography is more and less than the tale of this man's life. It is a description of his entry into his traditions, and those traditions are the master-narratives which fix for him role and identity, meaning and value. Each person can only become the character it is in us to become. But that character may have many possible versions. Each particular version takes its shape from the roles which are open to us in the stations of our history and the plot which currently gives it form and direction. In the narratives open to Raymond Williams, as the General Strike receded into the powerful miasma of folk-memory, he could join himself to his father and those self-confident men in the perpetual solidarity of a changeless railway and its beautiful, massive technology. Or, sharp-eyed, cheerful, watchful lad that he was becoming, he could leave those men and their work behind, leave the signal box and the beehives, and join a story with a very different plot, in which he wrote down what those men said, as they wrangled on the phone through the long hours of the night, about the strike, about the welcome they gave the great Labour victory of 1929 which went so badly wrong two years later. He would write down what they said but never wrote for themselves, and he would tell them what it meant.

Williams gave himself with an equal, unspoken passion to both narratives; he was held by both all his life; and neither he nor anybody else has been able to bring them together. You tie your heart as completely as you can to those you love; and in the name of freedom, you walk away, alone and for yourself.

Raymond the writer's story began, in all its inexorable innocence, several months before the General Strike. On 25 September 1925, at barely over 4 years old, Raymond Henry Williams, still of 'Llywnderw', was admitted to Pandy School.

The school stood – still does, though the buildings are new – a few hundred yards down from the Williams's home and garden on what was then the old, rolling country lane of a road from Abergavenny to Hereford. Term had begun on 1 September, and with Raymond's arrival there were seventy-four pupils. On the first day, the Headmaster had noted that 'thirty new books were introduced into the school and these will form the nucleus of the school library'.[18]

Violet James, as she was then, daughter of the farmer, later married one of the Higgs boys, joined at the same time as Jim, as did Albert Trevett's wife, another Violet. Violet Higgs, a spare straight woman with the ramrod carriage of the fine horsewoman she still is, remembered going to Pandy School in the old building.

Violet Higgs

... but of course they only pulled it down in the 1960s. It was like all such schools, built sometime after the turn of the last century, the date was on it, 1853 I think before the big Act of 1870, you see. But I don't know how many such schools there are still all over the country, I've spent my life in and out of them, a teacher myself, and then teaching teachers at Usk College ...

... It was a grey stone building, long, with high ceilings and high windows you couldn't see out of. It had iron railings along the front, which children used to put their

38

heads through and then get stuck and frightened, and Tom Davies the Head would have to turn them to one side and the other to get them free. The stream ran outside, when the floods came, the school was closed and the mud was washed over the classroom floor. The playground was only asphalted at the front, it was bare mud at the back where the boys played. The girls played in the front, quite separate.

Every morning Tom Davies would line up the classes, and we would walk in file, the 5-to-8 year olds in one group with Miss Williams in the little room at the side, the 8-to-10 year olds in the next (standards one to three) with Mrs Johns, and then the big children who didn't go to the County schools in Abergavenny but stayed on until they were 14 (standards four to six) with the Headmaster. There was a big heavy curtain dividing up the main room, Tom Davies teaching on one side, forever pulling at his long nose, stretch it into a trunk like an elephant we used to say, and the other teacher in the other section; if you sat near the curtain, smelling dusty like it did, you could hear both classes plainly and didn't know which to attend to.

The Reverend J.A. Hughes, vicar of the small and pretty church up at the top of the hill at Crucorney came in every week from 1920 until 1950, when he retired, to check the register and, at times, to address the children, on 'the reward of unselfishness', 'the life of William Shakespeare', and his personal passion, taught later to Jim, 'the movement of the stars'.

Tom Davies was a rare man, a strong but tacit Labour supporter, commanding respect always but gentle even when he caned children with a hazel switch cut from the hedges, upon the hand, across the seat of the trousers, and most painfully, across the back of bare knees. Such caning was frequent, brief, and unimportant. His authority turned on his long service in the village, his strong, craggy, benign presence, the power of his nose, his complete and Welsh devotion to education. Most strikingly, he gave classes in the evenings to adult illiterates from round about, and he and his wife, unsung and rewarded only by the respect of the villagers, coached the best pupils for the scholarship examinations taken each year to the Girls' County High School and the King Henry VIII Grammar School for Boys, four miles away in Abergavenny.

Jim learned to live, as we all do, by the all-dominating rhythms of the school year, of which the most apparent and obvious was the annual scholarship examination, and the proud announcement of the school's annual successes, so largely due to the efforts of Tom Davies and his wife.

The girls then as now did better than the boys, but, then as now, had fewer opportunities afterwards. In Jim's first May at the school in 1926, as the trains fell silent in the valley because of the General Strike, the school was told of two girls winning their scholarships to the County High. And Tom Davies was always thoughtful of what would best, as they say nowadays, develop the curriculum, noting in the school log during November of 1926 that 'with the object of further developing the individual system and giving opportunities for self-expression the Dalton

English course was adopted'. Self-expression was not then the blood-stained and fought-over concept it is now, and it seems a fair bet that young Jim, that verbal Anglo-Welsh-European, was lucky to come up against so progressive a teacher as Tom Davies. Indeed, during the summer term of 1930, Davies went for a fourteen-day course at Jesus College, Oxford, anticipating his star pupil's later performances at that other famous headquarters of the Welsh intelligentsia-in-exile.

Schooling was a hardy business in those days. Epidemics, harsh and sometimes fatal, would sweep through the classes so that, as in February 1927, half the pupils were away with flu, and it was frequently the case that twenty or thirty boys and girls were away ill. Only bad weather actually closed it. Jim, of course, lived a few minutes' walk away, but many of the pupils, including little ones of 5 or 6, would have to walk over the hill paths for three or so miles, small legs struggling through heavy snow, only to find the school closed.

And it rained, as only in Wales it can rain. In March 1928 the water ran fifteen inches deep along the road above the school, and Jim and his friends gazed in fascination through the back door of the school, set a little higher up the hill, at the brown water standing halfway up the metal legs of the paired desks. Every year, from 1927 until Jim left in 1932, the school closed for a day or two because of floods or heavy snow some time between November and April.

Not that hot weather was always the pleasure it might have been. When the sun baked the sweet fragrance out of the heather, it hit the heaps of the children's shit and the pools of urine lying in the pit toilets at the back of the school. Not until August 1929 were the pits replaced, to universal relief and acclaim, by flushing toilets. Tom Davies, wrinkling his long nose, noted: 'The unpleasantness and unhealthy smell caused by the old pit system has at last disappeared'.

The school closed readily, however, in response to the festivals of the locality: unlike English schools, it closed for all Labour Days. It closed in September for the great day of the Abergavenny Agricultural Show, and in Pandy, it also closed for the October day when the little village held its own sheepdog trials and ploughing match, and Violet James showed off her youthful horsewoman's prowess on one of the farm ponies.

As good schools do, Pandy had its own festivals as well. There were the annual GWR trips to Swindon or London for a dozen or so of the big children and the Headmaster; Jim went in 1931, but of course he knew the ropes and the railway by heart, and explained to the other children in that garrulous way he had how the boxes, the loops, and the bankers worked. Violet Trevett remembered the school shows and plays that were put on, as well as Harry Williams's keen interest in drama. Laughing, half in embarrassment, half in the pleasure of recollection, she described herself and two other little girls.

Violet Trevett

... quite little, only 7 or so, with blackened faces and homemade toppers singing 'we're three little curly-headed coons', and Jim laughing like he couldn't stop. Then later we did shows in Pandy, when Jim and Violet James and the others had gone on to Grammar School. Tom Davies produced *The Merchant of Venice*, and I was Bassanio – the girls took nearly all the parts, Jim wasn't in it, but Harry built the scenery. Then we did *Beauty and the Beast* for Christmas, but it was stopped by snow after the first night.

And in June 1930, we catch a glimpse of the future theorist of drama in the dramatised society as part of a series of tableaux taken from *Midsummer Night's Dream* performed by the Pandy pupils at the Abergavenny hospital fete. They won the second prize.

It was as good a version of primary education as one could get between 1925 and 1932. It was clear to everybody how bright a lad Jim was, but there was a formidable cadre of clever girls around him. His father had taught Jim to read before he even went to school at the age of 4, although he never taught him his own rich accomplishments as carpenter and domestic engineer. All his life, as his eldest son was to say, affectionately but appraisingly, Raymond Williams was simply awful as a practical man. All hammered nails bent, the screws of an electric plug were beyond him, and the only twentieth-century technology he ever mastered was the old-fashioned, portable, flailing typewriter. He never did anything much in the school garden kept carefully tended at the back of the school wall (all produce to the Headmaster). But he learned the melodramatic and self-serving history of Wales as assembled by the Welsh; he learned a poem per week by heart; he began Latin, with special coaching from the vicar; he made an awkward but sufficient stab at arithmetic, algebra, Euclidean geometry; he didn't actually read so very much, according to his peers, for there was only the Bible and the *Beekeeper's Manual* at home in spite of his father's zeal for education. But above all he learned to write, and to talk – 'Laborare est orare' as it happily said on the stone pediment above the school's big oak door. Talking was what Jim Williams could do, and even alone at home, the only child packed off to work at his books by the hour while his parents walked the Black Mountain paths in order not to disturb him, he talked endlessly, silently, to himself, so that the characteristic rhythm of that incessant interior monologue became who he was.

In the summer of 1932 the scholarship exams for the County High and King Henry's were later than usual. Not until early June did the hopeful candidates turn up at the two schools for their long day: an interview with the begowned Headmaster or Headmistress; a piece of written composition; some arithmetical problems; a general knowledge paper; and if the candidate declared a language, a piece of translation. Jim

41

translated some Latin sentences. Finally, a piece of prose or verse to read aloud.

On 8 July Tom Davies announced to Pandy School a record seven scholarships won: Raymond Williams, with Hilda Jenkins, Betty Hassell, Ethel Tompkins, Violet James, Esmé Groves, and Winnie Caldecott. It is a pleasure to record that Jim came out first of the boys applying to King Henry's, with a score of 204; it is an even greater pleasure to be able to tell Violet James, similarly top of all the girls, that she scored better on the day, with 218.[19]

3

THE GOOD TOWN
Abergavenny and the scholarship boy

In 1932, Abergavenny was a border town all right. South-west, over the first range of the Black Mountains, lay the Wales of the valleys, the embattled heartlands of the long strike, headquarters of Wales's best, and as it may be, most sentimental picture of itself. The deep clefts of the valleys each run up to the hard, huddled towns grouped about the pitheads then clustering at the tip of the valley fingers. The names read grandly like battle honours of the Labour movement: Tredegar, Ebbw Vale, Bargoed, Abertillery, Maesteg. The parallel lines of the valleys etch the landscape westwards, beyond Cardiff. Nowadays, after the grim and muddled resistance of the year-long miners' strike in 1984–5, after the revenge taken by the English Right upon its most long-standing class enemies in their minefield redoubts, the pithead wheels and winding gear are either gone completely or fixed in the shining perfection of themepark imagery. The sky is cleared of the hellish pall of smoke from the long terraces burning their own coal from thousands of domestic chimneys. The boarded-up shops and empty yards in the little factories, the street flotsam, the quiet, bear witness to the passing, wilfully brought about by foolish and rancorous politicians 200 miles east, of an historic order, and the powerful, noisy, dense and bloodstained way of life which it sustained.

In 1932, the terrific life of Wales lay in this order in the south. The coal poured out, upwards to Birmingham, down to the vast docks in Newport and Cardiff (at the turn of the twentieth century, *half* of all the world's coal was provided by Britain), and westwards along the littoral to the enormous steel rolling mills at Port Talbot and Swansea.

Abergavenny still stands on this border. When Jim Williams went home from school, he could look back at the evening sky and see the huge and rosy glow of the great blast furnaces on the coast reflected on the low bank of clouds, as the men in the mills – 'I have never seen such self-confident men since' – in their medieval visors and gauntlets, sweat-drenched and muscular, opened the massive doors for a minute.

The town described itself as a gateway – gateway to the rich agricultural land of the wide Wye valley as it opened into Herefordshire and

43

Worcestershire, gateway also to the sparsely populated and vaguely mysterious spaces of inner Wales; gateway long before that, a heavily guarded
and bolted gateway too, during the centuries of warlording, guerrilla war,
civil war, which is the history of the Marches, and of the people of Black
Mountains. The warlords and the kings came to the gate of Abergavenny
and met the Britons, the Celts and the Welsh there, for deals, for treaties,
for murder, and in battle.

Henry VIII was one of the kings; his officers came to the border, to
command and colonise for sure, but also to settle it and make it safe for
prosperity, their own in particular. The warlords had fought up and down
England and Wales for a couple of centuries, until Henry's father settled
all hashes in Leicestershire in 1485, and the son began to limn the features
of the modern state upon his country, to follow its money well away from
the Roman Church, and to educate the local élites of his scattered, incom-
municable fiefdom in the ways of London, Protestantism, and the ideas
of the Renaissance cashed into a securely indigenous currency.

The great strength of Raymond Williams's kind of socialism is that, like
the homegrown socialism of William Morris and R.H. Tawney, it commits
itself unequivocally to the side of the losers, and to living by their values.
The problem about any such commitment, inherited as it is from the forms
of Christianity, is its only sometimes forgivable aptitude for sanctimony.
In the famous interviews of 1979 transcribed as *Politics and Letters*,
Williams refers to Henry's establishment of the grammar school as part
of a deliberate policy of Anglicisation:

> What I did not perceive at the time but I now understand is that
> the grammar schools were implanted in the towns of Wales for the
> purpose of Anglicisation. They imposed a completely English orien-
> tation, which cut one off thoroughly from Welshness.[1]

It is an emphasis which becomes more prominent in all Williams's later
work and life. It is also a routine gesture in all cultural analysis by the
bien pensant progressives of a more recent generation. But such remarks
not only do very little analytically, they ignore the untheorised but highly
plausible possibility that historical progress may be simply unable to take
place without some version of the system now identified as imperialism.
In any case, Henry VIII doubtless intended his network of schools, broadcast across his country, to stabilise his rule, to ensure administrative continuity and a literate élite capable of running a competent bureaucracy,
to create an English culture, in form, language, feeling: of course he did.
And if he hadn't, who would rather have lived according to the previous
version of pastoral? In a state of beastly, nomadic warfare and under a
distant and arbitrary theocracy, redeemed only by enclaves of prosperity
built on sheep?

The royal grammar schools of England and Wales turned into one of the key class fortifications of the country's market towns. Abergavenny's King Henry VIII Grammar School was, by the time it was handsomely rebuilt in 1898, one such. The schools reproduced a local version of a posh education for the sons – and, a little later in the nineteenth century, the daughters – of local worthies, the professionals and the well-off merchants who were going to make sure that their children maintained the social standing that parental effort had won for the family. In the bursting economy of the second half of the nineteenth century, the strong, quick intertwining of its regions which the new railways made possible, and the surprisingly strong local feeling and allegiance which British capitalism engendered, these grammar schools did what schools are supposed to do: ensured the continuity of the parents' world into the world of the next generation, and stood as monuments commemorating those parents in the lives of their more prosperous and better educated children.

The schools proved, according to their parochial, at times philistine lights, historically flexible also. Their very first function had indeed been to 'Anglicise', and to do so in the name of a nation scarcely born. The grammar schools of Henry VIII and Elizabeth founded that part of a nation which discovered inspiration as well as status in study of the Trivium and Quadrivium of the sixteenth-century curriculum. From Wordsworth's Cockermouth in the north west of England to Dover on the south east coast, by way of the few main thoroughfares and the Midland market towns – Leicester, Derby, Coventry, Stratford, Sutton Coldfield, Stamford, Bristol, picking up Abergavenny, Hereford and Worcester on the way west – such institutions were set to create and establish a literate, mercantile class owing its ultimate allegiance to Crown not Church, and offering stable political leadership in its parish.

They had and have their stifling narrowness, local bigotries, and invincible snobberies. But they made, as they say, for continuity. Not only that; they provided for the necessary adaptations of history. When industrialisation produced a highly skilled, articulate and economically indispensable class of artisans as well as its desperate armies of wage-slaves, the grammar schools responded involuntarily to the impulses of Victorian philanthropy in its typically local and mutton-chop-whiskered versions, in order to accommodate the cleverest boys and girls born into this threatening and insurgent new class.

So the scholarship schemes came to life all across the country, and 'free placers' joined the children of the local traders, farmers, small gentry and any of the manufacturing households which couldn't rise to the fees of the new public schools, so misleadingly called because anyone could turn up there who could afford the bill. By the time Raymond Williams was a 'new boy' at King Henry's, the scheme had been running twenty-odd years, but Harry and Gwen still had to find the two guinea tuition fee – only eight bob less than a week's wages for Harry – every term.

Harold West

... it was a struggle while Jim was studying at home, Harry said. He could never have done it without help from the manager of the co-op. He let Harry pay for Jim's grammar school rig – blazer, dark trousers, cap, and the tie of course – so he'd be the same as everyone else. Two shilling a week he paid, right through school from 11 to 18. Course he was only just 18 when he went to University.

There were three sisters living in the three houses round the Williamses, Mrs Preedy, Mrs Bagley, and Mrs Watkins. Two of them had no children, and Jim was a sort of substitute-son. They would help with clothes for school, and they gave him a satchel to put his books in, as a present when he started. Of course at home, everything went on Jim, it was only natural, with him being an only.

As was usual in these local grammar schools, there were never big numbers of pupils attending; thirty-odd new boys joined each year during the 1930s, and each year roughly the same number took School Certificate and the Higher Certificate, the two levels of leaving examination, the first attesting to competence of a decidedly academic kind in the main subjects taught, the second – required by universities for entrance – to more specialised and even more academic adequacy in two or three subjects classified as either arts or science (but never both at once).

These antique divisions of knowledge, devised round about the middle of the nineteenth century, still hold in English and Welsh (but not Scottish) schools. But a different educational pressure was making itself felt in the aftermath of world war and the actuality of economic slump. In 1934 H.W. Newcombe, the Headmaster, noted to His Majesty's Inspector that he had the same eight staff members as he had when last formally inspected in 1922, but that school numbers had doubled to 169 boys. 'Border children' (in the school's own phrase) were now admitted, for extra fees, from down-county Herefordshire, and the average length of stay in the school had risen to four years seven months which meant that most pupils left after taking their School Certificate, and went to join their fathers in order to learn the business of the family shop or firm.

Fewer boys stayed on to become the school's sixth form, manning its cricket, athletics and rugby football teams, and recognised about the town as their future mayors, aldermen, magistrates, county councillors and head-masters. By the time Raymond was starting the two years of sixth form work towards his Higher Certificate, there were twenty-eight boys in the two sixth form classes, divided pretty much between English, French, Latin (Williams's three subjects for his Higher), History and Divinity, in the Arts, and Physics, Chemistry, Biology and Maths in the sciences.

These, indeed, were the subjects 11-year-old Jim faced when he began at the fine, low, redbrick building fronting the Monmouth road. It was a single storey building in the best late Victorian educational style, with a modest display of decorated pediment, brick mullions, scrolled gable ends, in keeping with the redbrick universities which were its peers, and politely imitative of the original Gothic in the colleges of Oxford and Cambridge to which King Henry's regularly sent its star pupils, and would in due course send its most celebrated alumnus, Raymond Williams.

Inside, the stone floors of the corridors rang to the solid shoes with their metal heeltips of boys and staff, to muffled shouts quickly hushed – school rules were strict about shouting and running in school buildings – and were faintly redolent of unburned gas and damp flannel blazers and trousers drying on their wearers after rain. It was not until 1935 that the governors, those grave citizens and ex-pupils, authorised £65 to electrify the school, and by the time Raymond left there was still no kitchen for hot lunches, and the meals were brought up from an Abergavenny caterer in military hayboxes, and unpacked for serving in the school hall in a dense miasma of boiled cabbage, grey beef and gravy.

The daily rhythm, and the annual one as well, moved with the pleasant severity and certainty of the railway timetable and the farm. Raymond would take the train down from Pandy at the special rate for the child of an employee of the railway. The other children, as Violet Higgs recalls, went in by bus. He left on the 7.50 a.m. down train, with his father, as often as not, waving briefly as he passed the box, and then walked, alone mostly, sometimes with his friend the Baptist minister's son, up to school to wait outside until, whatever the weather, the school caretaker unlocked the solid wooden doors and let the boys in at 8.30.

Prayers at 9 o'clock, all boys attending, ranged in the hall with the senior boys at the back, differentiated year by year down to new boys at the very front, looking up at the begowned and awful Head on his platform with the big lectern, the rest of the staff, mostly wearing their college gowns, sitting behind him in slovenly dignity (notably Mr A.L. Ralphs, English master there since 1914 and Williams's highly influential teacher). Anglican prayers, a hymn from *Songs of Praise*, school notices, off to lessons. Each lesson forty-five minutes, terminated by a handbell rung by the school caretaker; five lessons a day except Wednesday afternoon, for games; *quod semper est, quod ubique, quod ab omnibus*. Lessons, the teacher at the front of the class, behind a desk on a little dais, directing, telling, questioning, explicating with chalk and blackboard, hazed in a cloud of chalkdust as he wiped the board, then setting his class to do the exercises he has just described, the quiet, the scratch of pens, an arm raised, a question taken and dispatched, the collecting in of exercise books with completed homework in them ('please, sir, I couldn't finish it', 'please sir, I dropped my book in the farmyard, it's dirty, sir'), the bell, a shuffling and stretching and murmur of conversation quickly suppressed until the master – as they used to say – left and his replacement, Mr Ralphs, was awaited.

Mr Ralphs; English now, taught by an Englishman with a strong feeling for Welsh literature in translation, for Dafydd ap Gwilym[2] and the Welsh

47

medieval poets but also a strong philologist. Like all English teachers, he taught plenty of traditional grammar as invented by the Greek-and-Latin-trained classicists of the nineteenth century. That is, he taught the parts of speech, clause analysis and parsing, above all the names of sentence units – 'noun clause in apposition, come on, Williams, I AM THAT I AM, the most terrifying sentence in the Bible, verb "to be" plus *complement*' – and he taught semantics, the changing history of meaning, caught and held in that selective tradition of poetry and prose as taught in Welsh and English grammar schools, which was to be near the heart of his famous pupil's life's work.

That tradition began, between 1932 and 1939, with Chaucer's *Canterbury Tales*, jumped to Shakespeare, a great eminence with very little poetry around him except for a Caroline songster or two as chosen by the excellent Mr Palgrave for his *Golden Treasury*, and of course the giant Milton (*Lycidas* and a couple of books of *Paradise Lost*) half a century later (King Henry's naturally taking a Royalist line in the Civil War, Charles the Martyr having given Abergavenny its corporation in 1638). Then a brief pause in the eighteenth century at *The Deserted Village*, a glimpse of *The Rape of the Lock* and maybe a fragment of *The Essay on Man*, before passing through the great gate of Romanticism set up by Gray's *Elegy in a Country Churchyard*, and into the echoing vaults of the eloquent style as spoken by the Wordsworth and Keats of *The Prelude*, *Tintern Abbey*, and the *Odes*, all consummated in the taste of all those assuming their poetic sensibilities, like Mr Ralphs, at the end of the nineteenth century, by the mighty line of Alfred Lord Tennyson, and his tinkling accompanist, A.E. Housman.

These were the poems Raymond Williams was taught at school, of which he learned portions by heart for homework, to be recited, boy by boy, in class later that week. One may easily discern the framework of *The Country and the City* in its syllabus. One may also express some surprise that, with the giant exceptions of Shakespeare and Wordsworth, he seemed not to acquire any great passion for these poems, or for poetry. Neither then, now or on the rare occasions in later life when Williams wrote about poetry, did he ever seem particularly moved by it. He seemed deaf to the music of the pentameter, both to the magnificence of Keats or to what he later grossly misnamed as the 'cold wit' of T.S. Eliot.

Wordsworth was another matter and in particular when he too showed strong feeling for, and sympathy with, history's losers. Thus, in the crowded and estranging streets of London, Williams caught sight of Wordsworth's beggar:

> Amid the moving pageant, I was smitten
> Abruptly, with the view (a sight not rare)
> Of a blind beggar, who with upright face

Stood propped against a wall, upon his chest
Wearing a written paper, to explain
His story, whence he came, and who he was.
Caught by the spectacle my mind turned round
As with the might of waters; an apt type
This label seemed of the utmost we can know,
Born of ourselves and of the universe,
And on the shape of that unmoving man,
His steadfast face and sightless eyes I gazed
As if admonished from another world.[3]

Tintern itself was not far down the valley, though Williams was also curiously incurious: he never mentioned doing the sights of the sites, whether of Romanticism or capitalism: Mike Dibb, while making a TV exposition of *The Country and the City*, discovered to his surprise that Williams hadn't visited the country houses he wrote about with such enmity, and took him to Tatton. And for a partial Welshman, Williams also seemed to have acquired little feel for music, either from King Henry's school concerts and daily hymns, or from the many Eisteddfods he attended, in Pandy as well as in the town.

There were few books at home: the Bible and the *Beekeeper's Manual*, as he said, and a few half-reference and half-Wonder Books. The Williamses didn't know what to buy, which is odd, given his father's quick, conversational, political disposition. When he passed the scholarship exam for King Henry's so handsomely, in a queer, inarticulate but surely recognisable spasm of happiness, his mother went out and bought her victorious 10-year-old the Everyman edition of *The Trojan Women* and *Prometheus Chained*, as uncomprehended tokens of the learning to which her son had won access. The incident, as Williams later said, went undecorated into *Border Country*; one could hardly imagine a more abrupt testing of the doctrine of the universality of literature. Apart from these prizes, and such a vademecum as *The Home Lawyer* which Raymond bought at 16 when it had been suggested that he might become a solicitor, there were never many books around. Even in later years, people noticed how comparatively small his personal library was. It was piled up with review copies from thirty years of weekly reviewing, of course, but Williams never *bought* many books ('it took me twenty to thirty years, if it ever changed, to get used to the idea that books were something to be bought').[4] For a learned man, he didn't really read many either, and he was always sketchy and impatient with the necessary scholarship of bibliography, as his first publishers mildly pointed out. His hoards of words-and-ideas were stacked in his head; his reading was only a necessary prompt to these; his intellectual life was a matter of listening in to the torrential monologue of his interiority. Sometimes he turned it on to paper, at others to an audience. As many people noticed, from an early point in his lecturing career, his speaking voice would move into a rapid, undulating and at times incantatory fluency, as though what he said were spoken through rather than by him.

How does a person's disposition become what it is? Williams later spoke of his own propensity by the time he went to Cambridge for cheerful certitude, and the doubts, strains and tensions as only transpiring later. I would rather say that something in him responded fiercely and gladly to the stern, solitary regime of his childhood, to his father's severe, strenuous but live and forceful teaching, to his mother's insistence that he keep working, alone, hour after hour, at the compositions and exercises, the learning-by-heart and the preparations-for-debate which the boy brought home from school.

Within this discipline, the boy wrote and thought prose as much as he read it. On Holy Mountain he thought the prose into narratives, always writing intensely upon the pages of his imagination, but while the prose and the thought were fluent, the feeling in them was stiff and unpractised. His parents taught him solitary application and a proper acknowledgement of his own great intellectual gifts. He learned from them the special devotions of an only child, the heavy weight of loyalty, the namelessness of love, the irrelevance of happiness. As a consequence, a momentous self-confidence and a muffled, obscure and fearful resentment settled themselves as deeply characteristic of Williams's disposition.

Much later on, Williams came to criticise psychoanalysis, and the reliance of the bourgeoisie upon it, very sharply and accurately. As always, he sought to correct the over-individualising of social explanation in English-speaking thought, and to insist upon the inclusively social formation of lives and selves and histories. Yet Freud would not have had any difficulty with the idea that his essential protocols are mediated always by culture, nor with the fact that the coexistence in the Williams family of deep feeling and an utter muteness towards that feeling would make an only child into a man whose serene strength and darkly disappointed self-absorption proved more than a match for each other. Let it be said that Williams turned this daunting combination of attributes into a character of remarkable grace and poise, as well as one of needful elusiveness and concealment.

In 1934, his grandfather died, and his grandmother and Herbert Bird, purportedly his youthful uncle, in point of fact his half-brother, came to live at the Williams house. The change barely affected Raymond's position as only child. His mother guarded his studies as keenly as ever; his father, always keeping railway work and market gardening for his best social self, continued to teach his son but not his stepson. Raymond learned privacy, all through his body and temperament, learned to see from the Skirrid and the Kestrel the way his father's world joined the big world over the hills and up the valley, and learned to feel the heavy, thwarted anxiety which became the best his mother could do by way of love, and the dark inexpressibility of his father's, which corresponded to it, and from which he was released by work, by good signalling, by blossom and bees.

Harry never taught his son to garden well; he was always clear about the superior standing of mental over manual labour. Nor did he teach him the practical crafts – domestic carpentry in particular – at which he himself excelled. Williams later on tried to turn his devoted admiration for his father into copying him, but he was always a crude sort of gardener, best at wholesale cutting down of weeds than anything more patient and punctilious by way of raking, dibbling, pruning, grafting. (Yet when the privileged classes went in for such things, he was pretty hard on their pretensions, which was hardly fair.)

The lessons in how to think and how to use the instruments of thought were all in words, and words Williams was good at. The lessons in living, feeling, joining, were object-lessons, and Williams took them hard. They were there, but they couldn't be effortlessly reached like the language could. So he developed a symmetry in his way of being in the world, between an inexpressible privacy and a universal declaration of civic senti- ment. There's an odd little tale told by Peter Griffith, a later associate of his at the Open University. Griffith had known Williams when a student, and was working with him on a tutorial film. During a break in filming at the old Alexandra Palace (almost the last programme to be made there) he said to Williams that his own family came from the border at pretty much the same place, and since there were several Williamses in his genealogy, 'It's possible,' he proffered genially, 'that we're related.'

Williams stiffened in silence, and then with involuntary suddenness, 'Oh no, that's quite impossible.' Perhaps realising the discourtesy in his rebuff, he explained, 'But they'd certainly have known each other.'

Peter Griffith

This second statement was no more grounded than the first. What had happened was that I had, as they say nowadays, intruded on his private space, and he moved to defend it. The rebound from that was his insistence on community. Both were, in some sense, the products of *will* alone.[5]

This balancing of ardour against detachment, and of public against private life, with the ardour eloquently spoken for, and the detachment truly lived, meant that he saw the goodness of the way of life in Pandy and Abergavenny for what it was, but rarely lived in it afterwards. He could name what was bad in that good life as lived in public, but not what was bad about the life he lived in private. That is to say, he could plainly see the awful posturings and sentimentalities in the Eisteddfod as well as the moment when 'against his determination, felt himself caught up in that movement and pressure of the audience by which, in response, they became virtually part of the choir'.[6] But then to give himself, in public or private, to be generous of himself, was damnably hard.

Perhaps this is only what everybody finds who learns to treasure the life of the mind, that the fascination of what's difficult indeed dries up the sap of natural content, as Yeats swore it did. But Yeats kept 'blood, imagination, intellect' running together; doing so became for a time a mark of the well-lived life, and Williams couldn't manage it. He couldn't name his mother's speechlessness about love, nor his own indifference to her; he couldn't blame his father's colossal self-centredness, even though he saw it well enough. So he makes Will Price in *Border Country* into a nasty, carping bit of work, unable to write the one book he has set himself, and forever picking on the women in his life, his mother and his almost-sister, almost-sweetheart Eira, for incorrect attitudes.

It cannot, however, be doubted that the way of life in Pandy and Abergavenny, and at King Henry's and the sister school, the County High School for Girls, as this was lived during Raymond Williams's school life was as rich and plentiful as it was small and ordinary.

Days are where we live, nowhere else to go than to our parish. After all the class demonstrations and self-righteousness about country life and sports, it's a pleasure to hear Violet James (as she was) talk glowingly about the meet of Pandy hounds, or about the Scouts and Guides, or the great ritual of Sunday lunch at the farm, the gathering of family, the white starched damask of the big tablecloth.

Violet Higgs

Harry Williams was a friend of my father's. They used to share work in the fields, and Harry rented a piece of ground from us. The hounds met at the farm – we looked after a small park there. I rode to hounds from the age of 12 on one of the farm ponies. I *loved* it, I've ridden all my life, I still do. After the war our hunt amalgamated with the Monmouthshire hunt, but it was always, well, *local*, everybody came out, lots of people followed on foot, a few riders wore pink, but it wasn't that, it wasn't a snobbish sort of show, it was all the local farming families, and we all knew each other. There was no particular order or rank, you know, not with us. Sometimes my father took us just to watch the hunt. He had the first car in Pandy, a Wolseley ex-police car with a brass radiator and a canvas roof. Our saddler used to mend it. But I'd always rather ride.

But you mustn't think that was the only thing in Pandy. There were Scouts and Guides. Jim was a Scout and he looked well in the scout hat with the brim, you know. We had a joint party – the idea! – at Jill Festing's big house where we always met – old Mrs Festing ran the WI which Mrs Williams was a pillar of, for thirty years I should think.

... And there was the Drama Society, which put on plays at the Village Hall. Harry

Williams did the scenery. Jim wrote two plays,[7] I believe, for them, though I didn't see them myself. Of course, there was the football club and the cricket club, and the bowling green down by the school, where Harry looked after the turf ...

The bowling green and club: one of England's happiest sporting inventions, devised essentially, as all the recognisable versions of our sports were, during the colossal upheaval of nineteenth-century industrialisation, when the formless sporadic antics of antique games were turned into the neat and uniformed ceremonies, gravely conducted in well-kept urban parks, of their pre-television successors. Football stadia looked like factories around the little stretch of turf; the giant, civic crowds looked like the workforce going through the gates. Bowling greens looked like back gardens, with their neat little runs of white fencing, their herbaceous borders, the unbelievably close, thick emerald turf, the quiet knocking and clacking of the glossy woods. They pictured the huge class compromise of England and Wales at its elderly and aldermanic leisure, in shirtsleeves or linen jackets, murmuring over the tiny geometry of jack and wood.

The farms, the railway, the chapels and the school and all around them the modest mountains, were the material ground for this ideal culture.

Abergavenny, as befitted it, was a metropolis. *The Abergavenny Chronicle* was, and is, both archive and a sort of collective epic, a poem written by divers hands. Looking at what it tells us of life in the town, it is hard to resist Williams's judgement[8] that 'mobile privatisation' (which, as he agrees of his own coinage, is 'one of the ugliest phrases I know') has replaced something much stronger and much more communitarian in British provincial life since that life so flourished in Abergavenny, and in countless towns like it, in the 1930s. The geographical mobility of the car and the cognitive mobility of the television have together driven people back into their smallest social compass, making them spectators of everywhere, and active nowhere.

It is not nostalgic to say so; or if it is, nostalgia has much to be said for it. Abergavenny, when we have allowed for Anglo-Welsh snobberies, small-town philistinism, slump and the absence of a welfare state, was then a dignified town lining its two main axes, the Hereford to Monmouth road, and the road south-west alongside the river Usk to the valleys, all gathered tidily to its topknot around the green cupola of the Town Hall. From this small summit ran and run the orderly lines of shops with their wide canvas awnings stretching over half the pavements, their looped copperplate name-signs, the dark and solid pubs with their malty smell, the two small garages with two handpumps each for petrol, and a deep shed at the back for repairs to the town's modest cavalcade of Austin Sevens, Morris Eights, Hillman Fourteens, easily parked along the quiet, rainy street.

Behind the High Street, the big expanse of market, active since the fifteenth century, built into proper livestock pens for cattle and sheep and auctioneers in 1862, rebuilt proudly in 1925, the proud little classical Market Hall, where the merchants and farmers gauged the grain and paid on the nail outside, dated 1794.

Across a wide aisle, crowded on market days with bidders, farmers, shoppers, sheepdogs, stood a familiar township of temporary stalls, roofed with tarpaulin and furnished with trestles-and-plank tables. The Williamses shared one of these for the Saturday market – at very productive times of year, when the honey was plentiful or the fruit thick on the bushes – they rented a mid-week stall as well. They sold the honey, jam, bottled fruit, tinned fruit – Mrs Williams had bought an old-fashioned canning machine – eggs, and the occasional clamorous cockerel or, in winter, a sack or two of spuds. But they kept their son away from the stall, up at home and at his work. He didn't roam the market with the other lads while his mother ran the stall and his father, after catching up on sleep lost during the long night shifts, took over when he had the chance to come on by train the four miles from Pandy.

None the less, the boy's move to the grammar school inevitably meant his first step away from class and home had been taken. The narrative form of Williams's life – 'form' being the supreme abstract to puzzling out the meaning of which he gave so much time and effort – is figured in the strain to move away from home and the straining to return there.

It is a commonplace enough force-field, but the effort to make out and to measure the tensions kills everybody in the end. In the twentieth century, the diagram pictures that massive impulse which thrusts people towards the vindication of their own individuality, the freedom to fantasise the line of their own lives, the occasional opportunity to pick up those lives, and walk freely with them. But the same century has struggled to retain or reinvent the dream of home, of a place and its membership which will confer identity of themselves, without any irritable reaching out after personal discovery.

Williams later spoke of the grammar school as 'intellectually deracinating', but this is both a mistake and the paradox which posed his life-question. Abstract thought, the powers of theorisation and the habit of detachment, the very project of human enlightenment are exactly that: they pull up roots to examine and understand them. Education is intended to free the mind from the darkness of locality, its superstition, habit-learning, its denial of the possibility of progress and its grudging refusal of emancipation. Yet somewhere in the long passage which tore him from his racination, he found his oracular riddle: how shall educated thought conduce to customary knowledge? Or, how shall the progressive intellectual of the Left turn grand theory to the purposes of domestic settlement, of local knowledge and ordinary experience?

The very forming of such questions is itself a substantive contribution to the changeful science of human affairs, of which we stand always in such need, never more so than now. The lively culture of Abergavenny was as good a place as could be found by such a boy, and the man he became. It gave him a clear, courteous and openly conducted class struggle. It gave him a dependable education with a direct lead in English literature to the paradoxical necessity of combining ardour and detachment. It gave him Wales and England, linked by the bridge over the river. It gave him country and city, the shapely little city–state of Abergavenny, the busy market traffic pouring in from three roads.

In 1932, Councillor Truman, a railwayman and lifelong Labour member, became mayor of the town, and under his leadership the Town Council applied to be regarded as an officially 'distressed area', which would mean government aid and investment. The Council debated without acrimony the many shops and working premises in the town that stood empty, boarded up or their windows whitewashed along the quiet High Street.

But the brief skirmish which the *Daily Mail* feared as the insurrection presaging class war in 1926 was long gone, and the busy, pacific sound of local life offered the occasions of a decent, genteel and collaborative culture. In April of 1932 the town was electrified, and the Amateur Operatic Society produced their first Gilbert and Sullivan with electric footlights instead of the hot and smelly things which went back to Dickensian days (so, too, the regular boxing meetings in the same town hall). In May, the biggest Eisteddfod for miles around, pulling in all the best performers from the satellite Eisteddfods in Pandy, Crucorney, Llangattock and elsewhere to a massive, twelve-hour marathon of recitations, instrumental and singing solos, orchestral pieces, all completed by the grand, sweeping male voice choirs so 'devastatingly mounting', in Williams's words, 'that conscious emotional attack', and keeping up their relentless, bitter rivalries.

In early autumn, as always, as still, the Abergavenny Agricultural Show, for which the schools closed for the day, and the children filed happily on to the showground with the milling, sober and civil crowds.

> Let it stay hidden there like strength, below
> Sale-bills and swindling; something people do,
> Not noticing how time's rolling smithy-smoke
> Shadows much greater gestures; something they share
> That breaks ancestrally each year into
> Regenerate union. Let it always be there.[9]

They got another day off when the Duke and Duchess of York, later the King and Queen, made a royal visit to the town, and later on they took a big Saturday trip to Llanover Park on the other side of the Usk, the mighty Herbert family's home seat, in order to join the junketings in celebration of old Lord Treowen's eightieth birthday. Amidst these routine

55

confirmations of the omnipresence of Old Corruption, the reader pays tribute, as the *Chronicle* faithfully does, to the songs and music of the Railway Clerks Association smoking concert [*sic*], the Locomotive Welfare Fund concert (attended, among others, by Mr H.J. Williams), the GWR Ambulance Dinner, and the League of Nations Union meeting on disarmament. (A few years later, Jim Williams was their leading speaker on that hardy perennial at a public debate.)

Politics flourished besides Letters in Abergavenny. As well as the League, the Labour Social and Study Centre (next week – December 1932 in fact – 'Dictatorship and Democracy'), the Congregational Church put on three plays, as did the rival church of St Hilda's, both schools performed set pieces in the grand manner (the Headmistress herself producing an all-girls *St Joan* at the County High), and Jim, pottering off to Sunday School under the eye of his God-fearing grandparent, appeared in Pandy at the Sunday School concert, singing 'The Pipes of Pan'.

A working-class boy growing up in Britain between 1930 and 1960 (or so) was much more fully educated by his father's generation than was the case thereafter. The unboundaried spaces of social identity have been filled for nearly two generations by peers and pop, for better and for worse. But within the deeply traditional forms of farmers' town and railway line, of market garden and grammar school, young Jim Williams began to glimpse the outline of his contradictory twin, Raymond, and was both held by the closeness and geniality of his father's circle of workmates, and propelled just as genially out of that circle into a completely other world of which he consciously and conscientiously denied himself a similar membership all his life.

Only in and near Abergavenny did his thought and his feeling so flow through one another that he was at home, and like his beloved, inaccessible father, he was much more at home in the signal box than at home. In the bleak stone house below the mountain, there were such silences: the lonely silence of work, when Jim leaned back from the schoolwork lying on his grandfather's desk and stared unseeingly out of the window, listening to the long monologue of his consciousness; the harder, heavier silence of his mother and father at their meals, his father's peremptory, self-absorbed injunctions – 'more tea' – his mother's sharper admonitions of her son, her brief reports of sales of canned fruit or eggs, to dealers or in the market.

Until he was 14 or 15, Jim's happiest moment was to set off up the winding lane of the village, turning left before the Baptist chapel, under the low bridge, to clamber up to the high railway embankment, before daydreaming his way to the box with his father's snap tin and cold, sweet, milky tea. In the box, he remembered, there might be one of the local farmers talking, there'd be gangers passing, the heavy wrenches dangling across their shoulders, pausing to talk; there'd be the quick, convivial, always jocular exchanges with the train drivers themselves, the proud élite of the industry, the lines of their faces strongly etched by coal dust, their big hands hard as knobs of coal. And there would often be the quick walk, following his father, back to the station itself where they had all known young Jim since he could toddle, stationmaster, the booking clerk, the porter, the other signalmen, the man who kept the flowerbeds and repaired the heavy cattle pens, the platelayers who worked the length of the line from Abergavenny to Hereford.

Until war came again, these men expected their sons to follow them on to the railway, doing a bit better in terms of status and pay perhaps – a booking clerk got £4 a week to Harry's £2 10s – but learning the customs and discipline of the railway, like sailors or foundrymen, subjecting themselves and their sons to its hard labour and unyielding hours, until they were gathered into its continuities, until they died, usually in harness.

So young Jim learned their politics, and Raymond never forgot them, lived and died by them, too, with all the discrepancies such remembrance brought to the life of the mind and the privileges of the professoriat. The politics transpire directly from the way of work; it is an exceptionally pure example of what Marx called the relations of production expressing themselves in the ideas and values which those relations embody. The line from economic base to cultural superstructure is dead straight. The steel rails joining town to town, carrying livestock, human stock, chickens and honey; the telephone wires joining signal box to box; the massive engines snorting and chuffing past the neat flowerbeds and trim, gritstone buildings made the solidarity, the dependable discipline, the jokes and friendships what they were.

For Harry Williams, those values were under the protection of the Labour movement and the Labour Party. On other borders, in Italy or Germany or China, between 1922 and 1933, such links proved queasier. Socialist railwaymen disappeared or went to gaol. Here, with the coal valleys just out of sight, socialism looked a simple thing for men to pursue and plan for, and, very quietly, women to serve.

By the time Jim had started his fourth year at King Henry's, he was a cheerful, talkative, rangy lad with red hair falling in his eyes and the family's amiable Sealyham trotting up the mountain behind him. In class he was quick, eager to please, his arm shooting up in answer to questions, especially those from A.L. Ralphs, the English master, himself a man of capacious reading and as keenly responsive to new works of literature – he bought Joyce's novels and W.B. Yeats's poems as they came out – as he was to Palgrave and the Welsh Bards.

Ralphs was also the kind of teacher – he taught history as well – to keep the everyday facts of political life present in his classrooms. So when Stanley Baldwin called a general election in the autumn of 1935, Jim Williams was as aware of its implications as a powerful English teacher and a father who ran the branch Labour Party could make him. When the party had won the 1929 election there had been great rejoicing at home, and Jim, though only 8, was an instinctive supporter. By the age of 14 he wanted to be in the swim.

The Labour candidate in Monmouth was the 22-year-old Michael Foot,[10] just down from Oxford, and son of a big family of Asquithian Liberals whose commitment to a radical–moral politics was typical of the high-minded, publicly conscientious tradition of the English *haute bourgeoisie*, and the many recruits it sent into the intelligentsia. It is a tradition upon which Raymond Williams later expended not inconsiderable irony, and yet one which he could never place for himself, half-rejecting, half-joining it, never truly engaging with the significance of its Fabianism.

Becoming a Labour candidate in those days was an easy business. Michael Foot breezed in to see Jim Middleton, the Labour Party's national agent, asked about vacant candidatures, found that Monmouth needed one, and was unanimously accepted at the General Management Committee meeting soon afterwards. The sitting MP was, of course, a Tory, one Jack Herbert, scion of the great landowning Herbert family with their seat at Llanover Hall, and Lord Lieutenant of the County. The local farmers and their men were mostly Liberals (though the Jameses were Tories), the railwaymen were Labour, the women did as they were told, and the county always returned a Conservative until the excellent moment in 1966 when, with noticeably bad grace, the grandee Cabinet Minister Peter Thorneycroft gave way to the People's Party.

In 1935, however, young Foot hadn't a chance, but followed the well-known ceremony of initiations for Labour radicals of standing hopelessly upon the principles all good socialists of the day, including the Williams family, could cheer for: nationalisation of the banks and heavy industries (including railways – and twelve years later they jolly well were); raising the age of compulsory education to 14; a better and more generous scholarship system for access to grammar schools; the abolition of means-testing for unemployment benefits; above all, opposition to Fascism in Europe.

The Labour vote went up by 3,000, but Jack Herbert still got back easily, although not before Jim Williams and two friends had gone off to one of his public meetings armed with sticky questions of a most unexpected kind at that date, about pay and conditions for black workers in South Africa. Conservative public meetings until recently have been entirely genteel affairs by which the ruling class sought to take the politics out of politics, and serenely assume the polite complicity of absolutely everybody in the permanence of their rule. The boys' startling questions were positively rude noises in such a place – South Africa is ours so it must be all right – and so, it is said, a complaint about his fourth formers was murmured in the ear of the august Mr Newcombe, who sagely did nothing about it.

Young Williams had, however, entered politics. At about the same time, a happy accident gave him a much longer perspective upon that politics. His father went to see the vicar of the Church (of Wales; which is to say, of the Anglican communion) half a mile or so up the hill at Llanvihangel Crucorney, and asked him if he could give the boy some coaching in Latin. It was an initiative typical of Harry, born of the class confidence and intellectual assurance which he so successfully reproduced in his son.

The Reverend J.A. Hughes had known Jim since as a little fellow he went to the school which it was the vicar's duty to visit every week in order to check the register and, frequently, to speak to one or other of the classes or 'standards'. He knew that Jim was the only boy in the memorable year in which the school won seven scholarships, and had followed his progress up King Henry's (even soothing Harry Williams when the lad only came second in his first year of the relentlessly competitive rankings out of which such schools built their ladders of social opportunity).

So he taught Raymond extra Latin, well enough for him later to take the subject at Higher Certificate. But he also taught him astronomy. If the account in *Border Country* is faithful, the vicar was a fine teacher and an imaginative man whose religious faith was diffuse to the point of unbelief. However that may be, he kept a telescope which he could set up in the belltower; he had a microscope in his study as well, and collections of slides, of insects, butterflies, flowers, fossils, through which Raymond roamed as suited him. And he talked; talked perhaps as his fictional voice, the voice of Mr Pugh, talked of the Skirrid:

> The chapels are solid organisations, Matthew. The church here is not. I don't mean that their religious professions are insincere, but they could equally, it seems to me, be professions in almost anything – any other system of belief, for instance. What matters, what holds them together, is what their members do, through them, for each other. God, you might say, is their formula for being neighbourly ... I'm just a sort of outpost, they're the real local organisation, you see.
>
> They call that mountain holy ... because once in a time of persecution men met there, secretly, to worship and build an altar of the stones. We make too much of persecution ... Every cause, good and bad, has had its martyrs, yet there are some foolish enough to think martyrdom sanctifying. Just as I said outpost. There are outposts of everything: many of them are bad ...[11]

And then – I so much hope Hughes truly spoke these words –

> If there were a cathedral out there, but still the mountain would dwarf it. Yet the cathedrals, the universities. Perhaps I am too much away from them. Perhaps they are only the chapels, better built.

Only as institutions, sometimes, they seem more. That, at least, you must go and see for yourself.[12]

The talk, another monologue, between telescope and microscope, astral time and geological time, gave Raymond Williams a far vaster ground for politics than the Labour Party knew. Somewhere between the belltower and the study, the lens which held the heavens and the lens which expanded the surface of a fossil until it looked like the surface of the moon, somewhere on the walk down the dark hill with the shadowy bulk of the Black Mountains on his left, he learned that 'a life lasts longer than the actual body through which it moves', and came to feel the multiple lives of the valley, 23,000 years of them, and the life of rocks and stones and trees, move through his own body also.

So politics was only the most immediate of the voices of history as divided up by the academy: astronomical, geological, archaeological, political. But it was always the most peremptory.

On 2 April 1937, coming up to 16, Raymond Williams was selected as one of the leading speakers at a public debate staged by the League of Nations Union, the forerunner of the Union Nations Association of today, whose members were the most genteelly public-spirited and respectably progressive of the local worthies, and whose president at the time was the King Henry's English master, A.L. Ralphs. The subject was 'Imperialism', which leftist worthies of the present day, sixty years later, rather suppose themselves to have discovered for the first time.

Williams had this to say, essaying a little of the early relativism taught him by Mr Ralphs, voicing an excusable incorrectness as to being civilised, but hitting the gold in the target about his country: 'We must get at the native point of view because they do not always regard matters in the same light as we do. And they fail to see in what ways they are less civilised than we are . . .' and then a bit more forthrightly, 'Britain grabbed most of Germany's colonies for herself in 1919.'[13] A month or so later, the new king replaced his so very embarrassing brother and old imperialism broke into a fever of fetes and village parties to celebrate stammering King George and his placid queen. At the Coronation fete in Pandy on 9 May there was bunting strung across the road by both pubs, a modest Union Jack or two on the school railings, a church parade for the Guides and the Scouts (doubtless including Jim in his Scout hat, shorts and knee socks with chevrons), a dog show, a car and motorcycle rally, with ribbons on the headlamps and the brass and chrome gleaming. There were sports up at Crucorney, a direly comic football match with the men dressed up as pantomime dames and worse, high tea in the Parish Hall. At a quarter to eight everyone fell respectfully quiet, and stood up with a great collective shuffling as the strains of the National Anthem clamoured tinnily out of the loudspeaker specially rigged up for the day. Then the King's speech, painfully sincere and given great earnestness by the fearsome stutter for which the whole audience in the hall braced itself apprehensively throughout.

At the Maytime Speech Day at King Henry's, graced by one of His Majesty's Inspectorate to dish out the prizes, Raymond Williams was called up to take the Fifth Form English prize. The Headmaster, who could pick prize-givers as well as prize-winners – the previous year had seen Sir Cyril Norwood, President of St John's College Oxford, Chair of Royal Commissions – noted that the school had six boys at the University of Wales, two at Cambridge, one at Oxford, and one at Manchester, and his future star academic sat down in late June to take and pass the six subjects for his School Certificate.

Before the end of term, Mr Ralphs had seen to it that the two brightest of the boys about to go into the sixth form, Raymond Williams and his pal Peter Laycock, were awarded travel scholarships by the League of Nations Union to take them to Geneva in order to see the League itself in action. This was no small event. Boys and girls from Pandy simply didn't go on foreign holidays; bless us all, the excursion train to Barry Island off the south Wales coast was pretty daring.

They were to attend an international summer school of similar scholarship holders from 'all over the British Isles, USA, Germany and France, including two dusky negresses',[14] and Raymond took up on the trip with one of 'several delightful companions', on whom, however, he declined to enlarge ('parents and schoolmasters are funny people'). Margaret was a handsome, fair-haired and well-built girl from the County High who lived a little way south of Abergavenny, and Gwen Williams was always to prefer her vengefully to the wife her jealously watched-over son later chose.

A cheerful party formed itself spontaneously from the school, and did its duties commendably by the timetable. They sat and listened to the officials and the commentators appointed to talk to them, and Raymond's sympathies went straight out to a British Labourite called Arnold Foster (in a red shirt) and Konni Zilliacus, an Anglo-Jew in the Michael Foot pattern, energetically on the side of the Popular Front and the Left, cultivated, polyglot, voluble, wild-haired, and an idealistic opponent of the arms race all his life (including his long later career as a Labour MP). 'He seemed the first wholly cosmopolitan man I had met.'

They did the sights: the castle of Chillon, Chamonix, a glacier or two, a walk up Mont Salève, the Simplon Pass, and on every turn of the road, the splendid Lake – Wordsworth's education repeated, and Williams's mountain-and-valley-bred sensibility was struck with a proper awe at the momentous scale of the Alps. And they discovered Geneva café life, with an innocence the knowing little travellers of the nineties have lost by the age of 7. As Peter Laycock endearingly said, 'In Geneva I have seen as many as three or four of these small cafés standing side by side.'[15] So they sat happily outside, boys and girls easily and politely together in a way that would have been tutted at beside the river Fenny.

At the end of the stay, it was Raymond Williams who was chosen by their delegation to read a school report on 'Reform of the League' to its final assembly, with one Sir Norman Angell, no less, in the chair. But there was never any doubt that he would carry the occasion off with aplomb; he did so for the rest of his life.

On their way home, the Welsh delegation took three days' licence in Paris, 'where the Exhibition stirred up the fires of interest and controversy in us', which turned out to mean that Williams, Laycock and two of the girls nipped out to the international exhibition, gazed incredulously at 'a large cardboard cut-out of Neville Chamberlain and a fishing rod', sampled more cafés and, in young Williams's case, went for a pious look at the Soviet pavilion fronted, inevitably, by a massive piece of socialist realist sculpture with a noble duo of workers, one man and one woman. So he bought *The Communist Manifesto*, read Marx for the first time, and went home.

He was a sixth former – no slight position at King Henry's – *The Plainsman* and George Formby were on at the Coliseum, Garbo in *Camille* at the Pavilion, and on 15 October the Geneva Scholarship winners were to report to the League of Nations Union at the Memorial Hall in Frogmore Street, Mr Ralphs presiding. Raymond Williams, the *Chronicle* reporter noted, came in for 'hostile criticism' on account of his attack on the British Government and its 'eyewash' support for the League. We can bet that this strikingly confident and fluent 16-year-old was completely undaunted by his critics – and the town had plenty of people to share his views, what with the Labour Party's day school on Spain and even the Free Church Council moving a condemnation of the Japanese bombing of Shanghai. It is also a fair bet that the maturing Jim and his father shared some ribaldry, as they read the *Chronicle* on a Friday evening, at the egregious Brigadier-General Tulloch from the County Council, whose regular appearances on the Letters page, on education, on air-raid precautions, on Spain, on wages, were so dependably risible and provided such a rich and comical sourcebook of the fatuity of English ruling-class ideas. (The buffer Tulloch appears in a surprisingly kindly version as Major Blakeney in *Border Country*.)

The placid, pacific school and county year turned toward 1938, Munich and the war. In amongst reports of the meaty mixture of Abergavenny's choral music – the Choral Society's *Messiah* and the Baptist Church's *Creation* in February, Raymond Williams published his first film review, of Capra's *Lost Horizon*, with *Parnell* at the Pavilion, *Oh, Mr Porter* and *Kid Galahad* to follow in March as his ordinary weekly fare.

But the Williamses didn't go into Abergavenny very much with their son. Raymond, travelling daily to school, took the trip for granted; but even so, visits to the cinema were weekend treats – 'only once a fortnight', Violet Higgs recalled, and the grammar school boys and girls were certainly not expected to go together, except decorously on Saturday evening and never in the late afternoons on weekdays. Back in Pandy there was the Eisteddfod in March, with Owen Y Fenny (as he became for the occasion) masterfully and tempestuously presiding, 'every human feeling at instantaneous command', the beakily handsome face and long spidery arms dominating the village, summoning and cajoling, bending tenderly over or dismissing each performer, and weaving each into the network of eloquent greeting and reminiscence by which the village comprehended and recognised itself. And Harry Williams spoke vigorously at a Pandy protest meeting, opposing the new water scheme for the valley which would put the rates up and take water away out of the locality, eastwards, to the English. After all, as everyone still tells you round there, the BBC weather forecast until 1974 was announced as being for England, Wales and Monmouthshire.[16]

His son, however, took *his* politics continent-wide. To the staunch, unspoken railway solidarities forged and set in the General Strike, Williams added the broad commitment of the Popular Front, the generalised allegiances of which to anti-Fascism, opposition to the arms race, and the vaguely defined, vigorously hated class enemies provided by capitalist bosses agreed well enough either with Michael Foot's platform version of the Labour Party or, more to the boy's taste at the time, with the Communist Party. After all, as Williams said later, 'In the big industrial centres, there were organised and conscious ideological battles. But for many socialists, communism was a branch of the labour movement, and certainly if the press and the government attacked it, then it must be generally all right. There was a combination of acceptance and distance towards it.'[17]

The sixth-form politics Williams learned wasn't Party business; that came at Cambridge. It was a vivid idealisation of his father's class experience added to a no less vital but ungrounded sense that society was ruled by the wrong people, that they were stupid but replaceable, and that his own class had the vision of social justice and equality as well as the sheer intelligence to overcome them and bring about the good society now being adumbrated in Soviet Russia.

In the 1990s, one can only look wistfully back at a time when this idealism and this determination were common in the sixth forms of market town grammar schools to say nothing of such ancient seminaries of class power as Winchester College.[18] The famous idealists of the late thirties became national heroes if they died punctually in the anti-Fascist war of 1939 to 1945; it was only later that communism became a synonym for treason, and then largely because the Americans said so. That ardent

63

giving-of-oneself to place, family, class, and then finding the pull of history and politics just as strong but in a contrary direction is one of Williams's most powerful as well as most obscure themes throughout his work, to which the words 'loyalty' and 'tragedy' serve only as spotlights.

At this stage of his life, Williams's strongest feelings, of hope and energy and life itself, could run straight from all his father told him into the imaginative vision of the future provided by socialism and the immediate quest of the League of Nations to discover a structure for peace. For a schoolboy with his ambitions this meant writing and talking; politics was a mixture of stirring prose and good lives. So after a peace week meeting about Czechoslovakia at the Town Hall in April, Raymond submitted an essay to the Union which took the prize and which he had then to read aloud with the other winners to an open meeting. 'These are the pillars upon which world peace must rest. The architects have done their work; bricklayers and masons are needed now.'[19]

Well, Abergavenny was a long way (as Chamberlain said) from Prague. Indeed, one of the affecting details of the life which Raymond and his peers on both Left and Right at Cambridge enjoyed just over a year later was their entire lack of fearfulness at the prospect, and then the advent, of world war. The Somme notwithstanding, these young men and women had a confidence in the future which Williams never lost, but which those who grew up under the shadow of nuclear war could not feel.

The horizons of the Sudetenland or of Catalonia were still distant, and the warm, sunny, grass-smelling sports field borrowed from the town for the day (for King Henry's had no sports field of its own) was a better place to be than Geneva. While *The Scarlet Pimpernel* was showing at the Coliseum, and Anna Neagle as *Victoria the Great* was at the Pavilion, Raymond Williams put in a strong challenge while still only 16 to be champion of the school sports, the *Victor Ludorum*, winning the quarter mile in a respectable 58.6 seconds (on grass), and turning in an impressive 18 feet in the long jump, always his best event. But his puff gave out in the mile, he didn't finish, and that was that.

With a comparable blitheness, the brightest lad that Ralphs had ever taught positively raced through the syllabus for his Higher Certificate. A few days after the sports day, he sat for English, Latin and French (with conversation), the Reverend Hughes's coaching and Ralphs's devoted teaching were rewarded with distinctions in both subjects well before the boy's seventeenth birthday and he was placed first in the County's table of Higher Certificates. He had an enviably lighthearted and responsibility-free year ahead of him at school, together with the presumption that at the end of it he would go off to an as yet unnamed university. Oddly enough, it seemed not to have occurred to anybody, certainly not his dad, devoted as he was to the discipline of a long, formal education, to suggest he took a job at this stage and fattened up the family's modest revenue.

So he and his parents, his gran and his still unacknowledged half-brother went off for a few days in a pleasant Teignmouth boarding house, while Hitler and Ribbentrop made a monkey out of the wretched Prime Minister.

The Munich agreement was signed just after Raymond went back for his last year at school. On 24 September, the Left Book Club, an admirable venture started a year or two earlier by Victor Gollancz with local branches across the country running meetings as well as selling the designated books, organised a rally 'against Fascism and war'. Kingsley Martin, then celebrated and long-standing editor of the *New Statesman* and John Lewis, hard nut of the Communist Party, came to speak. Admission was threepence and sixpence, but attendance was decidedly disappointing. After the invited speakers, Raymond Williams brought up the rear. The League of Nations Union did its bit with a meeting in November, but at the same time, the county's Conservative Association called a very large meeting in the Town Hall, at which a strong resolution supporting Chamberlain's policy in Czechoslovakia was resoundingly endorsed.

Some time during that term, Mr Newcombe the Headmaster wrote to Harry Williams asking him to call and see him. Neither man mentioned this to Raymond. Newcombe put his view to Harry that because of the exceptional ease, rapidity and high marks with which his son had sailed through the Higher Certificate, he, the Headmaster, should write personally to one or two of the colleges at Oxford or Cambridge proposing that they accept Raymond on this recommendation and his excellent results, since it was by this time too late to enter him along the usual route, with college or scholarship entrance exams to sit in December. Those same results, gained a year earlier than most pupils, had already won the award of a state scholarship of £100 per annum plus his tuition fees.

The school had long had close links with the two grandest universities in what was then, of course, a very much smaller network. Jesus College, Oxford, had famously been the college of the cleverest Welsh boys of the diaspora – 'Go into the first court of Jesus and shout "Jones", and half the windows open; shout "Davies", and the rest do the same' etc., etc. Indeed, the same college had paid an annual tithe of £50 for many years to King Henry's. In the event, Newcombe wrote to Trinity College, Cambridge, a much less homely institution, equally celebrated for its intellectual alumni (Newton, Boyle, Wordsworth, Russell) as for its throngs of old Etonians.

Williams later came over all sanctimonious over these moves on his behalf by the Head and his father; fairly enough, they told him nothing of their plans in case they came unstuck and he was very disappointed.

Why didn't my headmaster send me to a university in Wales? That would have been an orientation that would have suited my life much better. It is no use going back over it, but it would have. But this is what he was there for, to find boys like me and send them to Cambridge. I don't say this in any spirit of hostility to him; he thought he was doing the best thing for me.[20]

So he was: young Williams was going to study English literature in one of the greatest universities in the world. The rest is a fit of a kind of fervour which overcame Williams several times in later life. *Of course* he hit off his own, best way of life in virtue of having been sent to Cambridge; he couldn't have fashioned his thought out of anywhere else.

Anyway, he was accepted on the terms of the letter, and that was that. He took this success, as he took his many successes, in his stride, and carried on at King Henry's for his last year, and a good deal of feting by the school.

He was playing rugby for the school's first XV, thirteen matches (one a week), seven of them won, notably against their rivals at Llandrindod Wells. Williams was playing in the forwards, mostly at number eight, occasionally at lock. Rugby-playing 17-year-olds in those days were nothing like as colossal as the mutants of today, with their 220lbs and eleven seconds for the 100 metres, but his height and spring as well as his doggedness and good humour made Williams, in spite of his boniness, a competent performer wherever Mr Sharpe put him.

At the School Old Boys dinner that year, however, his was the name on everybody's lips. Lord Raglan was guest of honour, and the noble lord had pretensions to being a bit of a palaeographer. His family held in fief the great white elephant of a castle on the border towards Monmouth town, a highly visible reminder of his family's equivocal history, poised between English and Welsh and doing well out of both, but finally settling comfortably for the victorious side while playing a line in local history about the 'barbarian savages' the Silures, and Glendower, 'Monmouth's public enemy number one'. He did it at the Old Boys dinner, and was at it again a few weeks later with a public lecture on 'The Post-History [*sic*] of Monmouthshire'.

The *Chronicle* had quite a taste for all this, and as well as reporting Lord Raglan in detail, used to run a local history serial across two-and-a-half long columns for weeks at a time. This was the sort of history Raymond Williams 'threw up on', but it has its grip, its narrative impulse, and it retained for all its tellers, even Lord Raglan, strong sympathy for the Welsh underdog and a form which gave positive weight to the values of resistance, membership, local bonds and loves, and in all its best and romantic versions, upon the free possession of the Welsh border landscape. Williams wrote a novel at about this time called *Mountain Sunset* ('which nobody is ever going to see') which, he feared, was infected by that sort of Welsh history. But there are worse histories with which to shape a young and idealistic socialist's imagination, especially if you are going on to write *Modern Tragedy* and *The Volunteers*.

These bumps of consciousness should appear on the map charting the growth of a thinker's mind, given that Lord Raglan spoke as he did to the alumni in the same February week that Major Herbert MP had the ineffable cheek to announce that he was presenting Holy Mountain, Ysgyryd Fawr, all 1,600 feet of it, to a surprised and grateful nation.

There was another speaker at the Old Boys' dinner, who praised Williams's remarkable exam results, his state scholarship and his place at Cambridge. This was Alderman W. Rosser, Headmaster of the boys' elementary school on the Hereford road, recently re-elected mayor of the town, former pupil of King Henry's and stalwart county councillor for many years in the Labour interest. Given his attributes, it is hard not to feel that this Rosser gave more than just his name to the Morgan Rosser of *Border Country*. The energetic, inventive, gay and genial part of Harry Williams is, of course, the moving spirit in Morgan, but the public figure, the solidly progressive and authoritative Morgan surely reflects this doughty teacher.

However that may be, the real Rosser drew sincere and public praise from his political opponents on the County Council for the way he constantly addressed what he took to be the best interests of the whole town, while never diminishing his absolute commitment to the principles of what used to be called, with honour, 'gas-and-water socialism'. He had a clearly representative function – and mayors mattered more then than they do now in the presently neutered condition of local government – which he discharged plainly; and he still spoke believably, to his pupils and townsfolk, of class reconciliation in circumstances of enormously improved public welfare and justice. Rosser's, one could say, was a fine example of that socialism which found its great moment in the years between victory in 1945 and the heavy freezing of cold war some thirty months later. Men like him – and once upon a time there were many men like him – gave the young Williams the political standards from which he started, just as Harry Williams did. If Labour governments couldn't match that, they didn't deserve any support. Whether such a hard line can really be held is one of the key judgements which must be at the heart of my biography, as it was at the heart of one man's life.

After the two giants of class power and struggle, Raglan and Rosser, made their obeisance, Mr Newcombe reported on Williams's trophies, concluding with the announcement that as well as the state scholarship, the school governors had decided to award the star pupil a foundation scholarship of £52 10s to add to his modest County scholarship of £10. Taken together, Raymond would have £162 10s plus his fees per year, quite enough to keep up with the young bloods of Trinity in the autumn of 1939.

The secular masses of the school year were decently observed, while the Siegfried Line was pointlessly completed, Winston Churchill kept up his backbench campaign to accelerate rearmament hugely, and the Spitfire went into serious production. The darkening politics began to throw their shadow across the honest little meetings of the annual cycle.

In March there was a protest meeting in Pandy village hall against the rates, but a little later, Raymond Williams was to be heard opposing that red-blooded old soldier Brigadier Tulloch, speaking against the stout warrior's hearty advocacy of conscription. There were several large and successful recruiting parades for the Territorial Army in the town, and when Lady Megan Lloyd George MP, the old man's daughter, came to open the Llanvihangel Crucorney fete for the elderly Reverend Hughes, she too alluded to the need for the best young men of the day to climb into battledress at weekends, just in case.

However, at the King Henry's speech day, Raymond Williams's name was much more frequently mentioned than Hitler's. Arthur Jenkins, a Labour MP from over the south-western hills, was giving out the prizes and thought aloud 'that we should never get to the end of prizes for Raymond Williams (hear, hear)' and 'hoped that he would have a magnificent career'. Mayor Rosser spread himself on the subject, expressing their communal pride in the young man (and quite right too. Matthew-Raymond is most disagreeably carping about all that in *Border Country*. What's the matter with him? People are proud of their own people, going away, doing well, getting on; they take a little smack of the success for their own lips, and why not?) Rosser correctly mentioned the legacy which would add to the town's contribution to the studies and well-being of their young hero, and then to his great credit wound up with a rousing speech, attacking the parlous conditions in schools brought about by Tory policies.

At his last school sports Williams again just yielded the title of *Victor Ludorum* to Tom Lawson, with another good long jump, and victory in the 100 yards to his name, and then immediately turned out to help Frank Hancock the Labour man standing in a local by-election against a National candidate (non-party, but Tory in truth). A Welsh Labour peer, Lord Davies, addressed an enormous meeting in the Town Hall, speaking against appeasement, and Hancock's Peace Pledge Union banner ('Is War Our Way?') brought him a respectable 11,000 votes in July.

Our way or not, war was declared on 3 September, the day after the Abergavenny Show had gone on as usual. Mrs Williams's Women's Institute joined eager forces with the WVS to shepherd evacuee children from the industrial cities certain to be targeted by the *Luftwaffe* into their strange new homes in the dark and silent countryside. And on 1 October Jim Williams biked up the gradual incline to Pandy station, put his bike in the guard's van and himself in an empty compartment of the train, letting down the sash windows of the compartment door with the long leather tongue of the strap, hooking its last hole on the polished brass knob which held it in place on the door.

The signal dropped as his father swung the long brass-handled arm in his box, the train chuffed and surged forward; his people, father, station-master, clerk, porter, ganger, waved from their positions of work, and Jim Williams went away to become Raymond Williams, Captain Williams, Dr Williams, Professor Williams. Change at Worcester for Birmingham; change at Birmingham for Bletchley; change at Bletchley for Cambridge. He went away, free, cheerful, confident; excited, independent, ambitious; to become a writer and a radical. He took with him, sick always for home and its absolutely safe solitudes, something longed-for and unrecognisable, something obscure and unignorable, sunk so far within him he couldn't even give it a name, and wouldn't name it if he could.

He didn't cry. Boys don't cry. Nor do fathers. And in any case, what would it be like when he came home? That wasn't what he had lost, what everybody loses, what it is the only true point of a good politics to find.

4

HIS CAMBRIDGE
Undergraduate Communist

The big first court of Trinity College – the great quad – is one of the loveliest sights in Cambridge, or any other university town for that matter. The gateway is pushed into the crowded jumble of Trinity Street, with shops, and neighbouring college fronts, and – in the 1930s – ordinary houses unevenly and bustlingly bundled together, so you aren't prepared for the sudden opening of the huge courtyard into sheer space, the great expanse of turf, the high, plain chapel facade on your right, the long, modest terraces of staff and student rooms making up the other three sides to the square.

Apart from the gate, and the handsome fountain in the middle of the grass, and the cricket-field size of the place, it's not particularly grand, and the rooms grouped around each doorway and its staircase are in some cases positively frowsty. Once Williams, the new student, went down the low, stone-flagged corridor past the panelled dining hall with its familiar heavy odour of institutional lunches and suppers, he would have found an atmosphere to put him comfortably enough in mind of King Henry's, Abergavenny; both institutions had, after all, the same benefactor. Only Wren's great library beside the river, with its cool colonnading and slender arches, made clear to the student a breadth of ideas accompanying an equivalent reach on the part of capital which together went far beyond the metropolis to the cities of Europe, Renaissance cities in particular, in which such visions of power in stone began.

Too great a feeling for such continuities, too much reverence done to the beauty of Wren's slender arcade, too solemn a contemplation of the tombstones of the great thinkers who made atheism possible in Trinity Chapel, turned into the values of traditional patriotic Toryism, and the young radical must have none of them. In truth, almost all his life Williams seemed proof against the deep feeling caused either by the visual arts – painting and architecture – or by music. It was as though he never learned those correspondences between masses of colour or waves of rhythm and the organisation of sensation into emotion. All his intense capacity for feeling, so much of which feeling remained unnamed for him, went into his compelling, moving picture of the best working relations of working men, and of a landscape, a clean, unviolated, known and loved landscape which gave those men their home and was the material, necessary ground of their labour. His best feelings flowed towards and through the stories which did that; novels and plays, mostly.

So Williams arrived in Cambridge with very strong predispositions as to what he was looking for. He only knew the other two boys from King Henry's, but his enormous self-confidence in his public life easily crossed from the little grammar school to the great university. Jesus College, home of the exiled Welsh in Cambridge as in Oxford, looked sufficiently like school – redbrick courtyards – and so did the ordinary courtyards of Caius, just next to Trinity, with its solid stone ramparts, the work of Waterhouse, whose pupil had designed King Henry's.

Work itself was sufficiently like school for Williams to make the same transition as he did in his social life. According to the pre-bureaucratic and unrationalised forms of ancientness prevalent now as then in Cambridge, there being no English tutor resident in Trinity, the college arranged for him to be taught outside its walls, by Lionel Elvin, a figure of some distinction who ended up decades later as Director of the London Institute of Education, and was always a Popular Front and Labour Leftist who taught the procedures of Leavis's and I.A. Richards' practical criticism and allied them in an unproblematic sort of way with decently left–liberal values.

It was a way of fastening form to content which did well enough for two or three generations, especially when given his special edge and flair by F.R. Leavis. A student was taught to discover in the words and rhythms, the images and music, of a piece of writing – typically, a manageably short poem – the qualities of mind and feeling characteristic both of the writer and his epoch; these qualities, standardly of intelligence, 'poise', inventiveness, wit, vitality, and above all of the vividly imaginative rendering of and giving realisation to an experience of some significance, were then used as critical instruments with which to measure the content of contemporary life.

It is an intellectual method with an exhilarating play and springiness to it. If you learn to be good at it, it brings with it an authority and a serene complacency which are very hard to challenge. 'Poise' of mind, ironic detachment, a zest for life, seriousness of intelligence are so obviously and absolutely good attributes to have now, or in any foreseeable polity. If you can turn the trick of reliably identifying their presence or absence in a piece of writing (or come to that, in a piece of speaking), then you will do much. You will have begun to ground a picture of yourself in terms of your ability to seek out the marked moral intensity and reverence for life in what gifted others write and say. You will have found a way of being serious in your own life, and of criticising without apparent self-interest the utter unseriousness, indeed, the triviality and, at times, the degradation of much of the life around you. You may even have found your vocation.

The trouble is, of course, with the arbitrariness of the values selected by those particular practitioners of the method in the Cambridge of 1939. Poise and irony were well enough with which to judge the merely social appallingness of Fascism, but something a good deal more robust would be needed to fight it. The values Williams found circulating as the currency of cultivation were those with which the great critics who perfected the method of practical criticism – the two Leavises – routed a local class enemy.[1] They attached the best values of a striving *petit-bourgeois* household – earnestness, probity, energy, hard work, enormous intelligence and deep religious feeling with no religion to express it – to the practical criticism of literature, and militantly destroyed any other way of seeing the subject. Those for whom literature was a cultivated adjunct to unearned income and those for whom it was a proving-ground for personal relationships were alike convicted and sentenced as fops, playboys and narcissists.

The sheer class confidence of this guerrilla appealed immediately to Williams, of course. But as he says, at this time he wasn't specifically conscious of Leavis, even if, like the Leavises, he was shocked at the revolting habit of the well-off of using their purported cultivation in the reading of novels and poetry to justify class privilege: Mrs Leavis had been boisterously scornful on that score in *Scrutiny* not long before.[2] And, also like the Leavises but ultimately in opposition to them, he was eager to attach *his* class values – solidarity, mutuality, common (not singular) feeling, settledness, sympathy – to the understanding of the narratives which constitute a society's vision of home. In the first case, this meant declaring for socialism; and in the realm of literature, for socialist realism. In England at that date it meant writing like the *Left Review*, which giants of the Left like Cecil Day Lewis, Jack Lindsay and John Lehmann (to whom Williams wrote) were compiling at the time.

Marxist writing about the arts and culture in the 1930s was illumined by a vivid light of optimism and certainty. It lit the faces and spirits of Williams and his friends, as one of them, the film-maker Michael Orrom testified in a film-memoir.[3] These young men and women invented communistic words to old music-hall and folk songs and hymns – to 'The Lincolnshire Poacher', 'A Tavern in the Town' and 'Our Class's One Foundation . . .' They went to listen to Paul Potts, the people's poet; they wrote poems and music which mingled personal love affairs with the march of history. They looked to modern literature to advance the cause of labour and they despised it when, as in T.S. Eliot and Ezra Pound, it turned to political reaction.

One of their heroes was Ralph Fox, a novelist and critic killed at 36 while fighting for the communist government on the Cordova Front in Spain in 1937. Fox was a novelist as well as author of *The Novel and the People*. Like Trotsky in *Literature and Revolution*, Fox believed that the great novels of the past should be recaptured and re-evaluated for a future in which all those excluded from such stories in the past and by the way the bourgeoisie was used to read them would be handed back these same books as their own. Fox wrote:

> There are rare occasions in history, in the personal history of each individual, in the common history of mankind, when the demands of life fully correspond with the dignity and intensity of man's desires. Such an occasion confronts us today ... The novelist who is able to understand this will rise like a giant above his times, re-create the epic art of modern civilisation, and truly inherit the tradition of English letters.[4]

The true heirs were, for the young communists of the day, those who saw truly that history was about to deliver the victorious dictatorship of the proletariat, and they would revalue past literature so that it told this truth, and write the new literature which would see its fulfilment.

At the same time, they saw that Stalinist accounts of socialist realism, plonkingly realised in heroic statues of New Russian Women driving tractors, were much too crude to cope with. They looked for a modernism which would be as free and playful, as conscious of contraries but as unified in creativity as the William Blake whom Randall Swingler praised so well in *Left Review*.[5]

So they went on to read Alick West's *Crisis and Criticism*. West wrote:

> The source of value in the work of literature is the social energy and activity which makes the writer's vision a continuation of the development of the power to see ... our perception of that value is the stimulation in us of the same social energy and activity ...[6]

which is to say that, by West's own Marxist lights, *value* is the correspondence of *praxis* as between writer and audience. The test of literature by the Party line was that it should be socialist and progressive in tendency, and that if it wasn't, it was to that extent less worth reading. Williams recalls that he and those of his political associates and friends reading English were much more heartily committed to *writing* the right kind of verse or prose, a kind capable of crossing class boundaries and speaking to the speechless, than criticising what had already been written. This meant that their canonical examples had to be modern, indeed avant-garde – 'Joyce was without question the most important author for us. *Ulysses* and *Finnegans Wake* were the texts we most admired, and which we counterposed to socialist realism.'[7] Very early in the argument, these young men wanted not only to square the sheer difficulty of modernism

73

with the popular temper, but also to enlist in their cause as many as possible of the political optimists among the moderns, what the wooden-tops in the CP of the day would have called the 'progressive elements'. Georg Lukács, as Williams was to discover for himself several decades later, was up to pretty much the same venture at the same time in Budapest, although in his case – and his case was Kafka – avant-garde modernism lost out.

The art form in the culture of the day which roundly reconciled these contradictions between difficulty and popularity, avant-garde form and proletarian content, was, of course, film, and film was no part of any Cambridge degree course in 1939, nor was it to be until Williams put it there rather more than thirty years later.

But it was movies which really gripped Williams, and the place to see avant-garde movies at that time was the Socialist Club.

Edward Williams

> Mind you, Cambridge was stuffed with cinemas at that time, and until well into the 1970s. There was the Regal in the market square, all single, big screen cinemas, of course – the Arts just down a side street – two more on the way up St Andrew's Street, The Cosmopolitan, the Rex out the back behind the railway line, the Union showed films regularly, and the Socialist Club. The Club showed politically correct stuff, as you'd expect – it's a concept with a long history – Vigo, Eisenstein, Lang, and also the avant-gardists as well, German Expressionist and so forth.

Williams found the Socialist Club at an early freshmen's recruiting squash, and his friends unite in describing its energy, variety and colour. The club had its own premises above a fish shop in Petty Cury Lane, a narrow road leading out of the market place. It had a dining room for wartime lunch and supper – fried fish from downstairs and mountains of chips – and was easily the liveliest milieu in the University. At that time, anybody with any intelligence in that generation was of radical sympathies if not specifically of the Left or attached to the Popular Front. The British government was in 1939 transparently cowardly and hypocritical in all its foreign policy, and it was foreign policy which as usual interested the young, reasonably well-off, intellectual idealists of the day. Moreover, the main undergraduate population of Cambridge was overwhelmingly male with the exceptions of the notably intellectual houses of Girton and Newnham. It came from English and Scottish public schools, cared nothing for scholarship, and dined, drank, cricketed, drove its MGs and Lagondas thunderously down King's Parade, and sent the echoes of its arrogant voices fairly slicing through the air of every college courtyard. Any serious student would have disliked and despised the gaudy uniform and uniform languor of the rich young men in the Pitt Club as a matter of duty even in wartime, and would have moved his political principles away from such people by instinct.

74

So the Socialist Club was an exhilaratingly cheerful place to go every day, for friends, for films, for cheap, filling meals, lashings of potatoes, sausages, sponge pud, as well as for the ineffable satisfactions of being on the right side, reading the right newspapers and being reassured by agreement on the right enemies: the very forms of Cambridge snobbery and exclusiveness, lived in negation. Williams met Matthew Hodgart there, himself later a celebrated Professor of English, John Maynard Smith, subsequently the greatest Darwinian revisionist of his day, Eric Hobsbawm, another now properly celebrated figure of the intellectual Left, Edward Williams, the composer, and Michael Orrom, later a film-maker with Paul Rotha and co-author of an early book on film with Williams, who arranged the club's screenings. He also met clever women undergraduates of the sort he glimpsed in Geneva; one of them a poetess, Anne Piper, who rather fell for him. Two others, Mary Rose and Winifred Lambert, writing in the student newspaper that autumn, reported the University Socialist Club as concluding, after a vigorous meeting, that 'the National Government connived at and even encouraged Fascist aggression and consistently refused to form a Peace Front'. And on 28 September 1939, Eric Hobsbawm, writing in the *Cambridge University Journal*, welcomed the 1,500 students evacuated from the University of London, including the London School of Economics, to take up residence opposite Peterhouse College in Trumpington Street, while the danger of Nazi Germany bombing the capital lasted.

The dangers were obvious enough, but the war, after all the fuss, was turning out phoney, and certainly of nothing like enough moment to distract Raymond from the keen delights of affronting the stolidities of non-radical opinion among the Cambridge undergraduates, to say nothing of a delightful sociability for which little in Abergavenny and less in Pandy had prepared him. University rules, to the freer radicals of a 1970s generation, look impossibly stuffy in 1939 (they lasted until the deluge in 1968). No women (or men from other colleges) in one's rooms after 10 p.m.; undergraduates must, on penalty of a fine, wear their gowns after twilight and would be chased by the University officers if they ran away naked; drunkenness in the street was a serious offence; sexual congress unimaginably worse. But in spite of this not-very-awful monasticism, and in spite of street blackout after dark once war had been declared, there were countless dances in Cambridge, some even permitting physical contact between the young men of the colleges and the young women of the town, and almost all of them held in the happily named Dorothy Tearooms, a large, rather dowdy expanse of parquet flooring upstairs, overlooking the corner of the old market place.

It was at the Dorothy one evening in November 1939 that Raymond, much influenced by recently having seen *Duck Soup* and with a pen in the corner of his mouth like a Groucho cigar, was selling tickets at the door to a Socialist Club dance (6.30 to 9.30) upstairs. Joy Dalling and Annette Lees, recently arrived in Cambridge from the LSE, had turned up to fraternise with the disciples of fraternity and equality on Joy's twenty-first birthday.

They made a good-looking pair of young women, strong featured, solidly made, their heavy hair turned back according to the fashion in thick rolls framing their faces and falling softly to their napes. Joy's hair was particularly luxuriant, red-gold in colour and setting off her serious eyes, good mouth, sharp and prominent nose.

She came from Barnstaple, born on 5 November 1918, nearly three years before Raymond. She was star pupil at the girls grammar school, collecting as a prize for 'the highest marks' in her last year a copy of *Money*, edited by J.M. Keynes and a rare trophy for a West Devon schoolgirl. Her family lived in a big house in the High Street (now demolished by a grim road scheme) and her father ran a successful coal haulage business clearing, as her brother Fred remembers, a thousand tons in Christmas week. They were a large, boisterous family, four sisters and three brothers, but the size of the family was no inhibition of a comfortable life, including the shoot which Charles Dalling rented up the coast, a weekend chalet at Christmas, and a Mediterranean cruise for him and his wife not long before his sudden death at the age of 48 in 1934. Mother took over as head of the firm and the Dalling Trust, and the older brother George helped to drive the deliveries while schoolgirl Joy and her mother did the books. They were all straight Labour Party people – Joy and her sister Ruth put their names forward for local candidatures – and Mrs Dalling was well known locally for her daring advocacy of methodical birth control.

So it was a pretty formidable as well as a pretty 21-year-old with whom Raymond danced that mild evening ('mind you,' Joy said, 'I thought he was a tutor'), and afterwards he walked back with Annette and Joy to Mrs Blackshaw's rooms over Hill and Saunders photographic shop in King's Parade, where they were billeted (under wartime conditions).

Annette Lees

On our return to the shop it was clear a party was going on on the ground floor – none of those LSE students, men and women, had been invited by us. Joy immediately turned them out. Only two students were billeted in the Blackshaws, Cambridge undergraduates, women, lived in College – Newnham and Girton. The Blackshaws did not in normal times take in lodgers at all – this was a wartime requirement. LSE students were a great novelty to Cambridge in those days – a mixed group with no supervision at all! So unlike the Cambridge undergraduates, Joy and I were very grateful to the Blackshaws for having us in their home, so we were not prepared to take risks over this and upset them.

They took to each other at once, but close friends or sweethearts in 1939 did not become inseparable and Raymond had other women friends. He would go round to Joy's and Annette's rooms, and sit smoking his pipe in complete and affable silence, while the women worked towards their finals.

From his arrival, he had thrown himself confidently into the politics of the old Cambridge Union. It is an institution not everybody knows about and, indeed, has now rather faded from its function of glittering prize-giver. It had, of course, no connection with student union politics as conventionally understood, and it centred upon its debating chamber, which mimicked in shape and furniture the Chamber of the House of Commons. Around the Chamber were the precocious appurtenances of a gentleman's London club – bar and dining room, smoking room, library, squash court, and latterly, a cinema. In the Chamber embryo politicians and a President in a white tie and tailcoat played at being Disraeli, Mill, and Lloyd George, devastating the house with ghastly shows of wit.

Raymond had learned debating and public speaking at King Henry's and the League of Nations Union. He was good at both, and earnestly ambitious (all his life) of reputation and recognition, of being known as writer and public figure, and also being recognised for his uncompromising radicalism and principle ('uncompromising' is always such a tribute in the lexicon of the Left). It took nerve, also, just turned 18 and without friends from posh schools, to carry the battle quite so straightly into that arena, but Hodgart and Maynard Smith were right beside him, and Hobsbawm was already writing about anti-imperialism in the *University Journal*. So the *Journal's* reviewer – for all performers read greedily the assessment of themselves in the weekly, world-weary review – was able to write haughtily on 25 November of Williams's contribution to a debate on rights for women students that 'Mr Williams might use his abilities to better advantage if he learned some elements of manners' (which must have gratified the Socialist Club) and in February 1940, debating 'that the darkest ages lie immediately ahead', the reviewer undeftly remarked that 'Raymond Williams read extracts from the *New Statesman*; he does not read very well'.

The put-downs were obligatory, but the socialists were never put down. Williams was unquenchable and highly visible, writing and speaking as copiously as in his heyday of 1970, and doing so with combative and youthful high spirits which come clearly through over fifty years later, and bear witness to just how hugely he enjoyed those two years at Cambridge, whatever the dark ages ahead. In a double column piece in the *Journal* called 'The Muse in Utopia',[8] he argued for an unfashionably unbreakable link between poetry and politics, and shouted cheerful and mischievous names at those who wouldn't heed him.

I would have put this down to prejudiced middle-class morality and damned it to the hell we are fondly preparing for such circumstances if I had not found that many quite progressive people ... stoutly affirmed that progress was a mere political programme from which it was best to separate poetry and spiritual values.

As things began to look so much grimmer over mainland Europe, the Left in Cambridge formed itself into a new federation uniting communists, socialists, popular fronters, and Labour Party members. Williams afterwards remembered the friendly homogeneity of the Left in Cambridge then, contrasting it with the virulent sectarianism of the Left's brief recrudescence in the late 1960s. In truth the communists were stupefied by the notorious pact between the Soviet Union and Nazi Germany signed by Molotov the Hammer and von Ribbentrop in a gruesome union of the two antithetical forces of the historical moment. Ready as ever to believe the unbelievable, communists prated on about the irrelevance of the bosses' war to the revolution, but it was a hell of a shock.

All the same, it didn't really touch Williams's breezy libertarianism – Hobsbawm took it harder, as he said, and swallowed it. Williams was ready enough at the time to write a rather jaunty piece for the Wall newspaper in the Club (a pious imitation of the invention of the worker soviets) saying that it would only be worth fighting Hitler in order to bring about socialist revolution in Britain, while in 1941, at the Party's behest, he wrote a decidedly less defensible pamphlet with Hobsbawm defending the Soviet invasion of Finland as politically necessary.

All this was mostly revolting student stuff. Williams's real energies went in writing journalism, at gleefully high speed on his own second-hand typewriter which so regularly stuck on the red ribbon it became a kind of signature, and preparing Union, English club or New Labour club speeches. In March 1940, debating at the Union 'that this house prefers drama to poetry' (which Williams always did), the reviewer wrote with the usual condescension, 'Raymond Williams apologised for his speech which was the least he could do; if only he would talk about the motion he might be quite good.'[9] After a bout of German measles and a concurrent article in *The Girtonian*, he made his maiden speech as nominated speaker in the Union on press freedom, vigorously standing up for the *Daily Worker* on 2 March, and for the Chinese Communist Party the following week.

Pausing to review *The Stars Look Down*, Carol Reed's rousing masterpiece which went straight to Raymond's heart, he launched into his first bit of political street-fighting the night of 15 March.

There had been a Socialist Club ticket-only meeting, 'Hands Off Russia', and, provoked by the provocative title, assorted class enemies with forged tickets had gatecrashed the meeting, heckled, burst stink bombs, and as the police always put it so nicely, 'there were scuffles'.

Afterwards, elated by all this, the club committee had linked arms and walked up Trinity Street, their voices echoing off the high front walls of Caius College, singing 'The Smoke of Battle' to the tune of 'The Lincolnshire Poacher'. Roused to ire by this further show of unpatriotic leftiness, the sportsmen had weighed in, in large numbers, and the Left was rescued by the unexpected help of two hefty RAF men. Eric Hobsbawm uttered a dignified rebuke in the *Journal's* next leader, directed at 'certain political people using the heartiest and least intelligent members of certain boat clubs to act as their stormtroopers'.

The weight of the war was becoming unignorable. At the end of the previous term, thrilled by the vitality and busyness of the Socialist Club, Williams recalled that when he joined, he had asked eagerly, 'Is this the only organisation on the Left, because I want to be with the reddest of the reds?' Typically he had been reproved for such a gush of enthusiasm – 'Don't say that' – so he had been invited to join the Communist Party before the end of term.

The Party ran a tight ship in Cambridge. They assigned their literate members, most of whom were reading English or History, to a 'Writers Group', and they watched carefully for promising recruits. They couldn't miss Williams. They were immensely self-important what with history being on their side and all, and he was clear at 18 that it was with a dictatorship of the proletariat that redemption would start. He helped along the big day by writing a rather striking little story about sugar riots in the West Indies and a trifling larceny in a Border village. He published it in a sixpenny magazine called *Outlook* along with pieces by Orrom, Hobsbawm and Alex Comfort. Writing was one form of activism, but activism was better. So when the Party dispatched him to the National Congress of students unions in April, he was glad to go, and when they told him he was to be the next editor of the *Cambridge University Journal*, in only his third term, he was startled but understandably gratified. It was a plum job in the student hierarchy; his personal ambitions and his political allegiance came together happily in the editorial chair.

Brian Simon who, like Eric Hobsbawm, was not only to become doyen of his academic subject (Education) but (also like Hobsbawm) stayed with the British Communist Party to the end, was then both local and national President of the NUS. It was a huge, tense, and apprehensive Congress, held in the brand-new Leeds Union building. H.G. Wells addressed the students, and to their applause reaffirmed student internationalism, their opposition to the imperialists' war, and their support of Indian independence.

A month later, *Blitzkrieg* started, the British Expeditionary Force was beleaguered, and Raymond Williams's leader in the *Journal* defended the Peace Pledge Union.

Cambridge's normal service was only grudgingly yielded. The *Journal* remained impressively awake to the crisis, and under Williams's editorship, with regular contributions from Maynard Smith and Hobsbawm, kept a pretty straight line of a Popular Front kind. When Williams dropped the local gossip column, which was the one item *all* students could be depended upon to read, and which he wrote himself, there was a flurry of protesting letters.

Williams's intellectual and social energy throughout the summer of 1940 was astonishing. As the Spitfires and Hurricanes took off in four-minute scrambles from airfields all round Cambridge into the blue, sunny sky and fought their historic battle across the route of the M11, and Cambridge itself was bombed in June, Williams wrote his regular 'Commentary' on University and on world affairs, pasted up the copy in readiness for the printer, reviewed the movies (Richardson and Edna Best in *South Riding* in April, *Hell's Cargo* in May, in which the dead Bolshevik hero is honoured by the fist salute given by a Royal Navy officer), and was even voted on to the Union committee, whatever he thought of their jokes and tail-coats. He spoke against public schools in a mid-May debate, backed the new literary magazine *Cambridge Front*, went out to dinner with Dylan Thomas who was visiting the English Club, all of them drunk on the lethal and then popular cocktail of gin and cider, and in one of the most improbable alliances British culture could imagine, was on genial terms in the Union committee with Jimmy Edwards, later an enormously popular BBC comedian whose turn depended upon a self-parody as a big-moustached and silly-ass RAF officer.

Not surprisingly amongst all this, he said to Joy in early May, 'I can't see you until after the exams', and duly took a First in the preliminary stage of the Cambridge three-part degree, the Tripos.

Just before the exams, after a German agent had been found shot in a shelter on a corner of Cambridge called Christ's Pieces, there was a symptomatic commotion when the President of the Union cancelled a late-Roman sort of debate, welcoming the end of Western civilisation. The national papers, always eager for a cliché, compared the motion to the notorious 'King and Country' debate at Oxford in 1937, when the bright young things had all voted against the flag. In his 'Commentary' column for 25 May, Williams wrote: 'The Rotarians said that the Oxford boys were just foxing. Ah, we subtle Englishers ... But then I'm Welsh, and wouldn't understand.'

His last 'Commentary' of the term was striking for its confidence, the range of its attack, its good-humoured tone. Some criticism of comrades in the University of Edinburgh, a review of the movie *Ninotchka*, and a breezy trailer for his next flourish. 'Next week I want to have a few thrusts and parries around the whole question of undergraduate journalism ... and there will be a special feature for women, and stories, and once again all the news of the University.'[10] But the next issue of the *Journal* did not come out until 19 April 1947.

Williams came back to a University in October chilled and sobered by Hitler's victories during the summer. The air battles had, it seemed, deferred invasion, but Churchill's celebrated speeches promising only 'blood, sweat, toil and tears' had an ever grimmer ring – 'if ... we are forced to evacuate our island home ... we shall carry on the struggle from His Majesty's dominions'. Conscription was now certain; you might as well make ready; Raymond joined the University's Officer Training Corps.

There was never any doubt in his mind that he would be an officer. Hobsbawm, who had taken his degree in the summer but was still in Cambridge editing *Granta*, later joined the Education Corps and quickly became a sergeant. His sight was poor and his principles strong; a year ago he had spoken up vigorously on behalf of conscientious objection to warfare. Williams was an athlete and was necessarily shifting his position on licking Hitler; in 1940 the communists, as Hobsbawm said to me, were beginning to feel uneasy.

Williams had moved out of his college into digs at 23 Malcolm Street, off Jesus Lane, close to the middle of town. He had spent the summer, as he had two years before, cycling and hitch-hiking round Britain with the remains of his scholarship money, visited Wem to see his hero Hazlitt's house, and this year joined a weekend summer school run by the Party on 'Communism and Popular Literature'. When he came back to Cambridge, even without the *Journal*, the Party secretariat had more than ever for him to do, and if it meant writing and publishing, or publicly speaking, he met it gladly.

He was to edit the *Socialist Club Bulletin*, which, as censorship laws and paper shortages closed about the students, was at first a typewritten affair duplicated from skins on a hand-turned Gestetner. In the first number of that term, Raymond kept up the cheery and conventional voice of his 'Commentary' column in the *Journal*.

> A lorry I was on carrying thirteen tons of bricks happened to break down in Merthyr and a few workers building surface shelters were overjoyed when we offered to dump our load.
>
> Our Welsh valleys still vibrate through the oppression and the misery on a nerve centre of socialism. We are, and our comrades everywhere must know it, a militant working-class.[11]

In autumn 1940 the business of Party zeal had to be kept up. It was army experience itself, and then combat, which really changed the culture of the intellectual Left. In Cambridge the old enemy was still so audible, hooting across the quad and bawling in the pub. Accordingly, buoyed up by production of Unity Theatre's left-wing panto, *Jack the Giant-Killer* (what else?), Williams once again went in hard for the target. 'This is the wretched crew that make up the top-hatted, top-heavy social system ... *We* are trying to discover the *people's* cultural system ...' and he quotes

81

gleefully from the show, without pressing too hard on the nasty words: 'Now's the time for a little liquidation. Take the Baron away and lock him up.'[12]

His Party duties were such that one is bound to feel that loyalists were thinning out in the secretariat's diaries. Joy used to complain that he could never say no, and certainly he had a crowded term. The first week in November included a full-dress paper to the Marxist English Group on 1 November on 'Culture and the People' (4.15 Staircase K, St John's Second Court); *Waiting for Lefty* to read with the Drama Group on 4th; R.H. Tawney and the Chinese Ambassador to meet and listen to at the Dorothy Tearooms on 6th; Pudovkin's *Mother* to watch and be reverent about at the Socialist Club on the Sunday; and *Kuhle-Wampe* ditto the next afternoon. *And* his editorials to write. In the editorial of 19 November 1940, we hear the prescient directness and truculence which remain the best of Williams. Writing on 'The power behind the press', he says, 'Idealism you are allowed . . . but truth about capitalism is forbidden . . . Once you know who owns the press, you know what to expect of it.'

But the political work, with its big simplicities and its background unease and fearfulness, was doing nothing for his academic efforts. At the start of the term, he had changed his immediate tutor ('supervisor' is the term of art) from Lionel Elvin to E.M.W. Tillyard, a grandee of the Faculty and founder-member of the committee which devised the Cambridge English Tripos in 1917, as well as a sufficiently energetic member of the Conservative Party to have addressed its Party association during Raymond's first term.

> We started doing the novel and I promptly produced the party orientation – that it was necessary to see any bourgeois novel of the past from the perspective of the kind of novel that must now be written in the present. Tillyard told me this . . . was a fantasy. How could you judge something that had been written from the perspective of something that hadn't . . . I would also talk about the romantic poets, insisting that they represented a project of human liberation which was going to be completed in the future. Then he would say that it was nothing to do with literature if some process was going to be completed or not.[13]

One might feel that liberation has *something* to do with literature while also reckoning that Tillyard comes off best in this exchange. This wasn't an irreconcilable clash of two metaphysics, as Williams hints; it was a blankness on his part, a blankness he later identifies and repudiates (in others) in *Culture and Society*. From early on, he would rarely confront an opposing point of view; he preferred either to deflect, or to ignore, or to assimilate it.

As a youngster, he was in a familiar bind, pulled by the foundations and rigidities of Party thought one way, and the strong propulsions of the literary history Tillyard stood for, the other. But there is, none the less, a penetrating, shadowy question at the bottom of Williams's then (and subsequent) determination to be in the right when obviously in the wrong (it was, and is, the least attractive quality of some of the Left's best people). The question asks how to reconcile heartfelt allegiance to what we believe to be the good, with the careful detachment enjoined by the absolutely necessary standards of rationality and judgement. Williams wanted with all his heart to join, and with that same heart to keep his distance. After making several blunders during his second year of study – a forgivable time to make them – he remained wary beyond words, and for years, of any more unequivocal enlistments.

Enlistment, indeed; that waited patiently for him, until he had completed his second year. In the meantime, the demands of political loyalty and the demands of intellectual inquiry began, for the first time in his life, to tear apart, and Williams with them.

The tempo of study in the so-called Tripos at Cambridge accelerates sharply in the second year. Williams having changed tutors from the genial left–liberal Lionel Elvin to this rather tougher egg (later his boss at Jesus College), could no longer hold together his political and his academic life. And the political demands increased. He continued to write his regular journalism in editorials for the *Socialist Club Bulletin*, which had by the autumn of 1940 advanced from the Gestetner copier into proper print, and looked quite neat. In January 1941, when deep snow covered the country and no traffic moved in Cambridge, he was delegated to attend the People's Convention, an indeterminate congeries of Left-sympathisers trying hopelessly to keep faith with the USSR and Peace Pledgers in spite of everything. The University's disciplinary officers, the Proctors, prevented a session being held at the Dorothy Tearooms, and being addressed by an anti-war MP, one Dr Pritt. Williams sprang on to high moral horseback.

> The power of the Proctors over members of the University is in effect unlimited. That is the first thing to get clear in all talk of a campaign for student liberties. Their power is only defined in terms of maintaining the authority of the University.[14]

Well, yes. There is here something of an innocence, something of heroism, and something wholly unrealistic as well. In all circumstances, he stuck to the right questions and the best principles. But such sticking simply won't stick in all circumstances . . .

A week later, the Labour minister in the national government, the celebrated Herbert Morrison, banned publication of the communists' *Daily Worker*. The young communists in their 'Writers' Group' promptly produced a *samizdat* version for sale on the streets of Cambridge. It lasted one day. They didn't know what was going on, and they couldn't find out. At times, as always has been the case for Marxists, ignorance was no inhibitor of confidence. It's ruthless to hold a man's views against himself at 19 but it's hard to excuse Williams in 1941 speaking quite so pratingly as he did 'about the enlightened methods used in the Soviet Union to correct young criminals', and even harder to look tolerantly upon his pamphlet written in collaboration with Eric Hobsbawm to defend the Soviet invasion of Finland.

The two students had been deputed to this task by the Party secretariat, given the Party line and a few (also Party) books, put in a room and told to get on with it. Hobsbawm said to me that he was uneasy with the task, but discipline held. The pamphlet contended that the invasion should be understood as a continuation of the insurrection of 1918, when Baron Mannerheim had called in the Kaiser's troops to crush Finnish workers, and 30,000 Finnish democrats were killed. So Hobsbawm and Williams declared that 'no true progressive can support [raising funds] for Finland's fight for independence'; the Soviets were rightfully supporting their stooge Otto Kunsinnen and his Finnish People's Government. And in March they, Dorothy Wedderburn, George Barnard, John Maynard Smith, all Cambridge young communists with grammar school scholarships, were out leading the campaign to 'Stop the War against the USSR', with the revolutionary weapons of posters, lobbying senior members of the University, and a meeting in the Dorothy Tearooms.

Given the amount of work Williams was putting into the *Socialist Club Bulletin* and Party devotions, it is no surprise that his academic work was going steadily downhill. In a May review of the touring show put on by Unity Theatre, he congratulated the company on being the only one 'which is a truly working-class organisation owned by common people', and in a grisly anticipation of the loopy Maoists of travelling theatre who came along in the 1970s, strongly approved Unity's political classes held for its actors, and its rituals of 'deliberate self-criticism from the whole staff'.

When, however, Party instructions moved a bit nearer his heart, he reacted as angrily as he always did on such occasions, and quite right, too. The secretariat learned that he intended to become engaged to Joy, and so Joy and her close friend Annette Lees were checked over for their Party suitability. Annette twinkles at the recollection.

Annette Lees

They said we were 'politically unconscious' – well, we *were*, to their way of thinking. Raymond was very angry at once, and that's why he left the Party. He said, 'They're not telling me who I can marry.'

His academic work, which had always been something his success at which Raymond took utterly for granted, was faltering badly. He was a well-known figure about Cambridge, and the Cambridge élite has always flourished in fierce competition as between intellectual and social distinction. Its glittering prizewinners were only victorious inasmuch as they combined both. Williams kept up his political intransigence as one essential class weapon; the other had to be his pre-eminence in exams. As this looked less and less likely, 'the easiest way to respond – one saw it again through the sixties – was to say all that was pedantic crap; that, my God, there was a war going on'. Tillyard, inflexible but astute and steady, merely replied, 'Then why are you against it?'

The point was well taken. All year Williams had, seeing that conscription was inevitable, providentially been a member of the University's Officer Training Corps, afterwards clumping off to Tillyard's tutorials in his War Office boots. He had learned simple parade-ground drill and the workings of the 303 Lee-Enfield rifle, the gas controls on the Bren light machine gun and how to find a six-figure reference on an Ordnance Survey map which, in a month or two, he would learn all over again in his basic army training at Prestatyn. He wanted, one would say, to have made the decision to fight the anti-Fascist war before it was made for him.

Operation Barbarossa solved the struggle of conscience for him and all other communists. Hitler invaded the Soviet Union; Stalin became an ally. Williams became formally engaged to Joy Dalling and let his Party membership drop into the past. The past itself retained sufficient grip to ensure that he was awarded what would for him have been a demeaning lower second class in his examinations, not helped by the fact that Tillyard, without telling him, entered him early for the final part of the degree. With four weeks to go, Williams handed over his journalism to Orrom, and disappeared from sight in a frenzied attempt to catch up. He didn't make it.

But Williams was going to marry this staunch, pretty, golden-haired woman, and anchor his life to her uncomplaining steadfastness. And he was going to war.

He left Cambridge in June. He was summoned, with two weeks' notice, to the Royal Corps of Signals depot at Prestatyn in early July. At the same time, showing a commendable faith in his future as well as *the* future, the Governors at King Henry's voted unanimously to renew Raymond's Exhibition scholarship of £52 10s, whenever he had completed his tour of military service.

5

GUARDS OFFICER

Come to Sunny Prestatyn
Laughed the girl on the poster
Kneeling up on the sand
In tautened white satin.

In July 1941 the beaches were closed and there were coils of barbed wire wound into the wrought iron railings on the prom in case the *Wehrmacht* tried their invasion on the wrong side of the country. But it was still a bonny spot, the high white hotels and wide russet roads, the handful of palms on the seafront, the curved steps up to the Grand quoting the *Promenade des Anglais* to this warm, moist corner of seaside Wales. There were soldiers everywhere with their peculiar squalor and brutality: the big plateglass windows of the hotels boarded against bomb blast, fag-ends in the arid fountains, the curious thick sweet smell of rooms which are slept in all the time by men who never take off all their clothes.

At the Royal Signals depot, out on the Rhyl road, the recruits lived in new, hastily assembled prefabs and Nissen huts, semi-spherical hives made from corrugated iron insulated with carcinogenic asbestos boards. The new model army of 1941 was a much better educated creature than its predecessor twenty-five years before and displayed from the outset a strongly democratic and civilian insistence that this wasn't just a patriotic battle against the Hun but a battle for a better country and a fairer future against the armies of the night. The new commanders were determined not to make the old mistakes, so they drafted the brightest young men they could find into the communications and knowledge regiments. The Intelligence and Signals corps throve on an intake of high-spirited, optimistic and energetic young men from an extraordinary mixture of origins: from the universities certainly, and also from technical institutes and evening colleges, from wireless workshops and telephone exchanges, volunteers from school staffrooms and elderly 33-year-olds from commercial laboratories.

This cheerful motley made, as armies will, its own way of life very quickly. Indeed, the same rapid creation of a culture characterised the whole remarkable training and mobilisation of the nation in what was to be well called 'the People's War'.[1] Signals and tank regiments alike took tolerantly enough to the demands of old army that all men perfect tiny and trivial movements of the feet on asphalt and inhabit the hysterical hyper-hygiene of the hut, but this trans- and inter-class traffic of millions of young men melded quickly into what Williams's comrade, friend and fellow officer Edward Thompson was later to call 'a resolute and ingenious civilian army, increasingly hostile to the conventional military virtues which became ... an anti-fascist and consciously anti-imperialist army [whose] members voted Labour in 1945, knowing why ...'.[2]

So OR4 Williams brought to bear his bit of preparation from the Cambridge OTC and learned to lay his kit out on his bed with his laundered shirts stiffened into a neat rectangle by the insertion of cardboard; he learned to scour the concrete floor and blacklead the iron stove to a matt metallic gleam; to box his blankets at 5.30 in the morning and run in his singlet down the hill to the promenade, the rapid rhythmic tramp of the boots bouncing off the hotel walls as the platoon doubled its two miles before baked beans, scrambled (dried) eggs and scalding orange tea in white pint mugs for breakfast.

And he learned wireless procedure and maintenance, learned to use the heavy, cumbrous old sets one man could barely lift, and the new portable ones; learned to run out hundreds of yards of cable and fit field telephones to them; learned Morse code, though always fumblingly, and what side-tone suppression and centre-tapped transformers were.

He was, of course, quick with the theory, plentifully fit and athletic enough to satisfy the Army's zeal for physical exercise, but he remained maladroit with screwdrivers and hopeless at either drawing or conceptualising electric circuits. None the less he was obviously what the Army used to designate, in its ineffable way, 'officer material'. Sure he was a writer, and wrote a short story called *Sack Labourer* while on a 48-hour pass in Pandy, but there were writers, actors, painters, and all sorts of queer folk in the Signals. What he was, was a leader, cool, authoritative, clear-headed. So when in November he went down to the War Office Selection Board at Barton Stacey near Winchester, and led groups of young men like himself through the mad sequence of tests – crossing a chasm with half-a-dozen planks and suchlike – there was never any doubt he would pass. His good sense, his natural distinctiveness, his keen ambition, all had long since convinced him that he would take a commission. That complex magnetic mixture of bravery and bravado which all boys with a bookish education from grammar or public school learned in his (and my) generation drew him irresistibly towards full-blown combat. In January 1942 he was posted to Officer Cadet School for the Royal Artillery, beginning just up the road from home in Shropshire, and then going a little later to the Artillery's main officer training school at Larkhill on Salisbury Plain.

The British generation which saw active service during the Second World War is now dead and dying; the youngest of the next generation to complete its compulsory two years in uniform was born in 1939. A minor literary and movie genre, the national service story, has receded as a matter of immediate personal experience. Some of the language lives on as folk-dialect; most is now comically unintelligible. But once upon a time this torrential rhetoric had young men of 21 fairly trembling with suppressed rage and fear as it poured over them in a high, ritual, uninflected scream a few feet or a few inches from their faces.

Now, on the word – MARCH – I want you only to take a step forward, *not* to march, I want you only to take a step forward, just pretend, got that? Some dim-witted piece of merchandise is sure to carry on. Now then, watch it. SQUAD – by the front – quick MARCH!

(Sure enough two soldiers march off and collide with those standing still, and one in front marches off out of sight)

Stop that laughing. I'll charge the next man I see smile.

All right, Horace, come back home. You nit, you nit, you creepy-crawly nit. Don't you hear, don't you listen, can't you follow simple orders, CAN'T YOU? Shut up! Don't answer back! A young man like you, first thing in the morning, don't be rude, don't be rude. No one's being rude to you. YOU. If you'd been paying attention you might've done it correctly, eh?

(To all) You'd better know from the start, you can have it the hard way or you can have it the easy way, I don't mind which way it is. Perhaps you like it the hard way, suits me. Just let me know. At ease everyone. Now we'll try and make it easier for you. We'll count our way along. We count together and then maybe we'll all act together. I want everything to be done together. We're going to be the happiest family in Christendom and we're going to move together, as one, as one solitary man . . .[3]

All those civil and civilian young men were cowed by this, obeyed it, once or twice were utterly broken by it, learned to copy and parody it faithfully until they cried with laughter, and concluded by living it right through their bodies and minds.

That was the point. Once this language was yours, then individuality was dissolved into solidarity, and more often than not the confident expectation of army cock-ups joined officers, NCOs and men closely together against the necessary and imagined 'they', who got things wrong from somewhere else.

Besides, not so very much went wrong. The British Army stayed and trained in large part in Britain. After the defeat at Dunkirk, when a third of a million men got away in the famous evacuation by the fleet of small boats, and with the conspicuous exceptions of the soldiers in Africa, Italy and Burma, the enormous numbers designated for the invasion of Europe trained for three years in their home country. Their morale was high, they got home sufficiently often, few had seen any combat but they trained all the time, and when it came to it they were quite good at soldiering.

Officer Cadet School for guns, tanks and infantry alike was a continuation of that same swamping of the consciousness with the language of command and the rules of procedure. There wasn't much conceptual explanation. There was just iteration, first of small movements of foot and hand, building by much the same teaching methods to the directing of artillery fire by the forward observation officer.

In a dark hut, at the further end of Larkhill Camp, was a shelf some 9 feet wide and 3 feet deep. On it, somebody with no aesthetic touch at all had constructed a *papier-mâché* landscape, more or less undulating and with a dry green sand glued to its surface to represent fields, a few scrawny toy trees, and some matchbox houses with a cardboard cut-out church 4 inches high in the middle. Underneath, invisible to the class of cadets, was a soldier smoking. When the tutorial officer gave map reference instructions by field telephone, the noise of a recorded explosion shook the hut, and the soldier puffed smoke up from below through a small hole at an appropriate spot.

Thus the cadets learned 'bracketting', to call down fire from gunnery positions behind them, and by studiously bisecting the angles at which their barrels pointed, gradually to bring the shells dead on to target.

> Not only how far away, but the way you say it
> Is very important. Perhaps you may never get
> The knack of judging a distance, but at least you know
> How to report on a landscape: the central sector,
> The right of arc and that, which we had last Tuesday,
>   And at least you know
>
> That maps are of time not place, so far as the Army
> Happens to be concerned – the reason being,
> Is one which need not delay us. Again you know
> There are three kinds of tree, three only, the fir
>   and the poplar,
> And those which have bushy tops to; and lastly
> That things only seem to be things.[4]

Raymond Williams had done the Army's curriculum: he had done foot drill, and blancoing his equipment with muddy green pigment at Cambridge; he had done lots more drill, small arms training, map-reading and wireless procedure at Prestatyn; now at Larkhill, endless drill of course, best-boots-you-can-see-your-face-in naturally, the checking of equipment by junior officers, of G108s (day issue) and G1098s (life-and-death issue); he had done schemes, exercises, and TEWTS, and finally he had become an intimate of guns, heavy field guns and their disposition alongside their miscegenated relative, the self-propelled anti-tank gun. But S-P gun training didn't feature much at Larkhill, run by straight artillery men whose view of the job was still that heavy guns were there to pound and flatten the opposition from some way behind the front line, after which the infantry went in and mopped up. This in spite of the fact that all the experience of previous British victories in the Second World War – in the Western Desert, in the Italian mountains, and still to come in Normandy, were of something much more mobile and uncertain, including dreadful artillery bombardments, for sure, but with changeable and erratic front lines, many feints and quick manoeuvres, long empty days and sudden swift advances.

Tanks, in this latest kind of war, were an unprecedented and essential kind of monster. The technology which came racing out of World War One accelerated astoundingly through the 1920s and 1930s to deliver at the moment of *Blitzkrieg* the fighter, the bomber, and the fairly-high-speed tank. Men, rifles and machine guns remained much as they were in 1918; until they marched over the conquered territory, the battle wasn't won. But the killing and the conquest were achieved by tanks on the ground, tons of fort-like metal with rivets big as a ship's, and aircraft above them.

Raymond must have felt a grain or two of the same excitement leak into his blood, for when asked to rank his order of preference for regimental posting when commissioned he put down 'anti-tank regiment' first.

His passing-out parade was on 4 June 1942, and he had sixteen days' leave before joining the 21st Anti-Tank Regiment, Guards Armoured Division, encamped on the edge of Salisbury Plain at Bourton. He sent a cable to Joy to meet him in Salisbury in order to get married. He forgot to say where they should meet.

Annette Lees

Joy had gone into welfare and personnel work in an aircraft factory in Birmingham when she took her B.Sc. Joy was only about 21, looked younger, but had the advantage of being very attractive-looking, with beautiful natural blond hair. This choice gave her freedom to stay with Raymond once they married, and she moved round the country with him.

The work of the personnel officers, required in any factory employing women, involved helping women, called up into industry, who often had not worked before. They could find the factory environment very rough at times. The Personnel Officer, however, supervised time-keeping and absenteeism and had to bring before a special tribunal women absent without good reasons. They were conscripted after all! The Personnel Department allocated extra clothing coupons to women involved in work on machines where oils, suds or lead could destroy clothing. There was concern about safety and women had to be persuaded if possible to wear protective clothing and caps (they could be scalped otherwise).

Fred Dalling

She followed Raymond wherever she could. When he was first posted to Prestatyn, she was in digs in Rhyl and they spent his 36-hour leave pass travelling on the local buses looking at the countryside. She went to the employment exchange at Rhyl and asked if they had any work. 'Yes,' they said, 'Right here. Come round the counter.' And she was there six months!

Annette Lees

So she went straight to her wedding in Salisbury from Birmingham, where she'd been working at an aircraft factory – I'd been in Birmingham as well, at J.B. Brooks at Five Ways and later Lucas. We shared a flat. Luckily there were no air raids at the time. I can remember Joy saying she was due to catch a train to Salisbury, but still had not had the telegram from Raymond to indicate where he would meet her. There was no choice of train so she left asking me to tell Raymond if he phoned that she was on her way and he'd have to look for her. She went to the nearest hotel to the station and waited and in no time he arrived there too! They married in a Registry Office in Salisbury and as they only took one witness, the taxi driver was persuaded to be the second one!

Raymond sent a telegram to his parents, but neither of them came. Travelling was a grim business in wartime, even for a railway family, and in any case Mrs Williams didn't want him to marry Joy and was never really reconciled to the marriage, nor Raymond to her.

Second lieutenant Williams R.H. joined the regiment on 20 June in heavy rain, and presented himself to his new commanding officer, Lt Colonel G.K. Bourne. The 21st Anti-Tank Regiment was one of several newly formed such outfits attached to the Guards Armoured Division, itself assembled in 1941 out of an incompatible medley of infantry and cavalry units. Some of the most élite and class-conscious regiments in the British Army – the Brigade of Foot Guards on one hand and sometime Household Cavalry regiments (the Royal Household, that is) on the other – were obliged to come together in an entirely new, traditionless division riding vehicles and using weapons of which they had no experience and upon which they looked down with a condescending scorn born of long and irrelevant confidence in their social status. The results were at times hilarious.

Peter Carrington was in the tank brigade dogged by the self-propelling guns of Williams's regiment.

Peter Carrington

The Foot Guards could be relied upon to do what they were told, and to do it conscientiously and efficiently. The tradition was less applicable to armoured warfare, or much of it. Where manoeuvre is required, so is speed and imagination and initiative. I never thought that our system was perfect for breeding those qualities. Individuals possessed them – splendidly. But the system itself was differently designed.

I have already referred to our warrant officers and non-commissioned officers, our sergeant-majors and sergeants. They were admirable men, but more in those days than today they were executants of pretty rigid orders, custodians of a fairly inflexible regime. They knew their basic infantry soldiering inside out. To find their Guardsmen separated from them by the steel walls of an armoured vehicle, apparently possessed of a will of its own, was disconcerting. Furthermore they themselves were in some cases less than rapid learners of new ways. There was also the simple fact that the tanks of the day were rather small and the Guardsmen particularly large. I remember one sergeant-major, a huge man of magnificent appearance, who seemed slow at responding on the radio – he commanded a tank – during training on Salisbury Plain. There was always a pause before he acknowledged a transmission, and one day, when his tank happened to be close to mine, I discovered why. When an officer's voice came through his earphones he stood to attention and saluted before tackling the microphone.[5]

Peter Carrington was not only a professional soldier in 1941, educated in the exigent and austere snobberies of the 2nd Battalion of the Grenadier Guards, he later became the sixth Lord Carrington and Secretary-General of NATO, always an old-fashioned Tory democrat who *liked* the New Model Army of 1944. He was writing about men whose whole life before they climbed into the Sherman tanks was defined and confined by the rigid conventions, fixed loyalties and arbitrary customs of Chelsea Barracks.

Williams's regiment, as I said, was a much more motley and civilian affair. By the time his battery went to war in June 1944, only the regimental CO Colonel Hulbert was a regular officer, and social class, even for someone as acutely sensitive to its stratifications as Williams, marked no clear divisions amongst the remaining twelve captains and tank troop-commanders. They included a garage-owner, a Maltese refugee, two other students like Williams himself, and an insurance agent, commanding a force of 785 men and NCOs, with a single Warrant Officer.

The enormous concentration upon the tank which caused the Grenadier Guards so much discomfort in 1942 or so was part of a reordering of British wartime strategy in expectation of an invasion of Europe, now that the Americans had joined in the struggle. It was helped by the dramatic and much-celebrated victory at El Alamein in North Africa in October 1942, at a time when the British Army was decidedly short of victories, as well as by the determination of generals who had watched the carnage on the Somme as company commanders not to permit pointless slaughter again. The trouble was that for one reason or another the inventive brilliance on each side of the Atlantic which produced the Spitfire and the Flying Fortress was missing in the production of the tanks. The American Sherman was nothing like as powerful as the German Tiger and Panther tanks. The enemy guns could blow apart the Shermans, which burned very easily, at 2,000 yards; the Shermans could do little except from the rear or from very close up. Victory on the ground in Normandy was as much due to the sheer mass of Allied armour as anything else.

When Williams began regimental training, however, these discrepancies were not much known about, and the Army was taking its time in training for its new, tank-founded strategies. For the first six months of 1943 he and his regiment trundled their ordinary field-guns and their S-Ps from Shaftesbury in Dorset across to Milton in Northamptonshire, from Thetford in Essex back to Gillingham in Wiltshire. On 22 April, just returned from ten days' leave with Joy in Birmingham, Lieutenant Williams and his brother officers put on a demonstration of tank mobility for their Britannic Majesties, George VI and Queen Elizabeth.

On 6 July the regiment was moved, with the Army's usual inexplicitness about its purposes, to the area of the North Yorkshire moors outside Scarborough. Q Battery, Williams's unit within which he would command a troop of tank-guns, settled into tents and billets at Birdsall, and four days later, to his great satisfaction, Williams was posted to Rhyl to do self-propelled gun and Sherman tank training at the Royal Army Military Transport School, and Joy got her instantaneous post in the employment exchange.

Tank-training in that hot late summer was a funny mixture. Inside the tank, with the flap down and your headphones on, your only thought was for navigation. The great mass of metal bucketed and walloped its way over the open moors of Wales or of Yorkshire, and the main thing was not to split your head open and to keep contact with your fellows through the infernal and inadequate periscope. With the flap up, steering just by looking, you were obliterated by noise and smell: the colossal roaring of the engine and squealing of the tracks, the black reek and filthy taste of diesel fumes. But then, when you switched off and the sweet and natural noises of the moors, the peewit, the lamb and the seagull became once again audible, the peacefulness of that lovely landscape rolled back, and the Sherman became as massive and immovable an object as the boulders themselves; you sat beside it, leaning back on the still-warm wheels, and sucked down the orange-coloured tea from an ungainly mess-tin.

Even out of battle, however, the tank which was your home could kill you. It could see little and hear nothing, and many soldiers were pressed into the mud when a vehicle reversing at high speed hit them unawares. Just after Raymond got back to his regiment in late September, a young second lieutenant, Alun Lewis, was drowned on exercises when a tank toppled from a light bridge into a river and trapped him inside. Thereafter, as Fred Dalling said, 'Raymond crossed his bridges with his men hanging on the outside.'

The regiment, as soldiers quickly and spontaneously will, made itself at home near Scarborough. Even in winter, barbed-wired and boarded up, Scarborough was a handsome place: the large Victorian bulk of the Grand Hotel had been commandeered, of course, but its old high and arcaded ballroom still made a hospitable mess to dozens of visiting officers, and walking-out in the wide, green Valley Gardens made for a common leisure culture of all ranks.

The exercises and manoeuvres began to stretch out and to become more specific. All the talk of the invasion of Europe was of 'when', no longer 'whether'. Heavy snow fell, as it always does across those moors, and the regiment was out for the first week in February, practising vehicle wading and disembarkation across the Derwent. The second week they were all down at Harlech practising firing on the range, and then back on 14 February for a ten-day exercise at Elleston Grange, followed by a debriefing of all officers in the Arcadia Theatre in Scarborough. So Raymond and Joy, who was in digs in Scarborough, went for a mixed grill at Charles's brother Frank Laughton's Silver Grill.

The regimental strength numbered 786, and on the last day of March the Prime Minister himself came to inspect them, and imply in his short homily that action was not far away. The order came to move to Doncaster at 06.00 hours on 1 May 1944. Joy, expecting their first baby in July, took a lonely train ride home to Barnstaple. Throughout the long, wet day, vehicles and men ground slowly on to trains and disappeared south, Bedford three-tonners loaded with boxes of ammunition and fourteen-day ration packs whined and wound on to the crowded A1, the Romans' own road north and south, and joined the huge multitude of men and munitions teeming towards D-Day.

So one and a half million men and their equipment were crammed into a corridor some forty miles wide running from Lydd in Kent to Lyme in Dorset. The weather was bad, and the days droned eventlessly by. The 21st Anti-Tank Regiment, of the Guards Armoured Division, was zeroing its guns at Lydd on 22 May – following that neat procedure to ensure that the idiosyncrasies of particular weapons were corrected – when Eisenhower himself, Supreme Commander, came to look at them in their base camp at Hurst Green. Everybody had learned from two years of training that warfare is a matter of long, inexplicable waits; interminable journeys up empty roads abruptly and inexplicably terminated; a few minutes' worth of vivid, grotesque, alternatively terrifying and exultant action, fatal for some, not statistically likely to be oneself. For thirty-six days the vast army waited, while a handful of meteorologists watched for the key conjunction of skies and tides.

On the evening of Monday 5 June wireless silence was enjoined on the whole force, and all units put on six hours' notice to move. As everybody now knows, the parachutists fell out of the sky into the small hours, and the invasion infantry, tossing on a swell at their moorings, and vomiting down the sides of their tethered landing craft, set exhaustedly off in the last dark of the night.

For the 21st Anti-Tank Regiment the waiting, with each man glued to the BBC News, began again. With everybody both bored and tense with fear and apprehension, and without proper training areas, it was extremely difficult to keep the regiment's fighting fitness at a sharp edge. There were training runs and vehicle servicing, but no leave even to the village pub. When the warning order came to move on 16 June it was a relief; little sleep for two days as the 21st joined HMS Landing Ship Transport 199 and cast off at last under Commander Stracy Connelly at 18.20 on 19 June.

Williams spent the night feeling dreadfully sick a few miles off Southend, with the rest of the regiment. So too the whole of the next day. On 22 June, D+16, at half-past two in the afternoon, they ran ashore in nearly six feet of water on Juno Beach, which had been taken and consolidated for the armour by the foot soldiers of the 3rd Canadian Division and the 50th British Division. The tanks shouldered their way ashore, pouring like waterfalls, and by the same evening were grouped a mile and a half from Bayeux, while the sounds of battle rolled dully in the distant north-west, and much nearer, in the deadly fighting twenty miles east, around Caen.

For six days nothing happened, and they didn't move. A strange little camp life improvised itself, the men stripped to the waist in the pleasant June sunshine, eating at a picnic table made from heavy wooden shellboxes propped on the eight-gallon jerrycans which carried water and fuel. All the associations for Raymond were with the orchards and pastures around Pandy. The trees were thick with hard green fruit; he was the one who spoke French, so he went across with the cans for milk and eggs from the little farm on the edge of Bretteville l'Orgueilleuse, a few miles up the road from Caen to Bayeux. Apart from his being tipped out of one of the regiment's bren-gun carriers when a small mine blew a track off, nothing happened, lots of nothing.

On the afternoon of 28 June, the regiment was deployed for action around the hamlet of Putot-en-Bessin. All tanks had their flaps down and were steering by periscope, but doing so in a highly cultivated landscape speckled with countless copses and intersected by dense and centuries-old hedgerows and deep lanes. Shut in the tank the drivers could see little and anticipate – sudden drops in the ground, for instance – even less. Williams recalled that the next day he was told to occupy a small wood, where the visibility was nil and which was being shelled anyway. He says he split his troop of four tanks in two, and never saw two of them again.[6] German tanks and infantry were attacked heavily on a one-mile front between Cheux and Grainville, and Q Battery were firing back both with the heavy Browning 50mm machine guns on top of the tank and with the enormous seventeen pounders carried by about one in four of the vehicles. This was the only gun capable of knocking out the Tigers and Panthers, and they accounted for one of each, but it also meant that the Battery was heavily shelled and mortared by Germans trying to destroy the heavy weapons.

Daylight fighting was pretty well continuous until 11 July, when they were pulled back for a break. With enormous reserves and the awful lessons of 1916 and 1917 always in their minds, the Allied generals were scrupulous in their care to avoid exhaustion as much as they could. This wasn't the Italian, still less the Burmese campaign. There were enough men and plenty of guns. The tankmen fought largely during working hours. At night, they dug a hole big enough for the five bodies of a tank crew, drove the tank into a position to straddle it, and slept underneath. Once or twice, so the tale went, a tank settled on its sleeping owners and crushed them in their sleep.

The fighting was, as they say, heavy; frenzied more like, but always sporadic. The S-Ps were in the front line, which wasn't at all the idea, and their Brownings, far from being defensive weapons, were being used in the chaos to take the ground ahead of the infantry, where Germans were dug in deep behind the high steep meadowbanks and coppices. The very bodies of both machine-gunners and tank commanders were dangerously exposed in open combat, but death and danger were vivid and immediate throughout the battle. One armour-piercing shell in the fuel or in the rounds of ammunition stacked along the inside, and the crew would be hideously incinerated; if the tank was hit but didn't blow up at once, the enemy machine guns would be trained on its turret as the crew piled awkwardly out. All around them dead cattle and unburied men bulged and swelled and split and stank in the warm July sunshine.

So they earned their week off. They had lost three tanks, not knowing – still nobody knows – exactly how many men were killed, escaped, or were taken prisoner. On 29 June Williams's two tanks never came back. His troop was being shelled and then was pulled out of the wood. If some of the men got out, they may have been captured, or having hidden themselves with the French, as soldiers everywhere long to do, they began to go home.

Desertion was rare in the Normandy campaign, and only a tiny piece of France had been recaptured by that date. Although plenty of soldiers got lost, they were quickly found and returned to their unit. The Royal Military Police were extremely efficient. The Battery's daily report only names three S-Ps lost, no deaths. But there again, they might not have known either. Yet it is still very odd that Williams never found out what happened to his men, and may explain a little of what he said, thirty-five years later, about guilt and war.

It was appalling. I don't think anybody really ever gets over it. First there is the guilt: about moments of cowardice, but also about moments of pure aggression and brutality. It is easy enough to feel guilty about when you felt frightened but much worse is the guilt once you've started recovering your full human perspective, which is radically reduced by the whole experience of fighting. Then you realise some of the things you've done . . .[7]

Nowhere is the commandment not to taste of the fruit of the tree of knowledge so clearly written as in the course of history. Only unconscious activity bears fruit, and the individual who plays a part in historical events never understands their significance. If he attempts to do so he is struck with sterility.[8]

Williams had been reading Tolstoy not long before; what lover of novels (on either side) would not have done? For truth, for sure; and for solace. And yet some people had to know what was going on, for on 9 July Caen was taken at fearful cost by the Allies, and after another whole month of the same intensity of battle, the Canadians, the Americans and the Free French forced a gap open at Falaise, and the Allies streamed through towards Paris.

That was the view from the staff. The 21st Anti-Tank returned from their rest on 16 July, the day Williams, R.H. was gazetted as full captain, crossed the river Orne two days later, fought in support of the Canadian infantry at Longueval, still only three miles or so from the beaches, and by the end of July was back near Bayeux at Martin-des-Besaces with a bunch of Irish Guardsmen and half-a-dozen prisoners 'very weak and shaken by the bombing'. Q Battery had lost two colour-sergeants and eleven gunners. The Battery commander was fluently plainspoken about (as they say) his *matériel*:

The FA trailer is considered hopeless by all anti-tank gunners (and was in 1942). Apparently no one has the slightest interest in a suitable tower for the 17 pounder, and consequently we are suffering from a slow, overloaded and cumbersome vehicle.

My guns are bundled into very forward localities and consequently see no tanks but are heavily shelled.[9]

They moved south to Vassy without incident as the Allied breakout westwards was at last achieved. While the regiment stayed at Vassy until 26 August, Captain Williams was sent on instructional duties with the 3rd Royal Horse Artillery, and only caught up with his comrades two-thirds of their way along the dashing advance from L'Aigle to Brussels, when the Guards Armoured Division covered 350 miles in six days.

Williams found them harbouring, as tank men say, near Douai. As he crossed Picardy and the Somme to catch up with them on 2 September, every signpost he saw was redolent of the dead of a generation before: Amiens, Albert, Bapaume, Arras. The regiment had come 250 miles since they crossed the Seine in the early morning of 30 August. Now, as Captain Williams took over 'A' echelon from Captain Beaty, they drove full pelt and with no hindrance another hundred miles into Brussels, parking the tanks beside the Basilique at three o'clock in the morning of 4 September.

Looking back, it was an historic advance, one of the great sweeping moves of the war. The last stretch was the most exhilarating, the top-heavy tanks swaying massively in their own swell, the tank commander standing in his turret, lulled and comatose in the incessant screeching and roaring din, on either side of the road the trudging soldiers, the only punctuation of the hours the suckling, scalding mugs of tea.

In Brussels, the cheering, jammed and glad-handed crowds thronged the tanks all night. It was wonderful. Completely strange girls were kissing tank crews with giddy abandon. The tanks were covered with flowers. Williams's own account of it, written a few months later, was printed in the regimental newspaper which he edited.

As we entered Brussels in September '44, the delirious welcome of the people seemed to become more feverish in every street. Thus while in Chaussee Ninove they had been content to throw lilac blooms, in the Boulevard Nord they began to throw bottles. There were bottles of champagne, straw flasks of chianti, flagons of beer and long tapering decanters of Benedictine. But the glories that lay inside them were not so readily appreciated as the patent fact that when they hit you on the head they hurt. My left eye was already showing signs of the bruise it had received back in Tournai from an under-ripe pear, and when I received a stinging blow from a champagne bottle just behind the left ear I decided that liberation was too rough a game, and got down inside the turret of my tank. I stayed there for a while, dividing my attention between the roar of the engines behind me and the boots of my wireless operator, who was hanging almost completely out through his hatch, when I saw thru the driver's periscope a pair of dangling female legs.

'God, this is the end,' I muttered under the noise of the engines, 'once they start climbing on we're done for.' I straightened out, and poked my head up through the turret. And then I saw her, small, blonde, smiling, and looking very embarrassed, as if the Lord Chamberlain had caught her trying out the Queen's throne at the palace. Her discomfort was so obvious that I had to laugh, and I suppose that was the best thing I could have done. She laughed back, and settled herself more comfortably on the turret. We were nearly at our objective, a pleasant boulevard in the north of the city, so we managed two more smiles at each other and then I ordered the squadron to halt and harbour. I climbed out quickly and watched them in, and then looked up at the turret again. She was still there, smiling, and holding out her hands to me to catch her as she came down. She was quite irresistible.[10]

98

Williams was delayed in Brussels, and came late through Louvain where a number of batteries found a cache of *Wehrmacht* champagne. On their way to Holland, they paused at Schoot to shoot up a house of which they had their suspicions, and 'one machine gun burst ... produced one Lieutenant-Colonel and forty-six other ranks as prisoners'. At Tessenderloo the regiment linked up with 50th Division and, in readiness for one of the most famous operations of the war, was issued with the new Condor II tanks.

'Market Garden' was to be the hop, skip and jump by way of the three crucial bridges at Eindhoven, Nijmegen and Arnhem, which would bring the Allies to the German frontier. In the event, as everyone knows from the book and the film, it attempted a bridge too far. For Williams's unit, it seemed to work just fine. His troop lost Gunner Smith as they crossed Zon bridge, and Lieutenant Tony Handford was killed at La Colonie. They were involved in the heavy fighting in which British and American soldiers captured Nijmegen bridge in one piece, and they stayed by the bridge for the last week in September, while the British airborne lost 8,000 out of 10,000 men at Arnhem. One brief foray on 20 September took HQ troop over the German border at Wyler Meer, causing the CO to vie with countless other claims for years to the improvised title of First-Allied-Unit-into-Germany.

Until after Christmas, that was about it for the 21st Anti-Tank. They were pulled back into a rest area for a fortnight in October, where King George came again to see them. They built log cabins against the winter. They held a regimental sports day on 27 October and Sergeant Penney beat Raymond into second place in the quarter and the half-mile. They finally moved across into Germany at Gangelt on 13 November, but although there is regular harassing fire mentioned in the daily reports from each troop – 'ten rounds per morning' – there was no engagement and no one was hurt. Even when the massive and desperate break-out by the Germans in the Ardennes offensive took place, the 21st spent Christmas at Kumtich, and apart from the sound of distant Spandau fire muffled by the heavy snow, and a few moaning Minnies exploding nowhere in particular, quietly sat out the Battle of the Bulge.

Throughout January the regiment went back to training in Belgium, there being no actual fighting they were called upon to do. For most of February it remained immobile at one hour's notice to move, and Williams assumed command of HQ troop, until on 24 February they watched the vast airborne fleet fly overhead on the way to cross the Rhine and drop on Germany.

It was another month before they crossed the Rhine themselves on 30 March, Williams resumed command of 'A' echelon and made good friends with a Dutch Army partisan attached to the regiment for the rest of the war, the genial, stout and bespectacled Baron Franz von Hövell tor

Westerflier, who went to prove the ancient truism that all foreigners have comic names.

The last heavy fighting for Williams's Battery took place on the road up to Enschebe-Gronau. By April 1945 there was no doubt about the outcome; Berlin was in ruins; the Red Army was taking an atrocious vengeance all over East Germany. But the discipline of the *Wehrmacht* held even among the boys and forty-somethings who had been added to the remnants of the front-line soldiers and ordered to hold the frontier. They continued, with pointless courage, to fight and to die at unpredictable points all the way up to the moment of surrender.

The roads of the advance were in any case jammed with men and vehicles, and the main military task for Williams and his men was to keep traffic moving and rescue wheeled vehicles from the boggy mud oozing across the battered roads. By this stage there were no German tanks left to fight, so 'Q' and 'Z' batteries were combined as an impromptu motor company with small arms they no longer had to use. At Schwagstorf they freed a wretched little prisoner of war camp with a bemused, filthy and starving population of about fifty Italians, Russians, Poles, Yugoslavs, and soon afterwards did the same for a concentration camp at Sandbostel in which, with happily poetic justice, they then imprisoned captured SS officers.

> That was satisfying – we had after all played some significant part in the political victory over fascism. But that satisfaction was soon cancelled. The SS officers would come up to me and say: 'Why did we ever get into this ridiculous war with each other, when it is so clear who the common enemy is?' By this time the Russians were in Berlin. I reported this back to my superiors, and was told: 'They could be right, old boy.' Many of them already thought that the Wehrmacht was a fine army, and that the War had probably been a mistake. An assimilation to the perspectives of what was to be the Cold War had started as early as March 1945.[11]

I think this is an example of a recurrent kind of bad faith in Williams's view of the world. In the regimental newspaper Williams edited a few weeks later, he speaks of his own necessary and righteous hatred for the *Wehrmacht* and, in a very full mail (which he printed) is rebuked for a lack of charity. But there is no mention of the Red Army, and I simply don't believe that the senior officers of a mere captain at the end of the nine months fighting they had seen since D-Day had even given a thought to anything except the end of warfare, still less the beginning of cold warfare. The remarks made in 1979 are another instance of Williams's twinge, which kept him so unremittingly in the waging of civil-*class* warfare, even when – most of all when – he didn't know who or where the enemy was.

100

For the rest of April they made 'steady, unhampered advance' until they got to Sandbostel on 1 May and quite rightly set the SS officers to digging mass graves for the dead and decomposing bodies of the camp victims. On 4 May all offensive action stopped, and the next day every enemy on the 21st Army Group front surrendered. The war in Europe was over.

Only a month later, the Guards were unhorsed by official order and reverted to that traditional mode of military transport, their own two feet. At a grand farewell on Derby Day, with the race being broadcast over the tannoy, Montgomery took the salute at the dissolution of the Guards Armoured Division on Rotenburg airfield, and the 21st joined the 7th Armoured Division, the Desert Rats. With the rat on their sleeves, the officers bustled off to an enormous party at the Kreishaus, Rotenburg, and drank as much of the champagne and cognac left behind by the defeated enemy as they could.

Williams was in tearing high spirits. The victorious army had captured a printing press still in excellent condition at Pinneberg, and in a flash he had set up as editor of *Twentyone*, the regimental newspaper, somewhere between the *Cambridge University Journal* and that much-lamented Labour paper, the *Daily Herald*.

Williams wrote great chunks of the paper, though he earnestly solicited contributions from the troops. He wrote editorials as Michael Pope, reviews and bits of reporting in his own name, a front page anonymously, and a short story as Peter Dalling. Joy appeared as a very demure as well as unnamed pin-up in one issue.

> The editor says there will be no statement of policy. I however am a free man. Without embarrassing either myself or you I may say that you are also free men. A free press is the best sign of a healthy community. A paper based on the partiality of merit alone would be the sign of a good regiment. This is a good regiment, and it is up to you, its members, to see that our paper becomes truly representative of the best that's in us.[12]

Such idealism and innocence speak from and to the heart. The newspaper, mostly in Williams's voice, betokened the best that was in the army, and the best that was in Britain, in the summer of 1945.

Williams warmly reviewed the visiting Russian concert and cabaret; as 'W.W.' (but the attribution is unmistakable) he warns his readers against political bias in the English press on both Left and Right; just back from a few days' leave in Brussels, he describes the re-emerging anti-royalism of the Walloons as well as sampling the cabaret, the races, and the strawberries.

In the fourth issue, 'Michael Pope' raised a storm by recommending that 'the memory of a man who died for fascism should be guarded only in contempt and hate, and never in reverence'.

There had been memorial services to German and British dead held in sequence in Pinneberg church, and Williams derided this as a 'mock sentimental occasion'. In the issue of 27 July, he defended himself vigorously in reply to a flurry of rather impressive letters reproaching him for lack of forgiveness, and lack of ordinary human sympathy. Astonishingly, Williams described himself as having been, 'three years before the war, a Christian pacifist. The Sermon on the Mount was for me the final embodiment of truth.' This is a corner of his personal history which he certainly never mentioned again. And he justifies the nursing of hatred by reminding his readers of the slogans painted on shattered houses near the front line during winter 1944: 'lead, Führer, we follow', 'Führer, we believe in you'. Williams goes on, 'They are not glorious dead; they are criminals executed by the conscience and the power of the free world.'

That seems a lot nearer to the spirit of the time in July 1945, than any move towards a construction of cold war feeling. So does the mounting attention and excitement apparent in the newspaper as the day of the British general election comes near. The comments coincide with the attention given to Army educational projects. The moment of victory was the high point of the success of the Army Bureau for Current Affairs. This was the high-minded body which had ensured that this 'ingenious and civilian army' (in Edward Thompson's famous coinage) had been kept informed of the plans being drawn up at home for winning the peace after the war, and ensuring that this post-wartime Britain might truly become a land fit for heroes to live in. In an entertaining little anecdote, Thompson also recalled the work of the ABCA which had sent to all regiments a summary and discussion documents on the Beveridge Report which outlined the welfare state of the British future. His squadron commander asked him to 'discuss it with the chaps, because it would be so difficult to speak against something when you know nothing about it'.

Twentyone vigorously reported that small corner of the nation's democratic debate with itself at a series of public meetings in the soft summer air and salt-breezes of the seascape not far from the Kiel canal. Gunner Kipling of 'Y' Battery appeared on the front page calling for Labour votes, and the boys sat around him applauding decorously. It is the decorum, the civic niceness of these young men which jumps out of those old Army snapshots. They look like Lowry paintings, better fed.

Edward Thompson

I can see now what was wrong with that generation. It was too bloody innocent by half, and some of them were too open to the world, and too loyal to each other to live.[13]

It was innocent, that generation, and it believed cheerfully in its own freedom. The headline of *Twentyone* on Friday 27 July is, half a century later, simple and stirring: 'Landslide to Labour'. Williams covers in his report the most newsworthy gains and losses, though he misses Charlie White's victory for Common Wealth in West Derbyshire, with Chatsworth at its heart, and Tom Wintringham, former commander of the British in the International Brigade who collected 14,000 votes for the Common Wealth Party in Aldershot (*Aldershot!*). But he spotted the 10,000 votes polled by an unknown farmer against Churchill, who stood respectfully unopposed by Labour or Liberal in Woodford. This was the genteel height of British radicalism this century, and just as seemly a symptom of its conduct as that handful of results is Williams's little bit of instruction on an inside page about the virtues and vices of proportional representation.

For a short time, the Regiment sat near the canal wondering apprehensively if it might be sent to fight in Burma. Then Little Boy fell out of *Enola Gay* upon Hiroshima on 6 August, and the rest of Williams's life was irradiated by its fatal after-glow. The Regiment was set to guard the canal itself on 29 August, and went to watch *Arsenic and Old Lace* in the mobile cinema the next day. Three weeks later, Captain Williams was sent with several dozen others to a tribunal in Brussels which recommended him for immediate Class B release in order to go home and finish his degree.

Merryn was 14 months old and Joy was 26 when Raymond got back to the Dallings' big house in Barnstaple. He hadn't seen Joy since his leave in April of the previous year, although she wrote to him every single day of his absence, and he had never seen Merryn at all. (A local woman in Barnstaple had said to the little baby, bouncing in her pram at the front door, 'Hasn't got a dad, eh?') He had been four years in the Army, in that powerfully male atmosphere, nine months at war, sleeping in, under and round a tank, three months in the faint delirium after victory, with another stupendous victory at home when Labour won on the scale it did. His life as schoolboy at King Henry's and student at Cambridge had been as masculine in its sociable bearings as it was solitary in its inner life. You could say that Raymond Williams learned his public gracefulness, his calm command and geniality from his striking success in the mannish life of school, university and army; he learned his terrific application, his solitude, his fierce privacy and silently passionate allegiance from his years of lonely study, his stiff mother and removed father, and from the all-comprehending enclosingness of his staunch wife.

Williams went back in late October 1945 alone to digs in Victoria Road, Cambridge, and returned to the life of a student in a town where, the urban legend had it, an undergraduate ex-major was arrested for being ungowned after dark by a Proctor's bulldog who had been his batman. Joy and Merryn stayed back in Barnstaple and so, married, a parent, a Captain and a third-year undergraduate, Williams set himself to put right the academic lapse in his second year in 1941, the only blemish upon the years of his success.

He took the option, in those days a very rare one, of writing a longish dissertation-style essay in place of certain examinations of the usual kind. He chose Ibsen as his topic, and immersed himself to the point of disappearance in Ibsen's work. He went back to Barnstaple only for a few days at Christmas and then in a kind of blur. He played 'Cheat' with the Dalling brothers, but couldn't bring himself to cheat.

The blur he was in was in its way enough of a crisis, in part of a kind characteristic of all the men returned from active service, whose simple, powerful purposes in warfare were to stay alive if possible, not to dishonour their duty to their comrades, and to remember, at times, the abstract but absolute commitment to destroy a fascism whose ultimate horribleness was only just coming into the light. Those were straightforward imperatives. Coming home, away from that close and adhesive life, away from bodies blown to bits and tea brewed up on a primus stove in the tank turret, thousands of the returning heroes were half barmy. In those circumstances René Cutforth, madder than most, yelled at his wife, 'Do you mean to say that the bloody army gave you lessons in how to be married to me?'

> 'Well, they told us what we might expect.'
> 'To hell with that,' I roared, and went off to the pub and stayed away for three days. When I got back, I said, 'I took off because I will not have my life interfered with.'
> 'Oh yes,' my wife said, 'they told us about that, too.'[14]

I don't suppose that anyone warned Joy that what the war would cause in her husband was not whisky but Ibsen; but it did. As Williams himself put it:

> He was the writer who spoke nearest to my sense of my own condition at the time. Hence the particular emphasis I gave to the motif of coming 'to a tight place where you stick fast. There is no going forward or backward.' [The line comes from *When We Dead Awaken*.][15]

Williams was stuck at the end of too many roads: war, university study, communism, the road to Pandy. He knew that he wanted to write but not what he could write about; he knew he had a novel in him, but not that he could write it; he knew he had a marriage but not how to live it; finally, he could sense that his life-project, to urge forward into a more general and generous future the deep, tacit values of his childhood, his father, the flowers, the fruit, the railway, was profoundly at risk in the Britain of 1945, and he feared defeat even as he longed for a victory with a longer future than had occurred to Attlee's Labour Party.

Reading Ibsen day after day, he could only write about him in a Cambridge idiom. One trait which characterises all Williams's writing is his thrift. He wasted nothing, and published almost everything except a clutch of three-quarters finished novels and a play: *A Map of Treason*, *Adamson*, *The Grasshoppers* and *King Macbeth*. His Ibsen thesis is still embedded in the later, three-times revised text of his famous critical guide book *Drama from Ibsen to Brecht*, and may easily be retrieved from it.

Wallace Stevens asks of a half-finished poem, 'Shall I uncrumple this much crumpled thing?' and Ibsen, by the time Williams had finished, at the age of almost 25, his 15,000 words, was a bit crumpled. But the marks of obsession are plain enough to read in the patient academic exposition.

So too are the marks of ingenuousness. For Williams rarely rewrote, regularly revised, and never threw away. As a result one can trace the archaeology of his composition quite clearly in the long essay on Ibsen. 'It is with the unity of his work that I am mainly concerned'[16] comes from the Tripos essay; so too does the treatment of Ibsen's late plays as extended dramatic metaphor rather than the exchange of putatively real characters. Both notions came from the dramaturgy of the day, especially Wilson Knight's Shakespeare criticism, and are none the worse for that.

A year or two later Williams borrows from his undergraduate friend Wolf Mankowitz the *Goon Show* insight that *Hedda Gabler* is a sort of farce,[17] and by the time the book is in print in 1952 he has added the key concept of his mature thought, the 'structure of feeling'.[18] But what marks the Tripos essay with Williams's own features is the combination of complete intellectual self-confidence (and confidence in judgement above all) with his absolute allegiance to hopefulness even in the teeth of certain defeat. This issues in a kind of life-axiom for him. Hopefulness is not borne down by defeat. Defeat is not failure.

Drama matters so much for Williams because, more than any other form except opera (and I don't believe he went to an opera in his life), it is a communal form of art. Among dramatists, Ibsen was his first key subject, because Ibsen dramatised heroism as hopefulness, even when – most of all when – the hero or heroine was pulled down to death by desire. Ibsen prefigured the essential tension between Williams's pervasive feelings of inheritance and his equally strong drive to break away and keep away, keeping other people away at the same time. Oddly enough, Ibsen's frequent heaviness of manner and diction, the striking of public attitudes against the social enemy – *Pillars of Society*, *Hedda Gabler*, *John Gabriel Borkman* – his generalised abstraction of resistance, accorded strongly and deeply with the currents and resources of Williams's being.

Most people, the philosopher J.L. Austin once said, think that being is like breathing, only quieter. For the purposes of this biography, let us say that Williams's being sought for a form which could contain and express the beatitude of belonging, and which at the same time comprehended the quick urge to dissent, to oppose, to break with all that is clumsy and cumbrous in one's inheritance, with mere convention.

Hence his lifelong preoccupation with form itself, and with form as devised by the accidents of social convention and available technology. At first sight, film looks an ideal match for his radical inclination to the ordinary, the natural, the unadorned, the quick, informal, shouldering-off of bloody old class, history and all that. But then the novel, with its weight of words, holds you down to experiences which, lived in your life, are heavy with the lives of those who preceded and surround you.

So the author of *Ghosts* and *When We Dead Awaken* was Williams's first man. The lies, the suppressions, the bastard, crippled children along with the drownings and immolations, the heroic personages destroyed by the past, gripped Williams with both terror and recognition: the 'tight place, where you stick fast. There is no going forward or backward.' But Williams also rejected this claustrophobia, and found in Ibsen in spite of Ibsen the undeflectable determination to keep climbing, to however cloudy an end.

The undergraduate Williams was conventionally wrong to name the unity of Ibsen's work as such. It was Ibsen's massive veeringness which caught him, and the playwright's dramatic, even melodramatic balancing of the gravity of the past against the unimaginable weightlessness of a free future.

This is the first theme of an undergraduate essay written in the familiar isolation of student soliloquy by the ex-tank captain, ex-communist, some-time Christian, always son and now father and husband, as a way of declaring what he was going to be when he grew up.

6

WORKERS' EDUCATION IN THE GARDEN OF ENGLAND

The intellectual life of Williams's Cambridge in that queer year he spent so solitarily on the other side of Midsummer Common was suddenly frozen and cracked open by the arctic temperatures of the cold war. The direct allegiance to which the undergraduate intelligentsia had given its heart in 1941 was split open by Stalin and Truman with consequences the world lived with for another half-century. Moreover, the bitter cold winds drove some into apostasy, as is well known, and others into a vehement defence of their own consistency, even in the teeth of evidence inimical to their commitment. For certain kinds of political temperament – Eric Hobsbawm's, Edward Thompson's for instance – it became all-important to stand up for the ideals of communism whatever communism did in practice, rather than to give an inch to the self-evidently horrible people trying to break the careers of those who did so.

No doubt life was much harder for those in the USA who hung on to the Hammer and Sickle, even if they appointed Trotsky and not Stalin their standard-bearer. But:

Eric Hobsbawm

Cambridge in 1946 was dominated by the triumphant-seeming fact of the new Labour Government which came out in the university as a sort of victory for the Popular Front line of the 1930s. We formed the Communist Historians Group in 1946, but of course in no time the feelings of complete hostility to the CP were so strong in academic life that there was no question of communists being promoted. If you had got a university job before 1948 you were quite *safe* – this wasn't Truman's and McCarthy's America, you wouldn't be sacked. But you certainly would be kept quiet and on one side.

Beneath these broad political oppositions, the smaller world of the human sciences in general, but English literature in particular, was divided by an ideological wall almost as thick as the Iron Curtain. F.R. Leavis, who won a university post for himself only at the age of 53, had by 1946 become the acknowledged legislator of his subject. Williams came across his magazine *Scrutiny* when he first went to Cambridge, although he had never met the editor. For five years of war, *Scrutiny* had continued to appear on time in spite of paper shortages, blackout, the natural indifference of everybody to the quiet conversation of culture, drowned out as it was by the din of propaganda and the urgently heeded communiqués. Often its contents were largely written by Leavis and his wife. But it kept up English, kept up its critical opposition to the worst of old English and, come to that, new capitalist culture; which is to say, opposition to the more repellent snobberies and gentilities of ruling class values and valuations, as well as opposition to the depredations of a civilisation given new self-confidence by the productivity of war, which foresaw its own untrammelled expansion into the self-indulgences of greed and possession as soon as the war was over.

Leavis saw with his fierce, austere eye the way the world was tending, and from a Cambridge college and a commonplace suburban house developed his doctrine of unremitting hostility to the forms and feelings of this entirely new kind of a civilisation, whose barbarism shone on its surface as soon as you turned it in the light. He also developed the instruments of close reading and careful contextualisation – 'practical criticism' – in order to effect this turning of a subject to the light, and with the judgements so wrested from experience offered to train (in his wife's phrase) 'an armed and conscious minority' in the effective struggle against a pervasive and lethal hegemony.

Coming back from the war, this was an exhilarating call to new, non-military, militant colours. There is no doubt that the call inspired Williams. Leavis was *the* source of energy irradiating the subject. The completeness of his vision, and the overwhelmingness with which he insisted that one's intellectual life must be fastened to one's avocation accorded well with the idealism with which socialists came back to build not just a better Britain but the best version of itself they could imagine.

It is important to add that others of a far less radical but just as English temper came back to be inspired by all that which in Leavis's work tends to political reaction, to sheer repugnance from the post-war world: his batty politics; his incomprehension before the necessities of social welfare; his ignorance of economics; his mere bookishness.

But Leavis's light shone brightly in the gloom of a wrecked national economy, the fuel shortage and wintry cold, the Arctic of international affairs, the enormous task of social reconstruction. Leavis had routed the mechanical English Marxism of the 1930s. Fired at once by his socialist formation and Leavis's high-minded project to rescue culture from capitalism ('though Leavis never called it that'), Williams determined to shape his own vocation in a triple response to the Marx of his memory and the Leavis of his last year at Cambridge; he would write his own novels as part of the remaking of culture; he would take on both Government and markets in the form of engaged periodical journalism; and he would teach the disinherited, the working men and women cut off from their own culture by class, by war, by geography, above all by the meannesses and cruelty of old Britain, the bloody-minded Britain such workers by brain as he was (and remained) were dedicated to replace.

It was a noble calling for a young man then; it remained a more than sufficient reason-for-being up to his death. At the end of the millennium, where the terms of living by idealism and vocation have long been on a starvation diet and are spectre-thin, that same vision now needs summoning up from 1946 and made once more to glow in the eyes of young teachers as it did in Raymond Williams's.

Not that he was much of a one for such diction. In conversation he shied off the higher moralising and would always undercut the apocalyptic imagery of old Leavis with his drier tones and sardonic wit. But writing and teaching looked, in 1946, to be the thing for him. He even cadged a couple of courses from Frank Jacques, Cambridge Secretary to the Workers Educational Association, himself an English graduate, socialist, an always genial, rather craggy encourager of young teachers ready to carry the word out into the wet and windswept Fens.[1]

So Williams did a ten-session course in International Affairs and another one on English literature before disappearing to Barnstaple when he finished his exams in order, as he told a disappointed Frank Jacques, to write a novel.

Williams had repaired his damaged academic honour in his finals. His answers to the special paper on George Eliot, for which he learned by heart great tracts of her novels, were clear in the memory of Muriel Bradbrook twenty years after she had marked them. George Eliot and Ibsen together brought him his first class honours and the offer from Trinity not of a fellowship, for they awarded no fellowships at that date to the still upstart subject of English, but of a £200 scholarship with which to pursue postgraduate research. At that date there were only twenty-odd British universities, staffed by people too old for conscription in 1940 but with plenty of years of academic service left after the war. An academic career was very hard to launch. The clever young men and women whom wartime had transfigured, and who brought a quite new egalitarianism and a radical view of the future of their studies found their way into intellectual life – I mean Eric Hobsbawm, Edward Thompson, Richard Hoggart, Dorothy Wedderburn, Bridget Sutton as well as Williams himself – by the stopping train and the domestic lines of university extra-mural education: 'outside the walls' as they used to say; 'adult education'. The *jeunesses dorées* at the ancient universities were undergraduates rather than adults, even when they were tank squadron commanders, and the adults educated by means of adult education didn't, well, they didn't (in a burst of candour) do work of full university stature.

So Raymond Williams and Joy, with a new baby called Ederyn to add, in August 1946, to his sister Merryn, were thrilled to see that the Oxford University Delegacy for Extra-Mural Studies was advertising for a full-time tutor in English at £400 per annum.[2] The job would be steadier than if Raymond had tried to provide for his family by occasional teaching of the same sort, while spending the bulk of his time writing. It would also be more demanding – three or four nights a week out at evening classes – but it left plenty of mornings at the typewriter. It wasn't what he'd origi-nally intended, but his novel was going wrong even though he could write it fast, and there was the wider programme of political journalism and criticism to pursue, which needed a dependable salary beside it. So when Williams later recollected[3] that 'it seemed unbelievably lucky as a job' he was surely right.

The luck went several ways. As a salary, it would do pretty well. As a job, it left time to write copiously and in seclusion – Merryn's earliest memories are of the typewriter clattering and thudding in her father's working room; it gave opportunity for editorialising in London the journal *Politics and Letters* which was to come in 1947; and extra-mural tutorial work at that date, carrying as Williams's did the escutcheon of the University of Oxford, was highly respectable and charged with political significance. It had strong links with the Workers Educational Association, organising mutual courses and certificating the three-year ones.

The WEA had been started in 1908 with a programme not only of extending educational opportunity for working men and women (but mostly men), but also of matching what was taught much more exactly to the experience of the students. It was a product of that excellently high-minded commitment on the part of the *haute bourgeoisie* to do what it could for those without its advantages in class and culture. If it had its inevitable taint of condescension, that was as vigorously repudiated by the first generation of the WEA's full-time District Secretaries as it later was by Williams.

Holding up its worthy Victorian pediment were the heirs of the great Victorian sages and philanthropists, especially T.H. Green and John Ruskin. Green, dead of blood-poisoning at 46 in 1882, was the idealist Idealist philosopher at Balliol who turned a whole generation of students to the work of improving the lives of the poor not in terms of personal amelioration but as the life-project of a politics. His students invented Asquith's liberalism and the Fabian Society, which for the first seventy years of the twentieth century wrote out the policy objectives of Labour's ministers-in-waiting. Ruskin – well, Ruskin is, with all his weirdnesses, still one of the folk-heroes of the British Labour movement, still serving to summon up out of the variety of his writing the noble image of a full education in the services of a fulfilled working life for all classes.

Following the path blazed by Green and Ruskin and William Morris came R.H. Tawney, key figure in the foundation of the WEA, whose rolling prose and principled disdain for the most hateful aspects of the British ruling class and its capitalism lit a light by which the whole Labour movement, Williams included, steered for years. Tawney's great polemics *Equality* and *The Acquisitive Society* speak cadenced and stirring maledictions over the enemy, and trust to the moral strength of their case to win the day. It isn't enough, as Williams saw. But it was a lot to have done, and Tawney's ethical socialism[4] pervaded the portals of the WEA, and gave to its tutors their always enthusiastic, occasionally sanctimonious commitment to public-spiritedness in all things, but especially education.

Thus and thus was the WEA tradition, and Eric Bellchambers, who came from a working-class family in the then railway town of Wolverton to run the WEA in Sussex and be Williams's local boss, was a fine embodiment of the old Labour and egalitarian tradition. He was a vigorous, trenchant man, blunt to a fault, with a strong zest for life in books and books in life, and wine and food in both.

Eric Bellchambers

For adult education the fifteen years following the end of the war were a mixture of promise and despair ending in the service being given an entirely new look, partly perhaps because the great British public – including the Labour movement and trade unionists – preferred bread and circuses but also because Government saw adult education as simply a leisure time activity, filling in time – the devil finds work for idle hands – or minds. The Butler Act of 1944 started the rot. In 1946 or 47 the Dept of Education issued what came to be known as the Green Book. It contained descriptions of courses and activities that the Department was prepared to support with grants. They ranged from courses of a university and WEA type to what were little more than leisure time activities. For many years Government had given grant aid to adult education courses provided direct by local authorities. This provision was permissive; under the Butler Act it became mandatory. Along with the Green Book came another paper, asking for development plans from the local authorities. These were to be prepared within two years and submitted to the Department for approval. The universities and the WEA now had competition; the local authorities were very soon offering all kinds of courses, from fencing to flower arranging, from yoga to antiques. In Kent the development plan included adult education centres. These were the brainchild of Frank Jessup, then assistant education officer with responsibilities for technical, further and adult education. Later to become Secretary of the Oxford Extra-Mural Delegacy. These centres offered great advantages, comfortable classrooms, warmth, refreshments at the interval, etc.; all in sharp contrast to the cold village hall or draughty school room. But each centre had a full time warden and it was imperative that the place was well used. Put crudely it was numbers that counted rather than the quality of the teaching or the degree of discipline imposed on the student. Just as the BBC and ITV companies give more weight to audience ratings so the centres became especially concerned about numbers and in some the WEA was regarded as at best a nuisance; an excrescence.

We were all working in a new climate. It was the precise antithesis to what had

111

gone before when adult education was thought of as education with a point and purpose, aiming at the creation of intellectual discipline, the mind engaged in an attempt to master a body of knowledge. The point is made very effectively in Newman's *The Idea of a University:*

> Recreations are not education; accomplishments are not education. Do not say the people must be educated, when, after all, you only mean, amused, refreshed, soothed, put into good spirits and good humour, or kept from vicious excesses. I do not say that such amusements, such occupations of mind, are not great gain; but they are not education. You may as well call drawing and fencing education, as a general knowledge of botany or conchology. Stuffing birds or playing stringed instruments is an elegant pastime, and a resource to the idle, but it is not education; it does not form or cultivate the intellect. (Discourse VI)

> There was a Gresham's Law operating in adult education. Just as bad money is said to drive out the good so those classes making the least demands made our work much more difficult – and more importantly – one sort of provision was seen as no better than another. Putting it another way, adult education once seen as a term of art was now simply the business of educating – or entertaining adults: a quite different thing altogether.[5]

Williams had things later to say, not altogether convincingly, about such a use of Gresham's Law, but for now Bellchambers's reminiscence will serve to identify the best and the most dismal tendencies of adult education in 1946. The seeds of its decline, far from permanent even now, were there to see through Newman's lenses. But its strengths were many and impossible not to elegise.

These are the proper uses of nostalgia. Nostalgia may as often vitalise as debilitate. Nostalgia is that urgent longing for what has been lost when the present feelings and circumstances lack the fullness a remembered past once provided. Longing for that fulfilment and the happiness of membership the past gave may leave us supine, passively convinced that things can never be what they were. This is the slope down to one kind of political reaction. That same longing can, however, as like quicken us to seek recovery of what was lost, knowing that if we can get it back it will be in a new form, transfigured into another pattern.

So to praise the adult educators of 1946 for their generous-hearted vision of a socialist education and a common and equal culture is not to launch the sentimental elegy McIlroy warns against.[6] Those men and women would have been incredulous that the magnitude and handsomeness of the Open University and all its works should come into such a flowering a mere twenty-odd years after they started up their classes on 'The English Novel', 'Problems of Peacemaking', 'The Common People 1789–1914', 'Culture and Environment' in echoing village halls and cold classrooms in antique schools beside the bypass. But because they had brought with them a post-war version of that old high-mindedness joined

112

to a vivid belief that socialism in Europe after the destruction of Fascism could be true, lovely and of good report, such a vision as the Open University came to realisation. It was founded upon the practical ethics of adult education, that picture of a solid education with a political ballast.

Such a formation was partly due to the powerful influence of the Army Education Corps during wartime, when on Thomas Hodgkin's estimate[7] 43 per cent of its teaching force (including Sergeant Hobsbawm) were either members of the Communist Party or else what were fastidiously known in those days as fellow-travellers. Their teaching was given focus by the syllabuses and discussion material produced by the Army Bureau of Current Affairs, and since there was nowhere for a communist's support to go except towards the Labour Party, it is likely that the ABCA did much to turn its pupils into the most democratic, self-aware and military-critical military since the New Model Army.

These lessons and this experience were taken straight into the expansion of Adult Education. Raymond Williams brought a reference from Frank Jacques, the WEA District Secretary in Cambridge, which spoke[8] of his 'great success' teaching his two courses (on international affairs and on the novel), and went on, 'I should have hoped to use him, but he went away to Barnstaple to read and to write a novel, and we have lost one whose promise had filled us with great expectations.' His former tutor at Trinity came up to scratch, making light of Williams's disappointing result in 1941, and reporting that Williams had taken the top First out of forty-six candidates in his finals, spoke good French, and was 'a man of wide reading and unusual capacity for hard work ... quiet and unassuming but determined and knows his own mind'.[9]

At his interview Williams was faced by a daunting range of representatives both from the Oxford Delegacy and the local WEA, among whom the most formidable were three men: the Lord Lindsay in the Chair, then Master of Balliol and keeper of the grand tradition of extra-mural education conceived as opportunity for working men. On one side of Lindsay sat Eric Bellchambers of the WEA, and on the other Thomas Hodgkin, Secretary to the Delegacy.

Hodgkin was a considerable figure. His grandfather A.L. Smith was a pupil and disciple of T.H. Green's, a celebrated historian and one of the authors of the formative report which went before Asquith's reforming Cabinet in 1908, *Oxford and Working Class Education*. His father was Provost of Queen's; his wife, Dorothy,[10] pupil of the famous communist scientist John Bernal, was already one of the best known crystallographers in the world, whose classical work on the structure of insulin was prelude to her Nobel Prize, her Order of Merit and her becoming an honoured and international saint of peaceful science, tireless in travelling on behalf of an anti-belligerent physics and nuclear disarmament.

Hodgkin himself, like his wife's parents, was an archaeologist, an anti-imperialist imperial administrator, and a communist. In 1946 he had just become Secretary to the Delegacy and a Fellow of Balliol; his great project was to develop an adult education for the incipiently independent nations of West Africa which would be as well matched as he could make it to what those Africans would need to know when their countries became their own. By the same token, he wanted tutors in the Delegacy not (crudely) to teach socialism, but to *be* socialists. That is, as he said a year or two before he died:

Thomas Hodgkin

> One wanted to get people who were politically progressive, yes. It is true that there is ... always a certain non-antagonistic contradiction about this ... On the one hand one believes that the people who are going to be most valuable ... in workers' adult education are those who have good political understanding, those who ask serious political questions, those who see their role as teachers as being concerned with developing political understanding and who are, in some sense at any rate, socialists. On the other hand one recognised another kind of criterion which is the criterion of academic quality, of how far a person is simply professionally good and, whatever his field may be, a person whose standard as investigator, researcher and teacher are as good and serious as they can be made.[11]

Hodgkin was a communist in the way idealistic men of the public-spirited bourgeoisie were during the Second World War. It was a fine strain in English social formation, but it wasn't the only, still less the best strain of progressive and leftish thought in 1946. A wide assortment of idealists, deeply influenced by what they had seen as well as what they had been given to teach came into Adult Education at the same moment, and took their lead from men as various as Hodgkin, Lindsay and Bellchambers, Williams's interviewing panel.

The Oxford Delegacy appointed seven new full-timers. They were supposed to consult with the then Ministry of Education about the suitability of new tutors, but there was a hurry and they didn't. The new men and women (but mostly men) were all pretty well on the political Left, several like Tony Maclean (who began in 1945) and Henry Collins, became close friends of Williams's; all were very bright, and all were dedicated to the ideal of a citizen's education, one which would not so much repair the deficits and restore the opportunities left vacant by schooling, as give to its students a quite new sense of common potential and collective self-realisation.

At the same time, of course, those who were communists gave some kind of allegiance to Moscow, were morally and theoretically anti-capitalist, and as a consequence volunteered for the front line of the just-declared cold war.

So there was a certain turbulence in the Oxford Delegacy. But it was a small and English-genteel turbulence, easily held within the rim of a teacup.

114

Thomas Hodgkin

I wasn't ever asked if I was a Party member. One felt it wasn't very nice to enquire what people's political affiliation was. One was interested in their political position; how they thought; how they felt; how they looked at problems; but whether they were Party members or not was not a question one would normally ask a person anyway. Someone who turned up for an interview whom one had never met before; one didn't know whether he was a Party member or not. Sometimes I didn't discover till very much later. In any case, one would never appoint someone because he was a Party member. Though, as I've said, it was very often the case that those who were, like Henry Collins, actual Party members, or like Tony McLean, someone who had been a Party member at some stage, and had later left the Party for whatever reason, but who had this kind of Marxist formation ... such people were in fact more intelligent and raised more interesting questions ... were to that extent more suited to teaching in extra-mural studies than someone else lacking that kind of formation. But it doesn't always work that way, of course.[12]

Certainly, there were rows. As the cold war began to freeze up, the Labour government, alert to the American horror of communism, took a passing interest in the danger of communist infiltration into Adult Education, especially down the long diagonal swathe of the Oxford Delegacy empire, starting from Staffordshire (where Lindsay was at the head of the movement which established what was later the University of Keele), hopping over Warwickshire, then taking in Oxfordshire, Buckinghamshire, Sussex and Kent. So when anti-communist scares blew around the universities, the pleasant little Wedgwood Memorial College fashioned out of a rather decaying old Victorian house in Barlaston village became the centre of a row, which turned on the political content of the many courses for trade unionists. English Labour–liberalism worked itself into a fine moral stew about academic objectivity and the lack of it, indoctrination, partiality and all that, and one communist tutor with a decidedly shaky administrative record got sacked in 1949.

It's hardly worth a mention were it not for the fact that in later life, particularly during those astonishing labours of autobiographical reconstruction which Williams shared with the editors of *New Left Review*, Williams reinvented himself as a communist tutor and dissident over whose teaching and syllabuses watchful eyebrows were raised. They were, as we shall see, but not for political reasons.

Cecil Scrimgeour

In the relevant years 1947–49 I was seconded by the Delegacy to carry the duties of Acting District Secretary to the N. Staffs WEA District. During those years I was obliged to play a central part in holding together a (by then) well established consortium of forces, i.e. the partnership of the WEA District, the three LEAs and the TCC [Tutorial Classes Committee]. The integrity of tutors was a vital element in the confidence holding them together, and that task commanded reasonableness

of spirit and clarity in understanding what was at issue. Raymond ... was sensibly
– and helpfully – aloof, getting on with his stint of work. My own concern was for
the good name and integrity of the WEA District as an open society. It was
effectively the linchpin of a delicate set of relationships for which many had worked
unremittingly over the previous decade, and its survival depended upon firmness
both of principle and practice. I have already put it on record ... that, in my belief,
the tutors whose behaviour had made for a slump in confidence and much dishar-
mony had been misguided about the responsibilities that demanded their loyalty
as teachers and colleagues in a widespread and open voluntary educational movement. I do not recognise the description of 'witch hunter' in any of those making
the cardinal decisions: Thomas Hodgkin, A.D. Lindsay, J.F. Carr, Wilfred Braddock –
to say nothing of myself. None of them was swayed by party–political prejudice,
though it would be true to say that they were all deeply disturbed by the evidence
of intrigue and manoeuvre practised by a group of tutors, small in number and
self-defeatingly.[13]

The simple truth would seem to be that in a post-war climate of great
ardour to make a better, a more equal and communal society, Adult
Education was thriving and exuberant in spite of bitter cold economic
weather. You could best put it by saying that without the work all those
tutors put in, whether Old-Right trade union Labour or New-Left sort-
of-communist, there couldn't have been the Open University, the happiest
and most creative public institution of the second post-war Labour
Government.

However public-spirited and communal the goals of the work, its weekly
actuality was dispersed, solitary and often damned uncomfortable.
Raymond got his job and was sent off on a three-year contract with an
annual rise of twenty-five quid, as the tutor in East Sussex, to teach literature to adult classes for the Delegacy and the WEA in the evenings. The
students attended, of course, by choice. The measure of their satisfaction
with their tutor was their feet.

Raymond collected Joy, Merryn and the new baby boy, Ederyn, from
Barnstaple, and took his family off to the not-dissimilar seaside town of
Seaford. They rented a ground floor flat in 'Betton', a plain, decent, brick-
and-slate house up on Southdown Road above the town overlooking the
sea. It had a fine big sitting-room with a wide window, but no central
heating, and in the two harsh winters of the first post-war years, when
coal shortages almost brought down the Government, it was hellishly cold:
'Raymond and Joy had to dry the babies' laundry in the oven', as Annette
Lees recalled.

Viewed from the British academic productivity deals of the 1990s, the
teaching in East Sussex for someone in Williams's position wasn't heavy.
He might be out three or four evenings each week (only two his first
year), and each class lasted three hours; but these classes were only
timetabled for two ten-week terms, with the odd Saturday thrown in. In
the summer there were two or three residential schools in Oxford, which

generally lasted a week or ten days, and were pleasurably intense while they lasted.

Once a tutor had built up a respectable bank of teaching materials and course preparations, he had plenty of time left for his own academic efforts, his novels, her plays, their life's work. But those were the days when teachers taught rather than searched and researched; Williams was comparatively rare in his avocation, even though he coincided with the now celebrated research efforts of Richard Hoggart and Edward Thompson in the same field, and while a whole clutch of textbooks came out of such work from other tutors. There was also *The Highway*, the WEA quarterly journal in which tutors debated their teaching with a fraternal vigour and high principle. All the same, Williams was exceptional among his colleagues for the austerity and stamina with which, from the start, he always set aside the first four hours of the working day to his own writing. Other days he would put in more like eight or ten hours, and always he discussed what he did with Joy, and she gave him her sociology classics from LSE to read for the first time.

It was a renewal of a lifetime's habit. His son, his daughter, his sister-in-law, his friend, his student, and me as well, all unite in affectionate recollection of his terrific incompetence with practical and domestic technology. The typewriter signified the limit of his manual skills. Father and mother had set him to work with pen and books and at a desk; they weren't having their son in any doubt about the precedence owing to mental over manual labour. He learned solitary application early and hard, and learned the habit of soliloquy with it, so that he spoke to himself and set it down on paper for others as part of the natural rhythm of his life. Such a habit, deeply and voluntarily instilled, often meant that he repeated himself or, having nothing much to say that day, he still said it.

He was an inspiration as a teacher. As he declared himself, what has always been called in the study of literature 'practical criticism', meaning very close analysis of 'the words on the page' ('reading very slowly', Terry Eagleton called it) was a tremendously liberating discovery. As I said earlier, its force lies in its apparent release of what, when identified, is self-evident. You read the words in their context, and by close attention to *how* things are said, you determine *what* has been said. What got suppressed at one time, of course, were the preconceptions which framed what you were looking for and at the very least inclined you to find it, or, more punitively, not to find it. Once this framework was also analysed, moral conclusions became less a matter of the self-evidential, and more a matter of preference or, if you'd rather, commitment. At any rate, that difficulty eventually brought Williams to reject practical criticism, and go straight for political analysis.

But as a teaching method, it is unbeatable. Leavis used to prefigure its ideal speech situation in the exchange, 'This is so, isn't it?' ... 'Yes, but

117

...' This is a picture of the best adult education: it is the exchange by equal persons of their understanding of their experience as focused in the 'third realm' of their common ground; in the case of the literature class, the play, poem or novel.

If there was an orthodoxy in Adult Education – and, come to that, in sixth form and university classes at the time – this was it, and Williams followed it; inspiringly. His first class as listed in the Delegacy reports was 'Problems of Peacemaking', which he had taught beside the Kiel Canal as regimental education officer, and now repeated at Bexhill, Eastbourne and Robertsbridge. But he had gone to Sussex to teach English, and so he did for fifteen years.

'English', however, as Leavis had redefined it so invigoratingly by the time Williams got back to Cambridge, was far more than a cultivated adjunct to everyday domestic life. It was a measure of the meaning and value of that life. That is to say, the great books and poems embodied and realised the best values of their day, and urged those values forwards for the renewal of the future; the student found and caught that embodiment by close reading and practical criticism; he and she then brought this measure up against the linguistic life of contemporary society, and judged it accordingly. If the language had gone wrong, it followed that the life itself had also gone wrong.

A zealous regiment of Leavisites went out at this date, Denys Thompson leading them in schools, Hoggart, Williams, David Holbrook, Frank Kermode, Stuart Hall, all amongst those doing the same work in the post-war decade in adult education. From his early days, Williams taught a general 'Literature' course, another one on 'Drama' alone, and joined these to his first 'Culture and Environment' course and his trade unionist favourite, 'Public Expression'.[14]

As in all such work, each class took place wherever the little concentrations of activity required it, in the bigger towns – Eastbourne, Brighton, Hastings; in villages – Bexhill was a tiny bit of a place in 1946, Cuckfield, Battle; sometimes in mere huts nowhere in particular, like a class he taught up on the Downs, in an awful Nissen hut formerly used by the Royal Observer Corps with a view from the door over the English Channel.

Peering through the mist of recollection with which the British Left hazes the memory, the cost, the sheer hard work of the great Labour government, it is now hard to discern the cold, the discomfort, the gaunt village halls and dreary committee rooms in which all that high-minded education of adults went on. And yet the mixture of physical misery and a devotion to culture and enlightenment is exactly the point. The Williamses, like most families of their age and income at that time, had no car, and all fuel was still rationed anyway. Three times a week Raymond turned out of the house into a couple of the coldest winters of this century round about half-past four to be sure of a six-thirty start twenty-odd miles away. Travelling by elderly buses or even shabbier trains, carting with him a heavy box of books, the WEA tutor picked his way cross-country to a village hall, a school room, the back premises of the local library, the annexe to a church vestry, and on occasions, somebody's sitting room, to meet with a dozen or fifteen people in order to talk about *Ulysses*, or Puccini, or the future of socialism, or the history of newspapers.

The best and brightest of the Oxford Delegacy's new young men and women were, as we have seen, politically committed and on the Left. They wanted to teach young working men how to grasp and hold on to their own future. They wanted the victorious Labour Party to give the labour movement its freedom from capitalism, and to hand it the culture and education to which it had so long been denied full and generous access. They wanted utopian versions of the future to point to, and in the aftermath of the war and the colossal sacrifices of the Russian people, the Soviets served that purpose.

The ideal of the WEA was to educate and to give the power knowledge would confer to working-class men. And that happened plentifully. The Oxford Delegacy and the WEA collaborated over many years on such courses: Arthur Marsh and Frank Pickstock (another railwayman's son who began as a WEA student and later became secretary of the TCC) were active pioneers of special trade union classes, while the famous row at Wedgwood College occurred precisely because senior trade union officials and Labour MPs objected to the political line being taken. Williams himself spoke of this old glowing picture of working-class working men's education:

> In recent years I have discussed D.H. Lawrence with working miners; discussed methods of argument with building workers; discussed newspapers with young trade unionists; discussed television with apprentices ... to me these have been formative experiences and I have learnt as much as I have taught.[15]

Well, so he did. Leavis's and Thompson's practical criticism of both culture and environment gave him his lead, and made it possible and pressing to use the words on the page – whether taken from *Ulysses* or the *News Chronicle* – to unsettle preconceptions about class or the purity of literature well away from politics. But since the making of English Literature as a serious intellectual subject at Cambridge in the 1920s, the preponderance of its students have been women, and its great significance has also been as a strong, sweeping current of liberation in the great tide of the women's movement as it has begun to come in over the past thirty-odd years.

Williams has been much rebuked of late for not seeing this. But in his classes at Bexhill, Brighton and Cuckfield, as John McIlroy and the record books attest, of the usual class size of fifteen to twenty, three-quarters or more were, as Williams unendearingly put it, 'commuter housewives ... who wanted to read some literature'.[16] That supercilious figure C.E.M. Joad, doyen of BBC's *Brains Trust* as first popular philosopher of the day, had the brazen cheek to write thus of women students in the *Tutors' Bulletin:*

> ... too many women make a bad class, lacking in bite and come-back, lacking, in a word, guts ... one gets the impression that the WEA tends only to get the women men don't want, the inference being that they are there not because they are impelled by a drive for education but because they hope for husbands or have nothing better to do.[17]

For them there was, exactly, nothing better to do, as one of his students bears eloquent witness.

Ruth Middlemiss

I can't remember all the books we studied, but Mr Williams made *Middlemarch* and *The Rainbow* live for me. In those days (as far as I remember) we studied fewer books. In fact we spent several weeks on *Middlemarch*, for which I was truly grateful. 'R.W.' honoured me by asking me to read out loud selected passages and I enjoyed this privilege immensely!

'R.W.' has (or had!) a musical voice but only a *slight* Welsh accent. It was the intonation that was so fascinating, though. He sometimes appeared to be *playing* a passage (not saying it). He was never aggressive or violent – just went on either reading (or explaining!) in those gentle honeyed tones! (We made copious notes all the time!) I found R.W's voice so soothing that sometimes I nearly went off to sleep! He wasn't a bit boring, though! He was just very fluent.

With regard to *The Rainbow* this was a revelation! R.W. made all the characters live for me! As I'd been brought up in a strict Methodist household (but a very happy one!) not one Lawrence book was on the shelves, although we had liter-ally thousands of textbooks between us. I felt a bit guilty about reading a 'forbidden' book but I must say I enjoyed it. I was – and still am – a great admirer of Lawrence's smooth style, although I don't like his attitude to women!

I was very interested to find that 'R.W.' had known Dylan Thomas well enough to go 'pub-crawling' with him! I told him that I thought Thomas had the most BEAUTIFUL voice I'd ever heard, although he looked like an unmade bed.

What was Raymond like to look at? Well, he had FADING GINGER hair (rather long, but combed back) and an enormous BROW! A real professor! Very scholarly! He was tall and broad and pretty slim and wore the most extraordinary colours with tweedy suits (i.e. dark blue shirts, yellow ties, green sweaters – that sort of thing). He also had piercing blue eyes! After the class he used to walk to the station (sometimes I went too, as I lived near there) regaling me with stories of Dylan Thomas.

I should think his head was in the clouds even at home. He struck me as NOT being a 'practical' person. Sometimes, on Thursday evenings, he would go into a sort of trance! No, he didn't go to sleep, but he used to 'waffle' in a very high-brow way – ABOVE OUR HEADS! (Then he used to pull himself together and come down (almost) to our level!)

I liked the way he kept all his things (books, notebooks and pens) in a haversack! (A very sensible way to carry things.) He was *tremendously* keen on T.S. Eliot and I remember an interesting few weeks spent on 'East Coker' (hope I've got the title right!).

R.W. was a very KIND man. I had to work overtime some nights, and turned up a bit late. One of the old BATTLEAXES in the class said 'Don't you know you *should* get here before the tutor?' R.W. smiled almost apologetically and told me not to worry! (He understood.)

He was COMPLETELY unflappable! One day we couldn't get into our classroom (the door was locked!) but he stood there smiling benignly until help appeared!

I wish I could take you back over 30 years to the TYPE of class we were! Average age 60–70; at 33 I was by far the youngest member. I wonder what our present 'young ladies' would have thought? Everyone was dressed in coats and hats (not to mention stockings!) and only GLOVES were removed for the class!

Raymond Williams coped with EVERYONE most successfully. He was a highly respected man![18]

Ruth Middlemiss had come to the Eastbourne class on 'Literature' held at 'The Glen', a respectable early Edwardian house of redbrick and dizzy little gables in Upperton Road. Those courses dealt, certainly, with Big Books: *Middlemarch, The Rainbow* – Leavis's 'great tradition' – but Williams developed a considerable disdain for the practice of many of his fellow-tutors who, clearly fancying themselves as university lecturers, fell into a mode of address soporifically learned when they were themselves students. They became accustomed to filling the first hour with monster platitudes of literary history, striding in seven-decade boots from Romanticism to Victorianism to Modernism. In an early essay of his,[19] first contributed to the house journal of the Oxford Delegacy whose headquarters were in Wellington Square just behind the splendid breadth of St Giles, Williams confesses that on his first course (of twenty-four meetings) on twelve novels and novelists, he had dutifully given a solid weekly lecture on the book in hand, the novelist who wrote it, her (the case in question being Mary Ann Evans) friends, intellectually gigantic ways (translating Spinoza, reading *Wilhelm Meister* and Kant in German), and 'well here was a portrait one had brought along; yes indeed, if one wished to be unkind, she *did* look rather like a horse'.

What he counterposed was, in spite of his expressed misgivings about the method, a course in practical criticism – 'reading very slowly'. So he planned a syllabus which led students from short extracts to longer ones to whole novels: from a paragraph by George Eliot (*Felix Holt*) to a short story (T.F. Powys or Lawrence) to a novel (*Bleak House*). English teachers worldwide will recognise this as The Way, and Williams repeated with piety the maxims of Leavis's 'English' as a discipline of thought: 'Literature, as a coherent record of human experience, needs neither apology nor external justification. It is itself, and its study as such remains one of the permanently valuable disciplines of any education.'[20]

One of the longest-standing habits of feeling is to relish the position of disapproved-of young radical. In the same paper, he writes with pleasure of having 'been told that courses like this turn administrators in their graves and throw the Ministry of Education into a conscientious flurry'.[21] This is all of a piece with his much later recollection of himself as chief ecumenicist in the Delegacy ('I was the only person to whom both sides spoke') between the public school communists whose intellectual perspective he shared, and the traditional Labour Party people who were, like him, from working-class families and had the same tastes in food and drink and enjoyment. Then he says, revealingly, 'I joined neither camp but I remember the experience . . .'[22]

It's not an attractive remark but it catches him right on the contradiction, declaring for community but denying membership. One of his colleagues is brisk about it.

Eric Bellchambers

In my experience Raymond wildly overstates the attitudes of administrators and the Ministry of Education.

He did little preparation. Since the method was simply to secure a response to certain texts it could be argued that preparation was pointless since he would not be able to foretell what was going to happen in the classroom.

This picture of Raymond carrying the banner of innovation – revolution in adult education is exaggerated. There were plenty of opportunities for experiment and innovation. There were conferences on such matters as the correlation of studies. And see the work of Cecil Scrimgeour on Drama; his course on The Partners in the Play, Author, Actor and Audience – and his studies of Comedy – Meredith, Diderot . . . and anyway the reference to food and drink is nonsense. As the eldest of a working-class family of six children I'll eat caviare and truffles with the best of them.

Williams' approach to teaching English was refreshing, novel, and demanding on the students. I believe his method was based on I.A. Richards and of course, Leavis. It involved an increasingly scrupulous examination of a decreasing number of texts. The Leavis canon was followed with but little modification. His syllabus consisted of about six novels with next to no reading list. This was in sharp contrast to the traditional Oxford extra-mural syllabus which was almost a book in itself. The syllabuses of De Vere, Emery, McLean and Jack Woolford consisted of several pages of explanatory text with even more pages of recommended reading. It has to be said that it would have taken a lifetime to get through all of the suggested books.

If it was a course on the Novel the novels listed for study would almost certainly be: Conrad, *The Heart of Darkness*, T.F. Powys, *Mr Weston's Good Wine*, L.H. Myers, *The Root and the Flower*, and maybe George Eliot, *Middlemarch* or *Felix Holt*, and Dickens, *Hard Times*. At one class I visited the two hours were devoted to a consideration of about twelve lines from one of Shakespeare's plays. Williams read out the passage and then waited for a response. This came about when, I suspect, one student found the silence unbearable. The real difficulty was the shock of the new. Just as the syllabuses of the Oxford full-time tutors had to be at least an eighth of an inch thick so by some unwritten law the two hours of each class had to be divided equally between lecture and discussion. Tony McLean, whom all loved and respected, invariably took one and a quarter hours to present his material and offer an analysis. Some students found it very hard to accept Raymond's method of teaching. Most of them liked to be involved but they also expected the Master to give them a lead. Some felt 'the hungry sheep look up and are not fed'.

An incident relating to this revealed another side of his character. An Eastbourne WEA Branch secretary complained to Oxford about his teaching methods, reporting a strong dislike of the long silences. Raymond got very angry about this, 'I will not have my competence bandied about'. This might be interpreted as meaning that in adult education the democratic process should only be allowed up to a point.

It has to be said that there was something of the prima donna about him; that he was preparing himself for the role of savant or guru. He was not exactly a loner but he did not appear to have any close friends – at the same time he was friendly and comradely when being the wise man – or the tutors' representative. In his early days in Sussex Clifford Collins and Wolf Mankovitz, friends from his Cambridge years, seemed still very close but they soon drifted apart and all went widely different ways. Raymond was a complex character. One other point needs to be made, Oxford had at least two other outstanding literature tutors contemporary with him; Pat Roberts and Cecil Scrimgeour.[23]

Bellchambers keeps a sceptical eye on his former junior, and it is true, as I say, that Williams kept up all his life this occasionally wearing class-consciousness, as well as nourishing a sense of himself as dissident, non-conformist, a bit unruly in front and behind the back of the boss. But then he *was* sharply dissident, just as he was also and conscientiously ecumenical, conciliatory and endlessly in search of a sufficient and honourable compromise.

His gifts in this direction were more and more admired and turned to by his colleagues, the longer he remained in the Delegacy. By the mid-1950s he was their spokesman on the Tutorial Classes Committee and elsewhere. As a tutor in his twenties, however, he followed, of necessity, the solitary, journeyman-of-letters kind of life enjoined by extra-mural teaching. He took the shabby, powerful old buses and the little local trains he knew so well to small headquarters of culture in genteel Sussex market towns, found the class secretary waiting for him with a list of a dozen or fifteen names, most of them women, few of them trade unionists, and through the dark, wet and windy winter evenings, took them around English Literature, or went on ahead and waited for them to shout for help.

John Levitt

His classes were always very successful. He was interested in the methods of adult literature teaching, and we had a lot of good exchanges of ideas over aims, methods

123

and all the other adult education shop topics. At the summer meetings I mentioned above, we always exchanged notes on the texts we would be dealing with in literature classes, for interest but, more practically, to see that we were not all claiming the same library supplies at the same time. So we knew each others' interests. On one occasion he shook us all by declaring that, in his Brighton class next session, he would be doing *Hamlet*. The whole session on the one play, and on the issues that it would lead to. And he did it, too, successfully.[24]

On the road, he saw little of his colleagues. The two most congenial of his professional neighbours were Jack Woolford and Tony McLean. Woolford was a social historian, also from a working-class home who had come to extra-mural teaching by way of Cambridge and the life-changing Leavis seminars. The manner of his memoir bespeaks the gentleman he was, and speaks also of the code of manners which characterised these men, teachers of a class of people who hardly glimpsed the politics which mattered so much to the mentors who so mattered to them. It was a code, one surmises, which took its grace and diffidence precisely from what Marxists used so solemnly to call the conditions of its production. That is to say, courtesy, accessibility, patience and painstakingness were all the products of evening after evening, from 6.30 until 9.30 in 'The Glen', 'The Beeches', the church hall, the infant school, the Victoria Court Hotel and at Kingsgate College, arranging a first, deeply puzzled and puzzling encounter between Ruth Middlemiss and her friends and *Heart of Darkness*.

Jack Woolford

Adult education as we practised it was a vocation, a total commitment. Formal teaching was a part of it but only a part: we mingled with each other and with students constantly and on a basis of mutual respect. I dare say there was a 'reputation' which floated around other people and their groups: trade unions, educational administrators and the like. As far as we were concerned, reputation depended on the long-term personal impression one made and that included lecturing in front of colleagues and knowing from inside, from within the extramural walls, how successful they were in other matters: witness their class programmes and attendance records and (in particular) the quality of the people whom they recruited to summer schools etc.

Raymond was, of course, a great theorist. His starting point was Leavisite: he had (like me!) attended Leavis's lectures and (like me) may have attended his seminars. But of course he was too independently-minded to be a disciple himself and he (obviously) developed his own ideas. He talked and argued endlessly about the content of curricula, about teaching method and teaching attitude. I certainly remember his arguments about 'the text, the whole text and nothing but the text' and his utter dismissal of such irrelevancies as literary history and biography. He believed in the virtues of unprompted response and strongly deprecated goggle-eyed admiration of and dependence upon the tutor by the student.[25]

I think Raymond was the most courteous man I ever knew. I only once succeeded in riling him (in 1949) and that was certainly all my fault. I do, however, recall many

124

many occasions when he gave me, as he gave everyone, his full, friendly and warm attention. Nor was it only a matter of courtesy. He was prepared to offer and to give practical help and that it might eat into his precious time was never a consideration. He was also tolerant far beyond normal standards at the expression of views which were very far from his own and his responses were always quietly, indeed, engagingly expressed. Even a rebuke, and I did once receive one, was offered in a friendly way, almost as an aside, and was not accompanied by any physical expression of distaste.

My most vivid recollections are of Raymond as a leader of tutors, appointed by consensus and with acclamation because he was prepared to take unbelievably endless trouble on behalf of colleagues (who did not always appreciate it) and could quietly argue administrators like the two Franks and the formidable Lady Sutherland herself into the ground. Whatever reservations he may have had, and I myself thought there were grounds for plenty, in the cases of some colleagues threatened with dismissal, he defended them with total dedication and more than one was saved as a result. This was perhaps the hereditary trade unionist. It was also very impressive by the best forensic standards.[26]

Tony McLean was politically nearer to Raymond, and perhaps personally also. At 25, he had gone to Spain as an interpreter with the International Brigade in 1936; there was no more honourable campaign medal on the Left, even though he was too hopelessly unmilitary to get beyond clerical soldiering. He was a public school communist of the pure and powerful formation which included Frank and Edward Thompson, as well as Anthony Blunt, strong (as one would expect) in the Army Bureau of Current Affairs, and then an early explorer of 'the politics of culture', of the allegiances in art eloquent of those meanings, public and private, which are true politics. Long before package tours, he made art history for the WEA a practical and immediate business. He and Eric Bellchambers taught the stained glass windows of Chartres on the spot, Henry Adams in hand, and did the same for Botticelli and Brunelleschi in Florence a little later.

McLean was a voluble, attractive, dominant man in and around Canterbury education, long before Lord Robbins's report founded one of the new universities in the city. He was more passionate than Williams, and less drily sardonic, as well as more gregarious – 'we all loved him,' Merryn said. He and Margaret McLean entertained endlessly at East Bank Cottage, and when there were day and weekend conferences at Kingsgate, the Williamses would come, and the children played in the garden while father did his turn in the town.

Gregariousness wasn't so easy in Seaford, and came less readily to Raymond and Joy in any case. Raymond sustained his writing regime sternly, and Joy patrolled its time and space faithfully, always warding off callers until one o'clock, keeping the tiny cubby-hole which doubled as a study in 'Betton' shut to the children.

Raymond kept on writing. *Brynllwyd* turned into *Village on the Border* with painful slowness. He came and went at it and on it, rewriting small amounts, rearranging the order endlessly, always coming up with a flat stop against the story he couldn't bear the novel to tell, the story all the other such novels had told ever since *Sons and Lovers*, of the bright young son of the working-class family who did well at school and went away to university in order to do even better for himself and the next generation. Williams wanted to find some way of coming home, but was too honest to pretend that he could come home for good.

So the novel whirred, and stopped and started. In between times, he wrote the critical guide to modern drama which had started life as his undergraduate thesis on Ibsen, and was to become *Drama from Ibsen to Eliot*, together with his practical textbook towards practical criticism, *Reading and Criticism*.[27] This latter came directly out of his teaching, and that teaching was in the direct line of Leavis's famous journal, *Scrutiny*.

Williams, it is important to note in the light of his later remaking of himself at a greater distance from his teacher, is quite straightforward in his acknowledgement of indebtedness. He makes it plain on several occasions.[28] What is more, he takes the lessons of the master together with his texts – Tennyson's 'Tears, idle tears, I know not what they mean', Conrad's *Heart of Darkness* – to serve as the lessons of the WEA. Indeed, he follows even more faithfully in the footsteps of Leavis's great collaborator–schoolteacher, Denys Thompson, and *his* guide to the evaluative study of literature, *Reading and Discrimination*. Like Thompson, who read the manuscript for the publishers, approved it strongly and suggested emendations, he ends the book with a series of exercises in comparative judgement (the then equivalent of bonkbuster novels in a fixed fight with James Joyce).[29] Most faithful of all, Williams takes the lesson of the famous Leavis and Thompson sixth-form textbook, *Culture and Environment*,[30] off to the housewives and trade unionists, and alongside Shakespeare and Yeats, analyses bits of newspaper editorials and advertising copy.

As I mentioned, he taught more than a few courses under the heading of 'Culture and Environment' over the years, and these were grounded in Leavis's and Thompson's own convictions that the popular press bought its popularity at the expense of intelligence, and was a, perhaps the, most, potent force abroad working against democracy. Williams's own experience, first of the *Abergavenny Chronicle*, second of the *Cambridge University Journal*, then of *Twentyone*, had left him with a deep and justified faith in the critical independence and first-hand experience of small and local journals and newspapers. In *The Long Revolution* he turned to the reconstruction of that ideal moment of the popular press in the middle of the nineteenth century when the insurgently self-assertive arms of the labour movement were so busy in the production of their own press and when the ruling class of the day did everything it could, and then vainly, to stop them. That nineteenth-century moment became for Williams not just a measure of present defeat (judged against the moment of the *Sun*, nobody could have foreseen in 1950 how complete that defeat would be), but a picture with which to keep up hope of future betterment.

This pull – between defeat in the present and hope for the future, between the moment of victory in an ideal past and the certainty of disappointment in the present – is at the heart of politics, and an armature of Williams's thought. It is, obviously, a classic trope – a defining *form* of political thought. Everything, of course, turns on the content: on the examples you choose to steer by. A present-day Labour Fabian steers by 1945: the National Health Service, public works and investment, gas-and-water socialism backed by huge popular assent. Williams steered by those best moments of the working-class past at which the class had roused itself to make its own order and institutions, and had on those terms settled and resettled its own stretch of the industrial and political landscape, a material, non-metaphorical landscape.

So Williams was at odds with the Leavis and Thompson settlement. Their ideal past moved from place to place, and time to time. It began in Farnham in the 1890s, where George Sturt was keeping his wheelwright's shop according to the best principles of a non-exploitative craft and a pre-capitalist sort of exchange. It moved, for Leavis, to Conrad's training ship *Conway* in the Mercantile Marine, as well as sideways to D.H. Lawrence's mining Nottinghamshire and Mark Twain's trading station on the Mississippi.[31] Raymond Williams treasured his such moments from his own Pandy, Abergavenny, his 'ingenious and civilian' army, and the WEA classes of the late 1940s.

He found parallels, certainly, above all in England of the 1840s; but he always found them tinged with his own sardonic detachment, his ardour for membership always cooled by his obliquity, the coolness of that deliberate, elaborated, formal speech, the unexpectedly biting jokes according with the habit of abstraction and withdrawal, the complete absence of spleen.

Professional collaboration took place on the train to Oxford, travelling to Rewley House to see the Secretary, Thomas Hodgkin, to review the reports, to attend the Tutorial Classes Committee, but above all, the high point of the Adult Education year, to teach at the annual summer school held, very properly, in the headquarters of the Oxford Left at Balliol College.

Balliol, massively Victorian, stands at the corner of Broad Street, one of the noblest university thoroughfares in the world, leading down past Trinity to Wren's Sheldonian theatre, Duke Humfrey's renaissance library, Sir Basil Blackwell's great bookshop, and the King's Arms. Since the time of T.H. Green it has been the Oxford bastion of un-Oxford progressivism, of liberalism and socialism, of anti-imperialism, also, and of anti-racism too. Its Cabinet Ministers have been many, Denis Healey, Edward Heath, Tony Crosland among them.

127

In the 1940s, A.D. Lindsay was still its Master, and the Adult Educators brought an assortment of three or four hundred students every summer to his college to hear, as they did in July 1948, Williams on 'the politics of popular culture', his old tutor Lionel Elvin on 'the culture of popular politics', and John Bernal, J.B.S. Haldane and Joan Robinson, all contemporary giants on the Left of their subjects, which were science for the two men, and economics for Joan Robinson. One hundred of the students came from the Oxford Delegacy's own classes, another hundred from other universities' extra-mural departments, seventy-odd from the WEA, forty from the forces, and the rest from another pillar of Victorian philanthropic education, the Literary and Technical (or Lit. and Phil.) institutes up and down the country.[32]

Surely these really were great days for such modes of self-education? The reports of the Delegacy are sprinkled, year after year, with such heartening names of the great, come to lecture for a fiver or so to this worthy mixture of suburban and municipal students, those such as Haldane and Bernal already mentioned, John Summerson, John Betjeman, A.J. Ayer, A.J.P. Taylor, Alec Clifton Taylor. These names, later famous and familiar on BBC television, and as the authorities of the Open University, turned up in their fleshly flesh to be heeded, revered and drunk, on the spot, and by a mere 400.

It is good to celebrate these occasions now, precisely because in so actual and material a way, they contrast with the excellently egalitarian broad-casting of broadcasting. Compared with Open University TV, the Balliol summer school was trifling: a handful of people listening to and forgetting unretrievable lectures. On the other hand, that egalitarian mixture of housewifery and earnest Labour students came to the capital of class learning, were made genteelly welcome in order to see, hear and even, at times, argue with the contemporary makers of intellectual culture. In the days before there was an intellectual star system, they heard (in Hertford College, just down Broad Street) – between 1 July and 8 July 1950, for example, Isaiah Berlin, Raymond Postgate, and Asa Briggs; in 1953, on 'Literature and Politics in the 20th Century', between 3 July and 14 August at Balliol, a couple of hundred heard old Leavis himself, Joyce Cary, Lord David Cecil, Angus Wilson, Richard Crossman, Tony Crosland, G.D.H. Cole, Edward Boyle.

At this respectful distance, the womenless names mostly don't mean much to people under forty-odd, so it is worth saying that these public-spirited figures spoke at such occasions out of a sense, a proper sense, of public duty, of what was owing to a public rather randomly represented by this small sample for their own considerable privileges, as well as what they would bear witness to, of the seriousness and endeavour of their thought.

They gave the lie, I think, to Williams's own brutal-seeming distinction, made on one of those train journeys up from Hastings, via Paddington, to Oxford, between 'English and History and Art and Ideas, which is what we do in the winter, and Adult Education, which we come in the summer to do in Oxford'.[33] Sure, there were rows of an office-political kind to have in Wellington Square, and Williams was right to sound bitter about the 'dreadful refresher courses', the endless rows over student numbers, the perennial hypocrisy of administrations. But those summer schools, this being bloody-minded old England and at one heart of its class-divided monstrousness, stood for much that was, and is, generous, even noble in the fought-over traditions of British education. Without them, as I have said, there could never have been an Open University, to say nothing of some fine books, Williams's among them.

As one would expect, the tutors of the Delegacy led their own departmental life in Oxford, as well as moving among the great. The Williamses always came to the summer school *en famille*, and Raymond got the necessary permission to live out of college while it lasted, carefully missing the rather intense sociability which always develops at conferences, when people break out of domestic routines, drink and talk fiercely, passionately, very late, and start up ardent friendships and love affairs which end abruptly when normal working life resumes its terrible, reassuring grip.

He had his gregarious moments, however. Jack Woolford cheerfully recalls the sort of concerts which the tutors would put on after the annual dinner, a dire mixture of songs at the piano, 'I say, I say' jokes, and duos of tutors tunelessly voicing old blue songs. It's a relief to record that several people remember Raymond, who sang excruciatingly, rendering that catchy folk ditty (it appears in *The Common Muse*):[34]

> They're shifting father's grave to build a sewer
> They're shifting it regardless of expense
> They're shifting his remains to make way for ten-inch drains
> To suit some local high-class residents.
>
> Now what's the use of having a religion
> If when you die your bones can't rest in peace.
> Because some high-born twit wants a pipeline for his shit
> They will not let poor father rest in peace.

For the most part, however, he did his teaching whether at summer school or in Sussex, and ducked off home. Home, like home in Pandy, was the fixed private order of his life to which the no less regulated order of teaching and administering was the civic complement. In the morning, nine till one, writing; in the afternoon, preparing classes; in the evening, teaching them. Or that's what he'd say, as we all do, pretending that there's nothing but virtuous hard work in our lives. But in Williams's case, with no examining, no summer term until the month or so in Oxford, three or

129

four classes per week sufficiently far apart in Sussex for the syllabus to be transferable, the time left unmarked was quite substantial; and he filled nearly all of it with writing.

Merryn Williams

> My mother did all the cooking, and she looked to the telephone so that Raymond wasn't interrupted until after one o'clock [the Williams family adopted the conventions of Bloomsbury, and used first names for all its members]. She was vegetarian, but for the family she cooked stews, salads, stewed apples, healthy eating. Then we used to go down to Fairlight Gorge near Hastings and pick elderberries to make wine. He liked the sweet ones, Sauternes, Barsacs.
>
> Raymond would come up to tell us bedtime stories when we were little, ones which he'd made up, about Rhoda Montado the garrulous parrot, Marmaduke the Monkey, and a surrounding society of snakes and gorillas called Adder-Adder-Adder and Bang-them-on-the-tum-tum...

So Joy Williams kept the order of the house in the most traditional way, and Raymond's work was the massive centre round which its ceremonies and routines turned. Once, early in their time at Seaford, Raymond had suggested to Eric Bellchambers that his wife should teach a short course in anthropology, having studied the subject at the London School of Economics. She taught six sessions, but when the tutor-organiser for the WEA called in on one to see how things were going, he found her reading aloud rather stumblingly from her student notebooks, 'and not a flicker of interest from the students'.[35] It was the beginning and end of her teaching career. Raymond always thanked her, a bit stiffly one might say ('I am indebted to my wife for her general help with the book'.)[36] He always said that she was pretty well co-author of *Culture and Society*, but it's hard to see it, though people said she urged him into writing the book and got him to read the sociologists on the LSE syllabus of the 1930s. She was oddly innocent. When Raymond's colleague Michael Carritt, whose brother was another mortal casualty in Spain, published an autobiography describing his subversions as a communist sympathiser in wartime India, *A Mole in the Crown* (as tricky a case of loyalty as you could find), Joy was heard to say to Raymond, 'Something quite awful. You remember that nice man Michael Carritt. It turns out that he was a spy.'[37] I think she was an open, shy, naturally straightforward woman who believed that resistance should be public and allegiances declared, as her husband did.

However that may be, Raymond's closest intellectual collaboration during his years in Sussex and Kent was with Michael Orrom, Clifford Collins (Henry's brother) and Wolf Mankowitz and the short-lived, well-named journal *Politics and Letters*.

Collins and Mankowitz had been friends of Raymond's during his last year at Cambridge. Both were pupils of Leavis, and ardent followers of his method and madness. But both shared with Williams the Left–

130

Labourist provenance which was the best political weather of the day, to which all three added the characteristic Leavisite inflection that an independent criticality playing over cultural matters was the guarantee of a moral politics and a necessity of democracy. Mankowitz shared with Williams the commitment to write new literature as well as to criticise it; eventually his writing career, of novels and of film scripts, carried him off into the upper atmosphere of success, even to Hollywood. For the moment of 1946 and 1947, when *Politics and Letters* began, he and Collins together were devoutly of Leavis's view that the health of literature betokened the health of a people, that that health was kept springily on its toes by critical journals, and that their active presence and vigorous partisanship conduced to the good life of socialism.

So Collins and Mankowitz raised money and subscriptions in London, and rented an appropriately shabby little room with a plank floor in Noel Street, Soho to serve as editorial office. Williams stayed in Seaford and wrote hard, while the two other editors piled in to stay at weekends, as often as not bringing Orrom full of schemes for movies – 'Raymond would never say "no",' said Joy ruefully – and planned new issues. Collins was intense, fluent, nervous; he had the clearest vision of the magazine of the three of them. Mankowitz was garrulous, talented, disorganised, irresistibly prodigal and energetic, and filled with optimistic schemes for movies, musicals, novels, political movements, chiliastic delirium. In the way of the day, they went boozing – Collins too much so – with the world of London letters, journalists, writers, the new broadcasting élite of the BBC, the new Marxist historians group. They brought back as trophies to their higgledy-piggledy office, brimming with rationed paper, books, carbons, newspaper, and bits of their wardrobe (Collins used to sleep there when he was tight), essays from Sartre, G.D.H. Cole, Leavis, Orwell (whose contribution they lost under the piles of paper).

They only ran four issues, together with one of a brother journal called *The Critic*. The journal kept up the prim separation of politics from letters enjoined by Leavis's *Scrutiny*, while it linked them thematically in the title. So Christopher Hill wrote robustly telling them to be proper Party members, and Williams wrote an editorial refusing. By implication, they played themselves off against Edgell Rickword's openly communist *Our Time*, just around the corner in Covent Garden. There was rationing and paper shortage, strike-breaking by a Labour Government, bitter cold and no coal, but the metropolitan drinkers-and-bellelettristes went unrepentently on debating the contribution of culture to the good life.

The magazine agreed well with the kind of intellectual energies and considerations which found political rather than cultural expression in adult education. It also fitted in well with the pattern of Williams's life. He was writing and teaching for the WEA: his practical arguments about that work went into *The Highway* and Denys Thompson's marvellous little quarterly *The Use of English,* which brought together debate on the teaching of English at every level of the discourse, from village primary schools to adult education whether of the WEA or the PhD. At the same time, Williams's theorisations of that experience went into *Politics and Letters* and, later, the Oxford-based journal *Essays in Criticism.*

That biographical pattern expresses itself in Williams's lifelong involvement with polemical journalism. *Cambridge University Journal, Twentyone, Politics and Letters, New Left Review, Peace News, May Day Manifesto, New Socialist,* even – with Bill Webb's unstinting support – the *Guardian,* were all and frequently the site of Williams's open, highly visible and dedicatedly candid declarations of partisanship in the class struggle of culture. Meanwhile, in quite another idiom, just as unmistakably his own, he sustained his long, solitary exposition of the theory of feasible ecumenicism: his increasingly abstract story of the future a seemly hopefulness may keep in sight on behalf of his most banal and powerful trope, 'ordinary men and women'.

The *engagé* writing is fierce and sardonic; the theorisation abstract and generalised. Yet both forms, personality-full as they are, curiously lack the personal presence, the metaphysics of fullness which it was his whole project to commend.

He believed that *Politics and Letters* stood for the still imaginary institutions of a future in which popular education and popular culture would flourish, not because of nor in spite of capitalism, but in themselves and in spite of themselves. Perhaps they have and did: The Open University, Channel 4, the best of comprehensive education, Marks & Spencer, Sainsbury's, CND, good hospitals, the Women's Movement, Town and Country Planning, the Arts Council.

Politics and Letters folded in 1948. Its manner was comically at odds with the modesty of its venturing. It was a tiny magazine of little moment except that it carried some rather good individual essays. It wasn't there long enough to strike an attitude. But Williams was always a touch solemn about his importance and his achievements, so he appraised those minor editorial doings on a grand scale, reproaching the Labour government for acceding to the conditions of Marshall Aid when the collapse of sterling's liquidity and then mere bankruptcy were straight ahead of them. As Williams later admitted there was no economics in *Politics and Letters*; that was because none of them knew any. The intellectual Left in Britain has always made much of the betrayal of its principles by the Labour Party without ever having learned to count. Williams was for four decades party to a critique of political economy with no economics, thus complementing a Right-wing enemy which had economics but no politics. Value without power matched itself against power without value.

The journal's early end was always a certainty, but he took it passing hard. In a period of hope, he radically misjudged what Attlee's government could and did do, and didn't forgive it. It's hard to forgive him, half-a-century on; or rather, one cannot ignore the gap which was obvious enough in 1948 between desire and feasibility. Attlee did so much; with another five years ...

Williams wrote his way indomitably past the journal's end. Settled and contented, in Seaford and Hastings, he wrote on and on, out of the end of the 1940s and into the publication of *Drama from Ibsen to Eliot*. He said of those years, 'I pulled back to do my own work. For the next ten years I wrote in nearly complete isolation.'[38] Well, yes, he did; but only because he wanted to. And he wasn't *so* completely isolated. He met with Freddy Bateson after 1950, and went on the Editorial Board of the Oxford rival to *Scrutiny, Essays in Criticism*, soon after it started.

Bateson was an interesting man, and a very nice one. Like Leavis, he got his Oxford job lateish in his career because of his vigorously anti-establishmentarian criticism. But he had a much stronger and less eccentric politics than the great man. Bateson had a bit of family money, had been to public school and lived in a lovely, low, Oxfordshire house in the village of Brill.

Eric Bellchambers

> He was something of a character. I never knew him to wear socks and he was usually dressed in a corduroy jacket and slacks. He had a pronounced stammer but this never prevented him making his points clearly and forcibly. His eyes were beady and he had developed a nervous squint. It was only fairly late in his career that he was given a fellowship at Corpus Christi. The difficulty was that though he had all the right connections he was anti-establishment. He was inclined to challenge every orthodoxy. For years he campaigned against Old English being a compulsory subject in the English syllabus. This made him unpopular with the traditionalists, but of course in due time he won.[39]

Bateson befriended and supported Williams in the 1950s, and published an early chapter from *Culture and Society* in the periodical. Williams liked him, their politics were close enough for friendship (Bateson chaired the North Buckinghamshire Labour Party); but friendship was not usually a close matter for Williams, so they remained no more than professionally and amicably allied. It was only Clifford Collins who became really close to Williams over these years, and that in part because Collins depended upon him so strongly and was so unable to run the ordinary, orderly life Williams himself cherished. Collins had been going to share the writing of *Reading and Criticism* but he got nothing much done throughout 1948, and Williams published it alone, a couple of years later.

I say he was happy over these years because he seemed so. His last child, Madawc, was born in 1950. He was writing copiously (including a trio of unpublished novels *Adamson*, *Ridyear* and *The Grasshoppers*); his

133

writing won respect in his trade; and in 1951 he was able, in a symbolic way, to discharge some of the load of guilt any combat soldier who had killed in 1944 carried with him for good.

After years of post-war occupation by US and Soviet forces across a dividing line imposed by the great powers with no indigenous voice heeded, Korea broke into civil war. The Korean president Syngman Rhee with American complicity had pretty well liquidated the actively oppositional Left in the South; the North moved in to help them, Dean Acheson ordered full American military support for the South and got the United Nations to back him. The Soviets, clenched and suspicious of absolutely everybody, withheld the veto. 'Police action' was authorised. The UN called up a multinational force. Raymond Williams, his name on the military reserve as a tank officer with combat experience, received his papers.

Fred Dalling

> Raymond was on the Specialist reserve, which meant you could be called up at a month's notice. My brother and I had been conscientious objectors in 1940 (our father was at Gallipoli) and Raymond knew this.
> We said, 'Don't register as a CO. You fought in 1944 and 1945, they won't believe you. You'll have to say you can't support the cause.'

Williams went to see Thomas Hodgkin. North Korea was, of course, a communist state and, like Williams, Hodgkin would have been, if anywhere, on the side of Kim Il-Sung. If Williams refused his draft, he would have to do a month or so in gaol. Hodgkin strongly agreed that Williams could have this month as his annual leave.

But this was a curious moment in British politics. The Attlee government, still desperately short of investment and quite unable to pay for a war, had fully supported the US in all cold war manoeuvres; the Soviets had indeed proved as unpleasant a non-combatant enemy as the Right could wish. All the same, a lot of men in and out of uniform in 1951 had fought with the Red Army as allies, and they were far from clear that civilisation as they knew it would be brought down by civil war in a country which, until occupied by US and Soviet soldiers in 1945, had been tranquilly united for a millennium. Rather than wish a series of treason trials upon itself, the Labour Government inaugurated a system of tribunals to which dissident conscripts could be referred.

Williams, a fluent, principled, intelligent ex-tank officer of 31 made a formidable witness. The Chairman of the tribunal, a 77-year-old Professor of Classics of some distinction called Arthur Pickard-Cambridge was entirely convinced by Williams's case. He discharged him from all military obligations.

Much exhilarated, Williams went back to Seaford where he and Joy decided to buy a house. His salary had recently gone over £800 a year, he didn't have to go to war and the Delegacy had declined his request to move to Oxford. H.P. Smith, his immediate boss, had written to Hodgkin saying that Williams was 'now at the height of his success in East Sussex and should remain for five or six years'. Hodgkin himself offered to stand as guarantor of Williams's overdraft when he bought their house, but in the event the Delegacy obliged.

Early in 1952 he and Joy bought 44 St Helen's Road, Hastings for £2,300.

7

OUTSIDE THE WALLS

In the spring of 1951 Williams sent the manuscript of *Drama from Ibsen to Eliot* to the publishers. He chose Chatto and Windus, publishers of a long and acclaimed list in literary criticism – which included F.R. Leavis, his wife, and many of his Cambridge collaborators such as Lionel Knights – at a time when the discipline of English itself commanded a unique authority amongst what are now called the human sciences.

It is a queer thing that the intelligent and cultivated discussion of novels and poems should have taken such a lead, but it was so. Partly this was indeed due to Leavis's extraordinary power both as a teacher and writer, which so fired pupils of an idealistic temper to do what they could for their country by teaching its young people how to read good books in order to lead good lives. But of course more than a genius was needed to give the study of English literature such way and weight. Politics had disgraced itself by procreating such abominable monsters as Fascism and Stalinism. You might also say that sociology, in Britain at least, took so long to get going because of its doomed aspiration to prove itself a science as good as the natural sciences, and vanished underground into the mining of hypothetical foundations and the production of numbers. Finally, you might also conclude, from scanning the intellectual conditions of immediately post-war Britain that philosophy, which in all good republics would naturally expect to be crowned queen of the sciences, had given itself over to a variety of moral and political refusals which, while they made occasion for some locally important discoveries about what could or could not be said about truth and goodness, entirely prevented any larger claims about how the world was and therefore how it ought to be, which high-minded young men and women had gone to University to argue over. Into what a later admirer of Williams[1] was to call this 'absent centre' had moved the discipline of literary criticism, and Chatto and Windus were the publishers who made of it a public institution.

There is something in this of old imperialism, and there is something in it of self-delusion as well. 'English', after all, was the subject which, at the various levels of examination taken every year by tens of thousands of school pupils, was considered indispensable to admission either to employment at the age of 16, or to the next level of education (and therefore of social promotion) at 16, 18, 21, or later. By the same token, English was the subject taken by many tens of thousands more school pupils who looked for *their* promotion, translation, or mere export, one way and another, in each and all the countries of that fifth of the globe which in the world maps of 1950 was still coloured in with the pink of British imperial rule. And although the English examination most of them took had no specifically literary content, those who wrote the syllabus and set the papers were suffused all through with that same literariness, while those who did go on to English literature at 'Ordinary' or 'Advanced' levels, were required, whatever their nationality or, come to that, their class, to prove to the examiners their sufficiently intimate knowledge of medieval Chaucer, Renaissance Shakespeare (two plays), and a changeable medley of poets and novelists stopping in those days well short of the present mid-century.

So there was a vast machinery for the international production and circulation of cultural meaning as defined by a smallish number of men and women, mostly working in or graduates of the Universities of Oxford and Cambridge. This institution was what sent so many Leavisite idealists off to teach, whether to what Marx called the 'rural idiocy' and rejections of an English village college like David Holbrook, or to the exigencies of British Council lecturing in Malaysia, like Denis Enright. It was the circumstance which impelled Denys Thompson, co-author of the classic *Culture and Environment*, to his quite extraordinary and radical series of school textbooks in English; it was the energy behind the founding of a National Association for the Teaching of English; and it was also what made Williams himself, years later and at the height of his fame, assume the Chairmanship of the Cambridge English Examinations Board, far and away the biggest of the imperial enterprises in knowledge.

But if 'English' was a grand cultural institution, it cut no political ice. To say so is a necessary corrective to Williams's own ambitions to speak so largely to and for a people. As he only discovered quite slowly, the idiom of an academic discipline cannot be made to speak to everybody. The 'sane, affirmative speech' which W.H. Auden sought for his poetry, which at their best the triumvirate heroes of adult education, Raymond Williams, Richard Hoggart, Edward Thompson, fashioned on behalf of two generations, bent to new values and gave a far wider reach and intelligibility, *cannot say everything*. Neither a body of poetry, nor a novel, still less a work of literary criticism or social history, can speak to a people of its common soul, its human future. A writer joins his or her singular voice to a common speech, and must speak it idiomatically. Balancing truthfulness against accessibility, the difficulty of things against making honest sense, is as much a matter of luck as it is of judgement. Williams veered a lot in both, as he was bound to, given the magnitude of the tasks he set himself. He missed chances, for sure; and he made bad mistakes.

So his first big book was quite a small thing. Cecil Day-Lewis, one of the best-known leftist poets of his day, was a senior editor at Chatto and Windus when Williams's manuscript arrived. He asked for cuts of 25,000 words down to 100,000, Ian Parsons, his boss, approved an advance of seventy-five quid (not bad for an unknown extra-mural tutor in 1951) and the book came out in October a year later.

The section on Ibsen was largely written, as we have seen, in that last undergraduate year. But the general case of the book ran somewhat against the grain of Williams's feelings for Ibsen. He contended that while modern drama was searching for a definitive naturalism – a form which would render everyday experience in recognisable circumstances – the conventions of naturalism turned too rapidly into artificiality to make the necessary tradition and a continuity of language possible. He saw Ibsen's later, poetic drama and Strindberg's efforts at a level of pre-cinematic fluidity of scenery as largely successful attempts to overcome this difficulty, and he praised T.S. Eliot's turning of the conventions of drawing-room comedy to religious account by devising his characteristically prosaic and conversational verse, in order to give the normalities of upper-class infidelity and allegiance a taste of the Furies and the tremor of damnation.

It was an uneasy business, struggling between the pessimistic view of *Scrutiny* that all contemporary experience was trivial because as inexpressive and unpoetic as contemporary language, and Williams's own deep feeling for Ibsen and for drama itself as the most communal, the most sociable of literary genres.

Yet the sociability was all in the words. Williams's book was all about words, rarely about performance. He hardly visited the theatre, disliking the London West End because it was a bourgeois playground, always preferring the cinema where darkness cut you off from connection.

The book was respectably if unobtrusively reviewed, in one obscure but homely case (*The Tutors' Bulletin of Adult Education*) hostile. Williams, with a promptness to anger in his own defence which was characteristic, broke the absolute maxim which enjoins all authors never to reply in public to reviews of their work, to accuse the reviewer of over-excitement and bluster. And a little later, in January 1953, one Kay Burton of Newnham College wrote a personal letter to the publishers[2] objecting that the section on Ibsen rested very heavily on the celebrated lectures given at Cambridge by Muriel Bradbrook in 1945–1946, and later published as *Ibsen the Dramatist*. Dr Bradbrook was for five decades a celebrated woman of letters in the Cambridge English Faculty, later Mistress of Girton, a quick, neat, bright brown button-eyed woman of notable catholicity of taste. Her lectures, then as later, were very well known and well attended.

Ian Parsons wrote courteously to Williams, attaching Kay Burton's letter, with its anxious observation of 'a striking coincidence of manner' as between what Bradbrook and Williams had to say about Synge and about Ibsen's *Peer Gynt*. Williams responded quickly and crossly.

I did not attend M.C. Bradbrook's lectures while I was at Cambridge ... the Synge quotations are those that everybody makes ... and the plan of the book at all points relating to anyone other than Ibsen clearly owes nothing to Miss Bradbrook.[3]

Kay Burton replied in April, having been sent Williams's rebuttal with its not-very-veiled threat of libel action at its end, to say that 'Mr Williams's letter shows him to possess that concern for integrity which prompted me in the first instance'.[4]

I don't know; the lectures were so very well known, and he doing his undergraduate thesis on Ibsen. And the closeness of treatment is certainly striking. He went to Leavis's lectures, with Mankowitz and Collins. Williams wrote damned fast and always used his authorities swiftly and silently; he acknowledged rarely; he scanted the scholarly conventions; it's a bit rum ...

While doing the proofs for *Drama from Ibsen to Eliot* Williams found himself a literary agent, John Johnson of E.P.S. Lewin and Co., to whom he entrusted the manuscript of a novel, *Adamson*, about a man adopting the identity of a suicide, but Parsons would have none of it. Even though he saw it was 'a most unusual book ... and clearly the work of a highly intelligent author' it had too many 'major defects', and prompted Parsons to ask a question Carmen Callil was to answer flatly in the negative over his last novel over thirty years later, 'Is Williams really a novelist?'

He had written *Adamson* quickly over the previous two years, after finishing the drama book. But his interests at the time were almost as keenly in the prospect of making a film with Michael Orrom, who had run the socialist film society at Cambridge and been his close friend and neighbour in Malcolm Street. Orrom had worked with Paul Rotha, he was making a name for himself, he contributed to the solitary number of *The Critic*. He had a book nearly finished on film, and he and Raymond set up their own little company to publish what became a joint work, *Preface to Film*. It sold a thousand or so copies, and Michael Redgrave liked it.

At the same time they put up a proposal for a twenty-five-minute film to the British Film Institute, a bit of Welsh magickery in which a young man, hearing voices in the hills, goes up to listen and returns to his village and his grisly witch of a mother to find that a whole generation has passed. Michael Stringer did some fine continuity sketches, and the realists at the BFI turned it down.

Nothing daunted, Orrom showed Williams a memoir he'd found in a

139

second-hand bookshop about the Klondyke gold rush, and Williams turned that into *Ridyear*, which was never published and which Williams never thanked him for, either. But most of their efforts (in the mid-1950s) went for many months into a feature film proposal built on a novel called *A Map of Treason* about undergraduate leftists of the 1940s which Williams had put aside, and on *Adamson*, which starts on the cliffs at Seaford but had, for Orrom, its true genesis in Conrad's novella *The Secret Sharer*.

Michael Orrom

The hero is a member of the CP who changes identity with a suicide whom he sees jump from the cliffs. The point of departure is that Adamson shares the suicidal feelings.

We talked across a whole weekend about it down at Hastings – I'd been earlier to teach a weekend school about film in Robertsbridge. When I left, Raymond promised more of the text. A month passed and nothing came. I wrote to prompt him, and got a one-line postcard, 'Doesn't convince me any more, I can't go on, Raymond'. Silence. I never could get in touch with him again. He *never* answered the phone. I was just cut off. I never understood it. It was very painful. I only saw him once more when I was filming in Cambridge ten years later. I found out his address and went to Hardwick. We had a beer in the pub, but he was very strained and embarrassed. So was Joy. Raymond always denied his indebtedness. Yes, he did.

Orrom was Williams's last collaborator from outside the walls of universities. Joy had got fed up with Orrom; she regarded him, Merryn said jovially, as Raymond's evil genius, coming to stay and going on endlessly about his film projects, stopping Raymond doing his real work. He was cut off abruptly, in Williams's way. Williams's scholarly interests and his personal preoccupations had in any case hauled him off down a more bookish as well as donnish track. He would not gainsay them. He had voiced the notion of a book about 'Ideas of Culture' to Thomas Hodgkin, and Hodgkin, who had taken strongly to Williams and obviously saw him as being as good a teacher in the field as they were ever likely to see, arranged for him to meet an editor from Oxford University Press.

But Hodgkin was running into trouble for reasons nothing to do with the resident tutor in East Sussex. It would be too much to speak of McCarthyism[5] and purges in Adult Education at this date, but Hodgkin had strongly backed a couple of tutors who were in various ways judged not up to the job, both of whom were Communist Party members. Moreover, there was no denying the drop in temperature brought in all corners of university and political life in England (Scotland and Wales, with strong CPs, were different) by the cold war.

Jack Woolford said it was all nothing to do with cold war, but that

Hodgkin virtually got the sack for appointing incompetent or unsuitable tutors. But Hodgkin's own recollection sounds a note of honest dignity which seems to me to be trustworthy.

Thomas Hodgkin

Once the storm broke ... one of the things that made me want to resign really was consciousness that one wasn't going to get good tutors appointed because there was so much effort to ensure that people who were left-wing in their convictions were disadvantaged ... And also, curiously, one of the things that influenced me was the fact that the person who, apart from Cole, was one of our strongest allies, David Worwick – the economist at Magdalen, he was very good and very helpful – I remember him driving me home after a TCC meeting and asking him, 'What do you really think about me?' and he said 'I think perhaps you ought to resign and give way to someone more right-wing in the general interest.' And I thought 'My God, if even David thinks that, it really is time I packed up.'[6]

Raymond, who was after all a long way from Oxford and further still from Barlaston and the Wedgwood College which was at the centre of the row, kept his usual distance from all this. Indeed, it was that very distance, a distance kept for the development of his own thought as well as one commanded by his temperament, which gave him his authority among his colleagues. Hodgkin was the administrative boss of the Delegacy, watched over by the Board. When he left he was succeeded by Frank Jessup whom Raymond actively disliked (which was very rare for him). A man called Frank Pickstock took over as organising secretary of the sub-committee which really directed the teaching programme, and Raymond was on good terms with him. Pickstock had been a railway clerk and stationmaster in the old London and Midland Railway and then got a scholarship as a mature student to Queens at Oxford to read philosophy, politics and economics (PPE) before soaring up the social structure during the war to become a major. He was a vigorous and trenchant defender of the WEA – blunt to the point of simplemindedness said a friend,[7] and a great wangler and schemer in these complicated local dealings between the grand incompatibilities of Oxford University, the extra-mural board, local education authorities, the WEA, the trades unions, and goodness knows what else.

The first allegiance among the extra-mural tutors was to that ideal conception of the WEA and adult education as it had fired so many of them during the war. As this ideal came under diverse pressures, partly from the middle-class women who wanted to read novels, partly from new government politics to promote local centres with a much less high-mindedly academic curriculum, Raymond was nominated during 1952 to act as a kind of senior tutor and shop steward on behalf of his colleagues. It was a tricky but unofficial post, although he wrote a comically contorted letter to Frank Pickstock wondering aloud about a rise because of it

– was there, he said, to be 'a formal announcement that Raymond Williams was to be informally regarded as Senior Tutor'.[8] Anyway, he filled the post with great assurance and what may be called forensic grace. His calm and lucidity in presenting a case across a formal divide of both interest and authority, are remarked upon by everyone who knew him and saw him in such action. Plenty of associates who, as we shall see, held very qualified views on both his intellectual distinction and on his political energies and class consciousness, joined in praising his incisiveness and clarity in the discussion of policy, and on his ecumenical and conciliatory power. The fierce little arguments at Rewley House over the place of the WEA in the general progress of adult education during the 1950s, to say nothing of the defence of the jobs of particular individuals, were frequently resolved by his gift, as I put it earlier, to talk past the sharp point of bitter contention towards some further perspective at which agreement would be possible, even obvious. I think this purpose suffuses much of his work, and explains, even justifies its frequent generality and vagueness. Wittgenstein remarks that sometimes a blurred concept is exactly what we need, and Williams's great pilings of subordinate clauses upon a moral predicate of benign and hopeful inclusiveness is an instance of this.

In the inevitably self-referential interviews in *Politics and Letters* Williams speaks of a period around 1950 as one of fatigue and withdrawal.[9] It's hard to detect it from here. He had a new house of his own, he had two books out, the public regard of his colleagues, and a whole range of new projects on the move. Freddy Bateson strongly encouraged him, and taught him much, as Williams acknowledged. 'His literary scholarship was continually finding me out in ignorance. Bateson ... used to say to me, "You simply are wrong, you have misunderstood this, you have not read that, you have used technical terms inaccurately."'[10] But then, with that grudgingness which is there in Williams and prevents his being properly generous to his peers, let alone his ever acknowledging the superiority of others, he goes on:

> I think this is a very difficult moment for anybody trying to develop a new intellectual project, because you have to be able professionally to take on people who have a different perspective, and doing so you can acquire certain characteristics of precisely that profession ... [and then, in an unappealing excess of egotism] I felt at the time that association with a professional organ was necessary for me, and that I had to be able to produce work that was valid in its terms.[11]

Well, he did. In 1953 Bateson published Williams's essay 'The Idea of Culture' and asked him to join the editorial board. The new project was Williams's most famous book. *Culture and Society 1780–1950* was on its way.

The long essay[12] is announced as swelling prologue to the imperial themes of the book. It begins with the results of a kind of historical semantics for which Williams had already been keeping notes (and asking his students to do the same). Such a semantics took key words in the formation of industrial society and turned up as much of their changing usages as he could find. 'Culture' was the first such inquiry, and if he later said, 'I don't know how often I've wished I'd never heard the damned word' (and who doesn't, just now?), at that date its heavy burden of contradictions lit the fires of anger and resistance in him, as well as those of enthusiasm. With fierce dislike, he chronicles the appropriation of 'culture' by those who declare themselves 'cultured' over against those others who aren't. He famously counterposes Arnold's idea of culture as 'the best that has been known and thought' (without jeering at it) against culture as a whole way of life. He calls Wordsworth powerfully to bear witness to this latter meaning, and memorably dismisses Cardinal Newman, though with blessings on his head. Finally, he connects the secular religion of culture which arises in the nineteenth century with the apotheosis of the artistic imagination codified by Coleridge, and in a sardonic coda, takes an address to a Working Men's College as a sign of times in which culture itself would be called in aid to prevent revolution and accommodate class to class.

The skeleton of the book is here. It is a specifically non-Marxist, labour–socialist protest against the triple assumption that culture as a well-ordered way of life has gone for ever, that present culture is in the hands of those who count themselves qualified to call themselves cultivated, and that their culture is what will redeem society from Jacobin excesses in the names of equality, liberty and fraternity.

The project was radical enough, in the smallish circle of those concerned with the condition of English in England. That is to say, it spoke to a significant fraction of the bourgeoisie about the clear limits of their own class formation. In criticising industrialisation and its depredations as they had, and in affirming the classic liberal values of individual freedom and fulfilment, they had never named the enemy as capitalism, nor remarked upon the degree to which their privileges depended upon the oppression of others, nor how the satisfactions of culture which they enjoyed and commended depended upon the class advantages deeply entrenched by the economic drives they elsewhere deplored. Against delusions it was so much in the interests of this class to maintain, Williams discovered an alternative and misunderstood tradition of anti-capitalists, wearing the homespun clothes of old romanticism, but declaring themselves for a different, equal and generous-hearted vision of a common culture: John Stuart Mill, William Morris, R.H. Tawney, D.H. Lawrence.

The primal energy of the book springs from its repudiation of the value-system and ideology which informed his degree course at Cambridge. That may seem a tiny enough beginning. But the small intellectual province, as I have indicated, ruled a biggish empire of consciousness. The English intelligentsia came into being, I suppose, as the empire really began to unroll across the globe and started to bring home its massive revenues, round about the early years of the nineteenth century. Up to that point there had been since the Restoration a metropolitan world of letters, a university-and-private-library world of scholarship, and a band of dissenting outlaws like Blake on the fringes of that society.

As empire began to recruit intelligence, and power to be both more concentrated in its purpose as well as dispersed in its geography, the intellectual class, of necessity recruited at times from households only recently arrived in comfort, was drawn into these deep currents. As *Culture and Society* brings out, the first preoccupation of the intelligentsia, politically speaking, was 'the condition of England'. Its education was profoundly formed by the narratives of the Bible and the ancient classics, but its natural wakeful life by the canon of English literature, especially its blank verse poetry from Shakespeare to Wordsworth.

As class politics began to dictate the terms of the English compromise which held pretty well, from the dissolution of the Chartist threat after 1848 to the advent of English *Poujadisme* under Mrs Thatcher in 1979, the intellectuals were hired to comment, analyse, make policy, and to prophesy. They did so on behalf of Reform or Old Corruption, for the new liberalism or the immemorial pieties, for capital or labour, and the shaping spirit of their collective imagination wasn't the new social science of Comte, James Mill or Bentham; it was the new novels of Jane Austen and Henry Fielding – and for the bang-up-to-date, the best-sellers of Dickens, Disraeli and the Brontë sisters – all this stiffened by Coleridge's conversational mixture of Hegelian idealism and propaganda for a clerisy.

This formation ran deeper than all differences. This was truly the English ideology. It was Williams's genius to feel it, feel its power and its explanatory force, and then to feel his mind more hugely and, as was perhaps inevitable, resentfully against it in the name of a different consciousness, of both class and generation.

The resentment and the repudiation it fuelled became fiercer as the years went by. During the first half of the 1950s, while he was writing this book, writing *Adamson* and *The Grasshoppers*, rewriting fragments of *Border Country*, writing *Drama in Performance* come to that, he kept up much of his faith in Leavis's method and even in parts of his historiography. Burke the arch-conservative, Coleridge the quietist conservative are both respectfully handled in *Culture and Society*. The anti-democratic and anti-Jacobin Burke is praised[13] (after weighing up his reactionary nature) for his whiggish old prudence about change, *any* change, and Coleridge – through the spectacles of John Stuart Mill – for his advocacy

144

of the clerisy,[14] for his rejection of material prosperity as an index of cultural health, for his anti-utilitarianism: 'Men ought to be weighed, not counted'. Even Carlyle, the strident conservative, author of that endearing phrase 'The Nigger Question' (and the essay that goes with it), gets off lightly, and is admired for *Signs of the Times*, for his hatred of the 'cash-nexus' and 'Mechanism' as forging the bonds of an unprecedented and repellent kind of society.

Williams had set himself the task of exposition as much as criticism, especially in his treatment of the nineteenth-century figures. He knew there was a long tradition out there, of liberal thought turned to the criticism of capitalism, and he set himself not only to master it by reading it for himself (in many cases for the first time), but to turn it to new purposes in the consciousness of a generation which had arrived in mid-century with much greater hopes for the future than the dark prophets of modernism – Eliot, Pound, Lawrence and their great pamphleteer F.R. Leavis – had ever allowed.

Those hopes were British – well, English – enough. Williams couldn't read German, and didn't read French for fun. He bobs respectfully to Marx in *Culture and Society* but he doesn't really use him. In any case, the congenial texts of the humanist Marx, *The Philosophical and Economic Manuscripts*, the *Grundriße*, weren't available in English until the late 1960s. He was addressing the local cases as ordered by the doctors of Tripos at Cambridge. Those he didn't know very well – Burke, Mill, Ruskin – he goes back to and expounds with striking sympathy. He takes what he is looking for or what he finds; he inexcusably misses, for example, Mill's great polemic 'On the Subjection of Women' and his remarkable, still disregarded last essays on socialism, and he seemed not to have heard of T.H. Green, who may surely be seen, if anyone may, as the first progenitor of the British version of the welfare state, the country's most benevolent gift to humankind.

All the same, Mill is a pivot in the book. He is taken very partially indeed as primarily the author of the fixed fight between Bentham and Coleridge,[15] which as Leavis's then very recent edition of the two essays had already pointed out, Coleridge wins hands down. He then appears as author of the *Autobiography*, but as nothing else, neither luminary of the new Civil Service, nor MP, nor hopeless husband, nor Rector of St Andrews.

The *Autobiography* is significant for Williams in a twofold way. First it describes personal breakdown as a consequence of the failure of an intellectual framework. Mill, with a supreme self-confidence not unlike Williams's own, sets about the book at the age of 48. In it, he describes his upbringing at the hands of his father James, a dogmatically Benthamite social philosopher who indoctrinates his son in a lethal mixture of public dutifulness and the utter supremacy of establishable facts and hard

145

reasoning as the ground of human conduct. Denied any expression of his natural bonhomie and tenderness, Mill understandably collapsed.

Williams knew this experience at first hand, with Ibsen as his companion in 1946, and later, shortly after the interviews which constituted *Politics and Letters* were completed but not yet published. He hinted at other such occasions. Like Mill's English gentleman, Williams faced out such threats with no break in his steady, calm manner, his steely discipline in matters of work, his courtesy. Mill retrieved himself by reading Wordsworth and finding there, in his splendid phrase, 'the very culture of the feelings'. This was, for Williams (in his caustic words), 'the saving clause in a bad treaty'.[16]

I think Williams makes a mistake here, both about the balm to hurt minds which nature (and culture) make available, and about value itself. What poetry did for Mill, the Black Mountains did for Williams. What each *was* sought out and healed an anguish in either man's spirit. In Mill's case, and in a way, in Williams's also, the balm was then administered on a national scale. Poetry, and the Arts, were offered by the curriculum as the softening, irrigating force which would make good the hard, dry effects of science. So, too, would a day in the country: on Holy Mountain, in the Dales, on the Northumbrian beaches. Value, that is to say, is both in us and out there. It is true that we desire Wordsworth or a picnic on Holy Mountain because we think these things good, and these things are good because they are what they are, and we desire them.[17]

But Williams also wanted to correct Mill's taken-for-granted preference for poetry (lovely, emotional, personal) over politics (hard, rational, public). Precisely, he wanted to repair that split in the English temper which kept poetry for private life, and as such true and trusty, and made politics the necessary realm of dishonesty, dealing, self-seekingness. Remoralise the Left, and it will, one day, turn the polity into the arena of a public poetry.

This astonishing hybrid of a book mingles expository primer, practical-critical study of practical critics, anti-English polemic of the discipline of English, and a ponderous but moving political prose poem. It was a life-changer for youngish readers in 1960 or so (including me). Its large, never-quite-grasped purpose was to find and recharge the lost veins of English romantic socialism, to make them glow again in the body politic. And it was to tear away the appropriation made by some thinkers of a history they turned to a reactionary cause not even their own.

Hence Williams's careful and incontestable criticism of T.S. Eliot, by the 1950s the most august contemporary jewel in the crown of English literature. The great poet and man of letters is accurately convicted of bluff and bluster,[18] of loose talk and disingenuous thinking. It was a revelation. And Leavis in turn is arraigned not only for bookishness in his definitions of culture, but for false history. Leavis's history lends itself to the darkest forces of reaction and irrationalism, only recently defeated in Europe. Worst of all, Leavis's whole view of the world, his theodicy, betrays the very radicalism which he had created in order to rout the genteel and self-congratulatory view of culture which had prevailed until his advent. The exhilarating triumph which he brought off in his programme of revaluations is then belied and sedated by his deep-seated pessimism.

So Williams moves towards his restatement of the doughtiness, the continued and material life of culture as lived in the practical socialism of the border country. In what are the finest pages in his book, he presents a political D.H. Lawrence, setting aside Lawrence's battier excesses and his grisly vituperation, and remaking the vision of a free homeland (which Lawrence himself gave up) out of their joint childhoods.

> Lawrence started, then, from the criticism of industrial society which made sense of his own social experience, and which gave title to his refusal to be 'basely forced'. But alongside this ratifying principle of denial he had the rich experience of childhood in a working-class family, in which most of his positives lay. What such a childhood gave was certainly not tranquillity or security; it did not even, in the ordinary sense, give happiness. But it gave what to Lawrence was more important than these things: the sense of close quick relationship, which came to matter more than anything else. This was the positive result of the life of the family in a small house, where there were no such devices of separation of children and parents as the sending-away to school, or the handing-over to servants, or the relegation to nursery or playroom. Comment on this life (usually by those who have not experienced it) tends to emphasise the noisier factors: the fact that rows are always in the open; that there is no privacy in crisis; that want breaks through the small margin of material security and leads to mutual blame and anger. It is not that Lawrence, like any child, did not suffer from these things. It is rather that, in such a life, the suffering and the giving of comfort, the common want and the common remedy, the open row and the open making-up, are all part of a continuous life which, in good and bad, makes for a whole attachment. Lawrence learned from this experience that sense of the continuous flow and recoil of sympathy which was always, in his writing, the essential process of living. His idea of close spontaneous living rests on this foundation, and he had no temptation to idealise it into the pursuit of happiness: things were too close to him for anything so abstract. Further, there is an important sense in which the working-class family is an evident and mutual economic unit, within which both rights and responsibilities are immediately contained. The material processes of satisfying human

needs are not separated from personal relationships; and Lawrence knew from this, not only that the processes must be accepted (he was firm on this through all his subsequent life, to the surprise of friends for whom these things had normally been the function of servants), but also that a common life has to be made on the basis of a correspondence between work relationships and personal relationships: something, again, which was only available, if at all, as an abstraction, to those whose first model of society, in the family, had been hierarchical, separative and inclusive of the element of paid substitute labour.[19]

It is a wonderful piece of re-creation, of his own and Lawrence's culture; it gives the definition of culture its looked-for material embodiment, its practice, and its soul. It repairs Williams's own losses: there was no quick making up between Gwen and Harry Williams. It dismisses with a lively scorn the domestic practices of the British upper classes. It shows exactly what Lawrence meant when he said, and is applauded by Williams for saying, 'Men are free when they belong to a living, organic, believing community, active in fulfilling some unfulfilled, perhaps unrealised purpose'.

For Williams in the twentieth century that purpose had to be at least realisable. Intent upon turning politics into culture, he blindly ignores the efforts of the best Fabians to make culture into politics. He sees the business of politics, of power and allocation and bureaucracy, as the product of culture, in most cases, ruling-class culture. The Fabians tried to turn that culture into efficient administration, regulated by just laws. So Williams misses a vital political cue. The conclusion of the book describes what realisation of Lawrence's maxim, and going ahead without a party, armed only with goodheartedness, would entail. He fails to imagine a virtuous judge and an honest bureaucrat.

Bits are clumsy, no doubt. They include fragments of the argument already published in *The Highway* and elsewhere, for Williams, as always, published as he went, and wasted little if he could avoid it. He sets out to repudiate the Eliot–Leavis line, going back to Arnold, that industrial civilisation has created an indiscriminate mass of people closed or obdurate to any but the easy, escapist pleasures provided for commercial profit and within which only a minority critically equipped against its blandishments and stupefactions can stand up for individual responsibility, keenness of response and the maintenance of a vital creativity.

It's a powerful argument: study the filthy lucubrations of the *Sun*, the ravings of the *National Inquirer*, the vacuity of *Neighbours* and *Oprah Winfrey*, and it's hard not to agree all through. Well into the 1960s Williams dismissed most of Hollywood as escapist pap, and wrote to that effect on his students' essays.[20] But he dug in against Eliot's class-based use of 'the

148

masses' as a category, and Leavis's book-based one. Once again, if implicitly, he stood by the pieties and dignified order of the village on the border.

By the same token he rejects mass communication as a term, but also because the phrase denies the civic and the political. One-way communication down to the masses is how capitalism pictures its newspaper and television industries; public communication would go (at least) two ways and would be just that: public, and publicly owned.

Finally, and rousingly, he stands up for the best of Britain against its bloody worst. In a reversal which certainly startled the mild-mannered teachers of English and their ex-pupils in the posh papers, he identified the creativity in all social resistance, particularly in trade unions, in their organisation of opposition to the blind imperatives of profit, in their strikes. In identifying culture as held, lived and renewed in common, he did not pretend to any easy consensus, indeed, emphasised argument itself as the form of the tradition, but he also named and rejected the British drive always to turn political culture into service with higher and lower servants, careers into the climbing of ladders, and the mobilising energy of social life as a balance between 'getting on' and disappointment at not 'getting on'. Those self-confident railwaymen of his boyhood came to stand for something fine and indigenous in British politics as they have always stood at the sentimental heart of the Labour Party. Those same men were deployed by Williams to dissolve politics into culture, and to turn culture into those institutions which bear witness to the creative, commonly expressive possibilities of everyday collective labour: committee procedure, the trades unions themselves, English common law, domestic custom and buildings, as well as the discoveries and theories of the (collectively produced) social and natural sciences. This was Williams's biggest conceptual challenge, to politics as well as to the custodians and gatekeepers of English literature.

Ian Parsons at Chatto was politely welcoming but lukewarm. On the first version, which he received in early July 1955,[21] he expressed anxieties about over-specialisation! But he accepted a finished manuscript which Raymond paid to have typed from the crumpled, double-crossed, heavily annotated, deleted and rewritten mass of the original on 26 March 1956, remarking to the author at lunch round the corner from the Chatto offices in William IV Street that he liked the book, it sat well on the firm's list, but he thought it would only do quite modestly, like another book he'd got coming out called *The Uses of Literacy*.

So Raymond received another £75 advance, and went off with the family to Devon for three weeks in April, while Parsons decided to cut out Godwin, Thomas Arnold, Herbert Read and 'the English Freudians', which presumably (and surprisingly) must have meant Ernest Jones.

The book had its roots in Williams's extra-mural classes, for sure, but it was a clear break with them, all the same. He had been one of the

Directors of Studies (with Lionel Elvin) at the 1949 Oxford summer school under the heading 'Democracy and Culture', had taught a number of courses in the south-east entitled 'Culture and Environment' (with a guide to the reading starting from Thompson's book which Denys Thompson himself published early in the life of *The Use of English*[22]). He had drawn some attention with two or three short essays in *The Highway*, contesting the Leavisian malediction of the ruin and poisoning of standards brought about by the pervasive commercialisation of everything cultural, as well as by the 'levelling-down' (in an ugly phrase) caused by the post-war version of democracy. To a man formed by the optimism of the Left in the 1930s, the solid experience of victory over the vilest embodiment of right-wing politics imaginable in the war, and the great surge of reconstructive, practical-minded hopefulness which carried Labour to power in 1945 and Williams himself into the radical earnestness of adult education, this was the worm in the bud, and a man like Leavis had no business to be feeding it.

So *Culture and Society* grew well above the small classrooms with their gloved, overcoated students looking for the 'non-specialist, concrete and human treatment' of literature.[23] It spoke for them, but beyond them also. Williams's output at this date, however, was as prodigious as always, and he also kept up his teacherly commitment to writing textbooks. He and Cecil Scrimgeour, who had been appointed at the same interview panel and was an eager Thespian, had been developing performance-based drama courses – Scrimgeour's, called 'Partners in the Play', culminated in summer school productions of, variously, *Twelfth Night, Major Barbara* and *An Enemy of the People.* For all Williams had had to say about the study of 'the words on the page' in his first drama book – many of those words in translation from Norwegian, Swedish, French and German, what's more – he briskly wrote *Drama in Performance*,[24] a handy guide of no great originality, crossing the centuries from Delphos to medieval Church drama, on to the Globe, jumping two and a half centuries to Chekhov and Ibsen, and ending up with rather perfunctory notes on performance as discussed in Brighton and Battle.

Drama in Performance was none the less a small measure of the striking intellectual and pedagogic busyness of adult education at that date. In the nature of this biography, it is mostly the discussion of the arts in general and literature in particular which has been noticed. But *The Highway, Adult Education,* the *Tutors' Bulletin*, the less local magazines like *Essays in Criticism* and *The Use of English* bear copious witness to thriving debate amongst the men and women doing the job in geographical and timetabling conditions which worked against collaboration, or indeed any sense that elsewhere in the country there were others thinking the same thoughts, teaching the same books, mounting the same arguments with housewives and with trade unionists, with school teachers, clerical workers, nurses, social security officials, probation officers, steel-workers, communists, Christians, weighbridgemen, lace loom operatives. Across the country, these people turned up once a week to hear Raymond Williams talk about James Joyce or the dismalness of the *Daily Mail*, Richard Hoggart talk about the methods of practical criticism, Edward Thompson about William Blake, Shelley, the deaths at Peterloo, Michael Barratt Brown about the labour theory of value, Bridget Sutton on the English Civil War, Arthur Marsh on the social and practical functioning of trade unions, Wolf Mankowitz on film and musicals, John Rex on the strange new subject of sociology, Raymond Postgate on the making of the canal system, Douglas Hewitt on Joseph Conrad, all of them in all they taught and did corroborating the best values of the new Labour politics in spite of the Labour Party, its defeat, and the rise of a Churchillian government founded on Attlee's successes.

I cannot keep an idealising note out of this roll-call, and I do not want to. Whatever the dreariness enforced by routine, the discomfort of the classrooms, the scattered classes and grim travelling, these were the best conversations of the culture of the day. No intellectual work can grow without a fertile ground: this is the power of the metaphor, 'culture'. *Culture and Society* and *The Uses of Literacy* came out within a few months of each other. They not only betoken, they helped to make the best British education, and the polity it nurtures, of the following forty years.

'After the songs of Apollo, the words of Mercury'. The little Apollonian corner of the culture occupied by adult education did its bit for manners and morality. But the monster polity of British imperialism was still seeking whom it might devour with its carious teeth. As *Culture and Society* went into production in the autumn of 1956, Anthony Eden, Churchill's successor in Downing Street, elegant, handsome, petulant, debilitated by an undiagnosed and leaking bowel, took his country to war. After four times rejecting his military adviser's plans to invade Nasser's Egypt in an effort to recover the nationalised Suez Canal, he threw an inkwell at the good colonel, who responded by cramming a waste paper basket over his head, and in November 1956 dispatched parachutes to Port Said, and a full invasion force behind them.[25]

Pretty well as he did so, the tanks of the Soviet Army blew to pieces the pitiful barricades erected against them by Hungarian socialists attempting, with desperate courage, to reclaim their own country for their own version of a kinder, less propagandised socialism.

The hideous clangour of nuclear war suddenly rang in people's ears. The two vast beasts of Soviet and Franco-British imperial arrogance reared up out of their separate bloody tramplings, peered at each other briefly and with indifference, and trundled back to their dens, triumphant in Budapest, humiliated in Egypt.

The everyday politics of culture as inscribed in Williams's and Hoggart's great books could not encompass the meanings of this sudden and vertiginous enlargement of the historical scenery. There was, abruptly, a lack of fit between the frames of mind devised to think about and celebrate working-class homes in Hunslet and Pandy, and the imminence of a new war lit by the blinding glare of a nuclear explosion.

There were protesting crowds out in the streets of British cities in a way unseen since the pro- and anti-Fascist marches of the 1930s. The rough old monster of Empire still commanded enormous support, however, and undergraduates at Oxford and Cambridge fought each other, as they did over Spain and Finland, and were impartially collected by cops and proctors. There wasn't much doing in Hastings, and Williams's self-containment was such as wouldn't, or not yet, take him up to London to the mass demonstration against the Suez adventure in Trafalgar Square. There was much more doing in the Yorkshire Ridings where John Saville in Hull, since 1934 a loyal communist of the Popular Front days, had joined with Edward Thompson in the extra-mural department at Leeds and himself also a vehement CP member, to circulate a slightly scruffy *samizdat* newsletter called *The Reasoner*, objecting to Stalinism whether in Moscow or Yorkshire. In the autumn, when the hideous circuses of Budapest and Port Said were staged, the two men were pleading for a campaign of re-moralisation on the Left which would oppose Khrushchev's murderousness as much as they did the British Labour Party's lack of nerve.

There's a comicality as well as a heroism about calling for such changes of heart from copying machines in Hull and Halifax. Not, however, to the lockjawed robots then in charge of the Communist Party in Britain. They would not permit such Party-free thinking, so Saville and Thompson broke with them, and quit just before they were thrown out.

Not before time, you might say. It was Khrushchev himself who, in the muffled jargon of his local party, had blown the gaffe on Stalin's unspeakable terrors, at the famous Twentieth Party Congress in 1953. It was by hoping for something a bit better after this burst of candour, that 10,000 Hungarians got themselves killed three years later. Once you knew about the Moscow treason trials, the eradication of the Kulaks, the willed famine, how *could* anyone have hoped for anything from the USSR?

Any answer must come close to the meaning of these men's lives, as it must to the whole project of intellectual criticism and opposition in the rich countries of a world only clear of cold war in 1989. Thompson and company remained in the Communist Party for the same reason that Williams joined with Tony McLean drinking in the Party's beaten-up little bar at the club in Hastings: for the same reason that both men taught, wrote, lived as they did.

John Dunn

Raymond allied to his own massive self-assurance the great strength of the Left, which is its identification with history's *losers*. He had a very good feeling for the way people are subjugated, a vivid imagination for how human beings get crushed. It is very important to have that direct relation to human maiming, and he had it.

But his political judgements were often culpably ignorant. His connection with human damage broke off – it was all in Britain – so he had no vision of what had actually happened in the USSR. He used those blocks of historical experience as counters on the board for an indefensible representation of how things really were at the time. What was called for by 1956 was a *very* frank discussion of what this meant to socialism.

There was too much credulity in that group of people. Their obstinacy and denial were wrongly distributed. They thought that to think in certain ways about socialism in its concrete detail was to surrender.

It would have been, they thought, to surrender to the enemy – to the English ruling class and its helots in the press, or to their far more repellent pay-masters in the USA, in the Congress for Cultural Freedom, visiting All Souls College, calmly admonishing the Left they too had joined when young and foolish, and now rebuked for its utopianism, its blindness to historical inevitability, its dated ideals, its sanctimony and awkwardness, its mere lack of taste and money. They detested Stalin but they stuck to the flag.

Faced by these reproaches, what man or woman of principles and pride would not have stuck to the old guns, turning them in their tiny redoubt to fire upon all those who betrayed the moral vision of Marxism? What Thompson and Williams sought was that vision as given perspective not by the ruthless bandits of October 1917, but by William Morris, stumping all over England, speaking to 800 meetings in the three years 1885 to 1888 and all in defence of an English socialism, a moral Marxism. What they had to cut out of their vision, and mutilate their thought in doing so, was their own clear knowledge at that date of all that had been done in the name of either Marxism or Socialism, done with such horrible cruelty and justified as historical necessity on the move again. Morris's odyssey ante-dated all that, and he was in any case English. He came to their relief.

The meetings had been totted up by Edward Thompson himself, in his long novel of a biography of Morris, published in 1955.[26] Once out of the CP, he and John Saville started *The New Reasoner* after the Wortley Conference of Socialist Forums was held in Sheffield in April 1957. Its editorial board included the novelists Doris Lessing and Mervyn Jones, the anthropologist Peter Worsley, the tough South African revolutionary John Rex, Randall Swingler, a well-known journalist and a dashing kind of nomadic chieftain of the Left in a mode now largely disappeared from British life; its intellectual orientation was towards the sort of economic history advocated by the doughty Communist Historians Group, Hobsbawm, Christopher Hill, Victor Kiernan, Rodney Hilton.[27]

At the same moment, four exceedingly bright young leftists linked up at Oxford, and set themselves to found a rather different kind of political mag. Stuart Hall we have met already; he went to Oxford in 1951 as a West Indian Rhodes scholar. His parents came from poor families; his father won a scholarship to become an accountant, his mother was adopted by a plantation owner. Hall has always been very handsome, irresistibly charming, smiling, even-tempered, and fluent to a fault. He was reading English literature, he wasn't a member of the Party but he had read *Capital*. He joined Al Alvarez' and Graham Martin's Critical Society, the first group ever to invite Leavis to Oxford, and he was taught by Bateson. He palled up with a Scotsman reading Classical Greats from Keele, another Hall called Alan, as well as with an enormously tall, craggy, friendly, antic kind of Canadian Christian-Marxist called Charles Taylor who always repudiated the more concrete-headed Marxists, and taught Stuart Hall the humanist side of the prophet, and about Hegel. They heard Christopher Hill lecture on the class-revolutionary meaning of the English Civil War, where they were joined by a nomad from the London School of Economics, Raphael – known as Ralph – Samuel, child of an ardently Jewish-communist family, with a kindly, sideways smile, and a thick mop of hair forever falling over the top of his specs which, even when going bald, he grew copiously from his parting so it continued to slide fascinatingly forward with the vehemence of his speech, to be pushed back and start its slide all over again.

Williams was, of course, often in Oxford over those years, and first met Stuart Hall in the winter of 1954–55. In the summer of 1956 the two Halls were planning a book on cultural politics and went to see Williams on his Devon holiday. They came back with copies of chapters from *Culture and Society*.

Stuart Hall

We appointed ourselves keepers of the Left conscience. There was Chuck Taylor, Raphael, Graham Martin and Gabriel Pearson then still CP, Alan and me. To begin with, Alan and I resurrected the Socialist Society in Oxford, which had been going strong in the 1930s. We found it still had a bank account with a decent credit; some of the Old Left had kept their subscriptions going!

At the end of the summer of 1956 Chuck went off to Paris to work with Merleau-Ponty and I went to London to teach English in a Secondary Modern school near the Oval, as well as some extra-mural classes down at Bexleyheath. We had set up *Universities and Left Review* just before then. [The grandly stylish title indicated the University origin of its editors and their hoped-for link with the pre-war *Left Review*.] We had *no* money for *U and LR*, but the first issue sold 8,000 [three times as many as *New Reasoner*]. There was obviously something on the move out there.

We first met in Chuck's room in All Souls. We were full of barmy schemes; Ralph and I were raising money to fly Sartre to England at the height of the Algerian crisis. It would have been quite easy.

154

They took an office in Soho and then, with bewitching flair and abandon, bought the premises. Money was no object; they took any amount from rich ex-members of the Communist Party from the 1930s and 1940s, 'fellow-travellers, Jewish, NW3 and NW8' as Hall put it, and 7 Carlisle Street, a pleasant, plain, late eighteenth-century terrace house, was theirs.

It was that key moment in post-war metropolitan street life when espresso coffee came to London. The building was more than an office: it was a club. It had a library on the first floor, crammed with new and old and conscientiously correct paperbacks (the intellectual paperback was now in the full flood of its amazing expansion, driven above all by Penguin's mighty flippers), review copies and Left Book Club stuff from the 1930s. It had editorial offices at the top. And it had the 'Partisan' coffee house. Raphael Samuel was the one who had been born and lived in London, and was streetwise. Raphael Samuel was also, as Stuart Hall remembered, crying with laughter, the most awful administrator, the most forgetful treasurer ('the bills were *never* paid'), the most chaotic bureaucrat ever, the papers piled high on the desk and floor, contributions lost under mountains of other contributions, the ancient, collapsing, wooden filing cabinet with stuff poked into drawers anyhow and a coat chucked on top. And all this was bad even by the standards of the political Left infamous for its administrative incompetence. (It wasn't until CND walked again in the 1980s that dissent in Britain learned a tidy bureaucracy.) Hall said, 'Nothing could happen without Raphael, but he was completely scatty. Chuck and I *forbade* them to start the "Partisan" as a coffee house, but it started all the same.' They bought a Gaggia espresso machine which roared and gargled and hissed loudly, as they do, and Samuel busied about Soho buying the coffee, while the studiedly camp Quentin Crisp, whose ditto bestseller *The Naked Civil Servant* so goosed the bourgeoisie, colonised the front-of-house and played chess there.

It was a long room with a platform at one end, and Samuel fetched Trotsky's great Jewish biographer Isaac Deutscher to lecture on the prospects for this new Left in the coming 1960s. Flanked by the crude murals and posters, lit by the hard white lights slung low from the ceiling, his papers were in the dark and he was only half-visible. It wasn't a bad symbol.

But the place fairly seethed. Hundreds came to hear the lectures in the gaunt basement-and-dining-room, two or three of them by Raymond Williams, and to sway to folksong and Woody Guthrie or Ewan MacColl protest songs picked out on an unelectrified guitar.[28] A model army of guerrilla discussion cadres formed itself in a trice, Left Scientists, International Forum, History of Socialism, Social Priorities, even London Schools Left Club chaired by a grave, twinkling-eyed, bearded young-old English teacher called John Dixon. When Williams came in 1959 a little after the publication of *Culture and Society* the place was packed, and

155

outside in Carlisle Street afterwards, as one of the leading members of the *U and LR* group recalled:

Graham Martin

> Ralph said, always considerate and courteous as he was in such ways, 'I don't believe we've paid your expenses', so he got down on his knees on the pavement and wrote the cheque. Raymond looked down, amused, and said, 'Well, I'm used to Left disorganisation but this is new.'
>
> I'd been down with Stuart to see Raymond in Hastings after we'd published some of the book in *U and LR*. After supper (a Saturday evening) we were talking away about some project, and Raymond said would we like a drink? He went to a cupboard and brought out a bottle of wheat wine – a beautiful warm amber colour, perfectly clear. On the Sunday morning, we went to the park with the kids, Raymond in an old heavy coat, and I looked across at him from a little way off and called, 'Raymond Williams, you look just like Wordsworth's Wanderer.' And he did. Not lonely, you know, just solitary.

The affinity with Wordsworth and Wordsworth's people recurs time and again through Williams's life. He was certainly Wordsworthian in his alienation from London, but when the two boards of editors from *Universities and Left Review* and *New Reasoner* decided on a merger in 1959, 'Raymond *always* turned up to the Board meetings.'

Stuart Hall

> The two journals had so much in common, and such differences. You can still read that historical legacy in the contents page. There were two generations for one thing, old CP and New Left. There was North v. South. Photo-journalism v. High Theory.
>
> After all, the collapse of the British Communist Party happened in the Thompsons' house in Halifax. Edward lost his magazine and was in any case such a firebrand. Raymond was the moderator always, talking *past* the rows, and I was in the middle.

So *New Left Review* was launched with a big turn-out at the inevitable Conway Hall early in 1960, with Doris Lessing and Iris Murdoch, celebrity novelists and new women, on the platform. Stuart Hall was to be the first editor at £500 per year (a lot less than he got at the Secondary Modern school by the Oval) with Janet Hayes as secretary, the only two paid officials.

It was a blissful dawn, all right. The magazine was to be the focus of a new, principled and non-doctrinal Left, stretching out reconciling hands to old CP, new sectarians, Labour radicals, and beyond that, to the well-disposed and educated new generation which looked for a way to combine decent, generous-hearted, egalitarian ideals with the vivid satisfaction of a world full of delicious consumer goods whose plenitude really looked as though it might help in dissolving class divisions in bloody-minded old Britain.

Following the magazine, with its snappy editorials by Hall, its sharp snapshot journalism, on Algeria or unilateralism in the Labour Party, or on the flowering of British cinema, its grainy black-and-white photographs, its reviews of pop, were the New Left clubs, scattered plentifully over the country, strongest in London, Leeds, Manchester (which also had its daring coffee-bar).

The sacred texts of this unprecedented kind of new political movement, combining as it did in its savoury brew old Popular Front and new popular culture, old political realism and even older Morrisian romanticism, new sympathetic internationalism and just-as-new social libertarianism, novels and wage-theory, sex and disarmament, were *The Uses of Literacy* and *Culture and Society*. It was a strong and satisfying mixture exactly because it included so much that until recently had been counted out of culture as not decorous enough, not classy enough, not *old* enough. The new movement of feeling caught up the simple happinesses of café sociability, of buying books and clothes and tickets to the cinema long before these had become another site of vicious competition and status-marking. It allied these gregarious pleasures to a cheerful, generous-hearted belief that politics really was for life and not just for politicians, least of all those grim economistic custodians of the Old Left and its mechanical activism.

Williams was quickly appointed pole star in this new little universe. He was grown-up; he was never at a loss with an audience, he was personable, and in his calm, distanced, cool and cordial way, he enjoyed the swift rush of fame. *Culture and Society* came out in 1958 to general acclaim. It was a startling book, but there was a space waiting for it. Reviewers knew how to read it. Given Parsons's doubts about the book, as a publisher (and a friendly editor) he must have been delighted with the range and the strong approval of just about every review. People had their criticisms, of course, about Williams's cloudier and more polymorphous sentences, but both the established luminaries – Stuart Hampshire, Anthony Hartley, D.W. Harding – and the new men – Richard Hoggart,[29] Frank Kermode, Graham Martin[30] – gave the book their serious attention and mitigated applause.

Hoggart's review shows that particular new man at his best. In praising Williams handsomely, but entering his careful criticisms, he also indicates their differences of disposition, of turn of mind, of ambition (come to that) which imply much about their future passage through the middle echelons of the British power structure, and the significance of that passage for those many people who have long looked to the two men for a lead in such a way of life, and for hints as to what one might do by way of acting morally and living well.

Hoggart, though he went on writing busily, stopped being a writer for a couple of decades a few years later, stopped also, you might say, being an intellectual. He never stopped being his own exemplarily principled

157

self, independent-minded, bluntly intelligent and knowing it perfectly well, but his public role, carried off as it was with his striking congruence of persona, personality, and personhood, was that of cultural diplomat and bureaucrat. He was the best embodiment I've ever seen of Max Weber's ideal bureaucrat – impartial, clear, confidential, extremely well informed, rational and upright in all things, *specific*.

In 1959, still a writer–intellectual, and an abruptly risen star in the just-emerging nova of the intelligentsia which replaced the old, closed élite of literary London, he turned these qualities to stern account when, after warm applause and strong approval for the book, he reproaches Williams 'only incidentally' for 'a recurrent note in Mr Williams's manner'. 'At such moments the rhetorical balance of the cadences, the rhythmic repetitive structure of the periods, the alternation of large general statement with biblically or classically simple metaphor, do produce a rather rotund quality.'[31]

Graham Martin recalled the same features of Raymond's speech more sympathetically:

Graham Martin

I heard him lecture on Joyce at a British Council summer school in 1955, invited by Freddy Bateson. He had a quality of voice I'd never heard in Oxford before. I don't know what he said about Joyce – though you can see the influence in *Border Country* – but the voice and the presence I always remember, eloquent, unhesitating, almost hypnotic.

There were colleagues in the Oxford Delegacy who later sharpened Hoggart's point, one of them the Resident Staff Tutor in Lincoln.

Graham Taylor

I never observed R.H.W. teaching an adult class or seminar group, only occasionally lecturing at Summer Schools or short residential courses. No notes. Fluently extemporised on his feet. Impressive. But unfortunately his delivery – 'elocutionary' style was poor. Quiet, sometimes inaudible voice, tending to mutter and mumble, lacking in rhetorical expressiveness. Also his involved, 'intellectualised' style made no concessions to and great demands on his listeners' capacity for continuous attention. He seemed to make insufficient distinction between his written and speaking style, avoiding the colloquial or dramatic, which are often so effective in oral communication. Also he refused to reduce a normally cerebral and 'intellectual', and (I thought) sometimes over-elaborate and complicated style to a more digestible oral form. In spoken (as sometimes in his written style) he seemed to 'wrap up' meanings which could be simplified without essential loss. He was, I think, suspicious of anything smacking of the simple and direct. Ironically, of course, he started the fashion for classes in 'Public Expression', including speaking, prevalent in the fifties.[32]

And another from the same stable said the same, more roughly.

Jim Fyrth

I have long recognised his stature. But I have never been a *fan*. This was because I so often found his writing, as you say, 'dense and impenetratable'. Not to put too fine a point on it, I often could not understand what he was talking about, and this seemed to be a contradiction (to put it mildly) in one who wanted to communicate with the class from which he came, and was constantly talking about the importance of language. In my own classes with trade unionists I have always spent some time on communication, emphasising the need to use simple but lively language. Trade union activists are too easily seduced by convoluted language which often hides lack of thought.[33]

Taylor and Fyrth object to more than manner or manners. It is substance which is at stake: first, the substance of an argument about what can be made specific, even factual; second, however, they object, as many did, to something in Williams's whole world view in which certain values were presupposed but which, in the general abstractness of his description, won a too-facile victory over their antagonists.

At the end of his review, Hoggart presses this incipiently painful point home, although he then turns it gracefully and quickly aside by making the difference between him and Williams merely, as it were, perspectival.

He queries Williams's opposition between 'solidarity' (*the* working-class value) and 'service' which, in its worthily unself-interested version Williams selects as the best of the middle-class values. (It is a timely note at a later date, when the middle class conspicuously renounced the latter value for a less exigent mode of time-serving self-service.) Hoggart, observing that 'solidarity' has its narrowing and exclusive aspect as well as 'service' its classlessly public-spirited realm, and himself as much a champion of the values of the 1945 Labour programme as Williams, ends by saying that in his belief life itself demands more working in the dark, more stoicism and irony than are allowed for either in Williams's idiom or his vision. It is a criticism which will come to sound louder and louder as, over the next thirty years, the Left in Britain missed its chances and the Right seized them.

It seems to be true that Raymond took little notice of criticisms. Several people report occasions on which he simply didn't read or didn't heed central objections made to some part of his work. He followed some inner rhythm, I would guess, according to which that monologue of oblique autobiography always being spoken in his head held now in a closer, now in a wider relation, the large abstractions necessary to social theory and the hard felt facts which give theory its life and force.

If he needed it – and he seemed to – the facts of life gave him a sharp jab dead on time. On 27 November 1957, Joy took a phone call from Pandy telling her that Harry Williams had been found in his signal box having suffered a severe coronary attack.

Raymond cancelled his classes and took the train, the long, rocking journey up from Hastings to Victoria, on the grubby buttoned seats underneath the washed-out pictures of the Prom at Eastbourne, then the underground from Victoria to Brunel's grand iron vaults over Paddington, westwards past the huge railway marshalling yards at Swindon, change again at Brunel's castle at Bristol, Temple Meads, under the channel to Newport, up to Abergavenny, very late, dark, and the last bus gone.

He describes it better than I can in the opening pages of *Border Country*. He comes home to a mortally ill father, goes back as his father fights towards recovery, returns in the spring, and is caught in fact by an early morning phone call, but in the novel, starting to go back to London again, by a railway official who recognises his father in him, with the grim news that his father is on death's edge again. He goes home. Harry dies, in his early sixties; hard life, hard death. Too much for his heart, as we say.

His father's death quickened and freed him, as he saw, with a detached fearfulness, from himself. Writing very fast after Harry's death in the early spring of 1958, he framed his novel with his father's death. A long time ago it had ended with young Will going off by train to become Matthew in Cambridge. Now, his father's life is repositioned; on either side of it the son returns.

In-between, Williams, with the thick skin of the writer protecting him from his own sobs at his father's funeral, deploys what actually happened around the deathbed – Annette Lees and Violet Higgs confirm it – in the fiction of his novel: someone dug the garden, someone else cut some railway sleepers into firewood, Raymond himself was told off to get the wreaths made, tried to do it all by telephone only to find that the local florist was keeping flowers back specially for Harry.

Matthew comes home to his father. They find a common speech. The women don't get a look in; Will is as insensitive to his mother in his thirties as he was as a lad, and is positively priggish to the sweetheart he never acknowledged but grew up beside. But he takes away with him his father's unique authority, his will-to-live as one ought to live.

Parsons at Chatto winced a bit in a well-bred way – 'your attempt to produce naturalistically the talk of inarticulate people is admirable, but it often produces phrases very difficult to understand'[34] – cut it a good deal, and went enthusiastically ahead. It was, Parsons knew, much improved on *Border Valley*, the title of last year's version. *Culture and Society* had been taken on by the New York branch of Oxford University Press, in Germany by Musterschmidt Verlag, and at home by Penguin. They had sold 2,000 copies of the hardback in the first year; Doubleday signed up for an American print run in paperback of 20,000 copies. Raymond Williams had become a house stalwart.

The hot rush of feeling which came with Harry Williams's death fused theory and experience together in Raymond's writing over that year. He was asked to contribute a chapter by Norman Mackenzie, a Fabian social historian, to a volume confidently called *Conviction*.[35] The other contributors were of a piece with Raymond – sociologists, social policy researchers, cultural commentators, MPs, intellectuals – Peter Shore, Iris Murdoch, Peter Townsend, Brian Abel-Smith and Hoggart among them who all shared a Labour or a more socialist view of the world. Together they represented the decent way of thinking proselytised by *New Left Review* that the cultural was political (and vice versa), and that the way to a better society in Britain was by dissolving its grim old class structure into the communality of a changed way of life grounded in an open education and the means of public communication which would support it.

Williams, in his contribution, magicked these bromides into a heartening polemic which started out, in strong actuality, with the bus journey from Hereford Cathedral library to Pandy. Culture is ordinary, he said, and said again; it is not the exquisite stuff of social discrimination used to keep us up and them down. It is ordinary. Its fineness is as plainly discernible in ordinary homes and lives as in great novels; indeed, he propounded the heresy that fine, even noble lives may coexist in the same household with awful newspapers and bad novels. This was not to say that you couldn't tell the difference between good and bad novels, only that bad novels (and newspapers) did not cause or entail bad lives. (He also doesn't say that the nastiest attitudes of *The Times* or the *Sun* may at other times fit perfectly the people who read them.)

Williams aspired high-mindedly but in plain and honest prose for better on behalf of each ordinary life, his among them. In a final break, he rejected Leavis's historiography: the lie-with-truths-in-it that democracy and industrialisation worked together to produce commercial culture and debased sensibilities. He repudiated the vicious condescension which expressed this as a 'Gresham's Law' of culture. And he spoke out for a more Labour culture to support Culture: open and democratic education, public support of the arts instead of private support by advertising, the common ownership of the means of public communication.

That was another epoch, with its own way of feeling about what was possible. It *was* possible, then (it *is* possible now). Where there's a will ... especially a political will ...

Williams himself, however, was now speaking on a much larger stage than the battered theatre of adult education in East Sussex could hold. After the 1960 summer school in Oxford, his transfer to Oxford was formally announced by the Delegacy; he had bought 47 Bainton Road from a colleague and after moving up from Hastings in July, took his family away in their ancient Vauxhall estate, laden with tent, pots and pans, for three weeks in Brittany.

8

MR RAYMOND WILLIAMS
AND DR F.R. LEAVIS

Even by Williams's prodigious standards it was an amazingly productive period, especially if one throws in the demands of moving house.

Culture and Society, like all Williams's books, was an archaeological piece of work. Embedded in its thick masonry, the solid treatment of this or that writer sometimes built into a whole apartment, sometimes a mere room, are assorted constructions from the past – the passages on standards for example – which had been used in a simpler, less heavily contextualised way in *The Highway*, or elsewhere. So with the third book in what he presented as a trilogy. *The Long Revolution*, the proofs of which he received together with those of *Border Country* at Bainton Road in the autumn of 1960, had a similar architectonic and method of assembly. He had, for instance, been writing the chapter on the history of the press for some time. His ruminations on the nature of creativity arise from discussions with a particularly good three-year tutorial class, twenty-odd strong, in Brighton. Some of the material on literacy and the advent of the novel appeared in *Essays in Criticism* in 1959, and his prescient (though conventional enough) sketch of a compulsory national curriculum – an idea nursed but not enacted until the Tories' Educational Reform Act of 1988 – appeared in synopsis in *Education* in 1960.

Although he wrote fast – or rather, typed fast, and thuddingly, on his battered and battering old typewriter (never electrified, let alone word-processed) – he revised copiously and by hand, covering the typescript with long loops linking interpolations, transposing paragraphs, deleting, editing, all the hieroglyphic devices of those pre-screen days. Indeed, a page of manuscript offered a metonymy for Raymond's domestic life. It was an extremely messy, strictly practical diagram of what needed to be done: confusingly difficult for anyone else to interpret, perfectly clear to the author.

He wasted nothing, threw little away, but reworked and replaced things so that his books were amassed out of the differently hewn, roughcast and manifold artefacts scattered around the crowded, cramped and rather cheerless studies which were his workshops. And he could leave nothing alone. He so revised the proofs of *The Long Revolution* that Nora Smallwood had to write to him from Chatto offering to split the bill of £80 for corrections between author and publisher!

Chatto had a very respectable fiction list – Iris Murdoch is still its queen – and they hustled with *Border Country*, getting it out in time for Christmas 1960, with a nice cover (Williams had been most specific in his demands for this during the summer) showing the signal box in front elevation, and the Black Mountains behind. It got, as the publishers wrote to him to say, 'a wonderful press', and this at a time when reviewing new novels was still a very busy activity in a weekly or fortnightly cultural press which not only published many more titles than now – *John O'London's, Strand, Punch, Time and Tide, Books and Bookman, The Listener* have all disappeared since – but whose book review pages took up most of the back half of their contents, with very little space for films, and none at all for TV or pop.

The literary culture of Britain was therefore English, and before English, London-Metropolitan, where London naturally included the two ancient universities only sixty miles away. Williams's novel, with its close re-creation of Harry Williams's working life, its angry retelling of the tale of the General Strike, its affecting invocation of old hopes about the nature and advent of a home-made socialism found ready and friendly recognition. Above all, reviews recognised its moral rendering of the dauntedly respectful economic historian who has gone away to be a university teacher but whose disappointing effort to write the great history of his people's economic diaspora in a sort of mixture of much smaller-scale Braudel and Institute of Community Studies ethnography, comes off humiliatingly second to his father's silently principled market-gardening and railway-signalling. Harry was the hero all right; his son merely the means to get the story told. What the intellectual might *do* to turn Harry's virtues into a larger, more social potentiality is excluded from the novel largely because, one would say, Williams himself had enough to do as a tyro novelist, with four versions of the thing mutually embedded in front of him, to get his father's life into the light, and his mother's failure out of it.

He did it, too. I remember buying the book the minute it came out, and seeing it, feeling it certainly as *good*, that is as confirming and celebrating some of my own deepest allegiances. These were made a long way north-east in a much better-off social class, but made similarly to a love of my family and of my landscape, as well as to the great names of mutuality and equality as lived under the just rule of our mother's small democracy. All of this, we believed, would surely be made manifest in an England, and a Britain, for which it was not then shameful to feel an undemonstrative patriotism. When Dennis Potter, who died in 1994 as the first unmistakably canonical writer for television wrote in his review of

Border Country, 'I cannot doubt that he has written a great book',[1] I could not doubt it either.

I could now. There's much that's heavy; there is, as we saw, a willed refusal to criticise Harry at all; there is the unfeeling and indifferent treatment of all the women including the hero's wife; there is Will's heavy priggishness. But *Border Country* remains a gripping read. More than that, it was not only centrepiece in Raymond's trilogy; with *The Long Revolution*, in proof as the novel came out, 'it completed a body of work which I set myself to do ten years ago'.[2]

The novel vindicated Williams's ambition as a writer. He recast it after Chatto refused his two other novels, one of which (*The Grasshoppers*) he urged upon Parsons as something upon which 'I have never in my life worked so hard ... I hope more than I can easily say that you like it ... and will publish it'.[3] Now his novel was out, and well spoken of; *Woman's Journal* [*sic*] declined it for serialisation, but Horizon Press in New York took it on. Now he was a novelist he had conspicuously justified his kind of cultural analysis, which had so reposed upon Leavis's old injunction to keep thought fully charged with the content of experience and unswervingly faithful to it. He had repaired in his own life the split in the academic divisions of labour between criticism and creation. He could stand, moreover, as an example to all those in the New Left who fervently shared Williams's view that personal creativity of this conventional kind – making your own art-objects (and being good enough to get them published or exhibited) – was a way of fighting back at the stupefaction of consumerism, of single-handedly refusing the categories of an alienating society and repossessing your own work. When *The Long Revolution* followed in March 1961, just a few months before Raymond's fortieth birthday, Williams became the leader, the celebrity, and the moral example the New Left was looking for, and for whom a space was marked out.

The years since *Culture and Society* and *The Uses of Literacy* had not only led to the formation of *New Left Review*, the founding of the 'Partisan' coffee-house on the club's premises, the spontaneous generation of the thirty-odd New Left Clubs up and down the country. Also, 1958 was the year in which the Campaign for Nuclear Disarmament was launched by an exemplarily genteel, high-minded and admirable group of Hampstead worthies, including Bertrand Russell as its non-titular head and Michael Foot as its resident MP.

CND of course became a vast international movement in the first four years of the 1980s. Heaven knows whether it did its bit towards ending the cold war. What it certainly did in those later years was testify to a big shift in what Williams famously called 'the structure of feeling' in a society, and gave expression to new feelings on the part of millions in the generation of the day that this unnecessary, perilous and extravagant sham was over.

164

In 1958 the structure of feeling was rather different and local to a much smaller fraction of (more or less) British society. The initiators of CND were grandees, intellectuals, writers, politicians, clergymen of that classically British formation whose philanthropic liberalism stretches back to the days of the First Reform Act, and those years in the 1840s when it seemed to many that the island might have its very own, full-blown and Jacobin revolution.

It was from those ancient days that the customs of what is called 'single issue politics' came. Single issue political movements are no more than they seem: the spontaneous and collective arousal of outrage, protest and resistance on the part of an informal, generally inchoate group of people who organise at large but without a political party in order to stop or to put right what is going wrong. Such organisations count on the money and time of those with enough of each to fill the offices of the movement. They need a charismatic leader or two to keep them in good heart, as well as appropriately blind and stupid opponents in government. They also exhibit a distinct aetiology, rising and falling in a few years either as some concessions are won, or defeat is obvious and people turn back to their own affairs. They are not insurrections. In Britain since 1832, they have included Chartism, trade union rights, Ireland (frequently), redundancy, unemployment, women's suffrage, housing, anti-Semitism and anti-anti-Semitism, taxes, wars and rumours of wars.

They must, to be believable, have numbers. In 1958, the founders had no idea what their support would look like. That is of the nature of single issue politics. They sensed, correctly, something on the move out there, something disturbing the deep sleep of a sufficient number in the somnambulist public.

When the Aldermaston marches began, starting out from the Atomic Weapon Research Establishment near Reading, and trailing cheerfully into London over several nights, kipping down in church halls and on the floors of friendly houses, it seemed amazing in 1959 that 100,000 souls could stir themselves so cheerfully to sing their dutiful, badly written songs and suffer the blisters during the forty-odd miles to Trafalgar Square.

The New Leftists were thrilled, as well they might be. Although they were themselves politically so self-conscious, they didn't have a programme, still less, as Peter Sedgwick scornfully complained,[4] a political–economic analysis which would remotely satisfy a Marxist. What they did have was, precisely enough for them, a strong feeling for the politics of culture, a politics in which feelings themselves were acknowledged as the defining feature of political commitment. If the tough eggs of the Marxist sects dismissed this as romantic utopianism, too bad for them.

Such keen and vivid feelings, nightly apparent in the motley lectures, songs to the guitar, daringly barbecued foods, and easy-going uniforms of the 'Partisan', looked not for messianic redemption or political murder by a party, but a longer, pacific, remoralising of civic life. Since the Labour Party was the only party with even a reflex response to the adjective 'moral', these new, soft-hearted but winningly cheerful herbivores counted themselves in on that side.

Man-eating revolutionaries couldn't stand this. But nor could they neglect CND, the only thing that had looked like a mass movement in Britain since the war. So they joined, and the ranks of the marches swelled to six figures, and Edward Thompson, steering what he said between old CP and New Left, put the New Left Clubs at the head of the quietly historic change in things.

> the Clubs and discussion centres will be places beyond the reach of the interference of the bureaucracy, where the initiative remains in the hands of the rank-and-file ... Their influence will pervade the Labour movement, as the Campaign is coming to pervade it; but because this influence derives from ideas it will elude administrative control. The bureaucracy will hold the machine; but the New Left will hold the passes between it and the younger generation.[5]

This was optimistic, and a bit over-excited, as Thompson tended to be at that date. But there was something in it. Membership of the New Left Clubs was academic – students and teachers, for sure, and pretty few workers; but even then the Labour Party, already eight years out of office, was mutating slowly into the party of the workers in the nationalised industries and the welfare state. Students and teachers alike shared an attractively sensible view that the capitalist state was a monolithic Thing, and that all that could be done about it was to use socialism as an argument with which to try to keep the Thing up to a semblance of its own professedly liberal standards. Nuclear weapons marked the lowest, most horrible, most uncontrollable and, indeed, suicidal plunge of those standards. A cheerful objection or two was in order. For the rest of politics, well, that was a matter of making one's own little enclave within which the civic virtues could sufficiently thrive and grow until those people picnicking there – one's children, one's pupils and students – could take on the hue of goodness, and bear their own, mildly Quakerish sort of witness to a good political life. The Williams family had joined the marches in 1959, and trudged with their new friends down to London, staying with Doris Thomas on the way to Leigh.

The Long Revolution, at least in its closing section 'Britain in the Sixties', spoke directly to the new friends they had met in this constituency. It was and is an odd book, like all Williams's books as much a collection of essays as a work with a single theme, unified by his entirely characteristic tone and style. The revolution of which he spoke took in partly the conventional usage of the term, as in 'industrial revolution', to mean large-scale change and upheaval directed not by political purpose but by structural and productive forces. But he remained enough of a Marxist to include the Jacobins' meaning of the word in his title, and in writing of 'a cultural revolution' he also intended to include the strong push of social classes, particularly his father's, to capture and possess the instruments of literacy, of public communication and cultivation, and to win their knowledge of these in the face of resistance from those who fought to keep the power and mystery of knowledge in their own hands.

Williams thereby set the class struggle down in the classroom, and thrilled a whole readership of students and teachers. He presages a revision of Marxism which would substitute – in a later phrase – 'mode of information' for mode of production, which is to say that the defining relation of power is capital-as-information rather than as manufacture.

He begins with his essay on creativity, not one of his more impressive efforts, cumbrously connecting an undefined 'art' to what Leavis once happily called, in a phrase Williams would have done well to thank him for, 'the inevitable creativeness of ordinary everyday life', and placing both in the undifferentiated airwaves of human communication. He then goes back to his familiar opposition between Culture with a capital C, the 'best that has been known and thought', and the culture of the anthropologists, understood as a 'whole way of life'. He displays this opposition to make porous the boundary between art and life, urging that in order to understand either they must each be returned to a context in which they figure as distinguishable elements in a totality. 'Totality' is an analytic concept with a long history, especially in Marxist thought,[6] but I believe Williams came on it unaided, even though Georg Lukács had anticipated him in another land and language.

In any case, he doesn't use the word 'totality'. He coins 'structure of feeling'; this is to be a 'term as firm and definite as "structure" suggests, yet it operates in the most delicate and least tangible parts of our activity'.[7] The formula gives him the theoretic centrality of the arts as especially formative of feeling in society; it gives him the connection between the honourable name of 'ordinariness' and exceptionality; it gives him his always-Hegelian instrument of analysis, which is to say, Williams's usably simple model of social change, in which feelings and meanings come through in each new generation and class in a general assertion of *difference* shaped by and shaping of all the key relationships of life. Such a model makes fearsome play of that at once theoretic, protean and sentimental word 'relationships', but it has the great merit of making our deepest feelings into the subject and object of history.

He illustrates the application of his term to his much-visited 1840s, repeating the excellent bromide that the great creations of those days certainly include the railway train as well as the trade union movement, and fastening this analysis to the then novel argument that to counterpose individuals to society makes for a misleading diagram of our lives.

167

He broached the sociology of the 1980s, which Anthony Giddens and Pierre Bourdieu, working in different traditions, were to bring to full-blown theory. (In 1969, talking to Bill Webb in Budapest, Georg Lukács said in the appropriate mid-European accents: 'People used to think there was a body–soul dichotomy. Now no intelligent person believes that. Eventually they will come to see that there is no individual–society dichotomy either.')[8] By his usual method, he sorted between words to describe different ways of being in a society (member, subject, exile, person) before plumping, as was to be expected, for some much more communitarian, reciprocally self-and-other-making picture of society than liberalism allows.

Throughout the lengthy first two parts of the book, Williams seeks, in sometimes very thin and abstract air, to catch and hold the way in which people shape their dominant meanings and values into a form, and how this form then makes their lives. He looks into the always palpitating and veering space between cultural form and the living spirit, and tries to measure it by writing a history of expressive forms in the nineteenth century: novels, newspapers, drama, everyday speech. Some of these are clumsy (the 'Standard English' chapter, in my view), and some of them are plodding ('Realism and the Contemporary Novel', which had been published in *Partisan Review* and *U and LR*). All of them are marked, however, by his strenuous efforts to grasp something at once slippery and profound. He strove always to see how the collaborations of language made for a world-reality which in turn made people in its own image; he then tried to catch the moment at which something new changed the making of the real; finally, he hoped that the new feeling would make for a new form capable of creating a better society.

He worked at these shiningly humane inquiries and homilies in a thick, at times downright dreary prose: 'It is certain that any effort to achieve a contemporary balance will be complex and difficult, but the effort is necessary, a new realism is necessary, if we are to remain creative ... [blah, drone] ...'[9] That kind of stuff made anybody restless and apt to impoliteness; still does. But it was always part of Williams's way.

Part III, which really got read and discussed in the clubs, is a lot brisker; it remains curiously unattached to all that precedes it. He starts with a perfunctory linking passage – a mere paragraph – and then launches into 'Britain in the Sixties', denying the official narrative that British democracy has been moving steadily towards greater and greater emancipation, with fulfilment and opportunity more and more equally available.

He rejects some of the basic terminology of this world-picture, its production of triviality and the propaganda of spurious wants and needs circulated by advertising, and decorously dismisses one or two of the wretched characters in the plot – 'consumer', 'manager' and 'the standard of living'. He stands up for strikers, which caused a hiss of indrawn breath

168

in the reviewer in *The Times*, and for communal services as against private choices. And he roundly rebuts the complacency of the day which asserted that democracy was doing fine in all its institutions, especially Parliament, pointing to the massive Labour support in the country's popular vote, substantially unexpressed at that date by numbers of representatives, and in an early use of an appeal first well-worn and then corrupted, contending for greater participation throughout the British polity. The repair of these distortions, which come through in the injuries of class, would, he thought, be much accelerated by replacing the House of Lords with an elected second house, contriving a far more egalitarian wage-structure, hauling more of private capital into public control, and above all – the theme of so much of his later life's work – recognising and using in the name of a whole people and its natural creativity the extraordinary fact of the new technology of public communications, dominated by television. Finally, he looks to the possibility of a new generation, feeling differently and building those different feelings into a structure of dissent, bringing about that next turn of the long, long revolution.

Where can a man or woman of honour be except on the Left? After Fascism and after Stalinism, it is still so plain that capitalism is itself morally repulsive, and liberalism either conscienceless or gutless in its public dealings much of the time. So to keep up the discipline of opposition and criticism to the roaring depredations of both was then and is now the prime duty of teachers and intellectuals. The danger, even the likelihood is that the habit of opposition becomes so settled, it is hard to work *for* anything official, or ever to see that power may speak for value.

It was a habit Williams sometimes saw in himself, generally in his fiction; and sometimes not. In the final section of the book, he was exemplarily poised, and direct in his expression, too. Insofar as he had written a political programme, it accorded well enough with the left hand of what Anthony Crosland wrote a year or two earlier in *The Future of Socialism*; it would be nice to see some of each programme enacted in Britain almost forty years later. But there was nothing in what Williams wrote, except for the surely crazy suggestion that Parliament be re-elected every two years, which the Labour Left would not enthusiastically support. It was a programme to which Attlee's great reforming administration of 1945 could have looked forward once the post-war reconstruction and its immediate tasks were completed. What Williams distinctively added was the realm of the cultural as expressed in the systems of public communication, and his powerful concern to make it possible for these truthfully to express the real feelings and best values of the common people of his society, as conceived by him at their best.

It is an odd book. Part of it is hurriedly put together without proper links; parts exhibit the self-teaching of someone puzzling out questions

169

better sorted out long ago by other people: T.H. Green was much stronger on the common good than Williams.[10] Quite a lot looks more like a text-book exposition rather than original scholarship, a tendency as strong as one would expect in a man who spent so much time writing alone, trusting only his own sense of direction, with instruction and collaboration from no one else. Like *Culture and Society* – not a trivial point this, but also expressive of something indurate in Williams which, precisely, *refuses* communication and exchange – the book is very badly referenced, the indexing perfunctory and the bibliography a disgrace.

Whatever its faults, the book caused quite a stir, and was even more fully noticed than its older sibling. It is a striking fact that by the time of the interviews in *Politics and Letters* Williams was so much more settled in and at ease with his position as leader of the Establishment of Dissent – an institution required of their nature by liberal societies – that it was with an audible self-satisfaction that he recalled 'a quite unforgettable degree of hostility'[11] in the reception accorded the book.

In point of fact, although there was certainly severe criticism, much of it came from serious people seriously disappointed with the faults of what one of the most sympathetic of them, Richard Wollheim, called in the more or less Tory weekly *The Spectator*, 'a work of great originality and power', and one which partook, in a term Wollheim used only approv-ingly, of 'the English dream', 'the ideal of collective, unalienated folk society, where honest men work together and create together, the ideal of Ruskin, William Morris, and Leavis'.[12] Indeed, it is indicative of Williams's state of mind in 1979 as well as his calm assumption that in 1961 his book clearly merited such prominence that, speaking of Richard Crossman's laudatory review which was given three full columns on the features and editorial page of the *Guardian* on the very day of publica-tion, Williams later dismissed the review and doubted that Crossman had read the book through.

Now Crossman, later a flashing sort of light in a Labour Cabinet and a big noise in both letters and politics, may have been foolish but he was not a fool. He made his criticisms, some of them like everybody else's directed against Williams's murky prose and abstract idiom, but called it, to the publisher's joy, 'the book I have been waiting for since 1945 – the book which no one of my generation could possibly have written'.[13]

But the later Williams could not, for the sake of his audience and constituency in 1979, tolerate support from such a senior voice in the Party, even though in more easy-going days he had known and liked Crossman. Now he dismissed him. He insisted on recollecting his work as having been pushed away into the margins of dissent. More than that, his intellectual habits of solitude and indifference became such that he rejected all criticism as merely the product of political and disciplinary blindness and partiality. So the traits of murkiness, the lack of specificity,

Raymond Williams with his mother, Esther Gwendolene Williams, Teignmouth, 1930

With his father, Harry Williams, Pandy, 1926

The house where Raymond Williams was born (photograph: Hilary Britland)

The Holy Mountain (photograph: Hilary Britland)

The King Henry VIII Grammar School for Boys, Abergavenny

With Joy at Trinity College, Cambridge, 1940; Raymond had wiped off Joy's lipstick, of which he disapproved (photograph: Michael Orrom)

TWENTYONE

NUMBER FIVE   FRIDAY, 27 JULY, 1945   ONE MARK

LANDSLIDE TO LABOUR
ATTLEE ONE OF POTSDAM BIG THREE

FIRST CLEAR LABOUR MAJORITY

Bracken, Beveridge, Grigg Out

Labour have won the General Election with a majority which has come as a sensational overthrow of expectations. With less than twenty results still to be declared, Labour has won 386 seats, against the Conservatives' 194. The Liberal Party got the dismal score of eleven, although over two million people gave them their votes. Fourteen Liberal Nationals were returned, ten Independents, three Independent Labour Party, two Communists, and one Commonwealth. The Labour majority is thus an absolute one of 151 over all other parties and groups (some of which will, of course, support them).

A few minutes after Mr. Churchill handed his seals of office to the King last night, Mr. Attlee arrived at the Palace to receive the formal royal invitation to form a Government. All the Labour leaders have been returned, and there is intense speculation as to the exact composition of the new administration. Its effects on the Potsdam meeting of the Big Three are a particular discussion point, as the new Foreign Secretary will have to fly back with Mr. Attlee to resume the conference with President Truman and Generalissimo Stalin.

Among members of the late Government who were defeated are Mr. Brendan Bracken (former First Lord of the Admiralty — defeated in Paddington by General Mason-MacFarlane), Mr. Amery, Sir Donald Somervell (former Home Secretary), Sir Walter Womersley, Col. Llewellin (Food Minister), Sir James Grigg. (Minister of War), Mr. Ernest Brown, Mr. Harold MacMillan, and Mr. Richard Law (Secretary of the Board of Education). Other notable personalities who are out are Sir William Beveridge and Sir Archibald Sinclair, the two lights of the Liberal Party.

Two bye-elections are already pending at Monmouth and Bromley, where the Conservative Candidates topped the poll but had died before the result was declared. It will be interesting to see how many of the fallen stars will cluster round these constituencies in an effort to get a seat somehow.

Many close results were declared, the lowest majority, being one of four at Worcester.

We are standing by as we go to press for the names of the new Government.

which are hourly expected to be announced.

NATIONAL SURVEY

Taking a quick survey of the country the following trends are noticeable. Labour has gained 15 seats in Scotland, and now holds 37 out of 71. Mr. Gallagher (Communist) and Mr. Maxton and Mr. Mcgovern (Independent Labour Party) retained their seats. In N.E. England Labour swept the board, although Sir William Beveridge (Liberal) was beaten by a Conservative at Berwick. In the North and Midlands all the big cities and towns have registered big Labour gains; in the agricultural districts there have been few changes. Manchester has gone over to Labour, only one conservative retaining his seat there. Traditionally Conservative Liverpool and Birmingham have returned Labour majorities. Mr. Churchill's son and son-in-law are among the defeated Conservatives. In East Anglia there have been big Labour gains, and in London Labour took 78 out of 97 seats. Not one Liberal was returned for the London area. Sir Richard Acland (Commonwealth) failed badly, but Wing-Commander Millington (Commonwealth) retained his seat at Chelmsford. For the other minority parties the only comfort was a Communist gain at Mile End. D. N. Pritt, standing as Independent Labour, got an 11,000 majority over the official Labour candidate, General Mason-McFarlane (lately Governor-General of Gibraltar and Chief of Military Intelligence in the 1940 B.E.F.) decisively defeated Mr. Brendan Bracken (First Lord of the Admiralty) at Paddington after a very thrilling fight. Mr. Attlee, Mr. Bevin, and Mr. Morrison were all

returned with comfortable majorities. Mr. Morrison's seat being a Labour gain.

In the Home Counties the swing to Labour was less marked, and in the traditionally Liberal West Country three cornered contests often let the Conservative candidates in on a minority vote. Michael Foot defeated Mr. Hore-Belisha at Devonport.

In Wales Labour held all its old seats with increased majorities, and gained seven more. Earl Lloyd-George's old seat was won by a Conservative.

DEPOSITS LOST

All over the country one hundred and fortyeight candidates lost their deposits; conspicuously absent from them was Mr. Churchill's opponent at Woodford (an odd independent with a plan) who polled ten thousand votes against Mr. Churchill's twentyseven thousand.

Approximate totals of votes are :—

Labour	11,500,000
Conservative	9,000,000
Liberal	2,250,000

FLASHBACK - B.L.A. ELECTION CAMPAIGN

Gnr. Kipling ("Y" Battery) says "Vote Labour" at an open-air meeting, at which all parties had their representative speakers.

BRUSSELS PARADE TOMORROW

The Regiment's contingent for the Guards Division Brussels parade — eight officers and one hundred and fifty men — left on Wednesday for the outward half of their 1600 mile trip. Major P. P. Shervington was in command, with Captain R. A. Johnson as Brussels Adjutant. It is not certain whether the Commanding Officer, who is flying back from leave in England, will arrive in Brussels in time for the parade.

On Saturday after a rehearsal, the parade takes place, and the Burgomaster presents standards or plaques to all regiments of the Guards Division, and to our own regiment. In the evening there will be two dances — the ball at the Hotel de Ville, where the Belgian Queen Mother, and the Belgian Regent Prince Charles will be present, and the dance at the 21 Club. On Sunday morning the Welsh Guards will adorn the statue of Manekin Pis in full-dress uniform, complete with bearskin. On Monday, our contingent will return. As faithful newsmen, we shall ask them for a full report, but as individuals, we who are left will suffer in silence and ask "What has Brussels got that Finnoberg hasn't got, anyway?"

REGIMENT TO FLY

The Regiment has been offered sailplanes in order to form a Gliding Club, and "Z" Battery are taking the lead in its formation.

Already a number of men have expressed their interest to learn, and it is confidently expected that once the planes arrive there will be a very large body of supporters. Non-flying members are discouraged — but anyone who has experienced the thrills of gliding should easily be able to persuade his friends to join.

Get out them wings, and them parachutes.

So The Ban's Really Lifted?

"Yes, Buddie, you're my man."

"English nicht compris."

"Don't look round now"

Maybe we're wrong. Maybe it's not fraternisation. We never could tell Estonians from East Prussians on sight — especially in swimming costumes.

Twentyone, the regimental newspaper

Delivering the proposal speech at the founding conference of the Socialist Society, London, 23 January 1982 (photograph: Andrew Wiard)

The cottage in Wales (photograph: Hilary Britland)

'The best cut tweeds on the left'
(photograph: Welsh Arts Council)

With Frank Kermode during the MacCabe Affair, Cambridge, 1981 (photograph: Times Newspapers Ltd)

Do first

Fixed forms
social & cultural authorities
and censorship
academies
market
bourgeois taste

discovery of unconscious (unconscious for 1)
language denaturalised
reformulation & questioned
narrative
self-reflective text

history < (ideology)

→ But this is modernism : a selected version
of the modern, which
offers to appropriate
the whole of modernity

20 HOW?

MEDIA Frontal/level   Changes in media
                        new media (photography, cinema,
                                     radio, television
                                     reproduction or recording
MOVEMENTS   New schools or manifestos (had been defining
25   now self-promoting Futurists
                                                                          himself
                                                                          etc

Next historical
level

METROPOLIS   New (metropolitan) cities
                        (imperialism)
                        ⎰ Paris, Vienna
                        ⎱   Berlin, London
MOBILITY   [CITY OF   ⎱ New York
            STRANGERS]
EXILES   ⎰ Exiles : Apollinaire & Joyce
                ⎱   to Beckett or Ionesco
                ⎱ Emigrés : from Russian revolution
                                 — formalists

                └ language theories REPRO | SYSTEM | SOCIAL SYSTEM
                 └ visual strangeness
                    narrative   clearly political
                    (state of mind etc

ANTI-BOURGEOIS Anti-bourgeois
                                    ⎰ Aristocratic
                                    ⎱ Proletarian

Brecht   DIVIDES   (Modernism divides politically
Mayakovsky
Picasso   — Brecht / Toller — communism
Silone   D'Annunzio   Johst / Benn — fascism
40   Lewis   ⎰ Marinetti — fascism
                Marinetti   ⎱ Mayakovsky — bolshevism
                Eliot   British — Yeats, W. Lewis / Eliot
                                                    / Pound + Modern)

Lecture notes, 1987

Raymond Williams with his portrait by John Bratby (photograph: Mark Gerson)

the generalised uplift in his codas, all become part of his signature, deep in the style that was certainly the man.

In the New Left Clubs, and within the talkative, friendly, authentically civic and big-hearted conversation of the bigger book-reading and middle-class movement of CND, Williams was undoubtedly man of the moment. Goodness knows if Bertrand Russell read the book, but Kingsley Martin, editor of the *New Statesman*, Michael Foot, Canon Collins, and the wonderful Peggy Duff, lifelong and indomitable peace-fighter, all on the main committee, certainly did. And Williams's ally, comrade, co-member of the *New Left Review* editorial board, career-long friend and critic, Edward Thompson did.

Thompson read it all right. His two part essay[14] on *The Long Revolution* was one of his most telling pieces of reflection upon political action and its meaning. He handsomely praises Williams as 'our best man', and that was indeed how the New Left decided to take him.

Thompson was writing his review through April and May of 1961. As always with that great man, and despite his admiration for his friend, the review is spikily personal as well as much harder on Williams's conceptual apparatus than anyone had been so far. He objected that no one could tell the difference in Williams's usage between 'culture and not-culture', and offered to give the too-inanimate notion of culture as a way of life the missing friction by Marxising the definition as 'way of struggle'. He then used William Morris as a trick by which to turn the intentional and expressive end of culture into 'handled experience'.

Thompson's hard thought, because a friend's, touched Williams's thinking more nearly, although, as Thompson complained, he rarely responded to criticism explicitly. At the time, there was the keen pleasure of attention and acclaim. The fame of *Culture and Society* still spread (as far as what was then Ceylon, in 1961) so that Williams was obliged to write to Chatto asking them to spread out their payments 'as Doubleday's advance pushes me badly into surtax'.[15]

Williams's confidence in himself, the severe discipline at the typewriter every working morning since before he first went to Seaford, since the first draft of *Border Country* written on his portable in the spare bedroom at the Dallings' house in Barnstaple during the summer of 1946, these qualities had never faltered. So he took success as it came, but for a single-income family in which the earner's salary on a fixed contract (renewed in August 1960 for another five years) was still measurably below £2,000 per annum, the royalties and advances were very welcome. If fame was not the spur, it was still a strong part of his proper ambition. The money was in any case a great relief, not least because the lifelong conflict in him between his communitarian and his privately ambitious parts was easily reconciled by the sacred name of family good when it came to his children's education.

It hadn't been a problem in Hastings, where Merryn and Ederyn passed the examination to the grammar schools ('our crazy Welsh names,' Merryn said, 'no one can spell them, they couldn't tell if mine was a boy's or a girl's'). When they moved to Oxford, Gwydion Madawc was only 10, bright but not as tractable as his elders. So the Williamses did as North Oxford did, and paid their children's fees to the local private schools.

Douglas Hewitt, who joined the Delegacy in Oxford having been a WEA tutor since 1945, looked at this move a bit drily.

Douglas Hewitt

> The thing about Raymond was that he was very ambitious and thought he ought not to be. He was a great believer in equality but he sent his kids to the Direct Grant school, and paid for them. Links with working-class culture are only a crux for the Left-intelligentsia in Britain where schooling is so important, and the private schools so clearly marked off. It sets up the conflict of privilege.

The business of committing one's own children to the undoubtedly more modest academic standards, less cultured culture,[16] conspicuously fewer successes in higher education which ordinary state schools exhibit in England and Wales came sometime in the 1960s to be an earnest token on the Left of one's best intentions for a more egalitarian future. (A generation later, Williams's pupil and *cause célèbre* Colin MacCabe outraged his whole staff at the British Film Institute by transgressing this principle, and had to take to the pages of the *New Statesman* in self-justification.) The Williamses walked through the taboo without a flicker.

It's a useful example of the clash of principles: family against public politics, getting on against neighbourly solidarity, private progress against civic identity, high culture against popular culture. There's nothing like it to break up dinner parties in Headington or Camden Town.

At the moment at which the Williams children went off in their school uniform, the National Union of Teachers was, to its everlasting credit, setting up what in 1968 would have been called a teach-in, but in October 1960 was just a hefty conference held at Church House, Westminster. In spite of its name, Church House is another of those *rendez-vous*, a large and official one close to the emanations from the Houses of Parliament themselves, in which the public-spirited and high-minded persons of society consider what is to be done about the fact that everything is going to the dogs.

It was a striking initiative for the NUT to take, not least because teachers had never really been part of those philanthropic élites but were now of a mind to become so. The conference was entitled 'Popular Culture and Personal Responsibility'. This was a bit doughy, perhaps, but so was popular culture in 1960, and none the worse for it. One moving spirit for the occasion had been Leavis's collaborator Denys Thompson, himself

172

doyen of that radical spirit in English teaching which had turned, in school classrooms as well as university ones, the weapons of close reading and practical criticism upon such innocent products of commercial culture as advertisements, the front pages of the newspapers, and upon far-from-canonical literature.

The conference was paid for by the NUT. It was a very good do. A bit self-important perhaps, but it was important that teachers assume and teach the responsibility they named in their title. (When the NUT tried to repeat it a decade or so later, the executive didn't vote the money. Nowadays one looks wistfully back at the Union's large-spiritedness in conceiving such a thing.) The best people spoke – men, of course, to a man, and spoke well – leftish academics (Richard Titmuss, Roy Shaw, Mark Abrams), artists (Richard Hamilton, Karel Reisz, Arnold Wesker), media barons and notables (Cecil King, John Freeman), and school teachers and administrators (John Dixon, Jack Longland). The two days were launched by the Secretary of State (R.A. Butler, bless us all) and closed by the knightly General Secretary of the NUT, the aldermanic Sir Ronald Gould. Raymond Williams was the opening speaker; he fired the first cognitive and political shots.

The conference was held during the weekend of 26 to 28 October. Church House was packed; the big auditorium held 800 people or so, most of them teachers, come from all over Britain in their best suits. Williams told them more or less what they could read four months later in *The Long Revolution*, and as he did so launched a new school and higher educational discipline, a discipline which fired their idealism and gave his listeners political and moral direction in their teaching.

Sitting in the audience were two sharp young New Leftists with degrees in English from Cambridge, who had been recently employed by Penguin to carry Allen Lane's great educational and democratic venture beyond the sixpenny paperback and the Pelican series. They promptly commissioned *Communications* as a topical Penguin Special; it became Williams's best-seller, and provided media studies with its first, and forever essential textbook. Denys Thompson, who had tipped them off, edited another Penguinful of essays from the conference[17] with a comparably long life, and a transcript of the entire two days was circulated in typescript by the NUT to its members, at 12s 6d per copy.

It did much for teachers' self-respect, that conference. It did much also to announce the permeation of New Leftism, that soft-hearted yet invigorating compound of pop and politics, new sociology, new movies, old lit. and old Labour, throughout the teacher constituency. It joined school to higher education informally, extra-murally of course, but actually as well. Those junctions have borne great strain in Britain since, but they have held. Not only held; on a cheerful day, one can see gossamer threads going out from the National Association of Teachers of English which, so to

173

say, came out of the NUT conference, to the sister associations in Canada and the United States, to Anglophone remnants of the old imperium, and leaving little traces of oldish-newish-leftish humanism even in Bombay and Johannesburg.

The autumn of 1960 opened, as I said, an astoundingly productive decade for Williams. Those ten years were perhaps the busiest, certainly the most exacting and public, perhaps also the happiest of his life.

Immediately after Crossman's review of *Culture and Society*, Bill Webb, recently appointed literary editor of the *Guardian*, asked Williams to do some reviewing. Webb was an English-with-German graduate of Trinity College Dublin, where he had been taught by the young Donald Davie who widened and deepened the interests that had led him to Leavis and *Scrutiny*. He hadn't had the job long but was to make of it, I would say, a success that went well beyond the readability and liveliness of weekly review pages. His rosy features and bushy beard, the charm of his twinkling-eyed way with you belied not only his sharpness of intelligence and insight, but also the no less sharp sense he had of his responsibilities – to the paper for sure, but to critical standards, to the political culture itself, just as *Scrutiny* enjoined. Over the period of his thirty-year reign, the *Guardian's* review pages carried the first but always deliberate thoughts on the books of the day of Williams (almost 300 reviews in three decades),[18] and of his best coevals, Michael Young, Hoggart, Kermode, Denis Donoghue, Richard Titmuss, Peter Townsend, a clutch of novelists – William Golding, Dan Jacobson, Doris Lessing once or twice, John Berger, John Fowles – as well as the two other stars of the *New Left Review* trio, Hall and Thompson.

Maybe science didn't get much space, but this Fabian–cultural formation, the new sociology, the old economic history and literary criticism, the politicians of culture, made for an impressive show over those years, made indeed for that programmatic aim of *Scrutiny* and Trotsky alike, an educated public with a distinctive style to its intellectual vanguard. Webb's loss to the *Guardian* knocked a big hole in the best that has been thought in Britain since. His was, you might say, the essential *Guardian* in spite of the *Guardian*.

Bill Webb

Raymond's first contribution was a leader-article on Young's *Rise of the Meritocracy*, and then another on *Joseph Ashby of Tysoe*. I had to fight a series of defensive actions on Raymond's behalf against the senior editors of the day – some of those impossible sentences! He *needed* an editor, and I was asking him at times to explore things *neither* of us knew much about ... It was Cold War time, so neo-Marxism in the *Guardian* was very exciting ...

Raymond found it hard to keep to 800–900 words, so I let him write longer

174

wherever I could make the space. He would run a couple of ideas of his own, do some real thinking in a review. He was tough but with a kind of openness and vulnerability, opening himself to attack. A kind of jokey ironising was always at a premium in Preston's *Guardian*. There'd be meetings of editors when others would groan at Williams.

He got fifteen guineas for the first leader-page article in those days, maybe eighteen for the second. (Old C.P. Scott used to make reviewers send the book back. All book receipts were entered in a leather ledger for a hundred years!) It was £100 per thousand words in 1991, £18 in 1961.

From 1964 on, there was a *Guardian* annual party for the literary pages. It used to be held at the National Liberal Club – where else? – in London, although the literary pages of the paper stayed in Manchester until 1975. Grand publishers like Billy Collins, Fred Warburg, Jamie Hamilton sat down all hugger-mugger with not only Raymond, Dan Jacobson, Frank Kermode, Hobsbawm and Co. but with young-sters who'd just done their first books, and there was a prize awarding in the middle of the do . . .

Raymond fiercely defended his own time. He was *driven*, I think, to do the kind of thing he did. I used to think he wrote novels out of political duty, a sense of the small number of *voices* in the contemporary novel, the loss of nineteenth-century polyphony. He complained like mad about Cecil Day-Lewis, then his editor at Chatto, cutting out the heavy bits from his own novels, and leaving in the bits where somebody moodily lights a cigarette. After 1979 another generation began to change the scale of things. Angela Carter, say, brought a bigger world and range of reference, Raymond was always on about 'English questions'. But I did a series for the paper on dissidents in the two Germanys between 1972 and 1975 and he was strongly interested.[19]

Across the mere eighteen months which included Williams's move to Oxford, and his second move a year later to Cambridge, he published *The Long Revolution* and *Border Country*, thrifty advance chapters of the first in *Monthly Review* and *New Left Review*, a chapter in Boris Ford's justly celebrated *Penguin Guide to English Literature*, a 'London letter' to the New York Left in *Partisan Review*, and a dozen and more reviews in the *Guardian* and the weeklies.

He also began to move towards his apostasy on the development of modern drama in which reactionary Eliot was replaced by progressive Brecht with a paper on Brecht in *Critical Quarterly*; he penned some first thoughts on tragedy in the same journal, and was well on the way with the second of his polyphonous novels, *Second Generation*. At the same time, the work at Oxford was a good deal heavier than in Hastings. He had his responsibilities as *de facto* Senior Tutor to meet, and was univer-sally praised for the forensic dignity and thoughtfulness with which he discharged these, even by those who viewed him a bit sardonically, like Arthur Marsh, or with outright enmity, like Hodgkin's successor, Frank Jessup. Williams sat in the chair of the tutorial advisory committee, was responsible for tutor training and class visiting, and was Resident tutor for three counties, including Oxfordshire. He had a class on 'Literature

175

and Society' in Aylesbury twenty-three strong, and the first year of a three-year course in Oxford on the novel with thirty-seven students, which was gravely visited and approved by Her Majesty's Inspector.

He was in demand all right; all of a sudden, he was further and imperiously demanded from a most unexpected quarter.

It used to be the way of the ancient universities not that they would, like other universities, advertise for new members of staff, but discreetly approach them, confident that no rational person could decline an offer of such grandeur. It was an assumption which only disintegrated under the Tory determination of the 1980s to hold down all public salaries, and vengefully those of the reprehensibly Left-inclined intelligentsia. In 1961, however, the assumption held. The English Faculty at Cambridge approved the proposal that a Faculty legate be sent to Oxford to ask Raymond Williams whether he would accept a lectureship at Cambridge, were one to be offered.

Williams would indeed be interested, he said, and the offer was duly made and accepted in April 1961. There is a slight taint of bad faith in the account Williams himself studiously developed of this transaction. He would say that a letter telling him he'd been appointed to the job came out of the blue, yet another token of old English class arrogance. This is part of his habit of contradicting the ambitiousness and the hope of reputation which he so strongly felt and fulfilled. He spoke of Cambridge with habitual belittling. But for a man of Williams's gifts and preoccupations, as well as his formation, he could hardly have preferred driving to Aylesbury in the dark to walking to the old School Lane lecture rooms in the morning, just off the main street of the city. He *couldn't* have wanted to go on with the evening classes, even though he was down to two a week plus the summer school; the pleasures of teaching students as bright as those he would meet at Cambridge would compensate more than enough for missing the 'dreadful refresher courses' Williams himself detested, to say nothing of the worthy bookish housewives so loving of *Four Quartets* whom he so much wished were miners, steelworkers, communists.

When he got the job, Jack Woolford said that he openly envied Raymond; Williams himself said, in anxious self-justification, to Douglas Hewitt, 'Douglas, *you'll* understand my going to Cambridge' and, Hewitt added, 'after his move he said unfriendly things about the Delegacy. They were resented.'

Douglas Hewitt

I have had a fair amount of choice in what teaching I have done and I have come to the conclusion that teaching adults is more fun than undergraduates. I am glad to have done both for many years, but if I had had to choose I would have chosen the adults. So I was surprised Raymond always said the same, though he tended to emphasise the politico/moral values more than my rather hedonistic view. His passionate advocacy of extra-mural work was therefore in some contradiction with his decision to go to Cambridge. Most people would have been happy to be translated to Cambridge and never felt the need to justify it. Raymond did feel this need.

In his letter of resignation,[20] Raymond wrote, 'in many ways I am very sorry to be leaving', but no one would have dreamed of criticising his departure for such a post. Merryn spoke of his enormous excitement and exhilaration when the news came, even if she and her brothers were a bit less exultant, only having left Hastings a few months. After he had gone, Frank Pickstock, organising secretary of the tutorial classes, wrote to a colleague:

In later years some of Raymond Williams's colleagues were better than him as a tutorial class teacher in the sense of drawing out individuals. Still, he had something else – not just an academic brain, but the personality and purpose of an inspired educator.[21]

It's not a sure distinction, but what Pickstock meant becomes clearer in Raymond's life, after he had moved to Cambridge.

In order to move, he had to pass beneath a fearsome portal. The only official welcome Cambridge offered him was the lead article in the house magazine, *The Cambridge Review*.[22] It was a review of *Culture and Society* and *The Long Revolution* by one Maurice Cowling, a patrician figure about the Cambridge History Faculty, a man of irremediable caste confidence and a strong dose of Pecksniffian Christianity.

This worthy entered the commonplace book of the Left by his ineffable grouping of Williams with 'English radicals, lapsed Stalinists, academic socialists and intellectual Trotskyites' whose institutional homes are to be found in 'the extra-mural boards, the community centres, and certain Northern universities'. It is a richly period piece of class insolence. The mixture of languor and *hauteur* – Cowling appears throughout his own article in the third person as a gentleman should – has by and large disappeared from English snobbery, even though *that* beast still has plenty of ravening life of a different kind left in it. It was a pity because alongside Cowling's carefully contrived and unremitting offensiveness, he had some just criticisms: like Cowling himself, Raymond didn't know, and didn't care that he didn't know, much about his class enemies. (As John Dunn later observed on Williams's behalf, a reliable class enemy is the dissenter's best friend.[23] The darts of 'elevated generosity' and 'prophetic fogginess' would and do stick when launched by other, less vulgarly indiscriminate hands. But Cowling's loftiness, his 'no doubt it would be nice if . . .', his crass political partiality, turn his review, as well he knew, into a merely social gesture of rebuff, one, as he did not know, Williams's own steeliness and his justified confidence in his qualities made him well able to despise, as it deserved. When he later spoke feelingly of Cambridge as being 'one of the rudest places on earth', 'shot through with cold, nasty and bloody-minded talk', it was Cowling's little effort he thought of first.

But there were friends too when he got there. He and Joy bought the house of the man whose post he was filling, David Daiches, who was returning to a Chair in his native Scotland, where he was his nation's greatest scholar of its most celebrated cultural product, its malt whiskies.

White Cottage, Hardwick was and is a long, plain four-bedroomed house, stoutly built in the early nineteenth century in a village three or four miles out of the town along the Bedford road. It stands on flat, windswept arable lands reaching eastwards to the Fens. In 1961 it had no dampcourse, the stone floor built straight on to the earth and a high water table. The house was always so damp the Williamses used to roll up the rugs in the sitting room when they went away; the water stood on the wall of the downstairs lav; the dark, narrow kitchen would barely hold the five of them, their beaten-up old gas cooker beside the antique coke stove against the inside wall.

The Williamses didn't care a jot for these disfigurements and discomforts. They didn't have a domestic aesthetics, nor any plan to enlarge the kitchen to make themselves a bit more room, still less to dry it out. They kept until they left in 1983 the ancient iron radiators with their deep ribs and thick pipes like ocean-going boilers. They ignored damp and dark and cold (and Cambridgeshire is frequently all three). So too they ignored the high, ivy-stifled front fence, the crabbed apple trees in the garden, the ghastly old wartime asbestos lean-to, which served as garage all the twenty-two years of their stay in Hardwick. As his son Ederyn, just 15 when they moved to the house, recalled:

Ederyn Williams

All of us were unpractical, technical incompetents. We used to read *all* the time. I taught myself to ride a bike at 14, while were staying at 6 Merton Street for the Oxford summer school. Merryn *never* learned to steer, bike or car. Raymond (and Merryn) disregarded the everyday things, so I learned to do them. He was hopeless, for example, with the motor-mower, and got so infuriated. Joy would say 'go and do your homework' to him.

The family was completely self-enclosed, but quite natural in the assumptions absorbed by us as children. Raymond took pride in what he did, but there was no pressure on us.

The family was more like a work-unit. It wasn't a family in which the language of the feelings was discussed, ever. We talked about *work*, and Joy was utterly given to the work of the family, she had no friends of her own at all. [Her domestic duties were her job. She didn't take any pleasure, say, in cooking, it was just her job, plain English food.] Raymond was one of the least status-conscious people I've ever come across. He was completely uninterested in cars and their appearance,

178

for instance. It just had to go. The last car he had was a ten-year-old Austin Maestro which I'm still driving.

He was dedicated to keeping his life extremely simple. He was modest. He didn't force his opinions on anyone, and did nothing just to *impress*. He wouldn't be impressed, either, or have anyone put something over him. Whenever he got a p.p. letter, he would say, 'If they can't be bothered to sign them, I can't be bothered to answer them.' It wasn't a question of grandeur, but a deep attitude. He had a terrific equability, an absolutely Victorian presence. He knew exactly that he was what he was.

No rituals either. He and Joy never wrapped up the Christmas presents, they came in the shop bag. You could say they were both low on ritual. Not mean, but non-ritualised. There was no tariff of presents. For their silver wedding in 1967 we just all went out for a Garden House Hotel dinner.

Of course, it was nice when there was a bit more money after *Culture and Society*. We went off camping each year in the old Vauxhall estate, with the back crammed with English foods, boxes of cornflakes, tins of corned beef, packets of tea, and the tent on the roof. Nine years we went camping. 1960 to Bandol, St Rémy, St Tropez. Two nights going down, stop at Juan-les-Pins, in 1961 on to northern Italy. We did the sights, sure, Orange, Tuscany, Venice, lived on steak and chips and what we brought. Mostly we sat scattered about the camp site in the sun, and read.

They were four miles out of town. Raymond had been appointed to a Fellowship at Jesus College whose small and pretty brick and stone courts with their quiet green gardens made for a more vernacular and homely home than his first college. He liked the familiarity of the wooden staircases and low beams, the flagged and cobbled courtyards with their neat lawns, and to begin with he attended, with a gleam of irony but real pleasure, the college feasts and ceremonies. E.M.W. Tillyard, his former tutor, now Master of the college, greeted him on his arrival with a fine old English barking bluffness: 'Williams, eh, Williams? Thing I remember about you is *boots*, Williams.' Not the Party line on the romantic poets, but his OTC boots.

The four miles were, however, his guarantee that he would get on with his own work, and do so out of the University. As in Hastings and Oxford, he worked every morning which remained free from lectures, and taught in college in the afternoon. In Cambridge, Faculty members have certain contractual obligations to lecture, but the content of their lectures is up to them. Nor is attendance by the students required. So the size of the audience is a measure of popularity, and on the whole of quality.

Williams launched himself straight into big topics: the English moralists from Blake to Lawrence (where he could rely on *Culture and Society*) in his first term (midday on a Monday), 'Aspects of Literature and Society' in three enormous bites, 1625–1785, 1785–1880, 1880–1910, across the whole academic year (on Tuesdays at 11 o'clock). Patrick Parrinder, as an undergraduate listener at Williams's lectures on the topic in 1963,

179

reproduced them as lucid notes. They refused the conventional metaphor of 'background' to 'literature', binding together the distinct, inseparable genealogy of thought, art, Church and State in arresting detail and with an exhilarating reach. Bacon and Hobbes, Jonson and Donne, are fastened not only to Puritanism and poverty, but to feelings and manner, and ultimately to tragic revolution and civil warfare.

The following year, 1962, he replaced the Moralists with Modern Tragedy, a book he now had planned and put up to Chatto as a proposal at the same time, trying as always to move very quickly from lecture notes to finished work, without the cumbrous but necessary conventions of scholarship.

> The first two parts [he wrote to Parsons] will not be technical analyses with footnotes but more like printed talks, then the third part a play of my own which I'm very keen on; it is based on the life of Milton, and comes through as tragedy, both personal and social.
>
> I know this adds up to an unusual book, but it might be read, don't you think? I just can't, now, go back to straight professional literary criticism, and anyway that has abundantly proved it can't handle tragedy.[24]

In the same letter he reports that he is looking for a typist to make the fair copy of *Second Generation*.

Joining the English Faculty at Cambridge in 1961 was, as the Cowling article indicates, a tricky business, quite unlike starting as a new member of staff anywhere else, including anywhere else in Cambridge. Williams captured a part of the Faculty's strange sociology when, writing an obituary for Leavis after his death in 1978, he remarked upon the way Leavis's circle 'serious, widely read and intelligent' as all its members were, were 'basically preoccupied with who was in and who was out, and in this, of course, even in negation, they retained and even emphasised the manners of their class'.[25] Of *any* class, one might add.

But the English Faculty was singular not in the bitter factionalism which was a product of these class allocations. It was only to be expected from the uses made of literacy at the higher levels of English cultivation that its members would judge one another as to be approved or rebuffed according to what they had read and how they had written about it. Lawrentians were not speaking to Joyceans, nor Jamesians to Hardyists; nor, rather later, Structuralists to standard bearers of the principles-of-literary-criticism; nor, today, traditionalists to relativists, the then-people to the now-party.

What was singular about the English Faculty was, first, a propensity intensified by the little monasteries of college life to ally very high but fragmentary intelligence, and the fluency that went with it, to a quite preposterous degree of moral scruple either over moral matters which didn't merit it or, more frequently, over merely personal or mannerly disagreements – modes of speech, idioms of argument and the judgements these led to – which really were more to do with social class than the life of the mind. Such disagreements were pursued with 'splenetic and vainglorious brawling', as we heard Kermode say,[26] largely because intellectual positions became so inextricable from personal life. Disagreement was disagreement over how to live. In some people – Leavis was one – there was a mad heroism in this insistence. In the Faculty at large it transpired as unfailing rancour, demeaning quarrelsomeness, a farcically complete inversion of those benefits of the cultivated life which the Faculty's great mentor, Matthew Arnold, had summarised as 'sweetness and light'.

The second singularity of the Faculty was precipitated from this more general climate of mutual enmities, even hatred. It was Leavis's presence itself, let alone that of his wife.

I have sketched something of the man when describing Williams's last year as a student in 1946. By 1961 Leavis was within a couple of years of his retirement, although he remained a member of the Faculty Board for some time after. The University had, not surprisingly, had its revenge on him by never awarding him a Chair, and widely accused of paranoia as he was, he had in a quietly English and academic way undoubtedly suffered persecution.

His disorientingly intense personality, vividly paradoxical, dominated the Faculty and plenty of the students. That intensity, the way he had of distinguishing a particular version of vivid, blazing, unaccommodating life in certain writers – Blake, Dickens, Lawrence, all of them just *too much* in their everyday dealings, too consuming of experience, too overwhelming of others – could carry people away, transfigure their sense of themselves, convert them. In the peculiar self-regardingness which Cambridge also engenders of its history, its class-formation and particularly among those who sincerely responded to those of its deep-toned bells which called them to true learning and study, Leavis's teaching was irresistible. If you could tell the quick from the dead in literature, you could tell them apart in life. Indeed, if in life they preferred dead authors to quick ones, they were dead anyway. And once you knew who was alive in literature, you could, as it were, earth their energy in your own body and soul, and live like them.

The history, the theodicy, and the politics to which Leavis's judgements led were, as I have said, quietly dotty. The way of life – unworldly, principled, blazingly honest, taking its pleasures domestically and its happiness from ordinary custom, provincial ways, unimpeded nature – had everything to be said for it, much of which spoke straight to Williams's heart. But he was far too steady a man to live at the high level of risk which Leavis's mode of confrontation with life and work required. His prudence and his equability were the epistemes of *his* history and politics, and they showed him plainly where Leavis went wrong.

Yet he became Leavis's successor as living example of high seriousness and political principle to the best young men and women coming to study his subject. There was much in him which responded straight to Leavis, his avocation, his utter uncompromisingness with bloody old England, snobbery, caste, all that. One of Williams's most telling bits of autobiography is a memoir of Leavis which Denys Thompson commissioned after the old man's death, in which Williams recalls an argument he had with Leavis about the syllabus, lending the story some of his happiest touches as a writer, bringing out their absolute difference of commitment to completely irreconcilable sets of principle, both fine ones.

Williams was, at the time, Secretary to the Faculty:

> The official business in which I had most to do with him was when a new paper on the novel had been proposed for Part II of the Tripos, and I, as secretary, had to convene a committee on it. I spent, in all, hours on the 'phone and in the street persuading Leavis to join it. He was quite sure he would not be wanted; I insisted that he especially was. He joined, eventually, and was very sensible and helpful. The crux was whether the paper should be the English novel, or the novel in general. He wanted the English novel only. A majority were against him ...
> 'But Dr. Leavis,' someone said, 'to understand the twentieth-century novel we have, for example, to read Proust and Kafka.'
> 'I have read them.'
> 'Then should not the students have the chance to read them!'
> 'It would be a misdirection. There is nothing relevant there.'
> 'But surely that would be for them to decide.'
> 'It would be a misdirection.'
> 'Because of reading in translation?'
> 'That too.'
> 'Then what about American novelists? Faulkner, for example.'
> At this point I have to hold on to my seat. I have the clearest memory of what was said next, and of the mood in which it was said: one of fierce pleasure in the argument but also of surprising conviction.
> 'Faulkner!' Leavis said. 'When the Americans moved in on Europe, after the War, they had to have a great novelist. That's who they chose, Faulkner.'
> Nobody knew, at the time, what to say after that. The general argument continued. Leavis could see that he was losing. Finally, with that open pleasure which usually accompanied what he supposed a decisive point, he turned to me in the chair.

'I put it directly to you, Mr. Secretary. The coherent course would be the English Novel from Dickens to Lawrence.'

He knew quite well that this was the title of my main current lecture course. He knew also, I think, that the course was an attempt at a sustained argument against *The Great Tradition*.

'All right,' I said, 'I think it is a coherent course. But a majority of the committee want some foreign novelists included, and I think their arguments are strong.'

... 'No, I am putting it to you, directly.'

'I could vote for either. They would be very different. But at the moment I'm an officer of the Faculty, trying to get the committee's decision.'

'To you,' he repeated.

The meeting resumed. Eventually a compromise was arrived at. He wrote after the meeting and said that I had 'done wonders with that committee'.

... 'If you had voted for Dickens to Lawrence,' he said later, 'it would have turned the committee.'

'I said I would vote for it.'

'You said for either.'

'Because that is my position. What I mainly wanted was a paper on the novel. Either would make a great difference to the Tripos.'

'You could have turned it.'

'No. The majority was clearly the other way.'

'You were not prepared to stand out and be isolated.'

'I have done that often. But on this it didn't apply. I wanted that paper, in either version.'

'I am taking the sense of your work.'

'Yes, and it is nearly all in a minority position. But isn't that the problem, working in any institution? So long as I can teach as I want, I have to accept a framework built by a majority I don't agree with.'

'No, you don't have to accept it.'

'Accepting it as you have. To continue the work. To put these other ideas in.'

He shook his head.[27]

The odd malicious remark about Williams was reported from the Leavis camp, almost certainly made by Queenie Leavis, queen of the night in her home town. The two men maintained an even, equal respect for one another.

It was the Faculty which seethed with detestation, and Leavis could not by his very own principles detach himself from it. Williams could and did. In 1964, Williams was doing his stint as Secretary to the Faculty Board at a time when a former friend of Leavis, a student of his, and a co-editor of *Scrutiny*, arrived to take up the senior Chair of English, the King Edward VII Professor of English Literature. Lionel Knights was a courteous, kindly and completely gentle man, bemused and horrified by the little boiling vat of spite into which the honour of his appointment had thrown him.

Before one meeting, the clerical secretary came to Raymond anxiously holding out a letter. It was from Mrs Leavis and addressed to Knights as Chairman of the Board. It made assorted formal complaints of a familiar kind in an inexcusably personal tone, and ended, 'I would wish you in hell were it not that, with your wife, you already live there'. What should she do with it? the secretary asked. Raymond crumpled it up and tossed it in the waste paper basket.

There is much that is symbolic in that anecdote: about Mrs Leavis, about Cambridge English, and about Williams. But he is the only one to come out with credit.

Still, for the first year or two of Williams's time in Cambridge, there was also commotion among the comrades. Stuart Hall had been editing *New Left Review* and running the office, handling Left Clubs correspondence as well as being deeply involved in CND, all on a tiny salary. The 'Partisan' meetings continued with their former flair, hundreds turned up for their dose of political charismatics in Bloomsbury hotels or at 100 Oxford Street where Humphrey Lyttleton played his joyful jazz. Speakers included Tom Mboya, Jomo Kenyatta's deputy, Tony Crosland, Doris Lessing, *Four-Gated City* just on its way. (Raphael Samuel was fired by a vision of Berlin night clubs in 1930; or so Hall said merrily.)

But Hall had been teaching three evening classes a week down at Bexleyheath, and he'd had enough. Charles Taylor was putting into the magazine a lot of the money which he had inherited from his French-Canadian grandfather, a senator in the Canadian parliament. Nobody knew anything about it, and Taylor never said a word. So Hall said he was going, and the first plan was that the *Review* would carry on with five editors. It had reached its twelfth issue, a huge one on housing, late and very expensively, with five editors. Two of these were bright new public schoolboys from Oxford, the others included Frances Kelly, Raphael Samuel, and Hall's deputy editor, an American with a bit of money and impeccable credentials from Students for a Democratic Society called Norman Fuchter.

The Oxonians were Perry Anderson, formerly from Eton, and Robin Blackburn. Anderson was and is of virtuoso eloquence, a serenely theoretic intellectual of quiet courtesy and steely purpose; he was barely 22 and rather rich. Blackburn, a beautiful, big, shock-headed youngster had an identical outlook, had read Sartre and de Beauvoir in French, had strong commitments to the Castro regime in Cuba where he and Anderson went off for Christmas in 1960, but was happy to serve as Anderson's junior. Both of them read and spoke at least three languages well.

Blackburn murmured that C. Wright Mills, the celebrated American sociologist whom he knew might serve as editor, but Hall backed Anderson and everyone was in favour.

Anderson had flinty views on what to do with the *Review*. He would ditch the uneasy mixture of up-to-date journalism, CND and anti-Tory polemics, investigative exposures and movie reviews, *ULR* moralising and *New Reasoner* economics. The new version of the *Review* would be a trans-continental and trans-Atlantic journal of neo-Marxist theory with a strongly revisionist turn, taking its lead from Sartre and Louis Althusser, a name then barely known in Britain, from early Marx and the unheard-of Italian, Antonio Gramsci. It would keep faith with the cultural emphasis that had made its signature, and which carried Williams's unique authority, but attach it to a more exigent and rigorous sociology than the old Marxist historians had ever read. Weber would be as much cited as Bernstein, Lévi-Strauss as Engels.

Anderson set himself the enormous task[28] of explaining, by way of a historically very lengthy, intellectually very terse analysis of the cumulative class-structuring of English society, the nature, magnitude, and utter becalming of its present hegemony and the state which perpetuated it. More raucously, his friend and ally Tom Nairn[29] wrote a fierce attack on the British Left, especially the Labour Party, as treasonously complicit in this state of genteel, anti-intellectual stupefaction. As Anthony Barnett, a pupil of Williams's in Cambridge between 1962 and 1965, and then for many years on the editorial board, said, 'When the Nairn–Anderson theses came out, they were the talk of the Left.'

By that date Anderson, whose succession to the editorship was perfectly legitimate, had coolly dismissed the old editorial board. With the exception of Williams and Ralph Miliband, they were all asked for their resignation. Some went in a dignified huff – John Saville; some went with a trenchant warning that theory was all very well but very hard to connect to living politics – John Rex; some went with righteous anger – Edward Thompson, who then wrote a long, eloquent and rather funny rebuttal[30] of the Nairn–Anderson theses to which Anderson fiercely replied,[31] when the need of the Left to heal its friendships was cryingly urgent.

Anthony Barnett

I was not a witness or participant to the takeover, but I talked about it with both Perry and Raymond. The picture that emerged was of the disintegration of the original *NLR*, after Stuart Hall found it impossible to continue. It was not viable. The Left may have marched in large numbers against the bomb, but it didn't read and it didn't write at the time. Thompson tried to oust the new editors and gaining

Raymond's support was crucial for him because with *Culture and Society* he had the public standing and the political breadth to condemn the takeover as improper. Raymond refused. He told me that he recalled saying that he hoped there would be 100 issues of *NLR* (this was when it was clear that there would be) and he sounded proud and felt vindicated. Why did Raymond refuse to move against Anderson and company? His recollection made clear that he knew it would be very hard to survive. His own magazine *Politics and Letters* had folded which I'm sure he never forgot. Raymond was always interested in survival. Second, and perhaps linked to this, he was fascinated by generations. Traditional leftists (in which I include Thompson) always believe *they* are correct and not only does this usually prove their downfall it is the central reason why they are so incapable of repro-ducing themselves – because they possess rather than hand on the baton. Raymond was different. He put life first. He watched out for change and was open to it. The new boys (they were boys) promised renewal and direction as well as survival – thanks to the fact that they had some money – for the *NLR*. It is easy to see Thompson as the radical and Raymond as the conservative. The opposite was the case. Raymond wanted change and embraced the new. Thompson was always resisting – it is unimaginable that he could have written a sympathetic and original book about the new culture of television. There may have been a third factor which should be added to ensure any account is not too idealised. Thompson had been rude and patronising about *The Long Revolution* when he reviewed it in *his* *NLR*. It might have given Raymond reason for a small smile to think that he had deprived Edward of a short counter-revolution.

Quarrels on the Left, quarrels in the English department; they have a comparable sociology. Both are rooted in very close working and intel-lectual relationships in which highly intelligent and articulate people hold passionately to noble ideals, and are quite unable to connect the good life they imagine to the damaged polity they can see. They hold also to a clear sense of what it would be to act well and efficaciously in that damaged world on behalf of its improvement, but they are quite unable to find ways of doing so. In such thwarted circumstances, the human propensity to rage and self-pity, personal blame and petulant vindictiveness are their readiest means of expression. For both groups, what is at stake are indeed matters of life and death, politics in an absolute sense. But for people like Williams and, indeed, Thompson, proper politics far outweighed the signif-icance of scholarly alignment and the moral stance this entails. What was at stake for them was the direction of a whole society, and what their whole intelligence could do to inflect it.

Even if they remained rather wary friends, one could see the moment of this passionate disagreement as indicative of a final divergence in the way a dedicated group gave themselves to the future. Thompson held to a native tradition of moral outrage and historical revaluation; he *hated* theory and completely rejected its new prophets. You could say he under-estimated the power of the new European capitalism just beginning to take shape; he certainly believed in the continuing actuality of his own

186

English tradition and trusted also in his indisputable mastery of its prose. His opponents were completely different, held almost to another metaphysics, even though they lived in the same small corner of political and intellectual life, in an island off the north-west coast of the mainland, thirty-odd years ago.

Only people with Raymond Williams's unusual calm and unusual capacity to absorb the turbulent feelings of others hold such groups together, or get beyond them. It takes a gift for indifference, as well, and this is inevitably allied to a proper egotism, a determination to do what you have resolved to do, and not let these people prevent you. Hence Raymond's powers of withdrawal, his lack of close friends, his absence of hilarity or gregariousness. Hence also his gift for talking past conflict towards a practical, working end.

It must have made him a terribly matter-of-fact father and husband; he couldn't possibly have been a lover. His massive pipe was scarcely out for a start – the White Cottage carpets reeked of pipe tobacco for twenty years. His fearsomely deep feelings were, as Cathy says of Heathcliff in a passage Williams later quoted quite calmly for its everyday truthfulness, like the living rock beneath; he hadn't that 'mind's recoil upon itself',[32] which makes possible passionate uncertainty, the loss of all gravity which goes with falling in love, the giving-of-oneself, the abandon. He was a sparing giver. He stuck to his timetable.

He stuck to it promptly with *Communications*, getting the book written, without a television, during his first year back at Cambridge. Merryn went off to the Perse, the best girls' school in town, Ederyn to Magdalen College School, Madawc to St John's College choir school, while father settled down in the poky little study with one small window at the back of the house, and thumped the old typewriter.

It's one of his best-known and bestselling books, even if it has its dull routines. Largely another textbook, readily grasped in both prose and method, it is successor to *Reading and Criticism*, but with the drastic change that it is addressed to a whole society, inviting its members to study themselves and acknowledge the immutable history which made them what they are, reminding them that the future is more tractable, if only they would grasp it for themselves.

So he goes through the history of the press, radio and television, as in *The Long Revolution*; commends the painstaking analysis of content (so many column inches to so many topics); tots up advertising, discusses effects, and writes out a curriculum. He ends with a small, touchingly optimistic manifesto – 'it is now more than ever certain that we shall have to get rid of a commercial television structure'[33] – and welcomes what was then called in the outline proposed by Michael Young 'the University of the Air' and later became the Open University.

It is an adult educator's document, and a school one also; none the worse for that, but unexceptionable. It came out of fifteen years and more of textbook-thinking and syllabus-preparation. The textbook manner stayed with him, as it was bound to, and kept creeping into later books. Hereafter, however, he imagined and addressed a very different student audience, and beyond the students, a much larger, more anonymous audience of well-disposed and public-spirited citizens. It is testimony to Williams's supreme achievement that he indeed found, created and held such an audience, held it, moreover, against the odds and across nearly three decades.

For the moment, the students who were his immediate and actual listeners, weren't classifiable, either, except as young men – and when he first went to Cambridge they mostly were young men – who were clever enough to get into Cambridge. Mostly, they had asked to be taught by Williams himself exactly because of admiring the work, of seeing that kind of intellectual endeavour as a way to forward the politics and idealism which fired them. They wanted Williams to *choose* them.

Charles Swann, a man of immense, rather gaunt height, a very bad back to match, all joined to a joyful delight in human weirdness which, what with his spine and his tattered lungs, he has to keep in good shape, was one of the first.

Charles Swann

I went to see Raymond in 1964 because I wanted to change to English from History, and to be taught by him. How should I prepare for the change? [Swann chortled with pleasure and then produced a wonderful Williams imitation, perfect in its laconic, slightly slurred intonation: 'Read a few tragedies.' 'Which ones?' 'Greek wouldn't hurt.']

You know, at points Raymond was fatally vague. I wanted to shake him and tell him to have a few enemies. *Modern Tragedy* was written to refute Steiner.[34] Why not say so? But he'd wind a match round and round in his ear, and light his pipe half-smiling, and say nothing.

Swann went on to become Williams's doctoral student. There was an imposing assortment of future academics sitting at Williams's feet in the early 1960s. Charles Swann with Patrick Parrinder, then John Barrell, but best known of course, Terry Eagleton, by 1993 the Warton Professor of English at Oxford but even at that eminence still as determined as he was in 1961 when he turned up at Williams's lectures in a grim barn of a lecture hall in the Old Schools, to make himself as impossible as Peter Pan, as mischievous as Jackanapes, as exiled and assassinable as Trotsky or James Connolly. And as allusively charming as Peter Wimsey.

All this, and as Stephen Heath said of his old friend and associate:

Stephen Heath

Terry was utterly bound up with Raymond; he was an absolutely militant agitator and detested, to his great satisfaction, by the college elders. When he finished his

188

degree in 1964 – Terry was then at Trinity as Raymond had been – Raymond was desperate for a second Fellow in English. He wanted to distance himself from undergraduate teaching. So Terry became the key teacher.

Terry Eagleton

Our group – John Barrell, Mike Long, Charles, and others would go round the same Williams lectures time and again. He asked me to come to Jesus before I got my Finals – Trinity had something for me, I was sort of negotiating with Theodore Redpath (he's now a wine merchant!), but he probably took against me. Then Raymond supervised my thesis – he was a bad supervisor, he wasn't a good undergraduate tutor. He wanted to get undergraduate teaching out of the way, so when Moses Finley ran classes for undergraduates instead of the old, one-to-one or one-to-two tutorials, Raymond did the same. I remember Stephen Heath, who had come to the college specifically for individual tutorials with Raymond, button-holing him and not letting go. I've never seen Raymond so defensive. Stephen kept at him, so finally Raymond said what a poor tutor he was. I held the troops down, disgruntled undergraduates would come to me for more of Raymond's attention.

The troops wouldn't always stay down. After Williams's death, one of his former pupils who became the best-known playwright of his genera-tion, David Hare, performed a studied indiscretion in a memorial lecture to Williams. He recalled the day in 1966 when a large group of students, admirers of Williams and powerfully upset at being denied access to their master, sat in his rooms and wouldn't move until he agreed to teach them.

David Hare

I have since been reminded that what followed was a strike. I'm not sure. Were things really that dramatic? I remember only an ultimatum. His third-year students told Raymond that they had been lured to the world's dampest university on false pretences. They had come for his personal tuition, and they were going to sit in his rooms until he consented to give it. I do remember his discomfort, which was profound. In the autumn of 1966, it was not an easy situation for the intellectual leader of the academic left to find himself in. It was downright embarrassing. In London new radical newspapers were being started. New political factions were forming in an atmosphere of wild optimism and vitality. The organised and disor-ganised left were taking to the streets. There was barely a new grouping that did not want Raymond's blessing and guidance. Yet on his own home ground his concen-tration was being disturbed by a small, self-righteous bunch of students who were demanding instruction in a subject in which they did not even any longer believe.[35]

He stuck to his timetable; he sat at home and wrote, and only came into college at unfixed and variable times, dodging students and frustrating them beyond measure. He had these powers of 'clenched withdrawal' (Eagleton's phrase), and they couldn't be revoked by anyone else.

So he had the first draft of *Second Generation* done by the autumn of 1962, and after Cecil Day-Lewis had praised it ('it has the *feel* of working-class life better than any other novel I have read for a long time') *and* sent a conscientiously detailed list of cuts, the next version was ready for Christmas 1963, was cut again, and the book came out as Harold Wilson won a majority of five for the Labour Party in October 1964. It starts: 'If you stand today in Between Towns Road, you can see either way: west to the spires and towers of the cathedral and colleges; east to the yards and sheds of the motor works.'[36] The city is, of course, Oxford, although the novel never says so. It is much more ambitious than *Border Country*. Williams attempted a 'condition of England' novel, comparable to those he admired of the 1840s, and attempted also to measure the moral and political distance between the life of the car-works and of the colleges, between the serious manufacture of cars (and the stoppages) and the serious manufacture of ideas (and what stops those, as well).

I am deeply attached to the book, but it has awful weaknesses. The end is pure sentiment: the young working-class radical dedicates himself in front of his family to working on the assembly lines, and then to writing the book of the work, *Industrial Estate*. (Williams is always good on the titles of missing academic books.) The conscientious sexual encounters are impossibly gauche – Williams was, so some women have said, quite 'without sexual presence', hence the much-noted omission of women from all his writing. Rose, the radical's adulterous lover, is made to stand in a physically impossible position, 'the fingers of both hands lightly linked over her thighs'[37] (try it). Assorted figures, especially Robert Lane, the young radical's thesis-supervisor, are made the targets of a quite uncontrolled class and, it seems, personal animus.

But it *is* about England; and Wales. It catches something of the country's somnambulism, its heavy sleep through the facts of decline, of the incipient failure of its politics, its grand class compromise, the end of the middle-class idyll. And the picture of the young radical, the second generation of working-class mobility (not necessarily upwards, either) is, even when clumsy, compelling. The drivenness of commitment, the unlikeability, the helpless hurting of others as Peter Owen tries to live the contradictions of work and class which are not just social–structural but identity-structur*ing*, is at once keenly recognisable, and one of Williams's grandest themes. Peter Owen cannot make a habitable 'structure of feeling' for himself. His tragedy will be that he will never be at home. Williams sometimes localised this predicament as one of loyalty. Some people have said that Terry Eagleton is not so far from being Peter Owen's prototype in both the novels in which he appears, and it may be so, but the same issue was at stake in the tolerance Williams extended to the new editors of *New Left Review*.

It *was* Eagleton-in-Owen, Eagleton, a marvellous mimic of Williams (and many others) who responded in not unkindly kind with this hilariously accurate parody, as lovingly hostile a critique of *Second Generation* as one could wish.

190

'But it isn't,' said Gwen, moving to the french windows in her blue sweater. 'It's the energy you give that breaks you. Don't you see? You take it this way and you see both ways, but in the end it comes down to the hard thing, that hard loss, the bitterness. And the growth pushes through that, but it isn't the same, not in the body it isn't. I fought and fought till it drained me but Dad wouldn't see it, he wouldn't make that bridge. It was a hard place to cross, to bridge that crossing, and in the end he couldn't, it was too much the other, he fell in. He fell in and you fell in with him, Peter, that's what I'm trying to say, don't you see it? You took the hard road and he took the soft road but you both came out together where they meet, where history meets. You can push the desire back and it will break you but it's all you've got, all Dad ever had, the hard thing at the crossing, that bitter growth.'

Peter moved quickly to the sideboard.

'Your growth, Gwen? Your bitterness?'

'All our growth, Peter. You, Beth, Daffyd, Dai, Jojo, Queenie – all of us.'

'And if we die, pushing back?'

'Then we'll push back, dying, Peter. Why else are our hands empty when that cold stream stirs quickly in the blood? You said it was desire, and so it was – but not that desire, not now, not in this place, in Wales.'

He turned slowly towards her, seeing the thin shoulders beneath the blue sweater, the dark hair sparse on the neck.

'*This* place?' His voice was light with anger. '*This* place, Gwen? Or your place? That cold, hard place, where desire meets and breaks? Is that what you want? What all of us wanted, for Dad? Breaking that deadness, that historical disqualification? Could I disqualify him when I was mortgaged myself, to you, part of that flesh? The hunger comes back and we feed it, but it's a new rhythm, a learned one, that cold voice of power. We were part of it, but now it's part of us all, of Daffyd, Jojo, Pinky, Evans the Post, Sarah-Alexandra, Mr. Rumbelow. We change the signals and the signals change us. Did you think you could break that circuit by giving me your body?'

She moved to the gramophone, thin in her sweater.

'My body, Peter? That cold growth of conscription?'

'Some conscript. Some enlist.'

'But now? Enlistment now?'

'Enlistment breaks the conscription. So we're equal.'

'As between friends?' She paused. 'Conscripted friends, Peter?'

He smiled thinly. She looked young as she stood before the french window, dark hair moving on the frail nape. He took the full glass from the table and held it to her, quickly.

191

'Well, Gwen. We can always learn a new enlistment.'

High in the darkness, a railway engine moved along the hard rails. Gathering speed, the long train pushed its difficult freight through the dim valley, out beyond the border, moving down the steep vales past the hidden farmhouses and factories, deep through the darkening frontier, into the wide skies of Cambridge.

Peter Owen was no tragic hero. He deserves this mockery. Indeed, the tragic mask, like its opposite, never fitted well on Williams's shoulders. *Second Generation* punctually fills up with hopefulness, the hope which came out of the Forces so cheerfully in 1945, and was never extinguished in this gradualist spokesman.

In October 1964 he had high hopes of the Wilson government everyone was expecting. The new *New Left Review* programme of Anderson, Blackburn and Nairn had its managerial side, its commitment (as Thompson noted ironically) to modernisation, to closing-down uneconomic branch lines of intellectual traffic. Wilson's famous party-rouser at the 1963 Labour conference promised 'the white heat of technological revolution'; it was a good advertising slogan for his campaign.

It struck a chord in Williams, and in any case he wanted to upset the neighbours. So outside his quite unmodernised house, he attached to the gate a five-foot high photograph of his cheerful Party leader as his choice for Prime Minister. All the family had turned out to canvass for Labour in 1959, and although by now Merryn had won a place at New Hall Cambridge to read English, and was living in town, the rest piled out again to scandalise genteel Hardwick by plying them with Labour leaflets.

Joy and Raymond had joined the Party when they arrived in Cambridge in 1961, and got up a subversive little constituency newsletter with rather routine articles in it against the bomb and the like, which was duplicated at the Party headquarters and randomly circulated amongst interested comrades. Years afterwards, in an unendearing way Williams had of implying that his smallest enterprises – a new adult education course, a Party newsletter – were disapproved of by the mighty, he used to claim that the word got back of Party disapproval of their little circular. The truth was the Party didn't have the money or the organisation to disapprove of anything. It didn't even have the *offices* – in those days they were London tenants of the Transport Union on one scruffy floor in Smith Square. It was a minor vaingloriousness of his to match the doctrinal indulgence with which he supposed that people would put him down as working class if he wore his old coat (just as he in turn would put them down if their accent seemed to him unwarrantably posh).

Anyway, the Labour Party won its small majority, and Williams turned out to speak for Robert Davies, the new MP for Cambridge, at a rather sparse meeting in Hardwick. He didn't, I fear, make any great impression on the city's Party. Clarissa Kaldor, whose beautiful daughter became a CND star and scholar of weaponry in the 1980s, was running the main committee rooms in 1964, and was in any case a commandingly *grande dame* of the Party of the old school; her husband, later ennobled for his trouble, was for some years Wilson's senior economic adviser.

Clarissa Kaldor

I don't remember *anybody* called Raymond Williams. We had a very large university membership in the Party in those days. I knew the economists of course, because of Nicky, and we discussed policy a lot, mostly with the LSE people. But our local councillors were so good, and it was *housing* that really mattered to us in Cambridge. It was a *practical* party, I would say. The old Left-Right business never came up. But all the people who wanted to get into Cabinet came for advice, of course. Cambridge has, after all, the best economics department in Europe.

So that was that. Williams kept up his anti-governmental fire from within his membership. At Easter 1965, the newsletter was circulated on behalf of CND's three-day Easter march from Bomber Command's HQ in High Wycombe via Uxbridge to Whitehall and Trafalgar Square on Easter Monday (ten shillings a head for the whipround). He urged the politics of the study group upon the Campaign and cursed the government for its anti-democratic bomb.[38]

It was the kind of writing commission he always accepted, along with the ceaseless journalism and reviewing. One of his pupils, David Hamilton-Eddy, even remembers giving him a copy of a small magazine of college writing and Williams helped them on with his good name by reviewing it pleasantly in *Varsity*, the student newspaper whose predecessor he edited himself.

While the Labour government moved towards its second victory, at an election called early in order to win a decent majority, and critics like Williams held their fire in acknowledgement of the parliamentary difficulty of a tiny majority, Williams's own writing drove on in the old, unsparing way. He had a couple of plays accepted for BBC television, and got a solid fee for them – £550 and £625 respectively – while he polished off *Modern Tragedy* which Chatto took on without objection, even though one of their directors, writing about Williams to an interested American house spoke of his sales 'as not, after the initial impulse, large, and we regard them as sound backlist items'.[39]

Modern Tragedy was a direct answer to George Steiner's *The Death of Tragedy* of which the argument, brutally summarised, was that true tragedy had become impossible amid the pointlessly overpowering statistics of world slaughters, and the levelling of social hierarchies. Williams replied without ever naming Steiner, talking as always beyond the point of conflict to another spot on a longer perspective at which agreement might be reached,

We come to tragedy by many roads. It is an immediate experience, a body of literature, a conflict of theory, an academic problem. This book is written from the point where the roads cross, in a particular life.

In an ordinary life, spanning the middle years of the twentieth century, I have known what I believe to be tragedy, in several forms. It has not been the death of princes; it has been at once more personal and more general. I have been driven to try to understand this experience, and I have drawn back, baffled, at the distance between my own sense of tragedy and the conventions of the time. Thus I have known tragedy in the life of a man driven back to silence, in an unregarded working life. In his ordinary and private death, I saw a terrifying loss of connection between men, and even between father and son: a loss of connection which was, however, a particular social and historical fact: a measurable distance between his desire and his endurance, and between both and the purposes and meanings which the general life offered him. I have known this tragedy more widely since. I have seen the loss of connection built into a works and a city, and men and women broken by the pressure to accept this as normal, and by the deferment and corrosion of hope and desire. I have known also, as a whole culture has known, a tragic action framing yet also breaking into these worlds: an action of war and social revolution on so great a scale that it is continually and understandably reduced to the abstractions of political history, yet an action that cannot finally be held at this level and distance, by those who have known it as the history of real men and women, or by those who know, as a quite personal fact, that the action is not yet ended.[40]

It is a dignified argument, egotistical as it has to be, although Harry Williams's tragedy now looks more domestic than social. Williams pursued it through *Dr Zhivago* with great conviction, and then rode his hobby-horse across *The Crucible*, damning it for faint-hearted liberalism, for its victimised hero (whereas *I'm* damned if John Proctor is anything other than a brave, defiant and active hero, speaking some of the most moving political poetry of the century). Williams scoops up his essay on Tolstoy and Lawrence from a back number of the *Kenyon Review*, canters round Ibsen again to make him emphatically tragic, and ends by printing, as he had threatened, the whole of his own play, *Koba*: not, as he'd planned, about Milton, but about Stalin.

It was a bold idea. It is an awful play. All the copious reviews said so, most heartily Frank Kermode, who rebuked him first for unevenness of treatment (two pages on Renaissance tragedy) as well as doctrinaire conventionality, and then for the 'disastrous badness' of *Koba*, its 'chocolate

revolutionary posturing'.[41] Williams intended the discussion of revolutionary tragedy to connect with his theorisation of long revolutions; this new
book was built into the grand arch of his ideas, the articulation of event,
experience and idea in a single frame of feeling. In other words, he sought
a unity of vision as grand as Marx's, as poetic as Ruskin's, in a new mode
of thought, a mode at once political, public and, according to the abstract
idiom of the century, mythological. To do this, to bring off this really vast
ambition, he couldn't just start, as he did, from a literary category on the
Cambridge syllabus. Kermode's bleakest judgement hits home (as
Eagleton, startlingly, agrees):

> ... the oddness of the book's structure seems finally to be self-
> indulgent, however strongly the general tone of sullen, incorruptible
> intelligence may seem to tell against such a judgement ... This
> book is in one way a learned argument ... and in another a work
> of imagination ... but the manner has certainly grown at once more
> severe and more selfish ...'[42]

He read the reviews as always; but he hardly ever acted on them (although
the play was dropped from the 1979 edition). The solitary dedication in
which he worked, the driven, onward and hardly reflexive march of his
writing had come to lack exchange, warmth, gregariousness; it had come
to want both a renewed grounding in personal experience and a more
immediate grip upon contemporary events.

9

LEADER OF THE
LEFT-IN-EXILE

In the chapter on 'Individuals and Societies' in *The Long Revolution* Williams reviews, as part of the 'imaginative sociology of his own' (the phrase was Stuart Hampshire's), a series of possible roles through which people live in society. To such obliging positions as 'members', 'subject', 'servant', he adds 'rebel', 'exile' and 'vagrant'. Noting that exile usually means those, like D.H. Lawrence, who leave home because it no longer is home, and refuse to return until it is transformed as he wants it to be, Williams says 'an equally characteristic modern figure is the self-exile', or as the Bolsheviks had it, 'an internal emigré which lives and moves about in his native society, but rejects its purposes and despises its values, because of alternative principles to which his whole personal reality is committed'.[1] He is urgent for change, this figure, but his dissent is fixed as part of the definition of his separateness. So he cannot join with others. (As Lawrence wrote in one of his letters, 'I will be wary, beyond words, of joining'.) This rebel, in Williams's brief definition, he aligns more or less with the revolutionary, who opposes the society in terms of the struggle for a different society.[2]

For the second half of his political and personal life, Williams veered between living as an internal emigré and living rebelliously. He had married himself completely to the values of the border country as lived by the railwaymen; strong, confident, settled men as they were, they belonged to the losing side of the struggle between labour and capital. Williams, like all socialists, was committed to the losing side out of his deepest childhood experiences. The values of the losers (to put it in that rough-and-ready way) were the fine things they were – solidarity, mutuality, fight, opposition, equal shares in difficulty – exactly *because* theirs was the losing side. But Williams's version of socialism, and that of the hosts of his admirers, dedicated the struggle to turning losers' values into winners' values – an utter contradiction, as so many victorious revolutionaries of the Left quickly proved. This contradiction is at the heart of the failure, as well as the defeat of the Left-intellectual project in Britain and other of the wealthy nations where it showed its flag.

196

In March 1966 there was a Parliamentary by-election in Hull. It was contested, among others, by an improvised group of incongruous idealists calling themselves the Radical Student Alliance, whose main campaigning principle was opposition to the Vietnamese war to which the Prime Minister declined to send supporting troops even when requested to by the senior partner of the special transatlantic relationship. The RSA candidate, Richard Gott, later taken on to the books at the *Guardian*, polled 263 piteous votes; the Tories were firmly defeated, and on the strength of this Harold Wilson called and won a general election with a ninety-six seat majority.

The still-Labour intelligentsia of the New Left hoped for much. A big majority, a full Parliamentary term, what now? Their great expectations went quickly down. There was a strike by the National Union of Seamen, and in variously shady ways the seamen's leadership were accused of being nasty commies and unpatriotic traitors to the Labour cause. It was an unsavoury episode, if no more. There was a freeze on wages, which hit the low-paid most, of course. There were heavy outflows of sterling as the overseas institutions holding it in reserve, apprehensive of an alien government, switched into other currencies, causing the nation's savings to leak copiously, and assorted public spending to be stopped. There was a novel attempt to plan the direction of the whole national economy, tying together management and unions in an unprecedented effort at incorporation and trans-class co-operation, all of which came entirely unstuck. Finally, there was no question of the Labour government doing anything at all about its continued pretence at being an independent nuclear power, as well as the fixed and front-line aircraft carrier for the USA flying its nuclear patrols twenty-four hours a day over Europe.

That was enough for Williams. The habit of opposition, rooted in his character, had in any case pushed him to the limits of membership when Labour won power, and thereby became obliged in virtue of being the nation's government to shift the centre of its own political gravity nearer to the fulcrum of the society. Wilson had once spoken of the Labour Party's being nothing if it was not a moral crusade, and Williams and Thompson, unofficial leaders of the New Left, had put their heart into political writings, the whole point of which was to remoralise a socialist project dishonoured by Stalinism. Their British socialism would reconnect power to value, embedding value not in policy but in culture, the way of life of a society.

There was, of course, a colossal self-importance in all this. These men called, in their quiet, dignified and modest-sounding way, for policies they wrote with a lavishly generalising hand during one long day in Jesus College, Cambridge. They offered to rewrite the guiding principles of what was still the eighth richest country in the world.

So Williams, with his terrifically unself-conscious self-assurance invited

Hall and Thompson to Cambridge to put straight the future of Britain. Hall had recently published a rousing condition-of-England article in *People in Politics*, the house journal of an outfit called Caravan Workshop, a bunch of survivors from the New Left Clubs as well as harbingers of the British version of a Woodstockian counter-culture. There had just been a big meeting of these excellent philanthropists, all of whom were fed up with the Wilson government. The three of them agreed that there was a surge of congenial feeling out there in their old constituencies.

So the Jesus College servants brought into Raymond's rooms great trays of excellent food prepared in the college kitchens and paid for by Raymond, and Edward Thompson lay on the floor and asked what they were going to put in the document about the Royal family, and they tacked out a framework for a *New Left May Day Manifesto*, to be published on 1 May 1967. It was privately funded and published according to the best Enlightenment principles by individual subscription, the list of subscribers being a roll-call of the young middle-aged Left luminaries of the day, including among its stars Iris Murdoch (before she voted for Mrs Thatcher and was enDamed), R.D. Laing, the union leader Clive Jenkins, and the Catholic priest admonished by Rome, Herbert McCabe.

It sold 7,000 copies at half-a-crown a time. It was magisterially confident, powerfully convincing to anybody – like most of us on the Left at that date – who didn't know much economics and only had experience of politicking in the endless committees and just-as-endless parties of the powerless but passionately interested sects. It was also, in spots, magisterially unfeasible, and this was inextricable from its unassailable moral rightness, and the structural completeness of its case. It presented an entirely smooth, sealed exterior to criticism. It was an example of wishing so strongly for miracles, that miracles seem possible. Like the African cargo cultists, believers in the *Manifesto* saw clearly a mirage which would redeem socialism. This magic thought bears Williams's signature.

> The Labour government of 1964 took power at the very moment when this system reached one of its crisis peaks, and in the very first weeks of its administration declared its determination to stand by the system, even at the risk of its other commitments to growth at home, and to the ending of stop-go cycles in the economy.
>
> The choice it faced was critically clear. It could break with the system as a whole, by taking powers to control trade and the movement of capital, and to appropriate, in the real national interest, British overseas private holdings of foreign shares and securities. These crisis measures would have enabled the situation to be held, as a preliminary to creating new institutions to control production and distribution, and to end capitalist power. Yet any such policy

could be a direct attack on the centres of irresponsible power in the society, and would be opposed and sabotaged by interlocking financial interests with power gravely to hurt the British people. Nobody can pretend that such a choice, though in fact the only socialist choice with any chance of success, would fail to involve strife, bitterness, and temporary economic dislocation. It is easy to imagine why some nerves would fail.[3]

This is Williams answering to both sides of his character: the ambitious public policy-maker, eager to be heeded in the power élite and to count influentially; the radical critic whose uncompromising opposition to power keeps faith with the powerless and the losers, and gives them hope that they will be spoken for by power itself. It is another case of honour rooted in dishonour, a structural consequence of an imperative, brave and self-deluding argument.

The programme itself is richly impossible. Surely he knew this? It seems not, or not yet. The idea of a newly arrived Labour government with a majority of four at once 'appropriating' the control of trade and capital *from London* is plain comic. There would have been no sterling left in the corner of any vault. What on earth the 'new institutions' would have looked like 'to end capitalist power' only Spike Milligan could have said. Of course, it is 'easy to imagine' why some nerves would not fail, but the nervelessness in question could only be so in relation to uninhibited effrontery and ignorance.

It is hard, now, to speak so harshly of a document by which I, a minor supporter at the time, was impressed, convinced and stirred. It is also a matter of some importance, as well of justice to those involved, to understand the strong feelings on the part of these few academics, intellectuals and writers that their ideals and principles might make a difference to the world. For a start, their lives as teachers and the way they taught were shaped by their picture of a valid democracy in which rational and educated publics shall determine in open debate the way of life of a good society. Second, their kind – my kind – of remoralised socialism rested upon a sort of gallant Quakerism, in which bearing witness was a self-defining necessity in a faithful political life. Finally, we believed to our credit that Britain herself remained closer to certain basic political decencies than most capitalisms, and that she might even be moved by such an appeal to bring ideals and actualities closer together.

If there was innocence in all this, it is nothing to be ashamed of. But there was also ignorance, culpable ignorance, and self-delusion, too. Let the judgement of Gareth Stedman-Jones stand, a mild and kindly historian with some command of economics, and for years a member of the *NLR* board, colleague of Williams, loyal soldier of the Left.

Gareth Stedman-Jones

When I was at Oxford we started up an undergraduate magazine called *New University*, which later became *The Messenger*. It was very Williamsesque. People had *Culture and Society* and *The Long Revolution* on the mantlepiece as sacred texts. We held a special discussion session on *Communications*, set it against the Labour Penguin special, *Signposts for the Sixties*.

But I came to think that Williams kept faith with socialism for sentimental reasons. He never had a very assured relation with history; history merges into autobiography and mythology – his view of the General Strike, for example, was crazily simple. And there are large amounts of self-deception in the *Manifesto*. Lots of Left thinking, my Left, is profoundly evasive about policy and about the Labour Party. How would *they* have spent council money?

In the small, warm, acrimonious and companionable enclave of Leftism in 1967, whether at the border of the Party, or over it into the wild variety of tiny socialist sects, laden with initials (CPGB M-L, IS later RWP, RSA, RSSF, IMG ...) this was not how the *Manifesto* seemed. It was amiably reviewed in Harold Evans's *Sunday Times* and *Le Monde* among others, by people outside proper politics and policy, and the moment looked ripe for what the New Left always calls an intervention.

A substantial committee of the old hands began to coagulate, with an impressive platoon of bright new characters – Charles Swann as treasurer, Eagleton certainly, Bernard Sharratt – another Catholic, Bob Rowthorn – a proper economist, Michael Rustin, Norm Fruchter, mad, voluble Peter Sedgwick shouting abuse from outside the door, John Morris, Robin Murray, a couple of dozen nearly all of them men but nobody noticed, Juliet Mitchell married to Anderson, Mrs Murray, Mrs Rustin, gathered at NLR headquarters, at Jesus College again, nostrils flaring and eyes bright at the good words 'movement', 'manifesto', 'mass meeting'. Neil Middleton at Penguin asked for a new, enlarged version of the *Manifesto*, to be published next May Day with a big launch and a weekend conference. There were about three months in which to do the rewriting.

The magnificent, tireless Three, plus Rustin, sent out a round robin asking for money. The scheme was to rent an office (300 quid) and an officer (£1,250 a year), and for something like £2,500 restore the life of the gone New Left Clubs in a small flowering of conferences, discussion groups, working parties, a bulletin, all the worthy, laborious, and exhilarating work of politics-outside-politics, the heedful busyness which civil society must have if it is not to fade away into the perfect acquiescence all ruling classes desire.

The work was all right; Williams loved the work and could write with his prodigious readiness. So 'Raymond's young men', as Joy called them, trooped in and out of Jesus and Hardwick, bringing their two or three pages each of analysis of individual areas of the vast, simple, propaganda fresco Williams was to assemble.

200

At one point he laid the piles of offerings in the order in which he would take them along the edge of the long dining table, and walked broodingly round the four sides of his display. The headings were all there, all coherent: poverty, inequality, welfare; the new insurgent and expansionist international capitalism; the new imperialism; the dominance of the City; the problems of the State and the Party. There was now a proper economic argument from Rowthorn and Michael Barratt Brown to stiffen the vacuities of the first version. There were exact figures, for poverty, homelessness, the frauds of overseas aid, from Dorothy Wedderburn, an old soldier from the Cambridge socialists in 1940, and Peter Worsley. But there had to be an at once collective and single voice, speaking with the resonance and assurance of these many voices who all felt the same. Williams was the only one who could bring off the trick of such heteroloquism.

So he wrote a 200 page book in three months (not by any means for the first time). He recast the thing, he drew together its parts and locked them in a single frame, above all, he suffused the prose of the *Manifesto* with his own inimitably calm reasonableness, his authoritative assumption, expressed in those steady, slightly sleepy cadences, that the unimaginable only needed saying to become real; that honest Utopians were always abused as ludicrous by the enemy; that the enemy was never right.

You can't say he wasn't right; you can only say it couldn't possibly have been done. Poverty in Britain was exactly as the *Manifesto* said. Those were social facts, for sure; they are shamefully worse in the 1990s. The key conceptual move of the economic analysis was, first, to show how capital, as Marx had predicted in another insurrectionary year 120 years before, was now the mover of world history, but to go beyond the platitude to demonstrate how tightly and completely its structure interlocked ('interlocking' was a favourite metaphor in those early days for structuralisms of many colours) in a system whose intentional and self-aware agent was the new superpower, the international corporation. The *May Day Manifesto* popularised this concept right across the Left, and turned it into the indispensable explanatory demon of socialist criticism – so much so that when, years later, Paul Hirst and Grahame Thompson[4] established by a careful dismantling of the figures and the policies how much more shadowy and intangible the local effects of these monsters were, they simply weren't believed. No international corporation has the beginnings of a record to match the cruelty, oppression and wanton incompetence displayed by those solid agents of the historical process, the nation–states; but never mind: corporations prefigured the last enemy, capitalism itself, and the arguments pivoted on them. The strength and simplicity of the case not only persuaded a commando in the Parliamentary Left over the years, it so addled its collective pate that, between 1980 and 1983, it was led by Tony Benn almost to bring the Labour Party to an end as an electoral force.

There was, however, one nation–state in particular driving the whole system: the USA, which always figured much more villainously in the political narratives of the Left than the home of Gulag. In part the USA brought this on itself, especially in 1967. The discrepancy between the noble principles of the Declaration of Independence and the tonnage of bombs then falling on Vietnam was publicly measurable exactly because those principles still carried weight in the Constitution, and when it was linked to the waste of the cold war years, then the agents of the free world and the commanders of the B52s deserved all the abuse they got.

There was something else about the USA for the *Manifesto*-writers. The USA was everybody's byword for enormous consumer productivity. Every leader-writer mocked the country for its so-called materialism, for its sheer abundance of material goods. Williams, indeed, was exceptional among them for rebutting the charge made by the comfortably-off in the 1950s that the good old working class, instead of continuing to prove its honest brains and worth by taking the bus and using the mangle had rather gone overboard in its pursuit of such material goods, long enjoyed by the bourgeoisie, as cars and washing machines.

This was well done by Williams. Washing machines and accurate contraception did more for the freedom of women than equality in gender-language or the casting-off of high heels. But there was a split in the political consciousness of many on either side of politics, between acknowledging these great public goods and seeing, correctly, just how much abominable and trivial junk was produced by the new, American-created abundance, and the advertising industry which gloated over it. And then the only answer to William Morris's question, how shall we ensure that we only produce what is beautiful or useful? is to prevent such production emerging from the market and ensure that the *Manifesto*'s unspecified institutions for the control of production and capital would do the job.

Whatever reverence must now be done to the idea of the market, it remains true that somebody must ask for production not only to be rational but morally worthwhile as well, and that a society should not produce what is useless or lethal because markets say so. Marxists have always been strongest on such diagnosis rather than prediction or solution. They were in this case also. It was true that the USA was doing everything wrong, and doing it cruelly in Vietnam and Central America. Thousands of Americans thought so. It was true that the moral depredations and inequities of this new global capitalism were as repulsive as the *Manifesto* said they were, in Britain and in the world at large. It was true that to understand this process demanded a political model in totality, Marxism's most important contribution to social theory.

To understand, however, did not mean that anybody could grasp the levers of control. There were no such things. Still less could Britain, one

wealthy-enough country, resign from the totality and do everything differently. (It couldn't do such a thing above all because of the truth of the
totality argument, clinched by the economist contributors and made clear
and commanding by Williams's exemplary exposition.)

The largeness of both the manner and the error came from something
still shared, in negation as it were, by the New Leftists with their natural
opponents. They still thought naturally of Britain not only as a potentially
decent place but as an immense world power, in spite of the way they
themselves so clearly documented the decline of that power. Hence they
believed the country could effect such massive changes in its policy, structure, essence, and start a new kind of society. They never reckoned up
the stupefying costs of this, in literal cash and capital, let alone in terms
of the other national economies to which Britain was inalienably bound.

But the serene assurance, the high-mindedness, the smooth finish of
argument and answer carried us all buoyantly along. Nobody even noticed[5]
that in the vicissitudes of popularity and despite the humiliating devalu-
ation into which the Government was forced while Williams was doing
his rewriting in the autumn of 1967, the Labour Party was trundling pass-
ably on. The *Manifesto* men made much of the crisis – another salivatory
word in the New Left as well as, I fear, throughout Williams's own work
– in Party membership, but that was only on the same gradually down-
ward slope it had slid since 1950. Worst of all, the *Manifesto* claimed, and
all of us followers devoutly believed, that there really was an incipient
tendency in the civic feelings of large numbers of honest citizens towards
a much more radical kind of socialism than had ever been tried in Britain.

So when the manuscript was typed up by Charles Swann and packed
off to Penguin, there was still much to be done. An informal kind of
conference was held in November, at which enthusiastic and sensible plans
were made for a rather larger occasion at University College, London at
the end of April just before the Penguin was launched. A *Manifesto
Bulletin* was started on the spot, with distribution to a small number of
member groups sprinkled mainly across London, a few others in Hull,
Leeds, Brighton, Cardiff (where, as the local convenor said spiritedly, there
were only three members but all of them dedicated). A committee to
direct things came spontaneously into being with its first preoccupation
being to organise for a much larger membership and political visibility.
Committees and conferences come naturally to this fraction of the politically minded bourgeoisie; too much so, as Robin Murray pointed out.

The model for such occasions was, in spite of its unpopularity, the
Labour Party's national conference and love feast, at which secret deals
were done at the back of the hall, affairs started, old friendships sundered,
the character of one's enemies assassinated and one's crown prince
saluted, while miles away below the hot lights the neglected speakers,
their faces glistening, bashed out the dismal clichés. There used to be a

radical belief, still formally observed and shared by heirs to *May Day Manifesto* that the Party conference should take policy decisions which will bind Labour governments to obedience. But nothing could have been less like an Athenian forum or an ideal speech-situation, nor less equipped to judge and vote rationally, than the Party's annual and gregarious birthday beano.

Allowing for the diminuendo, the same was true of the *May Day Manifesto* conference. Assorted people made vigorous proposals for the big day, and these were typed out on to reproductive skins, as always, by the tirelessly obliging women of the organisation, peeled back, rolled on to the ink-heavy Gestetner drums and spun so that the ink was driven out through the cut letters onto copying paper below. Then the faithful women wiped the drums, stacked and stapled the copies, and posted them out with Raymond Williams's name on the bottom, together with that of a senior trade unionist called John Morris.

The two men calmly declared, in antique typescript:

> The May Day Manifesto analyses the society in which we live. It is now clear that we shall not change that society if we rely entirely or mainly on parliamentary political parties; we also need continuing and connected effort outside Parliament.[6]

The statement continued by invoking the large but uncoordinated number of bodies of people which, if brought together, would find a new strength and direction (statements like this are always strong on those two nouns) as well as a new efficacity in their local strivings. And the same people were reassured that if any such creative new grouping could be brought about, this would in no way impugn or dissolve the identity of their existing memberships (the initialled sectarians of what the French punitively call *groupuscules* are of legendary self-protectiveness).

Their general invitation was followed by more specific proposals, basing the movement itself on three theoretic arguments: Ralph Miliband's *Parliamentary Socialism* (in which the old new reasoner announced that parliament is done for as far as socialists are concerned, having been turned into an irrelevant ranting-house by the capitalist ruling class); Thompson's 'Revolution Again' (a piece of platform uplift which does not show off the master to good account); and the youthful Perry Anderson's pamphlet essay *Problems of Socialist Strategy* (immediately and immortally parodied for its over-blown theoreticism by Peter Sedgwick). Stephen Yeo, radical historian, wound up the circular by saying, with an agreeable self-correction, 'We, at least I, would like to see a fully-fledged and effective alternative to new capitalist politics', and asked gratuitously about the local Labour parties, 'should we leave them to rot or use them ourselves?'

All this excitement was mounting towards the April conference. It was turned almost into delirium by the unexpected thrill of world events in that amazing year. On 31 January, the feast of Tet, the Vietnamese guerrillas after infiltrating thirty-six of the regional capitals of South Vietnam and sixty-four market towns in complete secrecy with an enormous quantity of light weaponry, rose in a huge insurrection against the American occupying forces and the Southern troops. They fought with amazing heroism and were only defeated by a show of American firepower, televised all across the United States, which revolted and turned against their Government crowds of young people. In March President Lyndon Johnson announced on American television that he would not seek re-election, and it seemed as though those same radical crowds had brought him down. On 6 April, in savage confirmation of the need for continued vigilance against the evils of racism, Martin Luther King was shot by a sniper in Memphis. A world-historical climax gathered in the imagination of the big-hearted, always self-deceptive and honourably idealistic Left.

'Where may a person of honour be except on the Left?'[7] The men and women of honour came to Gower Street, thrilling at the thought of a replay of 1848, but one in which the morally best side won. Within just a few days, that thrill was compounded by the French detonation touched off, most thrilling of all, in the universities. The new Penguin was on sale, there was a party at *The Dolphin* and another one at Gower Street, there were seminars on absolutely everything, including real live workers from the Institute for Workers' Control,[8] another inspiring sign of the times, there was an election of a standing committee, the taking-of-motions and referring-back, the inventing of compound motions ('composites' in the jargon) and the rulings-out-of-order. There were blinding rows, and sex, and booze.

What there wasn't was Raymond Williams, nor Hall nor Thompson. The big three never showed up. As Brian Darling wrote with mild reproach in a letter to the *Bulletin* afterwards,

> I felt we missed our senior figures. Not so much for their superior speaking ability nor fiery activism – rather for their experience in chairing plenary sessions and particularly on the Sunday afternoon I felt the crippling absence of Raymond Williams' unifying skills, his ability to see and seize what unites factions rather than divides them and to insist upon this unity before the conference terminates.[9]

It was always true. That was exactly Williams's great gift, the gift of the great politician he could have been, if it wasn't for his drive to privacy, his nailing himself to the avocation of writer.

Life's like that on the Left. Leaderless, the conference became quarrelsome and fragmentary. It fell to pieces. It was bedlam. Robin Murray tried to write a detailed implementation of socialism for Great Britain, typing furiously through the night, victim of that special dementia which assails working conferences. It was duplicated in the small hours, and the 'fantasy strategist' (as Bernard Sharratt, who was there, called him) looking white and drained saw his resolution chopped to a quarter of its size, and then passed as a generalised malediction spoken over the corpse of parliamentary socialism.

Somebody else berated the conference from the platform for not discussing whatever it was, himself having missed that very discussion the day before. Life's like that, too. Busy leftists, or lazy ones, or – goodness knows – ones bored by the show, turn up late or push off early. There were other disappointments: several hundred people registered, but nearly all of them from London. The Situationists were their usual loopy selves. The tough eggs of the Left sects, especially the International Socialists, announced their presence with their studied offensiveness, and plenty of people were offended. A number of the papers presented were raggedly done, and as always at these occasions, debates debated nothing. They were merely the sequence of the items on an agenda, grossly distended to take in the whole globe, and protracted to screaming point by the patient tolerance of the English liberal intelligentsia which rarely interrupts and believes everyone should have their say, even when what they say is tripe. Mike Rustin, a youngish Old New Left hand, solid Labour, with his scrunched-up face and owl specs looking like the school swot, was quite marvellous at conciliation, but he didn't crack the nuts who wanted the *Manifesto* to become a campaign, and to run doomed candidates in the next general election.

However, however, everyone went home to watch the news, pleased that the conference had happened, and soothing themselves with a warm soup filled with local initiatives, positions clarified, and high expectations.

The news, when it came in, was amazing. In Paris, a routine student protest and occupation of assorted university buildings boiled over, as everyone knows, into the colossal commotion of open street-fighting with the sinister stormtroopers of the French riot police. The dash, flair, quicksilver adaptation of the students, and it may be, a certain temperance on the part of some policemen, gave the students what looked on television like the edge of victory. When the student riots, their graffiti wit and their vast open debates at the Sorbonne on the horribleness of consumer capitalism metamorphosed into General Strike and brought out old De Gaulle, beside himself with fury, to call the students dog-shit on television, the quiet London intelligentsia fell into delight and envy.

Williams kept his counsel. Thompson kept his distance. Thompson thought, and said, that although these people were OK if a bit hairy, they'd no idea about a properly worked out, rationally chosen revolution. After most of it was over, Williams said something untheoretic – there was plenty of theory about – but sympathetic, to the effect that he was no longer young,

but it is worth saying that these young people are the only generation I can bear. All they can do, perhaps, in these next few months
is shout at the puppets, mock the wonderland, take their casualties.
I can't say anything easy.[10]

That was the best of him; that's what he was loved for.

For the rest of 1968 through until the middle of 1970 he answered the
periodic calls first from the *Manifesto* committee and thereafter from what
became the National Confederation of the Left.

By the time the French insurrection was blazing fiercely, the *Manifesto*
groups were looking round agitatedly for their own piece of action. Being
English, they even ran a conference on 'Where is the English Student
Revolution?' at University College again, whereupon a London art college
obliged with a sit-in, and more energetically but still a trifling teacup of
a stir, the students at the London School of Economics, led with romantic
flair by Robin Blackburn (temporarily on the staff) forcibly took down
some offensive new gates of iron set up by the authorities to keep the
wrong people out.

Even by English standards, the newspaper outcry at this was excessive,
and the urgent need to put down revolting young people insisted upon
with more than usually large flecks of saliva on the pages of *The Times*
and the *Daily Mail*, as well as on the jaws of distinguished public figures.
But the London *haute bourgeoisie* and its hired mouths had the wind as
thoroughly up as their identical peers had in 1848, and the Yellow Press
foamed eagerly at the creation of a genuinely home-bred stereotype, the
revolutionary Marxist student.

The cartoon came in useful for donkey's years; as Colin Crouch, a
steadying student voice at LSE, said it would at the time. Quite falsely,
the cartoon pictured students and universities down the left-hand side –
I wish it were true – and was used thereafter to damage them, the socialist
idea, and the Labour Party, which as usual didn't know what to do about
it all.

The *Manifesto* movement picked up enough steam to persuade itself
that it had a future. A 'Socialist Charter', calling for reform and extension
of the Labour government's timid and short-winded policies was published,
and found a few hundred signatories. A forceful and articulate bunch of
broadcasters, well-known and youngish, set themselves up as the Free
Communications Group with a neat, pocketable journal, some famous
names (Bill Webb and Neal Ascherson among them) and, naturally, a
conference in King Street in January 1969, with Raymond as its lead
speaker, and a clutch of *New Left Review* editorialists to reply. At home
in staid and unpolitical old Cambridge, a group of young Fellows and tutors
established the Cambridge Left Forum, with Eagleton, Rowthorn, John
Dunn, Lisa Jardine, on its books; so Williams spoke to that, also.

It is very hard to keep up a proper scepticism when a crowd of small signs and twinkling wonders seem so brightly to be pointing down the way you ardently want to go. What with the grand march and demonstration against the Vietnamese War and American misconduct outside the US Embassy one mild autumnal Sunday in October 1968, it seemed so tangible that a new feeling was abroad. A widespread rush of mature and fervent sentiment through crumbling old rigidities might at that very moment be surging towards a humane collectivism, a rejection of capitalism's neglect of poverty at home and cruelty abroad, a hope for the possession of one's own job in factory or shop or school, for a voice of one's own in newspaper and television. And so it truly might. It was Williams after all who had taught the power in history of the sentiments, and the importance of grasping an epoch and its key moments in terms of the structure of feeling which both framed and impelled it. If there was indeed a new feeling abroad, it was the duty of the Left to catch it on the wing.

So Williams planned with the *Manifesto* committee for a new conference, 18 to 20 April 1969, at which the National Confederation of the Left would be baptised. He chaired a preparatory commission in the *NLR* office at 11 Fitzroy Square, the *Review* having much discussed the theoretic links between a student intelligentsia and the historic role of the working class as *the* agent of revolutionary change ('little motor and big motor' as the Parisians had coyly put it).

The motley troops of the Left duly converged on St Pancras Town Hall on 18 April. They wrangled unamicably for two days, antique Stalinists still banging on about the moral superiority of the USSR, the central debate about the redemption or damnation of the Labour Party again unresolved, the correct expressions of mutuality quite failing to conceal raucous indiscipline, the delights of fissiparousness, the routine insolence. Williams was by contrast once again at his best. It was the summit of his authority. His quietness, his calm combination of reasonableness, conciliation and steeliness kept his audience of 600 as attentive to the impersonality of things as was possible. He battled for unity, the great simple of all political movements and appeals. In the end, everything turned on a proposal to prepare themselves for some kind of electoral intervention, but whether that would mean candidates actually standing was not decided. Michael Rustin voiced eloquent doubts,[11] and everybody clattered out from under the great gloomy Victorian vaults and went home.

They had all been Londoners, really. The *Manifesto* ran a conference in the Leeds Trades Hall, another piece of Victorian splendour still iron-black and unrestored in those days, but it was a bit of a flop. The virulence with which the *groupuscules* declared their mutual hatreds and rivalries, the sheer competitiveness of the Trotskyite factions, whose allegiance to Trotsky's manifold inheritance was strictly to his anti-bureau-cratic tendency and, given a chance, probably to his killer ruthlessness, all this made 'confederation' hardly confederate; plain uncomradely; down-right chaos. There were desperately serious people there, backing Williams as indeed their best man for such a job. I have dropped their names in a small downpour. The real puzzle is why they did it. (I'd do it again.) A Williams biography is one attempt at an answer.

The *Manifesto* appeal had raised enough money to pay an officer a poor salary. The plaintiveness of his report for the last effective six months of the movement – although as always the movement wouldn't lie down after its death – repeats the story of the extra-Labour Left in Britain since the days of its ancestors in Hyndman's Socialist Democratic Federation and Morris's Socialist League.

In September 1969 the *Manifesto* committee, now on the premises of Martin Eve's Merlin Press issued its 'New Intention' (Williams was excel-lent on titles). But the hapless Secretary's report[12] lists the old weaknesses of leftish administration: no constructive handovers, missing information, lost lists of members and helpers, malicious gossip, continued absences on the part of key members. As the Secretary said, and Max Weber before him, if the movement was to be anything, it had to be competent bureau-cratically. It could not expect its people to do this kind of extra-mural politics until midnight every day of the week. But the *groupuscules* liked nothing better; the people they had to recruit in order to thrive were quickly fed up with five-hour committees and a political life with no room for their families, their games, their jokes.

So the *Manifesto* and its Confederation quietly and quarrelsomely lapsed. They didn't run candidates in the 1970 general election, although in a tiny way they probably helped in the Labour Party's defeat. Williams didn't care; he *wanted* Labour to lose. Bernard Bergonzi, a sometime discovery by the Oxford Delegacy who went on to become a much-respected Professor of English, saw Williams some time before that blazing June when Wilson lost, to everyone's complete surprise:

Bernard Bergonzi

I remember seeing him at dinner at the house of John and Gillian Beer, when I got a strong sense of the intensity of his disillusionment with the Labour Government. The next General Election was talked about, and RW expressed some concern that the government might *not* be defeated. It could have been a Tory speaking. RW seems to have taken it for granted that a Conservative Government (as was duly elected) would be preferable to the continuation of the Wilson government.[13]

People said Williams looked and sounded tired by then.[14] I don't know. I met him in Hardwick in July, and he'd never looked fitter. He'd been out long-jumping with his sons at the St John's college long-jump pit in

Grange Road, and jumped eleven feet two inches. Not what he'd managed at Abergavenny in 1938, but, as the boys had said, pretty good at 49! And he had to think the last four years had been worth it, whatever act of faith that took.[15] Being in the right, and right about it, was a wide plank in the platform of his self.

As always, he'd kept up his hammering discipline at the typewriter. Back in November of 1966, while preparing the first *Manifesto*, he had written to Ian Parsons,[16] outlining an enormous writing programme. He had sketched out a plan for a two- or a four-volume study, 300,000 to 400,000 words in any case, drawing a long historical bead on Marx's classical emphasis on the relation of country to city, going on to tackle this relation by way of the novel as *the* literary form with which to render cities (the second volume), and proceeding to further studies within this framework of 'War, Empire, and the Future'.

Parsons quickly settled for the four-volume plan. At the same time, Williams mentioned that he was beginning the third novel of what had become the Border trilogy but was not to be published for another thirteen years. Lastly, Parsons asked for a revised edition of the drama book. However, since its many mutations into its published form, not only had Williams written *Modern Tragedy*, but the work of Bertholt Brecht had won a remarkable victory over the English-speaking stage. Eric Bentley (who had ten years before refereed *Ibsen to Eliot* very critically) published his best-selling translations, the Berliner Ensemble had been to London, old Popular Frontist school teachers had put on *The Chalk Circle* and *Galileo*[17] as school plays, and Williams's textbook demanded drastic revision.

A revised version was politely requested by Parsons for early March 1967. Williams put in one of his dauntingly, dauntlessly hard stints of writing. He had just finished as Secretary to the Faculty, but he was revising the textbook in the form of new drama lectures, moving Brecht to the heart of things. That was during the summer term. In the spring term of 1967 he was giving three separate series of lectures on the novel – 'Dickens to Lawrence' on Mondays, 'Critical Problems' on Tuesdays, 'Conrad' on Fridays. He was in the middle of his eight years as editor of 'The New Thinker's Library', a touching resurrection of an old-fashioned adult educator series published by Watts (he scarcely ever declined a commission). He turned out his monthly review for Bill Webb at the *Guardian* during these same weeks, and a magisterial conclusion to Eagleton's collection of essays trying to hold together Marxism and Catholicism for the happily named and heretical journal *Slant*. Amid all this he polished off Brecht, using him to demonstrate the possibility of turning naturalist drama into radically historical drama, transforming biography into political tragedy (and comedy too, though he didn't say so). Lukács's apothegm, made to Bill Webb in Budapest two years later, about the dissolution of the individual-society dualism, found its first English expositor.

Williams had been working and turning the question over as both a philosophic and a political one for years. On 15 March 1967 the BBC broadcast at prime time on its main channel the second of his plays for television, *Public Inquiry*. You could call it his agreement with Lukács.

You could say also that it was Brechtian; it certainly has its tragedy. I'd rather say it is Williams's own style, a poetic idiom made decidedly statuesque by the transposition of his Border Country vernacular into a major key not always innocent of the idealisations of socialist realism, but strong, rhythmic, moving for all that.

The play depicts a father and son, both signalmen working the same box. The son stays late at a union meeting in order to clinch a vote for working-to-rule, while his father covers for him in the box, falsifying the record of his son's absence. Flurried and overtired, he makes a mistake which one of the drivers should have spotted. There is a crash, a driver-friend of his is killed by staying at the controls. At the public inquiry, the father is censured and retired. At the last moment of the play, his son pulls him back from attempting suicide in front of the express at the accident spot.

During his training as a young signalman, the senior official training Tom Lewis says severely,

> That book, Lewis, is like Judgement Day. The entries you make in it are the whole truth of your life as a railwayman. You're a young man now, but I want you to remember this, through your whole working life. You can no more write a lie in that book than you could cheat your own father.[18]

The play dramatises that judgement in the terrible strain of loyalties between duty to the railway and to the union, old generation and young, father and son, the one in the other with no chronological precedence, working their unheeded, natural dynasty so that the long connections (as the train timetables call them) and their promises are all kept by the society which makes them. The link holding those connections, and keeping them safe, is one man in an endless series of such solitary men joined by the track, by the telephone, by 'duty and accident, the first two words ever made me tremble' ... 'and you can just happen to look up, this shape that you're passing, and there's a man in the window, a stranger, looking down and watching the train'.[19]

Williams never published another television play, although he mentions in one of his *Listener* television reviews an early version of his novel *The Volunteers* as starting life in that form.[20] But after March and after revising *Drama from Ibsen to Brecht*, he took a header into the destructive element

211

of politics, and didn't return to the surface of academic or novel writing until the wild and, in places, deadly festivities of the globe in 1968 were played out.

He made the diary of his responses to that year immediately and candidly open, for by then he had accepted the invitation held out by Karl Miller, sometime Leavisite dominie and always Scottish democrat, to provide a monthly television column for the BBC's weekly *The Listener*, of which Miller was then the audacious editor. Academic writing – the four-decker for Chatto and Windus – and the novel which became *The Fight for Manod*, had to wait.

At the start of the autumn term of 1967 his promotion to Reader was announced in the University. 'Reader' is a quaint and agreeable token in British universities awarded to cheer those people up who have written a lot for other people to read but who are not yet going to be given the grand old honorific of professor, with which some other, transatlantic countries make so deplorably free.

Throughout that academic year he continued, amidst the demands of genteel insurrection on the campuses and the public plottings of *May Day Manifesto* in the University of London, to give his lectures on the English novel. At the start of the next year, in the autumn of 1968, Williams gave the first lecture course in the history of Cambridge English to include films. He lectured on dramatic forms and tragedy, on a Monday morning, and poked in two extra sessions of film extracts and discussion on Friday evenings.

It caused, in the stiff, contentious old Faculty, a bit more contention, but 1968 was a good year in which to get your innovations accepted. Besides, Williams was becoming anxiously aware that his four-volume project had made little progress. The first volume was to have been called *The Novel and the City*. So Joy, dedicated as ever to the work, sat at the back of his lectures in Mill Lane on 'The English Novel from Dickens to Lawrence', and every Friday at eleven o'clock, as Raymond put his head back and talked unseeingly out at his crowded audience (for by now his was the mantle of Leavis, and the students flocked to hear the lesson of the master), Joy switched on a tape recorder and turned the rough short-hand method she had learned in her various wartime jobs to transcribing her beloved husband's words.

They took them home, and she dictated in the tiny study at the back of White Cottage while Raymond transcribed and typed, deleted and edited, enlarged a little but not much, so that by 11 July 1969 the manuscript was delivered to Chatto, who coughed up a handsome £250, and in April the next year *The English Novel from Dickens to Lawrence* was published on each side of the Atlantic.

Williams got his usual full round of reviews, including (for the first time) the august *New York Review of Books*, which gave him a lofty enough para by an English critic who had already reviewed it elsewhere.[21] All of them were a bit taken aback by the racily conversational tone of the book, which he had deliberately retained from the recordings, letting the sentences run on and on without punctuation, following the long, sinuous line of the spontaneous speaking of his meditations, eyes rolled back in his head. This was his most mannerist manner, the one by which Dennis Butts and Graham Martin were so mesmerised at the Oxford summer school years before, and which his reverently irreverent students, Sharratt, Eagleton, Swann, Parrinder, mimicked so faithfully.

The book was an unacknowledged correction by Williams the class-warrior to Leavis's *The Great Tradition*. It misses out Henry James, and puts Thomas Hardy, great chronicler of the labouring country class, in his place. It puts down Bloomsbury and all its works on class grounds, and exalts Lawrence not as the great individualist, but as the incomparably inward celebrator of mining community life.

There was one powerful new concept in the book, going far beyond the limits of a few novels on a university syllabus. The advent of the industrial city was the main fact of the industrial–capitalist revolution. Seeking to accommodate its tumultuous and terrifying vitality, the transience of its encounters, the thrill of its coincidences, its astounding permanence, Dickens assembled his unprecedented idiom, almost as though he were inventing a new language, one in which innumerable dialects blend and separate, each betokening its vivid form of life. He hears and recreates a jostling, incomprehensible hubbub of voices, compounded of street-jokes, legal diction, thieves' slang, salon gentilities, and the true languages of love and death, and turns them all into a single poetry.

This unprecedented idiom is then put to work to discover 'the know-able community' hidden in this unprecedented city. Such is, for Williams, the passionate quest of modern society. He turns Durkheim's anomie and Marx's alienation upside down, insisting that the great English novelists, led by Dickens, presage the determined longing of us all to recover from the narratives of our culture versions of that pastoral home where we may lead the good life of homely politics.

As always, he searched his own experience (and in this case experience was the novels in hand) for harbingers and reflections of the ideal border country, the home on the border we can all leave and which can still be restored to us. This is the best of Williams and what movingly speaks from him to so many people; the quest for community, we say; but it's only a slogan. Williams names that in all of us which longs for that lost beati-tude, insisting that it *is* always lost and yet always to be found. Let us call this not the cry of the weaned child, but the resolution of the unappeased and peregrine spirit determined upon the public discovery of home, the remaking of a happy land.

He wrote abstractly, affectingly, endlessly, of this. In his ordinary life he kept breaking any chance of the connections, blindly keeping them behind him, in Pandy, on that actual border. Keeping his own dreams soft, he trod hard on other people's. He at once affirmed and denied community. The ideal was only real when he wrote. This was why he could treat conventions so lightly. It was the ties of his ideal world which were so real; the real world couldn't match up to them. I once asked rhetorically (in Williams's absence), 'Who, who does he talk to in Cambridge?' Years later, Patrick Parrinder, one of his students closest to Williams, said to me, 'I've got a bone to pick about that. Why not make the answer, his students?' Not if he could avoid it, he didn't.

Terry Eagleton

He sat at home and *wrote*, he never went anywhere. I was in his room once and MIT rang up to ask him to go there and talk, and he just said no, he couldn't, because of his opposition to the Vietnamese war. But it wasn't that. There was his absolute commitment to Joy and the family, but also his clenched withdrawal. I saw the students one by one get frustrated. It was something you couldn't get to, but I didn't really try. The nice way of putting it was to say it was part of his natural dignity, the less charitable way, his pride. Hence the lack of proper acknowledgements in his books, the lukewarm references, the un-generosity.

But always the ambiguity, and always the courtesy.

Bernard Sharratt

In 1968 I wanted very much to be taught by Raymond but my college couldn't get him as an official supervisor. So I wrote him a note asking if I could join his seminar group on tragedy. I was just handing in the note at the Jesus Porter's Lodge when the porter pointed across the courtyard and said 'Here he comes.' Williams came into the lodge, obviously in a tearing hurry, the porter handed him a great pile of mail and said something like: 'There's an urgent message from the Arts Council, your taxi's waiting, the Master wants you to phone him – and this young man's just left you a note.' Williams immediately put down his case and the mail, visibly stopped in mid-flight, relaxed, smiled and said, 'Well, what's in the note?' I explained, and he waited until details of times, reading etc. had been sorted out. Then paused to ask 'Are you sure that's all?' Then finally shot off to his waiting taxi.

Williams liked much about college life; he said so. He took his responsibilities towards supporting the subject in the college by increasing the number who taught it very seriously. He got Eagleton his Junior Fellowship and when Eagleton so mortally offended the Faculty they wouldn't keep him, he made sure Stephen Heath stuck. He turned up regularly to college feasts, and used them handsomely to provide the public hospitality he infrequently provided in private. But the only person with whom he became anything like close friends in the college, apart from the band of outlaws, his best graduate students, was Moses Finley, the Jewish-American Classicist who so famously turned his subject upside-down by applying Marxism to Ancient Rome and Greece.

Williams moderated his anti-ritualism, happily enough, for big occasions. In 1969 he submitted all his work for the award of Doctor of Letters, for when he began in adult education one degree was enough. But a Cambridge D.Litt. has indeed its resonance, a recognition carefully weighed and then publicly made by one's peers in the subject. So in July of that year Lionel Knights took him and John Holloway forward to receive the degree from the Chancellor beneath the sumptuous classicism of the Senate House ceiling, and Raymond jolly well bought his own red doctoral robes to wear for the day, and afterwards, as Father Christmas for his grandchildren.

Even with Finley, however, he kept up that complete manner, finished, stated, more than a bit ducal. It had little spontaneity or vividness. Even when, as often, he ran off a flow of sardonic anti-Cambridge jokes and listeners (on his side, of course) rocked with laughter, he would, like a good comedian, not laugh with them but pull his mouth down in a sardonic, pleased smile, quite unbitter. As Sharratt says, if he had no sparkle, only that carved gravity in the way of him, this manner *was* Raymond Williams. His was, somebody once remarked, a character 'which had externalised its own conflicts'.

One doesn't know what to make of that. Can the mind precipitate the inner into the outer? The distinctions make no difference. Or does it mean the inner is somehow more fundamental than the outer? The courteous cordiality, the polite listening, the rhythmic flow of speech in college meetings, in tutorials, in the lecture hall, were of a piece with that practical, working matter-of-factness in his domestic life. His strong dislike of psychoanalysis was no accident.

There is no enigma. There is only the conduct of the man, and any understanding of him as of anybody else carries the judgement in the description. He was, it is handy to say, like his father, though far less liable to silent anger. But like Harry, he did what he did, and everybody went along with it. He held together paradoxically different, even contradictory qualities with striking consistency. He spoke often and movingly of strong emotions, but he rarely showed his own. He commended openness, and kept his peace. He praised giving, and took much from a wife who gave unstintingly. He sought for places to put his loyalty, but could only find his past, his landscape and his family to trust. For a man who loved difficulty and ambiguity, he seemed to have no regrets.

Terry Eagleton

There was no domestic dissension that I ever saw. It was – well, it was a highly conventional marriage. Joy played her own part in the *egoisme à deux*. She had that bright, impersonal manner, and Raymond never showed the slightest awareness of the asymmetry of the relationship.

215

Stephen Heath

It could be a difficult atmosphere, for me as a visitor anyway. Everything revolved around Raymond's work. Joy seemed to have put herself entirely at the service of that and it was hard to find a way of relating to her outside of this role of supporting him with it.

I used to go out to see them quite regularly, especially in later years when they lived in Saffron Walden. Whenever I phoned, almost invariably it was Joy who answered and she'd be off to get Raymond before I could say more than my name, before I could say anything *to her*. If I went to supper, it was taken for granted that Raymond and I would go off on our own to talk immediately the meal was over – that was the order of things. I was embarrassed but there was no opening for anything else, Joy in a sense *absented herself*.

I knew Merryn a little when we were both students – she would come to Raymond's and Joy's parties for the Jesus English undergraduates – and I used to wonder what the strains must have been on her, as a young woman, between a father of immense presence who was so much in demand and a mother who – publicly – presented herself so much in terms of Raymond ...

Raymond gave the impression that Joy was very nervous – he couldn't go out after dark because she was nervous of being left and didn't like being out at night either. Travel was a problem because Joy was afraid of flying. I was in Paris once when they came through on their way to Italy where Raymond was lecturing. They arrived on a train full of – I think – Scottish rugby supporters come for an international. It was very amiable but noisy and Joy was apprehensive and really quite tense until we got to my flat. When they left, I was talking to Raymond on the platform. Joy had got on the train which was suddenly shunted a few yards and she was utterly distraught. But I think Raymond used Joy as a protection for his own nervousnesses as well, he didn't like going out at night, he didn't like flying ... She shielded him and he seemed to use her as a shield. They were very dependent on one another, they went everywhere together.

The deep structure of Williams's life was practical and factual. The facts are the man. That is to say, what mattered first was his writing, and the solitude in which he did it behind the safe barriers of Joy's protection. That way of working *was* his marriage, and the form of his family life. This does not mean he neglected his children. Not in the least. They were parts of the practical, necessary interconnections of work at home; his love for them lived in his ordinary carefulness. Teaching, friendship, collegial life and politics were similar frameworks built more lightly around that core.

So style touched Raymond only lightly in the great efflorescence of fashion which unfolded in 1968 to push him into longer hair, knee boots, a Russian astrakhan fore-and-aft. And as Dafydd Elis-Thomas said much later, 'he always had the best-cut tweeds on the Left'. He and Joy lashed out on a Charles Eames leather armchair to put down in the dank sitting room among the older Williams's bits and pieces. But they hardly looked round, or poked a finger into the sodden window frames. It was home enough, Cambridge, a place to work.

He craved another place to work, nearer home, his Border home, and Joy craved it for him. Sometime in 1968, Raymond's mother reported that the baker who still called at the house with the order had told her of an old cottage ten miles up the road at Craswall, an English name on the very frontier. An old lady who had lived there for generations had gone gently mad and was now in an asylum. The roof had fallen in. The family had thought the place was owned by the hospital.

So Raymond bought the ruin for £1,000. He had the change ready in the royalty account. Merryn was well on the way to her doctorate, Eddy had finished his degree at Cambridge and would shortly have his doctorate in computer work from Oxford. The money was to spare. At the last minute Raymond was summoned by the farmer-relative of the old madwoman for an extra hundred quid, and Raymond duly paid up.

He had another refuge, from the university, from home. They did up the cottage in a rough-and-ready way over the next couple of years; ungifted in the poetics of space, Joy and Raymond sprinkled it with uncertain furniture from local sales, tatty old Welsh prints on the stairs, the queer arrangements of a tiny balcony three feet above the sitting room where an extra bed could go at a pinch, a cheap loo. But the curve of the dry stone wall held the low, stout cottage into the massive rampart of the escarpment of the Black Mountains like a ship carried high on a big sea. The grass paths draw you away from the cottage into the mysterious and delicious arbours made quite naturally by the young trees, larch, hazel, blackthorn, crab apple like the Normandy *bocage*. The big pines behind them keep you safe.

10

WATCHING TELEVISION

In 1968, at the very pinnacle of intellectual dissent and political street theatre in Britain – elsewhere, especially in Chicago, the audience had poured on to the historical stage and turned acting into action – Perry Anderson published his famous polemic, 'Components of the National Culture'.[1]

In it, Anderson mounted a full-scale indictment of that broad spread of British intellectual life which lay between the arts and the natural sciences, summarily convicting its practitioners in history, philosophy, politics, psychology, sociology, anthropology of a narrow empiricism, and a resolute Anglo-Saxon hostility to theory amounting to downright Philistinism, all dominated by a bunch of mainland European immigrants on the run from all that theories of society and human nature had done to their countries.

Anderson implied a diagram of academic inquiries in which each was separated from the other by the divisions of labour as segments in the arc of a wheel. But the wheel had no hub and no drive. Deprived of either Marxist or Weberian theory, the 'absent centre' towards which all intellectual disciplines must converge left them immobilised for the lack of the concept of totality. They did not know how to connect their empirics to the grander movement of history, and they wouldn't learn. English intellectual life remained contentedly inert, calm in its refusal of self-criticism.

Two disciplines were expelled to the margins by the very fact that they had struck up an illicit and clandestine liaison with totality: psychoanalysis, shamefully dominated by women, and English literature. Needing as a matter of urgency a home-bred theorist who could rescue old English inertia (the essay is powerfully, but of course implicitly patriotic), Anderson found one in Raymond Williams. Seeking social theory and intuitively requiring totality, Anderson pictured Williams as finding it in Leavis's literary criticism.

Leavis seized language in literature and placed it in life. More particularly, he found embodiments of essential life in the writings of certain singular figures. He then contrasted that vitality with the debilitated form

218

of linguistic life around the present, tracing a line of steady deturpation from the idealised communities of this highly specific literature – Bunyan's Elstow, Mark Twain's river-town on the old Mississippi, Conrad's training-ship *Conway*, Lawrence's Eastwood – to the consumerist meaninglessness of 'technologico-Benthamite' barbarism in the mid-twentieth century.

Williams, as Anderson saw it, set Marx against Leavis, identified consumerism as capitalism, and replaced the handful of vital and vitalist writers with the emancipatory heart of the best men of the British working class. He restored a future to social criticism, where Leavis only had a past, and replaced individuals in dynamic social structures.

Anderson's essay, I can testify, was utterly intoxicating and prodigiously eloquent. As he later admitted, it was a bit much; his own speech tic 'and so on' became the trope of his essay. But the essay caught the moment. And it confirmed the appointment of Williams not only as intellectual leader of the Left in Britain, but as its star involuntarily caught up by that weird aureatic force in contemporary society which seeks out, identifies, projects and discards celebrity. Anderson did his considerable bit to place Williams in the nova which exploded in 1968, and was made intelligible to us all as a constellation of bright lights.

A world so instantaneously and unevenly available on television and by way of journalism must be made to *mean*. The enormous industry of culture produces meaning as its key commodity. Our way of seeing the world as shaped by the actions of responsible individuals fits exactly this machinery contrived for making things intelligible. Its habits of magnification, both technological and intentional, turn individual agents into stars as these are needed by the moment.

In 1968 Williams became a star. It suited him well enough; he enjoyed the role in his deprecatory, sometimes sardonic way. He had the steadiness of temper and distance from others to take celebrity in and on; he had the egotism also. Anderson didn't nominate him lightly, and Williams accepted nomination, for the time being, willingly. But it confirmed in him that neglect of criticism which his powers of withdrawal had always permitted him. The recognition he was accorded was such that, as David Hare remembered, everybody on the Left wanted him as name or presence in or at their party during those years. At the same time, it excused him from listening to or reading other people except when he happened to light upon something which lit the way ahead; as happened with Lucien Goldmann or Sebastiano Timpanaro.

This meant that he was little touched by fashion except, so to speak, when the glow of admiration from his audience turned him gradually in a new direction. This happened palpably with the Marxism he fashioned out of the dissipation of radical energy after 1972 or so, and the bitter sediment it left in the feelings of some highly political nomads in British universities. But the solitary dedication of his writing out at Hardwick together with its complement, his position as leader of the Left-in-exile, combined to cut him off from ordinary intellectual exchange. For example, it was in those years hardly conceivable that a figure of his talents and interests would not have read Wittgenstein, whose influence touched every one of the human sciences. But I am sure he didn't.

So was Gerry Cohen, then at an early stage of work upon his exemplary study of Marx,[2] when in January 1969 he presented a paper[3] on Williams's textbook *Communications* to the Free Communications Group, a clutch of energetically Leftist broadcasters and journalists. Cohen restates what is now generally accepted as Wittgenstein's irrefutable demonstration that in talking about our feelings with one another we can see we understand the feelings of others and of ourselves without having to suppose that to do so we must share those other feelings in some kind of perfect facsimile. Cohen quotes Williams as he makes this mistake:

> To succeed in art is to convey an experience to others in such a form that the experience is actively recreated – not contemplated, not examined, nor passively received, but by response to the means, actually lived through by those to whom it is offered.[4]

He is in good company in this error; it is almost exactly how Tolstoy puts it in *What is Art?*

It may seem a bit abstruse to take Williams to task for philosophical mistakes in the course of this biography. But much turns on it, not least because in his best practice – particularly when writing in his direct, caustic way about domestic television – he surpassed his error and, speaking in ordinary language, corrected the conversation of the culture in what Wittgenstein had contended was the only means by which the job is done. In theory, however, Williams made the mistake so many people make, that we know what we feel by introspection.

Williams was held to this traditional mistake not least by the intense nature of his own feelings of privacy. This is the paradox. He looked into his deepest feelings, and he trusted them absolutely to stand for the best feelings of others. He would have responded with blank anger to Wittgenstein's medicine:

> The temptation to say 'I see it like *this*', pointing to the same thing for 'it' and 'this'. Always get rid of the idea of a private object in this way: assume that it constantly changes, but that you do not notice the change because your memory constantly deceives you.[5]

If the private object in question were Williams's deeper feelings and the allegiances which were their object, he simply couldn't have performed this salutary thought-experiment. But the personal exposition of private experiences is a delusion because we could never determine if what was being expounded were true.

Psychological or emotional words do not name private experiences which we alone can know. The language of feeling, like any other language game, is only made intelligible if we follow the rules of the game. We all of us learn the right way to use emotion words, and we also learn that there are many right ways, only one of which is to describe or report on our state of mind. In Williams's case, for sure, he was often invoking his feelingful allegiance in the hope that others would feel something like the same; what he was doing therefore was persuading (as he didn't understand). He was not producing in others a facsimile of his feelings. Talking about feeling is just another language-game, and as such it is reciprocal, sociable, public.

The oddity is that Williams so neglected an argument which established the necessarily public, conversable making of the structures of our feeling, since such facts were what really constituted his own deep values. Worse still was his acceptance of the fallacy that art, like all other modes or genres of communication, has as its common purpose the 'transmission of valued experience',[6] and that the 'only practical use of communication is the sharing of real experience'.[7]

What can this mean? Not only is this absurdly restrictive, it repeats the old fallacy, and in doing so leads to wrong moral actions as a consequence.

This is the importance of this short detour into ordinary language philosophy. Sticking to the fallacy about the identity of feeling would mean that to 'share valued experience' must be understood as *to feel exactly the same way*. There is no interpretative translation, there is either reproduction or (even more important to Williams) the recognition of affinity (this is what solidarity is for him). Since it is obvious that people do not 'share' identical or facsimile feelings, there are only three courses of action open, two of them morally repugnant, one of them politically vacuous. You either try to force people to feel the same, or you blame them for not doing so; or you pretend they do when they don't. This was the triple error of the old new Left. Williams, never a bully, was naturally led by his distaste for quarrelling to this third choice.

Wittgenstein locates a central symptom of Williams's general habit of writing and thinking in disregard of the bibliography of the day; what he did was simply to keep on writing, to use the books he happened upon as prompts to new thoughts. He always called himself a writer; a slightly priggish touch comes out when in the conversations with his inquisitors in 1979 he gave himself the title of writer 'not professor; I have to remind myself I am that'. It is another instance of John Dunn's acute criticism that:

John Dunn

Williams's experience in Cambridge was not, for him, experience at all. The truths of his experience were in no sense Cambridge-dependent. He never made any sense of spending twenty-odd years in an extremely privileged university. He never found an appropriately defensive account of what it was to teach at Cambridge.

221

Writer, not teacher? But writer with a steady and taken-for-granted income quite independent of his writing. And a university teacher quietly working his way up, as his father would have ardently wished, from Lecturer (in 1961) to Reader (in 1967) to Professor (in 1974), obviously concerned and conscientious about the progress of his subject in college and university, pressing (as did old Leavis) for progressive change in its syllabus, finally bringing films within the purview of a once radical, long since conservative system of curriculum construction.

In the academic year of 1968–69 his lecture course on dramatic forms and tragedy included Eisenstein, Bergman, Pudovkin, Lang, D.W. Griffith. The films were shown on Friday evenings to be discussed on the following Mondays (Mill Lane, 11 a.m.). In the spring term of the next year he gave four lectures with a following hour of discussion, much along the lines of his and Michael Orrom's old textbook *Preface to Film* and the Brighton evening class which went with it. By 1971 and 1972 he had run drama into film, and lectured on 'Strindberg to Godard' for ninety minutes on a Thursday afternoon at 5 p.m., with plenty of time for watching film clips and, in a manner unusual in the Cambridge lecture hall, with plenty of (as they then said) audience participation.

Writer; teacher; star of the Left; intellectual; journalist. He was his father's son. Like Harry, he had good, steady work with a large firm which paid respectably if not exceptionally, wasn't subject to sudden dismissal in times of general economic hardship, left plenty of spare time both in and out of official hours for other forms of work, as well as allowing its practitioners to use what they had put together in earlier years as often as they liked. Instead of signal-box-keeping, honey-making, dahlia-raising, apple, plum and pear-growing, eggs, cockerels, potatoes, carpentry and joinery, instead of these: literary criticism, political theory, novels, the odd television play, political oratory, extra-Parliamentary politics, *Guardian* book reviewing, commentary in the journals of opinion, and for four years from 1968 to 1972, monthly television criticism for the BBC's house weekly, *The Listener.*

The variety as well as the sheer application of his labours at the typewriter make Williams seem, without any deprecatory echo, a small businessman of letters. Running the job from home with low overheads (Joy for secretary, his own, almost unheated study, tiny home telephone bills), he took in almost every commission irrespective of whether it paid, but always watchful of the deal (as Carmen Callil once said in a memo at Chatto and Windus, 'RW is no mean slouch at business, I must say').[8] Keeping his own accounts and tax returns and reproachful, also, of publishers who were late and inept with theirs.[9]

So there was never any doubt that he would accept Karl Miller's invitation to do a monthly television column for *The Listener*, particularly since he had written *Communications* without taking a daily newspaper or having a television set in the house! The Williamses got their first set, Merryn remembers, 'sometime in the early sixties, I think it was after the Labour Party got in'. But in spite of the mountains of work Raymond took on after 1967 – *May Day Manifesto*, the National Confederation, the books, the reviewing, the teaching, he got his writing cleared in his daily, unyielding 9 a.m. – 1 p.m. stint at the typewriter, characteristically setting Sunday morning aside for the television criticism (it not really being work to write about TV).

The confident ease and off-duty nonchalance with which he took to such hack labour brought out the best in him. Williams had always spoken in his journalism with a quite different voice from his critical and theoretic idiom. His lecturing manner, 'putting his head back and speaking' (as Eagleton put it) in that strongly and rhythmically undulating way, a way close at times to incantation, with his eyes rolled upwards in his head, the deeply incised and geological landscape of his face kin to the bards and seers of his people, was quite unlike that of his double, the journalist.

The journalist was racy, sardonic, hard-bitten, cynical as a journalist should be. (This journalist has a brother, hero of *The Volunteers*.) The journalist started from and with the news of the day, and of the world. He was laconically up-to-date. He was a socialist, so, anti-capitalist. He watched the hard stuff, knew the good stuff, was understandingly contemptuous of the rubbish but took nothing for granted, least of all the judgements about the rubbish. As he said himself in his professorial address and in professorial accents:

> Only dead cultures have scales that are reliable. There are discernible, important and varying proportions of significant and trivial work, but for all that, today, you can find kitsch in a national theatre and an intensely original play in a police series. The critical discriminations are at once important and unassumable in advance.'[10]

So it was that, in the middle of the exhilarating public commotions of 1968 and Williams's propulsion into the centre of them as far as the Left and its student constituency were concerned, he picked up *The Radio Times* and the *TV Times* each Friday, marked what he would watch in the following week, and made sure he did so. Indeed, once the telly was so belatedly installed, the tiredness of which he so often wrote together with his drive to privacy together dropped him in front of the set pretty often, and much more than Joy.

David Holbrook

I'd known Raymond since Cambridge in 1945, such a serious, mature man, he was a good example to us. I wrote to him for good advice when I was going into Adult Education in 1953, and got it. Then he found work as a supervisor for me in Cambridge when things were hard. He got tired. His students used to complain he went to sleep when they read their essays to him in tutorials. I'd roll up at Hardwick, and Raymond would be watching the gymkhana on telly. I had the impression he watched for *hours*.

I couldn't stand so much telly. I don't believe he knew what was on unless it was for the *Listener* piece. I mean, he'd leave the set on while we tried to talk, and it just flowed over him.

But Williams, as Frank Kermode said, was a pro. If it was his byline, the stuff was bang on time. He started in August 1968, just before the Soviet tanks crushed the Prague Spring under their tracks, and he fought back at Robin Day when on *Panorama* he 'tells us that the Czechs are struggling for things we've already got', and 'I tell him to keep his "we" to himself'. In 1968 you could still just about hang on to the hope that a decent, workable socialism might yet emerge from Dubček's daring in Prague or Kádar's terrible patience in Hungary.

It's Williams's calm, casual, completely authoritative bloody-mindedness at home, however, which most sharply reminds us of what's so much missing from British journalism. The ruling class, for instance.

It is the combination of those quiet voices, those composed manners, those relaxed drawing-rooms, that keeps suggesting there is nothing whatever to hide: all is purest rationality and normality, whatever cruel or stupid (as well as reasonable) acts they may happen to be engaged in. The appearance of frankness, of that cool but always available politeness, is the most efficient collective disguise I have ever encountered, and for my own part I have given up asking it questions. I look for the answers in what they do.[11]

Williams's television journalism is much more than a matter of making such calmly insubordinate noises from the back of the room, cheering and necessary though these are. When he turns to a Dennis Potter play – *Lay Down Your Arms* – he rejects the 'orthodox analysis' of the working-class scholarship boy 'making his way into an Establishment which at once fascinates and revolts him', shouting rude names at its stupidity, contemptuous names which he learned from the education the Establishment decided to give him.

Williams turns caustically on this, and on the Freudian-derived analysis of the hero as projecting personal difficulties of guilt and dislocation into externally directed anger and aggression. What Potter dramatises for Williams is a much more than personal 'crisis of identity'. In a sketchy play, Potter is presented as addressing exactly what is being omitted in the general election contested that same week: the 'basic structure of society and its possible policies'. Not only this, but framing the dramatised conflicts, between father and son, between classes, between views of the political actions (Suez and Hungary in this case), Williams places his 'structure of feeling'. Only this time he does not make this a Thing mysteriously transmitted and received. He makes it an argument in words, about feelings as created in a drama for our recognition. Don't take Potter's play personally, Williams says; take it historically. Don't feel it as about your son, or about you; feel it as about your history, and how to make it yours. Don't see it like them; see it like this, instead.

This is the mode of criticism, the mode of critical pedagogy, and it is what makes Williams's television journalism, in spite of the murky bits, so much much better than the writing of such house comedians as Clive James or Nancy Banks-Smith. They are extremely funny, but *only* funny. Williams keeps humanism going, keeps the big, necessary words clean and audible. He puts side by side what television itself put side by side one May evening in 1969: African women hopelessly trying to wave a huge swarm of locusts from their crops, and a chimpanzee in a jacket raced across the Atlantic to advertise Tetley's Tea and the *Daily Mail*.

'What had produced this conjunction? It was ordinary BBC-2 planning: a repeat of *The Years of the Locust* followed by a 'progress report' of the Transatlantic Air Race. The *Horizon* film was television at its best: serious, practical, mobile – a detailed showing of the return of the locust plague, out of the Arabian desert into a belt across Africa. The people fighting the locusts had the everyday commitment and comradeship of a clear and uncomplicated social purpose. I remember the Eritrean, a former fighter-pilot, flying his light plane through the swarm that was bursting on his windscreen like machine-gun fire: his calm eyes and voice, his hands on the simple controls. There was a very similar pilot, an Irishman on Aer Lingus somewhere over the Atlantic, being interviewed about the Air Race. It took him several seconds of embarrassed decency to bring out the word 'stunt'. He didn't want to be offensive; he just knew the difference between that and Alcock and Brown. It isn't often we get so complete and transparent a festival of the society so many powerful interests are trying to establish.'[12]

Class, always, is what grips and moves him, and class in art. It brings out the harshness in him, as when writing about the magnificent adaptation of Tolstoy's great novella *Resurrection* in December 1968, the news of the world's great year all in by then and most of it stained with disappointment whether in Paris, Prague or Saigon, he writes with exceptional bitterness of the connection he saw, lived as he saw it, and wanted us to live with him, between art and life. In *Resurrection* art turns into the irreconcilable, bloody collision of 'the morality of revolution as opposed to the morality of conscience and charity'; whichever side Tolstoy was on finally, there's no doubt where Williams stood.

He writes elsewhere in this remarkable sequence of his Sunday thoughts, taken on the run, of 'art jumping us'. Yet it wasn't often that, it seems from the page or from the life, that art really did jump Williams. Ricks's remark that Williams's habits of mind largely lacked that habit of the 'mind's recoil upon itself' has its truth; the terrific self-assurance of *The English Novel from Dickens to Lawrence* or of his treatment of Arthur Miller in *Modern Tragedy*, of Ben Jonson in *The City and the Country* are tokens of this certainty. He is hardly ever disconcerted by art, mostly on top of it, and history too.

But then class cuts him open. He watches Dmitri try to make atonement to Maslova, and he sees the prose, the feeling, and the bodily movement become one. He sees that the best television is live like great drama in live theatre, and he asks for nothing better on behalf of the watching millions. This response is the more marked because, immediately afterwards in the same week he catches ex-Marxist David Mercer adorning a man's, a writer-man's self-pitying demand for sex from his beaten mistress, with the names of history and insurrection, in order to give his plight and play a bit of stature. Williams dismisses him with contempt, as so much of

> that rough, cursing monologue, overriding precision as it overrides what others might say; that howl for attention to the isolated body's hairs and juices which converts the cries of history – the banners, the barricades, the revolutionary crowd, the name of Che – to its own angry echoes.[13]

This is angry and quick, Williams spontaneously rejecting television's degradation of one of his primary allegiances. This is why his television criticism is so readable and so good. He talks aloud from his sitting-room on how the world looks to him through the screen which reveals it. Best as always on the side of those who have been wronged, he can be wrong (like any of us) when his sympathies and the action on screen come together as victory. Casting himself to speak on the same side as – on behalf of – the put-upon, the exploited and the oppressed, the losers of history, leaves him at a loss, at a loss and not knowing it, when he comes up against losers who have won. 'In its central intention, or at least in its declared intention, the Cultural Revolution seemed to me one of the most hopeful things that have ever happened in the world.'[14] It had been a documentary, in the summer of 1971, called *Ping-Pong in Peking*. The producers were in time for the alliteration. Max Hastings, of all people, fronted it. And when we were told, in ruefully incredulous accents, that all the factory executives did physical work, Williams was rather too quick in reply. 'The requirement to go to the country and do physical work is not, for me, the difficulty. In very different conditions I find I have to do the same to keep sane.'[15] They were different, all right. Rotovating a few beds of nettles up the hill at the cottage in Craswall wasn't what the Red Guards had in mind.

One can see what he means. But the unreality of the attempt 'to abolish the divisions between intellectual and physical work, between town and country, between the executive and the operative' still knocks you back. He *must* have known that all that stuff about Chairman Mao and the blooming flowers was dangerous twaddle; the imperative to solidarity stopped him thinking. He was still doing the same thing when, a few years later, he gropingly tried for a halfway sympathetic interpretation of Year Zero in Cambodia, as declared by born leader Pol Pot in 1975.

> Many people draw back at the spectacle of forceful repatriation to the countryside and the very brutal discipline employed to enforce it, although it could be argued that these were a consequence imposed by a revolutionary seizure of power in a situation made so exposed by a previous history ... The real tragedy occurs at those dreadful moments when the revolutionary movement has to impose the harshest discipline on itself and over relatively innocent people in order not to be broken down and defeated.[16]

Yes, many people do indeed draw back. This is language filthy with dishonest use on the tongues of Soviet and Chinese policemen. Battling always to hold the connection with his side, Williams agrees to describe arbitrary cruelty as tragic necessity. It is not just culpable ignorance at work here, it is venal self-deception, and I treat it with a heavy hand because here the lapse has so disfigured even Williams's, the best face of the Left-intelligentsia, the man who could be depended on to judge the events of the day justly.

The excellent and emulatable generosity of the Left carried it to the losers' side. But that Left could not imagine how to win without recourse to a theory of terror, a theory which, incorporating mass murder, cruelty, revenge and the death of justice, causes these same monsters to dissolve into its pure abstraction. It's all right if it's theory. The abominable thing is that that same view is taken straight from such guides to humanism as Robespierre and Lenin, and then sunk deep in the cortex of Western Marxism.

Such a blinding aberration is at the heart of the conceptual and practical glaucoma of the Left intelligentsia. But while the intellectuals of the Right, who *did* touch power in Britain and North America, made a much worse mess of things, the old British New Left, living always with the actuality of defeat, could and did direct their best energies into the success and exhilaration of opposition. As we see, this habit of opposition has its limitations as an intellectual and practical method, but (as Edward Thompson said) there is always so bloody much to oppose.

At home, in permanent opposition, Raymond kept his counsel, his nerve, his temper. One afternoon in the spring of 1970, before going home to Hardwick for the television, he had an appointment with a not-so-young German student called Rudi Dutschke.

Dutschke had been a radical student leader in Germany at the height of university dissent in Europe in 1967. Lanky, with thin, good-looking features and tousled hair, he was less dazzling and fluent than his Parisian counterpart, Daniel Cohn-Bendit, but even more uncompromising in his criticism of West German consumerism, and its far deadlier predecessor which Federal German and the Democratic Republic were bent on so unfederally and undemocratically forgetting. He was shot and critically wounded in the head and chest by enemies of a neo-Fascist and forgetful tendency for his pains. He survived. The police put it to him that if he stayed in Bonn or Berlin someone would try again. He applied to Williams and asked to write about Georg Lukács. Williams, with characteristic solidarity, took him on. Dutschke had had the speech centres of his brain damaged by the attack, and had to relearn parts of his own language. Williams talked to him at length, but reckoned that, living quietly and with plenty of therapeutic as well as academic help, he could do the work.

It wasn't only up to Williams, of course. His recommendation went forward to the Board of Graduate Studies, and as Williams himself said, 'I have seen hundreds of research students admitted, and I have known no single case in which there was so much checking and counter-checking.'[17]

Dutschke was a star and a symbol from the dread year of 1968. The Tory government had a horror of such people, and they weren't going to let in some sort of German Spartacist if they could help it. Still, Cambridge was Cambridge; the University, as Williams also pointed out, at least knew by its investigations a great deal about Dutschke. The Home Office admitted him, on condition that he consorted in no way at all with political adults.

Not an easy condition to meet if the subject of your scholarship was a book called *History and Class Consciousness*. England was in one of its regular throes of moralising about leftishness and radicals, fearing revolution and giving it a man's name, the eddies of 1968 still surging a bit in its emotional backwaters. So they put Dutschke under surveillance and chucked him out at the first opportunity in defence of the constitutional principle that liberal states shall do what they like with their liberties, especially if rich trading partners tell them to.

Williams fought the decision all the way to a National Council for Civil Liberties protest meeting in Central Hall Westminster on 14 January 1971. Cambridge, as Cambridge does once it has accepted you, defended its man manfully. Over a thousand academics petitioned on behalf of Dutschke and academic freedom, and Williams spoke ringingly for them all when he invoked the essential internationalism of university research:

> For me as for others this is an intrinsic value of the university, and the effects of this case have very deeply shaken it. Very crude definitions

228

of national security and very alarming prejudices about people stereo-
typed as foreign nationals, have shaken that value, and have alarmed
many respected and welcome members of the university, at very
different stages of their lives. I felt this so strongly, during the Tribunal,
that if I could I would have declared myself foreign or stateless, since
if being British meant being what these definitions and prejudices
indicated, I no longer wanted to be it. Yet my whole life and work is
here, and the threat must be fought in a different way.[18]

In June 1970 he had gladly bade farewell to Wilson's Labour government;
seven months later his deepest feelings, always silently eloquent on behalf
of his private definitions of home, started to pull him off the border back
into the safety of a more distinctive Welshness. 'I want a culture I can
breathe in' he said to me and in print a few years later, but then, as he
declared in Westminster and repeated to his own Cambridge, 'my whole
life and work is here'.

1970 had been a bad year for trying to feel at home in England, or
anyway those corners of England which took strong colour from the
metropolis. What was wrong with the metropoles wasn't so much their
xenophobia, as their hatred of the Left. Kick Dutschke out, certainly.
After the petitions and the meetings, the short-lived paragraphs of outrage
in the *Guardian* and the *New Statesman*, the government hustled him out,
still frail and convalescent, as well he might be after bullets had been dug
out of his head, and Denmark offered him a quieter hospitality.

Not so very long afterwards, he died, having overturned no governments.

On the other hand, as balanced history books say, back in February
there had been a so-called 'Greek week' in Cambridge. Greece at the
time enjoyed the rule of a bunch of colonel-gangsters who, troubled by
the tide of messy and incompetent democracy which seemed to be rising
in their homeland, assumed power by courtesy of tanks rather than
elections, with a general view to tidying things up, putting a few leftists
inside, smartening society and cleaning up the Parthenon.

Such a policy was always attractive to plenty of indigenous and emigré
militarists in southern England, and somebody with money to spare had
joined with the Tourist Board to back this 'Greek week' in Cambridge in
order to put down the revolting students' sanctimony. The said students
had reacted gratifyingly by staging a sit-in on the premises of a travel
agency. Then an evening-dressed sort of reception for local worthies and
assorted grandees was arranged, with Greek food and dire Greek music,
at the Garden House Hotel. The hotel stood along a cul-de-sac beside
the narrow sluice of the river as it meandered in towards the colleges. It
had a pleasant seat upon small lawns with plate-glass windows giving onto
the water and willows.

229

The communists would organise a protesting demonstration, with Haben Naqbal as its pleasant, talkative convenor. There were few police, and a couple of hundred students, chanting, as students used to, at the class enemy. Bricks, inevitably, flew, and a plate-glass window was satisfyingly smashed. Robin Marris, a senior member of the University and an old New Leftist got in as a guest by way of his cashmere overcoat and, having been an RAF pilot in wartime action, took rather ill the old buffer spluttering amongst the debris, 'I didn't fight in the war so that hooligans could insult me and my Greek friends . . .' John Vincent, a historian Trot at the time although later the only Professor of Modern History to write a regular column for the *Sun*, egged on the crowd from the back with a bullhorn so that a wretched proctor was bashed on the head. There was a fistful of arrests, the police and the proctors cooked up the evidence between them, and seven or eight students went down for a few months to the accompaniment of some well-modulated raucousness from the Judge.

Bob Rowthorn, then as now the best-looking economist in a not very photogenic class, was one of the prisoners and the son of a cop.

Bob Rowthorn

The police and the proctors fixed the evidence. They decided who the ringleaders were from the lists of known political activists. The junior proctor was anxious about this, but they got the right people, the guilty ones, as well as a few who were innocent. One poor Christian lad went down for six months! and somebody got two years, greatly to the surprise of the police. They thought it was a marginal affair. When I was arrested, I defended the police to the others; my father was a policeman. I said they weren't pigs or Fascists, just on the wrong side.

The CP set up a defence committee, with Williams and Goran Prinz-Pahlson, a lecturer in Swedish who would shortly stand up for Dutschke, as members. Williams drew a guarded moral for a piece on the police in his *Listener* review. He is wry at the expense of British TV cops – 'those snapping egos . . . taking over, glaring and rasping at each other . . . the growling, insecure, status-conscious lot [on *Softly, Softly*].[19] The student in the TV story gets off lightly; Williams's own student is doing time. Williams knows plenty of decent policemen, like everybody else, it's easy to feel sympathy with them, but 'does the BBC have to put itself so simple-mindedly on one side of the argument . . . as naturally, as casually as, say, it supports King Hussein?[20]

It was a question which recurred, fourteen years later, when the Royal Yorkshire mounted police, bussed in from all over England, charged striking miners on the field of Orgreave, and ran them down with clubs. What Williams began to see in 1970, in fact, was the outline of a new kind of British state. It would be a state opposed to statism; joining in the popular hatred of state 'interference' it would enormously enlarge its invisible pervasiveness by backing the popular approval for strong authority, law-and-order, the suppression of dissent and nonconformity. This new and exceptional state would draw its legitimacy from what Stuart Hall would call its 'authoritarian populism';[21] Margaret Thatcher would be its embodiment.

One can see those thoughts coming through the slow, massive, rather battleship-like movement of Williams's mind[22] as he turned in late 1970 and early 1971 to address himself to a literary sibling and unavoidable fellow-pedestrian with whom he had never been on the best of terms.

Frank Kermode was editing his remarkable new series 'Fontana Modern Masters' in which, at that date, various luminaries in the European curriculum had received a tailoring job which left them cut down to a much smaller size. Weber, Lévi-Strauss, Marcuse, had had their surgery. Kermode invited Williams, though with absolutely no iconoclastic requirements, to take on George Orwell.

Naturally, Williams did. The commission paid respectably, the venture was well-publicised. Between 25,000 and 30,000 words was nothing to him, even with the journalism and the four-parter for Chatto. Moreover, as he said himself, 'In the Britain of the fifties, along every road that you moved, the figure of Orwell seemed to be waiting',[23] and there were bones to be picked between them, about socialism, about Britain, about dissent and about what it was to be a writer, a novelist, and a celebrity.

The similarities are easy, though Williams doesn't even acknowledge them, let alone take them easy. Both men wished to speak as directly as possible of bloody-minded old Britain, the horrible actuality of its class injustice, its somnambulism, its dead refusal to face up to its own awfulness. Both wanted to find a prose and a form which would accommodate these facts. Both wanted to live intensely the politics of everyday life *as politics*, and to write about them in a like manner. Both felt right through them the bonds which tied them to their history.

Orwell did and felt these things; but Williams repudiates him. It is indicative that two of the most prominent American intellectuals of the present day, Richard Rorty and Michael Walzer, honest and true men both, chose Orwell as their truthteller, the voice in whose accents they hear the plain truth told about the cruelty and monstrousness of politics. It must be because class is still so unusable an ideological concept in anti-socialist old America. Yet Walzer can rejoin to Williams, in a fine essay:

> 'As for *1984*,' Williams told the editors of *New Left Review*, 'its projections of ugliness and hatred ... onto the difficulties of revolution or political change, seem to introduce a period of really decadent bourgeois writing in which the whole status of human beings is reduced.' 'The difficulties of revolution' invites comparison

231

to Auden's 'the necessary murder' – a line that could never have been written, Orwell rightly said, by anyone who had ever seen a man murdered. So Williams's line could never have been written by anyone who had actually experienced those 'difficulties'. It represents a refusal to respond, intellectually or emotionally, to the central events of the twentieth century ... Orwell was the very model of a 'national–popular' intellectual, perhaps for that reason he sensed that a democratic politics was more readily available, more immanent in English life, than any Marxist analysis could allow. At the same time, he worried that the defeat of democratic politics might open the way for a hegemony far worse than anything the bourgeoisie had ever achieved.[24]

But Williams, in the last two chapters of his brief book, lets the hell out of his temper at Orwell's 'stale revolutionary romanticism', his 'incomplete humanity', 'the lonely confusion of the adolescent' (with a concomitant 'guilt about lovemaking' thrown in), 'the disillusioned and embittered prophet of the forties'.[25] He even blames Orwell for inventing the 'anti-hero' of the fifties, that aggressive young hero of working-class upward mobility, covering his bourgeois assimilation with his 'generalised swearing'. For Williams, as ever, form is the crux, and the form of Orwell's novels – in particular *Animal Farm* and *1984* – is in Williams's analysis, reactionary, lethally class-bound. As Raymond said to Merryn more than once, what he hated about *Animal Farm* was that it pictures the oppressed as *animals* revolting against *men*.

And yet, and yet ... Williams is too honest to overlook the classic, calm essays on popular culture, the radical journalist of *Tribune*, the heroic Schweik of the Catalonian front. So he falls back on Orwell's contradictoriness, a fact of history much more than of identity. That contradictoriness was briefly resolved for Orwell when he went to Spain: the alliance in that war between the monster Fascism and bourgeois capitalism was plain to see in the sunny light of the daytime bombing of Guernica. The contradictions of history were dissolved into the happiness of honourable action.

Then Stalin's Soviet Union became an ally, and Orwell had to settle for a contradictory patriotism, sufficient unto the day. Williams couldn't take that, and in rejecting it, had to give up in this particular polemic, his belief in long revolution coming out well.

In other West European countries, where elements of the old order collaborated with fascism and new alliances had to be made in the necessary resistance, other choices were possible. But in England capitalist democracy survived with its main contradictions intact, and then the pretence or hope that it was social democracy, or was about to become so, lasted longer than was good for anybody's reason.

Even after the profound disillusions of 1945–51 and 1964–70, the pretence or hope survived. Yet no such illusion is static. If the only effective social contrast was between 'democracy' and 'communism', then some sort of accommodation with capitalism – that capitalism which was 'on the point of' becoming a social democracy – was at first temporarily and then habitually conceivable. Having made this accommodation, and the corresponding identification of 'communism' as the sole threat, it became harder to see and to admit what capitalist imperialism was still capable of doing: what, in the years since Orwell died, it has done again and again, in repression and in war.[26]

I suppose this is another instance of Williams's over-fastidious recoil from Fabianism. But here he has lost his touch with the ordinariness of culture, as well as denying his own, never-failing hopefulness. The people, *his* people saw 1945–51 as years of great achievements in democracy; so does he in so much of his writing in the late 1950s and early 1960s. Even Wilson had his moments: a mere half-a-million unemployed; the troops back from East of Suez; compulsory redundancy pay; consumer protection; tenants' rights; sexual freedoms; all enacted. They don't look much, but you could call them victories in a long revolution.

Orwell summoned up some obscure rancour in Williams's spirit. My guess is that its source is Williams's keen sense of just how alike Orwell's work and his own really were, and how unsolved and irreconcilable the difficulties with which Orwell grappled and which Williams saw so clearly were. Of course he never fell into Orwell's kind of crassness about 'the mighty loins' of the proletariat, nor his more dewy-eyed fustian in *The Lion and the Unicorn*. But these weaknesses cannot be extricated from Orwell's strengths, which were the vividness and detail with which he saw things and the heartening robustness of his invective. Williams was a much more accomplished thinker, and he saw the sheer difficulty of politics much more fully. But he too pictured a highly unspecific kind of iron command economics a very long distance from the work people do, and his proper patriotism only avoided flag-waving by being tied to twenty miles of railway line and a few hills in a county which for centuries had no single mother-nation.

One can only call Williams's attack on Orwell a personal one. That is exactly because he took his reading of certain key authors personally. 'Structure of feeling' was a concept designed to catch the point of intersection between art and historical experience as individually, and therefore as socially lived. Williams's project since *The Long Revolution* had been to grasp a cultural history as experience; that is to say, to interpret the movements of change caught and held in the peculiar lenses of art (especially novels) not just as they were lived by their makers – Dickens,

233

Hardy, Lawrence – but insofar as they consciously and non-consciously dramatised the best values of their day in such a way as to make them renewable in a better future.

It was a risky business; for to study feeling as it articulates as action is to risk becoming quite sterile with abstraction, like a golfer studying the rhythm of other people's swings until he locks himself tight with self-consciousness. Williams turned to the new French theorists who offered a method by which to escape the rigidities of personality.

Lucien Goldmann had come to Cambridge in May 1970, the parodic French intellectual, Gauloise in his hand and at the lip, open-necked shirt, leather jacket, thick accent, cheerful, voluble, prowling the seminar room with hunched shoulders. Williams arranged for his return in 1971; Goldmann died suddenly at 57, before he could return. In a commemorative lecture a year later in Cambridge,[27] Williams spoke of the pressing need for a theory which would take him beyond literary criticism and the old English objections to those foreigners of a French or German kind, who would insist on using hard words, and abstract structures of analysis.

It was more than the sociology of knowledge he was after; it was a method by which to catch the moment of genesis in 'the active processes of learning, imagination, creation, performance',[28] and their continued presence and renewal, or their fading and loss, as past is transformed into future by divers hands. What Yeats called 'the fascination of what's difficult' now drew Williams forward and a little away from the everyday politics which had filled so much of every day since the first *Manifesto* in 1967.

Early in 1972 he went off briefly to the Istituto Orientale in Naples. Fernando Ferrara had boldly initiated Cultural Studies there, amid a medley of philological and linguistic courses for sometime 'oriental' students – meaning the short distance to the shores of the Eastern Mediterranean – and for many more of the hordes of the nomadic Italian students, surging from university to university in the hope of finding a bit of room and a professor to take care of them.

The Istituto Orientale is housed around a black-paved quadrangle in some of the colossal, black, thick-walled and pigeon-spattered houses of downtown Naples. Down the hill, the high narrow street opens on to the huge vista of the bay, with its complex legacy of the panorama paintings of Thomas Jones, the Neapolitan sewage system, and the base of the American Sixth fleet.

Williams went, with Joy and by train, the long trundling journey before high speed diesels reassuring his geographically timid disposition with its familiarity: Calais, then the Venice express through the Simplon Pass, the frontier guards still checking passports along the carriage corridors just like the old war movies; change at Milano Centrale, vaster by far and more splendid than Euston or Paddington, on south to Rome and Naples, sidling by the deep blue sea itself, springlike even in January, the pink almond blossom out beside the line.

Naples itself was, is, a third world city, enormous, sprawling, filthy, its industry, its poor and its myriad, tiny peasant farms all jumbled together around its crammed and ancient heart. Early in Raymond's stay there was a student strike, a little later a lecturers' strike, finally the porters and caretakers came out and the lifts stopped working. When he came back he said to Nick Garnham, rangy *flâneur* of the academic boulevards, 'When industrial society seizes up, Naples is what things will be like.'

At about the same time, Garnham, then a BBC producer, made the first film about Williams's work (Mike Dibb followed it up in 1979). Redolent of a modest radicalism then agreeably present in the Corporation, Garnham juxtaposed some simple, striking images of privilege and the lack of it in the Cambridge of town and university, tracking Williams as he paced the handsome iron gates into the pretty courts of Jesus College before taking him back to his father's signal box to ruminate a little on the changes of work along both borders, and the changelessness of class preference that goes with them.

Williams, dashingly attired in shin-high polished boots, leather Dylan cap, heavy and voluted riding mac, strode with his slightly prancing walk from the new libraries on Cambridge's handsome Sidgwick Avenue site to a sheep-filled road near Craswall, and talked with an awful stiltedness on the way to a directory-full of the Cambridge Tawney group – Tony Giddens, Bob Rowthorn, daughter Merryn – as well as the signalman and shepherd in Pandy. Topped off with a Carl Davis soundtrack and a chat with Dennis Potter, it made a stylish enough programme, not without its banality.

Apart from a few strays – one of them, a piece called 'Distance' written during the Falklands engagement, perhaps the most important piece he wrote about television – Williams finished his four-year stint for Karl Miller's *Listener* just before Christmas 1972. He had, for the first and only time, accepted one of the countless invitations that flowed from the United States and done so, a bit strangely, at just the moment at which Richard Nixon, having swamped the wretched George McGovern at his re-election, bombed Hanoi and Haiphong right through the autumn of 1972 and across Christmas up to the ceasefire which began a couple of weeks after the Williamses arrived in California.

Williams had declined before this warm invitations to turn up in Columbia in Edward Said's department, pleading his objection to the Vietnamese war. This time he allowed himself to be persuaded, as he and Joy took their only flight in a Jumbo, and Raymond hid himself away in the department of Political Science on the lovely Spanish campus of Stanford out at Palo Alto, and came home each day to a neat little flat in Escondido to watch American TV.

He hardly noticed California, the giant, golden and beautiful co-eds, the gay gays putting on the new style, the other end of every kind of world from Naples. He and Joy turned out for an early springtime march against Nixon; apart from that and being dazed by the endless iteration of the ads on television, he fished out his old portable and wrote *Television: technology and cultural form* in six months.[29]

It's far from being his best book, although the best thing in it is probably his rebuttal of the view that technology rules the world and drives history, together with his rough taxonomy in Chapter 3 of the forms of television. It looks as though he was following his engrained habit to write another adult education textbook – indeed, the Open University quickly canonised the new book as such. He rapidly classifies the arguments about the causal relations between technology and culture, pointing out, in a favourite example of his, that Strindberg imagined a script for cinema before the invention of the cinematograph, indicating that form both follows and shapes what the technology will do, and that culture, understood as power and capital, tries always to make technology do what profit and politics prefer.

Joy, willing horse as ever, did the programme counting and allocation at home and in Escondido. The exercise was copied in countless classrooms no doubt, but is not much fun to read. Raymond added a compressed history of electric and electronic media while Nick Garnham advised him when he got home on how the world developments might go. At the beginning of April, Williams tucked the 50,000 words into their suitcases and he and Joy went down to Oakland to take one of the last two day trains back to the east coast, changing at Chicago and catching the QE2 back across the Atlantic just in time for Raymond to buy a new tie in order to attend his daughter's wedding.

The spring term of 1973 had been an official study leave from the university, although he had taught some graduate seminars during his visit to Stanford. He was back in time to hold consultative classes on modern literature on behalf of students who were writing short dissertations instead of taking a particular examination. It was an innovation in those days – regular practice, now, of course – and one close to his heart, which he and Knights had fought for. But apart from the huge chore of marking the papers, those sessions were his only duties to his students in 1973, and there were the novels to keep up with.

In April of that year, Chatto published the second volume of the four-parter he had proposed in 1967. The manuscript was completed, with his usual punctuality and prodigality, in July 1972, and at the same time he had reported to Hugh Brunner in William IV Street that his new novel *The Volunteers* was ready and written.

Like anything worked on for so long it stays in the mind, and now

236

it's finished I'm a bit frightened of it. It follows a group of people through the Europe of the next forty years. It took a lot of thinking and feeling as well as writing, so I suppose I'm a bit drained.[30]

Chatto had their doubt about *The Volunteers*, and Ian Parsons, astute and courteous as always, required cuts to the manuscript of *The Country and the City*, as well as reproaching his famous author for careless talk about George Eliot.

'Wretched' seems an odd objection to use even if you – unaccountably – take this piece of George Eliot *au pied de la lettre*, instead of the piece of ironic pseudo-comic evocation it so patently is. And this leads you into a digression which reads horribly like a piece of Marxist propaganda (old-style) for the rest of the chapter.[31]

Williams took the cuts quietly, though he never put right the perennial objections to his cavalier absence of scholarship in the matter of the bibliography which, Parsons added, was 'much more like a reading list for first year English students than a bibliography by a senior don, and frankly would, I think, expose you to some ridicule from reviewers'.

Christopher Ricks, never an admirer of Williams, was stern in conversation about *The Country and the City*.

Christopher Ricks

There is such bullyingness and deadness in the prose. Look [he opened the book, at random, at pages 20–22]. There is this grand use of anecdote, and then 'of course' 'significantly' 'it is interesting that' ... But these are arguments that have to be *made*. He never works for them. It's like a slide-show – 'Here we can see' ... 'Next slide please' ... 'And it is then interesting to see' ... Nahum Tate, Pomfret, Pope.

The argument can indeed be made. Two admiring pupils, sympathisers of Williams's method, lined up also to criticise something too flat-footed about the book, Williams's angry determination to read all the pastoral art and literature of England as a long lie about the country poor (Wales hardly gets a look in, the Rest-of-the-World two short chapters at the end). John Bull and John Barrell, trenchant leftists both with a future to come, took strong exception to the way Williams 'forced the literature and history ever further apart', and this 'in the face of Williams's ever more urgent attempts to see them as inseparable'.[32] Williams, they said, invoked 'real history' when he meant Marxist historiography, and Barrell criticises an anachronism in Williams's method whereby a poet or novelist is required to see the connections of his local action to this wider 'real history' whether or not anybody could have thought such thoughts and turned them into poetry in such a time.

The book, Bull remarks,[33] is dedicated to 'the country workers who

237

were my grandparents', and woe betide any writer who fails to see the blade of capitalism cutting the marks of suffering in the faces of those who, at two, three or four centuries distance, were comrades and copies of his grandparents. In what one may think of as pre-theoretic literature, which is to say a literature unaware 'of the distortions in the history of settlement', this makes Williams treat his subject poets – Herrick and Ben Jonson in particular – like 'an Intourist chaperon in the early days of the Cold War'.[34] Once again, Williams confidently offers as clinching his case the deeply rooted truths of his own feelings; but these feelings were more and more confirmed in the solitude of his writing and reading, without recourse to collaboration or to the heeding of criticism. He detested the large, last enemy, capitalism, and it walked everywhere abroad, seeking whom it might devour. Hence the steady motion of his intellectual confidence into grand theory across the 1970s; hence also some intellectual mistakes, which he largely ignored when they were pointed out to him.

Yet his was a large and protean mind, in which imagination and its narrative propensity were every bit as strong as his theoretic faculty. Theory and method led him astray, it may be; but something in him which was his best self as a writer added the looked-for corrective in his later novels.

It is surely the novelist's touches which made *The Country and the City* appeal to such a range of readers. John Bull is funny about the unwitting self-parody of Williams's first chapter:

> This then is where I am, and as I settle to work I find I have to resolve, step by slow step, experiences and questions that once moved like light. The life of country and city is moving and present: moving in time, through the history of a family and a people; moving in feeling and ideas, through a network of relationships and decisions.
>
> A dog is barking – that chained bark – behind the asbestos barn. It is now and then: here and many places. When there are questions to put, I have to push back my chair, look down at my papers, and feel the change.[35]

But it was exactly this personal note which spoke clearly to many for whom literature really was experienced as oppression at worst, boredom at best. The best pages in the book are those which, with a not-impressive cheek, Williams simply lifts from his lecture-book *The English Novel* of three years before, and drops gently into the new work. He is splendid as anthologist of social change as registered by Dickens and Hardy. Dickens could see and understand the chaos of railway-building in *Dombey and Son* like Williams saw the possibility of the new town in *The Fight for Manod*. Williams's readers thrilled, as they did to old Marx himself, at the names he is prepared to call the landowner barbarians praised by the pastoral poets. Like Williams, like Marx; both knew that the vile new cities and the new capitalism brought both freedom and misery, abundance and want, cruelty and joy. Then both name for what they were the misery, want and cruelty which was most people's inheritance.

To do this Williams has to abuse local knowledge and experience to the advantage of grand theory, or mere propaganda. He must ignore the peculiar circumstances of the unpolitical poet, and ring his works against the criterion of democratic progress. And yet the sweep of it all, the crowds of writers, the confident banner waved by Williams's narrative cannot but have its exhilaration. His was a call to arms, not a cultural history. The *Eighteenth Brumaire* rewritten as a vast guidebook to the English landscape, you might say, the Puritan become cavalier.

If history is the struggle of classes, it will repay you, however. If your side does these things to minor pastoral poetry, you can't complain when reaction – the Thing – strikes back.

Well, it was another book done; back to work. The Master of the College wrote to Williams in a collegial sort of way while Williams was working for the Labour Party during the general election of February 1974. He told Williams politely that he wasn't meeting his duties to teach a certain number of hours to college undergraduates every term, and would he please do so. Williams wrote back amiably to say that of course he would. Shortly afterwards, his promotion to a personal Chair and Professorship of Drama was announced, courtesy of the Judith Wilson fund as from 1 October 1974. His salary was to be £6,651 per annum. Cambridge professors have no duties to their college to teach house undergraduates.

239

11

THEORY AND EXPERIENCE

He ascended to his Chair shortly after he acquired two grandchildren: Kirsti was born to Ederyn's wife, and Merryn, her doctorate on Hardy long since tucked under her arm, had married a quiet physicist called John Hemp; David was born on 26 June 1974. His mother was then a tutor at the Open University, for substantial sections of whose work in English and Education Williams had become such a potent point of reference.

The Open University, as I've said, was one of the Wilson government's most handsome accomplishments. It was situated emblematically near the centre of the most utopian of Britain's post-war new towns. Milton Keynes was planned as a technological utopia, smoothly grassed and gleamingly housed in two or three storey buildings scattered over the slight undulations of middle Buckinghamshire. The OU was next to a show comprehensive school of fierce progressivism and striking success; its students came by mail from all over the country, and it dispatched the reading and returned the essays from outreach offices controlled, with great efficiency, from the centre.

Graham Martin, its second professor of English, built the course in its early stages on the rock of *Culture and Society*, the historiography of *The Long Revolution*. The reading and the writing were further directed by the specially made television programmes, broadcast by the BBC early on Sunday mornings; as Williams said in a quiet eulogy to the success of the Open University written for *The Listener*, '*every*body can drop in on these courses'.[1] Access to the courses was completely open, competence determined by performance.

Thus, adult education in Britain turned into the egalitarian university, and Williams's work, his way of seeing the benefits of a citizen's education and the networks of trustworthy communication upon which an intelligent democracy must depend, not only turned up in the OU curriculum, it offered a way of judging and valuing the whole undertaking. In the teeth of the new managerialism and the crude profiteering enjoined upon universities, Williams's central concepts were transformed into guiding lights. The idea of a university as promulgated by John Henry Newman

240

and given its polemic edge by F.R. Leavis became in Williams's hands an ideal of mutual social learning, of public communication serving enlightened publics, of a common pursuit of truthfulness and of emancipation by way of a whole curriculum, taking in the history of iconography or solid geometry, astrophysics or the apprehension of the past through the lenses of half-a-dozen novelists.

Williams's inaugural lecture as Professor of Drama to a packed audience on 29 October defined his field with a grand sweep, an allusiveness, a sardonic largeness which betokened his ambitions and his achievement, as well as lending themselves to the affectionate parody in which his students could never quite excel his very own efforts.

> Again I heard, as if for the first time, what was still, by habit, called dramatic speech, even dialogue; heard it in Chekhov and noticed a now habitual strangeness: that the voices were no longer speaking to or at each other; were speaking with each other perhaps, with themselves in the presence of others. But there was a new comprehension, in which a group was speaking, yet a strange negative group; no individual ever quite finishing what he had begun to say, but intersecting, being intersected by the words of others, casual and distracted, words in their turn unfinished: a weaving of voices in which, though still negatively, the group was speaking and yet no single person was ever finally articulate. It is by now so normal a process, in writing dramatic speech, that it can be heard, any night, in a television serial, and this is not just imitation. It is a way of speaking and of listening, a specific rhythm of a particular consciousness; in the end a form of unfinished, transient, anxious relationship, which is there on the stage or in the text but which is also, pervasively, a structure of feeling in a precise contemporary world, in a period of history which has that familiar and complex transience. I don't think I could have understood these dramatic procedures as *methods* – that is to say, as significant general modes – if I had not been looking both ways. I could have seen them, perhaps, as techniques: a professional viewpoint but in my experience not professional enough, for it is where technique and method have either an identity or, as now commonly, a significant fracture, that all the hard questions of this difficult discipline begin.[2]

'This difficult discipline' and its hard questions; drama, now, but he had hardly been to a theatre for years. What he professed was a way, a method for sure, but also, like Leavis, like Michael Oakeshott, a moral commitment to hearing the language of his kind of poetry in the conversation of that corner of humankind which was his society.[3] He hearkened to the poetry of ordinary culture as heeded and set down by writers of all ages, but heard, by Williams, at its best in the strong and heartening speech of

241

working class life this past couple of hundred years. Wordsworth, Dickens, Hardy and Lawrence had heard it; Leavis had found them listening but then twisted what they said into the way he wanted them to say it, which wasn't Williams's way. Williams himself had heard it, in his father's rare speech and along the railway line, had heard it then in those same writers, had heard it abused and condescended to by another, brayingly putting-down mode of utterance, and now listened for it intently in a medley of voices from a dozen different borders.

This *was* his subject, and this his 'full field'. Looking across Europe and North America then and now, one might see the first thinkers of the day searching for metaphors with which to turn this ungraspable interplay of language and feeling into theory. Jürgen Habermas,[4] like Williams, keeping up faith in the old enlightenment name of common emancipation, would be one; Michel Foucault, sombrely translating all speech into the mind-forged manacles of discourse, another. Williams, often accused of murky jargon, kept to the metaphor of drama and its idiom, dramaturgy, but told collective experience as a single tale, a metadrama immanent in many dramas, whose conversation either impelled or delayed the next curve of a long revolution.

This was his epic story, the narrative of a culture told through glimpses of whatever caught his eye and ear. One thread of this narrative was entertainingly pulled out in a *Listener* piece, where Williams pieced together the single story of a myriad advertisements, that happy handsome couple, their delighted children, their enchanting cat, dog, car, home and holidays. In *The Country and the City* there are many stories, some hateful, some subdued to a mere murmur, some lovely and of good report, all gathered into one. As, however, the brief radical spasm of 1968 and the next four or five years settled into political indirection, Williams seemed to withdraw a little more from the intense variety of day-to-day storytelling, and bent himself to producing his story of all the stories. This is a way of saying he sought a grander theory of his endeavours. If drama could be used as metaphor for that untidy, unfinished, sprawlingly inclusive conversation of the culture, then he needed a theory of conversation itself.

In this he strikingly anticipated the conversational turn of all philosophers in the 1980s, when Richard Rorty and Jacques Derrida[5] together would announce the end of philosophical reason and the advent of conversational reasonableness as the only measure of good sense and workable politics. But Williams had of course a sterner as well as a less philosophic, more political purpose. There was only one theorist and his name was Marx.

So in his theoretic labours between 1974 and their culmination with the publication of *Politics and Letters* in 1979, he battled to strain his own powerful intuitions and strong feelings about the sources of daily life through the hard filters of materialist doctrine. In part, of course, he took

242

Marx's lead, as had so many of his own and the next generation, exactly because Marx provided the historical and structural explanations which one-piece-at-a-time empirical and liberal history could never attain. Since it was clearer than ever before that something massive hauled everybody along willy-nilly in its wake, Marxism was the most inclusive story on offer as to what was happening. But of course Williams owed more to Marx than finding him useful. Class and Party together taught the old man as dogma, and Williams had been drawn back by the irresistible currents of the moment to reaffirm a churchy Marxism he had always repudiated in the past.

He became not a heretic but a hermeneutician. If the absolute presupposition of what it is to be a Marxist is a belief in historical materialism, and if the moral precept issued by this datum is that one do all in one's power to help the proletariat to revolutionary victory, then Williams's contribution would be to clarify the theoretic instruments and regrind the lenses guiding this strategy. Materialism must be reclaimed for a modernised Marxism precisely in order to hold the key connection between thought and life, academic privilege and the still so obviously exploited and resentful members of the working class.

So he wrestled with certain key concepts of old Marxism in order to load them with the words which really mattered to him – meanings, values, tradition – and thereby keep those words out of the hands and mouths of the enemy. He began this task in a singular paper delivered pretty well impromptu (then tape-recorded) at a conference in Montreal to which he was inveigled from California in April 1973, and made all the vast journey by train.[6]

There he took the conventional Marxist distinction between economic base and cultural superstructure which had so provoked Leavis in the 1930s,[7] and dissolved the one into the other. In antique doctrine, the economic base was pictured as the material actuality which determined the superstructure of cultural life, ideas, the 'means of mental production'. Capital, in short, produced the political ideas, the novels, and the paintings, as well as the iron and steel. Williams, committed to feeling and understanding culture as the place where life was really lived, resisted the notion that that life was merely superstructural to the hard facts underneath.

So he took from Gramsci the idea of 'egemonia' or the power of culture to saturate consciousness with its forms and values, insisting in the high, dry abstractions of the day that hegemony and culture are coterminous. Then he re-presented them as the key site of political struggle and one in which what is struggled over – taste, creativity, books that are good for you and television that is bad for you, love and death themselves – is all every bit as material and materially produced as wage packets and automobiles.

243

None of these things are mere objects; all are points of realisation in a network of productive, exploitative relations. A television programme is an image made up of 625 lines of black and white dots coloured by three primary interceptors; it is a set of embodied meanings; it is what producers, cameramen, presenters, editors, programmes colluded to manufacture; it is the nine o'clock news; it is a site of struggle.

In all these ways of seeing, Williams teaches us to follow the jostling contradictions of his three historical currents, those trade winds of value which blow through every life, fill every pair of lungs and oxygenate the blood and brain with their contrary directions and temperatures. These three are the clusters of values he identifies temporally as 'dominant', 'residual' and 'emergent'.

They indeed look like Hegel's categories of argument: thesis, antithesis, synthesis, and to be called Left-Hegelian is, in the curse-book of the *groupuscules*, a mortal insult. But if we skip the saloon-bar duelling, this trick of Williams's gives us purchase on much. It brings the *valuing* of life, which every word we speak insists upon, to the centre of our thought, and insists that such thought is of its nature at once historical and political. The values one sees, and renews by living, are in inevitable contestation with other values; some of these values will defeat others. These will be class victories, and Williams triumphantly reclaims his neo-Marxism as the method for the study of culture by setting aside the ceremonies of tasteful study of the texts. That pedagogy pretends only to the genteel suppression of politics from the arena of culture. It does so to the advantage of the genteel. Once culture is seen as the struggle over values, and values themselves as the field-of-force of social life, then personal life irradiates the realm of culture. Academic thought turns into historical action.

It is a paper of some technicality, abstruse and jargon-heavy. Yet it seems to me one of Williams's most important efforts. Marx is its point of genesis, the thoughtful air Williams breathes. But the significance of the paper goes well beyond the effort to keep the church alive. Held down, at times, by the ponderousness of his two idioms – Marx's and Leavis's – in this paper he joins with that submarine movement in the thought of the day which tried to catch life-on-the-move by placing it in the mobility of common language.

The philosophers, in their odd dialect, had led the way. Quine[8] had borrowed from set theory to show how inquiry does not work down a list of items like an agenda, but *within* a set of propositions like a field. A proposition is no more than an element in a system and as such always corrigible. So much for Kant's analytic truths which we know by observation to be true. So too with Kant's synthetic truths, which are true by definition or 'tautologically'. For no definition can be shown to be a perfect translation of its first term. Thus definitions from direct experience are always liable to modification.

Williams would have flinched from that last scepticism. Otherwise, he too commended to others to see that whatever is begotten, born and dies is always mobile, changeable, mortal, and that only by trying to grasp this changeful, ungraspable totality will we understand anything, and then only in passing.

As Williams took this line of thought further, always seeking to vindicate and ground materialism as a necessary premise, he undermined his very own venture by thinking what was strictly unthinkable in Marxism, before solving the problem by calling what he had just done 'materialist'. He turned to a book published by Perry Anderson's company New Left Books, the publishing house Anderson had set up to help bring to fruition the *Review*'s ambitious project to theorise and Europeanise British thought in the human sciences.

Williams picked up Sebastiano Timpanaro's *On Materialism*,[9] showed in his treatment one or two unexpected signs of strain, but used Timpanaro as the occasion for re-declaring a kind of materialism synonymous with a rather stirring metaphysical vision.

> So why then a materialist pessimism? There is ground for a sense of tragedy in the long and bloody crisis of the ending of an imperialist and capitalist order. But at the most basic physical level there is only the contradiction intrinsic to any conscious life process, and this is not a settled but a dynamic contradiction, in which life is not only negated by death but affirmed by birth, and practical consciousness at once defines and redefines its proper limits.[10]

He takes Timpanaro as translating materialism into human conduct set in nature and natural processes, with human nature freed only from these by its historical capacity to collect and criticise evidence. This gives him the cue to endorse Timpanaro's suspicions of psychoanalysis, to deprecate the contemporary ecstatics of the method then murmuring pentecostally in *Screen* and *Signs*, and to join Quine in placing all questions and answers within a natural holism where explanations will never have enough evidence to count on.

There is a sardonic stoicism in all this which socialists might have done well to cultivate, and which is the strength of Williams's long and muscle-binding immersion in the concrete of theory over these years. But there is a briefly dogmatic slumber knocking out part of Williams's wits. In hanging on to materialism as the 'test of political fidelity'[11] [*sic*] Williams marches snoring down a cul-de-sac. For he seizes upon Timpanaro's challenge to Chomsky and his ambition to explain the phenomenon of language neurologically, and vaguely gestures towards 'an account of language' which would adumbrate 'the outlines of a productive materialism'.[12]

One can only conclude that *Keywords*,[13] which he published in 1976, was in his view an elementary contribution to such an outline. He had had the book in his workshop for years, started it in adult education, intended it to appear as an appendix to *Culture and Society*, and with his characteristic husbandry towards his own books, kept up the file until it was publishable.

It was a glossary, heavily partisan in both selection and treatment, of the key words of his kind of cultural and political history. So: 'art', 'bourgeois', 'culture', 'democracy', 'intellectual', 'management', 'nature', 'radical', 'subjective', 'wealth', 'work'.

He begins, as he always begins, from his own life, and his return to Cambridge in 1945 to find the people there simply 'not speaking the same language',[14] setting himself to compile a lexicon of these differences, and their origins in historical uses as inflected by class, place, *power* (which isn't aired). Pitting himself, with his usual assurance, against the *Oxford English Dictionary* itself, he says:

> Anyone who reads Dr Johnson's great *Dictionary* soon becomes aware of his active and partisan mind as well as his remarkable learning. I am aware in my own notes and essays that, though I try to show the range, many of my own positions and preferences come through. I believe that this is inevitable, and all I am saying is that the air of massive impersonality which the Oxford *Dictionary* communicates is not so impersonal, so purely scholarly, or so free of active social and political values as might be supposed from its occasional use. Indeed, to work closely in it is at times to get a fascinating insight into what can be called the ideology of its editors, and I think this has simply to be accepted and allowed for, without the kind of evasion which one popular notion of scholarship prepares the way for.[15]

The editor, R.W. Burchfield, replied promptly and angrily, calling in aid from his New Zealand working-class background.[16] Yet Williams's autobiographical point, apart from this tedious insistence on sticking that point into absolutely everybody on the assumption that they are on the enemy side, still stands. An East Sussex student of his, Mr W. Heyman, had given Williams the paperback fascicles of the *OED* in three large cardboard boxes, and he had leafed through them entranced as his project gestated in his mind in 1950.

It was a long bringing-to-birth. By the time it arrived, twenty-six years later, *Keywords* purported to chronicle the 'variations and confusions of meaning' in a 'structural' history of these 'strong and persuasive' words. But the creature had become deformed over time. As so often with Williams's work, its development from often intellectually rough-and-ready origins, in which ideas were rapidly arranged on paper in readiness for the evening classes, meant that later reworkings and adjustments remain embedded in that primitive form. By the time he published *Keywords*, his own thinking had gone well beyond its method to the holistic inquiries ventured upon in 'Base and Superstructure'. And while the volume has its uses of a lexicographical sort, it is vitiated by nonchalance about the whole question of ideological distortion on the author's part, and by a series of more or less grievous errors, for which he was much castigated by Quentin Skinner.

Skinner's article[17] was commissioned by Christopher Ricks for *Essays in Criticism*. Once again, Williams must be rebuked for having failed to educate himself in certain important scholarly arguments bearing directly on his work. Marxists, even revisionary ones, read too much Marxism. Skinner rebukes Williams for quite failing to distinguish between possessing a concept and knowing a word. For one may possess a concept without having a word for it, and one may use a word without there being a matching concept ('culture' itself tends that way).

Not only that. Strong or 'appraisive' terms (Skinner's adjective) may be correctly or incorrectly used. There are rules of actuality governing their use, and rules for their application also. Appraisive words, that is, have a sense and a range of reference and what J.L. Austin called 'perlocutionary' force, which is to say they define attitudes (you can't sneer with a sincere use of the word 'courageous'). But what Williams misses, and misses because this delayed work hasn't caught up with his own later thinking, is the holistic nature of meaning.

This is, again, Wittgenstein's great discovery: that words mean what they mean in the game of their use, and that usages twine themselves about themselves in such a way that they cannot have what Williams claims to provide, a word's 'own internal structure'. Skinner convicts him of a failure to see that some disputes over meaning arise from an extension of a term's applicability, a widening of its use; other disputes are settled by agreeing to a new but different application of an old term. Finally, Williams is demonstrated not to have noticed the constitutive force of language such that, as it is the point of his friend and comrade Charles Taylor's work to establish, social reality is itself made out of our linguistic institutionalisations. This is our truly human constitution. Although Williams often seems to assume its truth, when he is busy with making sure that Marxism and materialism hang together, he forgets his critical training and himself hangs culpably loose.

This second detour into the errors of his philosophy is not merely, as they say, academic. It is not only that there was a certain unthinkingness in some of his theoretic labours, in the 1970s in particular. It was also that he bent such efforts towards what his very own thinking had made redundant. *Keywords* (as Skinner says) has many subtle and memorable insights in it – this was, as David Hare remarked, 'a phenomenally clever man'; but the book is misconceived. Pretending to be a lexicon, it is a partisan

247

list of usages which caught his eye. It came out of the notebooks for evening classes for sure, and was then hitched to his later efforts to reaffirm a pure historical materialism as correctly framing his own singular and powerful inquiries.

This is apparent, for example, in the entry for 'Idealism' in *Keywords* which garbles the original technicalities of the word in the Berkeleyan philosophising of the eighteenth century, jostles a series of contradictory uses together without any indication that people know the distinctions perfectly well, and peters out helplessly, saying that *'idealism* is obviously a word which needs the closest scrutiny whenever it is used'.[18]

Although he objects in this entry and in the parallel one on materialism to the merely polemical use of the words, he is intent, none the less, on restoring Marxism to itself and himself. There is consequently no doubt as to which of the two words he votes for.

> The point that matters, in relation to the history of the words, is that *historical materialism* offers explanations of the causes of sense (iii) in *materialism* – selfish preoccupation with goods and money – and so far from recommending it describes social and historical ways of overcoming it and establishing co-operation and mutuality. This is of course still a *materialist* reasoning as distinguished from kinds of reasoning described, unfavourably, as IDEALIST (q.v.) or *moralistic* ...[19]

In a substantial corner of that English and American intellectual life which defined itself as the opposition, it was still hoped that moral preference could be made synonymous with science, and that the holy alliance could, as the books of enlightenment taught, bring human society to a condition of virtuous rationality.

Williams's own route to such a science was unscientific enough, and none the worse for that. He had long ago set himself a body of work which also constituted a way of living. This meant that, as they say, his work was his life, so much so that by the time he was in his fifties he did very little other than work. He saw the children and the grandchildren – Merryn's second was born in March 1978 – he taught a few graduate students, he lectured, he wrote, and Joy and he took a summer holiday.

His subject was always the connection between social experience, especially his own, and imaginative grasp.[20] But social experience largely meant, as far as his own was concerned, his everyday life up to his leaving for the Army in 1941, added to his strictly intellectual life thereafter. This compression, however, conscientiously directs him not to understanding for its own sake – the traditional project of pure inquiry – but to discovering the usefulness and beauty of that early life as it may be turned to the common weal, and its improvement. As D.H. Lawrence put it, 'One writes out of one's moral sense; for the race, as it were'. In other words, Williams wishes earnestly so to think about that experience and its representativeness that the understanding thereby won by thought and theory can be turned to human benefit. He will so measure his own life, his father's life, and the life in the books he chooses that he may lend his imaginative grasp to those who, if things turn out well, will hold and pull the political levers.

To help win this long day he attempts to give his vocation, as seers will, the name of natural science. So he dubs it 'cultural materialism', a ringing oxymoron which gave a licence to many later disciples for shows of righteousness. He surely didn't need the term, and nor do we. As Richard Rorty contended a little later, why on earth should all sciences fall into one of only two categories? Williams's very own holism had already made the notion of a cultural materialism redundant; Quine and Wittgenstein had long since shown it to be an error.

To be accused of error in the Marxist cadres of intellectual opposition was at that date – 1976 to be precise – a way of life. In the beginning of that year there was a little clash of arms in the forest which had signal consequences for Raymond's intellectual life. Terry Eagleton challenged his intellectual father to mortal combat. (Christopher Ricks remarked mordantly that Williams, in the gospel according to Eagleton, was to play John the Baptist to Eagleton's own Redeemer.)

Eagleton published an essay in *New Left Review*[21] damning Williams with inaudible praises for 'socialist humanism', 'romantic populism', social-democratic tendencies and other corruptions of the day. Even though much of what Eagleton says is justified and subtly said, I would rather count the charges to Williams's credit. Williams is indeed a gradualist and provincial: good for him; but his early 'Left-Leavisite' revisions had for some time been replaced, in *The Country and the City* and elsewhere, by a novel totalising of both his theoretic play and his cultural specifics. Williams wanted by now to imply a whole society in every grain of culture. On the other hand, such a cultural astrophysics could not accommodate the haughty requirements of Eagleton's coda: 'criticism must break with its ideological prehistory, situating itself outside the space of the text on the alternative terrain of scientific knowledge.'[22] At this distance, listening to such prattle, one wants to shuffle and cough and, crouching, leave the room. Eagleton, like so many comrades of the day, was riding hard after the high horse of Louis Althusser, who taught once again that Marx's ideology-critique was a true science, and the key to all political theory. Williams swayed a bit under the assault. He even wrote *Marxism and Literature*, his unreadable book.

Anthony Barnett, long on the board of *New Left Review*, loyal, cheerful, outspoken, came quickly to defend somebody who was, he believed, utterly essential to the maintenance of a humane language of socialism.

THEORY AND EXPERIENCE

Anthony Barnett

The manuscript arrived just before Christmas 1975. Francis Mulhern expressed his concern that it was an act of parricide. But Perry was enthusiastic and keenly supported publication. I read it over the holiday and was unhappy. I've a great interest in culture but not in literary criticism. It was Raymond the socialist that concerned me. By chance, I went into Blackwells and found a copy of *Modern Tragedy*. I don't know what would have happened if a copy had not been there. Anyway, it changed my life in a way that few books have.

The opening of *Modern Tragedy* is about political violence. Anyone who is interested in doing something to diminish the cruel inequalities of our society has to be concerned with the question of change as more than temporary alleviation. And change involves force. Political force, electoral force, economic force and physical force. At what point, if ever, is it justified to take up arms?

That was one element of my sudden interest. Then there was Raymond himself. He was someone I found impressive but remote. But I knew he was a key person for the *Review* to which I was then very attached. First, the great issue of revolutionary change, national self-determination and the role of force, and second the small question of the journal that defined my own political position. And I read *Modern Tragedy* and I was both inspired and ashamed. Here was a participant in the Normandy invasion who had seen, watched and weighed violence and who could write about its cost, its necessity in the last resort and the nature of that last, tragic resort. He could write against violence without relinquishing his commitment and without being a pacifist.

Then I re-read the Eagleton. Behind a masquerade of clever and sometimes sharp literary criticism there was a put-down on just this issue. Williams was not 'antagonistic to bourgeois state power', his thought strikes 'political strategy dead at birth', he was 'contaminated' by reformism and thus, unable to appreciate the 'revolutionary rupture' and was pathetically 'reticent' about 'insurrectionary organisation'. Eagleton, whose trigger finger had never squeezed anything more dangerous than a beer glass, was using the *NLR* to lecture a tank commander who had helped liberate Europe from Fascism about the need for him to be less reticent when it came to insurrection.

It was a poor joke if a shameful one for socialists and possibly evidence that literary criticism is more prone to ludicrous pretension than any other discipline. It became for me a resigning issue. *NLR* was elitist, who could deny it? But I always defended the *Review* by saying that it was difficult because it dealt with difficult matters. It was hard but it was not dishonest. It was remote from England, but it engaged with the world and its leading intellectuals. This justified its pretensions. Eagleton's attack was everything people said the *Review* was that I had said it wasn't. It was clever dick, fast with words and loose with realities. It was horribly *ad hominem* and luxuriated in being knowing and superior. It was shallow about a man who was deep, it mocked the very difficulties he pronounced and I knew to be true. In short, it sold the pass – it was revolutionary chic.

The *Review* could publish it – magazines need clever articles – but if it did so without a rebuttal or a reply I would leave. I worked like a man possessed, trying to get a measure of the literary criticism so that I could get to the politics. It was very painful. I wrote a 20,000 word essay that included a theory of the intellectuals that showed what kind Raymond was. Perry killed it with tutorial firmness, and then, when I produced a third draft, tried to pass a motion of censure that evaporated under a counterblast from Fred Halliday. But that draft was OK and Perry phoned to make up and support its publication.

Barnett's piece initiated a long movement of reparation by Anderson and his fellow-editors which culminated in the interviews published as *Politics and Letters*. Barnett agrees with Eagleton that Williams dissolves politics into culture, and understates class struggle, and then he drones on a bit about the idealism/materialism antinomy. But what counts so much for Barnett and his generation (me too) is Williams's direct engagement – as a matter of experience and 'structure' – with the expressions and embodiments of power, whether political, imaginative or both. The happy accidents and the moral luck of his life brought him up against his father, the railway, the border, the tank, the Nazis, and English literature. In these he found and from these he made a theory of politics which he addressed to his times. It is the making of a life into a way of thought, a mode of both explanation and envisioning which is Williams's grand achievement.

And it has a true grandeur. Williams broke with the traditional academic regulation that intellectual inquiry should keep apart judgement and allegiance, that ardour must be distinguished from accuracy. The greatest thinkers of modernity – a list which would include, I take it, Dewey, Sartre, Wittgenstein, Rawls – would have recognised in Williams an endeavour like their own: to wring out of the painful disorder and broken language of everyday experience a truer order set to beautiful words, but words taken from the real language of men and women, not dictated by a fixed prayer book.

Williams bent his life, together with the literature he read as a commentary on that life, to that common task. Seeing this, we can see and feel the love he inspired in those who understood the magnitude of such a task, and the likelihood of defeat in it. Barnett, Eagleton and Anderson wholeheartedly agreed upon that, and so did Edward Thompson, come home to make up the quarrel in the same issue.

In the spring of 1976 he wound up a two-hour BBC2 debate on advertising which Tony Roberts had produced. I had been asked to front the debate on the anti-advertising side, and Raymond and I got to Pebble Mill, the BBC's Birmingham studio, punctually. Well over two hours late, the enemy turned up in an emerald green Rolls Royce. Peter Marsh was thirty-odd, stout as a seal, golden-curled, shiny green-blazered, not bad-looking, appalling. It was jam. The sharks mouthed their teeth in the usual way, and Williams wound them up:

> how is it that we have such a powerful advertising industry and such an unsuccessful economy? ... The period into which we are moving

is one in which there is going to be a situation of absolutely finite resources. It is very significant that we are hitting this with things like water, like energy, *like capital*, at the very moment when we are still celebrating, as if we are children, happy consumption of pleasant objects which we all enjoy, but which are trivial compared to those basic ones.[23]

As we left, I asked Raymond about Eagleton's attack. 'I think he might have sent me a copy before it was published,' he said, imperturbably, but I think he was a bit hurt, even so, by Eagleton's swashbuckling.

To my mind, the two novels he published in 1978 and 1979 were his best answer to Eagleton, agreeing with some of his criticisms as well as refuting the likelihood, or even the desirability of 'scientific knowledge' of life which, as a theorist, he could still invoke in *Marxism and Literature*.

He took the latter book seriously enough even if his friend Gwyn Williams said in his irresistible Welsh stutter, 'I d-d-efy you to read it without going round the b-b-bend.' It has good things in it, the best being his revised 'Base and Superstructure' paper which I have already discussed, and its separation of the values force-field into 'dominant, residual and emergent'. But it is a fearsomely jargon-heavy book, cleansed of practical examples, solemn, abstract and opaque. It was one in a series of 'Marxism and ...' books which Williams began to edit for Oxford University Press with Steven Lukes, but which never got very far. The recrudescence of Marxism in Anglophone intellectual life ran out of steam before Marxism's professed defendants in Eastern Europe gave up as well. Lukes himself cogently criticised the topic into a moral dustbin,[24] and meanwhile the best of Williams's attention was elsewhere, on two novels, possibly materialist, possibly not.

He had a bit of a row with Chatto over *The Volunteers*. With a not uncharacteristic business ruthlessness, Williams had on the advice of a new agent called Woodings given the manuscript of the novel to Eyre-Methuen. Norah Smallwood, doyenne at Chatto, was angry and hurt, and wrote to Williams saying so.

> I am astonished that a reputable publisher like Eyre-Methuen should poach in this way ... is it even a wise move on your part? ... If your heart is set on this move, we must accept the situation as gracefully as we may.[25]

A little later, Williams replied saying coolly that Eyre-Methuen were indeed to publish *The Volunteers* and that the manuscript of *The Fight for Manod* was on its way. It was delivered on 12 May 1978, and Chatto, swallowing the affront, coughed up an advance of £500.

The two novels, as we know, had been in the writing for some years, *Manod* a project conceived soon after *Second Generation* as the end of a trilogy. In the event, the action is set at a pretty well contemporary moment. Matthew Price is now hero of the Welsh intelligentsia, the man who has reinterpreted the Welsh industrial diaspora for his people, and given them back a fighting historiography. But he has already had one heart attack, and has another during the action of the novel. Peter Owen, the unlikable, attractive young radical-at-Oxford in *Second Generation* is even less likable here but with a pungent radicalism and a painfully sharp, contemptuous wit. Robert Lane, in 1964 teaching politics and sociology in Oxford, is now in the advisory echelons of a Labour government at the Department of the Environment.

He asks the two Welshmen for advice (!) on a proposal to build a utopian new town, a sort of Milton Keynes in Northamptonshire with a dash of Baltimore's Harbor Place. Manod's original is at Caersws in the Severn Valley, here moved thirty miles south.[26]

The two men go to live in Manod, to ask the people what they think, and to uncover shady land deals running back to Birmingham, Brussels, Bonn, but fronted by a ghastly local builder-developer, and his gorgeous, robotic wife. The new town is intended to manufacture and to test in its normal working a complex, novel system of communication technologies. The human needs are plain, as the older hero of *Border Country* declares in a fine statement at the final big meeting before the Minister of the Environment, the interested investors, the EEC functionaries, and the two Welsh consultants.

'... the crucial factor – you must really appreciate this – is who the people are to be. For this is a country bled dry by prolonged depopulation. Not far away, in the valleys, there is a ravaged and depressed old industrial area. If it can be clearly seen that in these new ways, bringing the two needs together, a different future becomes possible, a future that settles people, that gives them work and brings them home, then through all the dislocation, through all the understandable losses and pains of change, there could still be approval, significant approval; not just the design of a city but the will of its citizens.'

'You are eloquent, Dr. Price, but I don't quite clearly follow. Are you saying that this city should be confined to Welsh?'

'I don't mean nationality. I mean that the storms that have blown through that country – storms with their origin elsewhere – should now be carefully and slowly brought under control. In one place at a time, one move at a time, we should act wholly and consistently in the interests of that country, and those interests, primarily, are the actual people now there, caught between rural depopulation and industrial decline, the end of two separated orders, and there in Manod, if we could see it, is a real way beyond them. But only a real way if it belongs to the people on whose land it is being made.'[27]

It's a very good novel, much sparer and more fragmentary than the first two, the dialogue constantly stirring the reader to a vivid realisation of how hard it is, as they say, to communicate. But Williams takes this difficulty far beyond the chronic banality of 'communication problems' to the thick, obscure obstructions in the veins of people's bodies and feelings as they struggle to get clear what they know and how they can act upon that knowledge.

At the end, if we reduce a rich and immediately recognisable wide world to a diagram, the action possible is shared by Matthew Price and Robert Lane: the one economic historian, spokesman with a rare probity and incorruptibility of his people's intelligentsia, and the other scholar-bureaucrat, sometimes Fabian and Oxford social theorist, now planner-managerialist in the power élite. Peter Owen, the hot, sharp, angular radical is left to patrol the margins of actual social organisation, driven out of community by his own passionate uncompromisingness, rehired by a different system of communication for what Lane well calls 'the long complacencies of denunciation' after he has hunted down profiteering in land deals based on illegal breaches of confidential documents.

Lane and Price foreshorten the arc of Williams's thought into a tense praxis. Lane summarises what is surely, for all Williams's obvious dislike and suspicion of Lane's kind of man, Williams's own judgement upon England, upon Britain, now.

> The whole of public policy, is an attempt to reconstitute a culture, a social system, an economic order, that have in fact reached their end, reached their limits of viability. And then I sit here and look at this double inevitability: that this imperial, exporting, divided order is ending, and that all its residual social forces, all its political formations, will fight to the end to reconstruct it, to re-establish it, moving deeper all the time through crisis after crisis in an impossible attempt to regain a familiar world. So then a double inevitability: that they will fail, and that they will try nothing else.[28]

Towards the end of the millennium, the prescience of this is very startling, the confident hopefulness of Price's speech very moving. If there were a politician, now, still speaking like that, and meaning it ... But to do so there would have to be an entirely different way of thinking about belonging and entitlement, and a different history too, because having forcefully dramatised in *Manod* the long emptying of the valley, the elderliness and childlessness of those who live there, Williams makes Price invoke the sorcerer's power of the word to belong, 'belongs to the people on whose land it is being made'.

And who are they? as Lane asks him. Battling a year or two later with the same idea, Williams briefly acknowledges the miscegenated nature of all peoples in Britain, in Europe, the world and the universe, but then denies it; or rather, catches hold of the indefinite concept of cultural identity in order to reaffirm something, anything perhaps, which will make for community and solidarity in such an uncommunal, solidity-melting moment of history.

He sees this bit of magic for what it is, himself. *Manod* and *The Volunteers* bear witness to Williams's protean capacity to see the criticism of his own beliefs and not to forestall it, but to put it directly and irrefutably. As an American friend says to Price near the end of the novel,

> 'Come on, Matt, you want it to happen. You want that city to be built.'
> 'Well, I want that country replenished.'
> 'That country? You mean Wales, or that valley?'
> 'Well, I could even say Britain, if you pushed me. I want the pattern to break, to some new possibility.'
> 'But that's what's wearing you out. You can't push a whole system.'
> 'Neither push it nor settle inside it.'[29]

Price, no doubt, comes to stand for something Williams saw as his own best possibility, although as Williams once said to Francis Mulhern, he felt 'a coarse, hard bastard' beside Price who is, even at his best, more than a bit morose, grudging, distant. But he defines for Williams, who as absolutely everybody had always noticed assumed the manner and manners of a man much older than himself from very early on, a way of being in an always alienating world. Price is neither a revolutionary like Peter Owen, not an internal emigré like Lewis Redfern, youngish hero of *The Volunteers*. He is an elder. He continues, in the uncertain health of ageing, to work for the future of his people, knowing he won't see the outcome, listening to their hopes and plans, and hoping things turn out well enough for them in the end. He is father and magus, who in virtue of his wisdom takes into the wide space of his heart the passionate contradictions of class and capital as lived by the people and landscape he watches over.

No heart could hold so much, and his is split open. Robert Lane says openly to Matthew in bed at the hospital what we feel – what Williams makes us feel – ourselves.

> Well I saw it, suddenly, as a kind of heroic absurdity. Heroic, certainly, because at all times and in all places you keep saying the same thing, and the right thing. But absurd, also, because of its wild incongruity. Saying it there, to them, and as if you had only to say it. There, within that last, disastrous and quietly spoken carve-up, that final operation of the prevailing forces and the decisive priorities. And within it taking part in it, you just sat there, stiffly, and you were talking still, as if it were the beginning of the world.[30]

255

The words in these three long speeches I have quoted from *Manod* are Raymond Williams's, but the voice is quintessentially that of Henrik Ibsen. The old man speaks through middle-aged Williams for probity and against corruption, for the honest way against the rotten one, 'as if he had only to say it', no matter whether one was stuck in a tight place, no going forward or back.

I think Williams *was* stuck by 1978, stuck because he believed, rightly, that many people felt like him, but not enough of them with the power to make much difference. So the longing on behalf of others for a better life, the success and recognition now so abundantly accorded him, the readiness and stamina in writing won by years of disciplined practice, the slow disintegration of old socialism itself, the hatefulness of so much in political life, all, all these scarred his own heart and gave a terrible inwardness to his description of Matthew Price's coronary.

Williams had his own warning. During 1978 he too experienced that 'rising heavy pulse through his neck and shoulders ... the long constriction of breath'. It was at a Jesus College feast; he went white, straining for breath, stood, walking stiffly and slightly halt. He made light of it, fighting as always to recover privacy, eager not to be touched too nearly or intrusively. He was helped to his room, recovered quickly. Not until the next day did he go to Addenbrooke's Hospital, took some tests and came home refusing, Merryn recollected, to say what had been said to him except that he wasn't going back. Impassively, he remembered his father stricken in the signal box, went on smoking his great stove of a pipe, ten or fifteen loads of the sweet weed every day, and bided his time.

I love *Manod*; it's his best book for me; I can't see its many faults. But it's a passive book, curious in a man who had thought so long about the connections of political thought to action. It sold quite well, and won a Welsh Arts Council prize. It was also translated into Russian and in 1981, bound in with Barry Hines's novel of his own screenplay for the Ken Loach film *The Price of Coal*, published in the USSR with a print run of 100,000!

But it told only half the story of Williams's political feelings at that date. *The Volunteers*, part dreamy wish-fulfilment, part a running, bitter commentary on the way we feel and see through the spectacles of contemporary British politics, is the other half. Both, Bernard Sharratt said, are an uncompleted argument with Eagleton and his generation, Eagleton as he spoke so insubordinately in 1976.

So what comes through so piercingly in *The Volunteers* is a bitterness largely suppressed by the sad acceptances of *Manod* ...

> the cold pleasure of the game of deception, the probably collabo-
> rative wit of two insistent false trails, had somewhere inside them

an unusually hard edge: a certain settled bitterness; what I thought of, indeed, as an older kind of bitterness.[31]

Williams gives the bitter young radical leader in *The Volunteers* the best lines; but really he stands behind the shoulder of another Robert Lane figure, the MP-become-charity-spokesman, travelled, urbane, wealthy, duplicitous, dedicated. Mark Evans prefigures a loss of innocence, a necessary feel for compromise, an exceedingly complex if not tangled loyalty field – of sex, age and class – a final courage which to our enormous surprise commands Williams's admiration; his allegiance, even.

'I think you're living your destiny, Lewis.'

'Volunteering for it, you mean?'

'If you want to say that. I'd say you were more a pressed man.'

'Pressed by you, you mean? Is this how you recruit?'

'No, basically pressed by yourself. I'm just, what do they call it, a providing agency.'

I went on staring at him. I was past assessment; past trying to understand him. The line between observer and participant, that I'd always theorised, had been turned so effortlessly. I'd broken secrets to him; I was helping him burn his compromising papers. And right in the middle of this shared and satisfying voluntary act I was turned, without hesitation, into another and much more difficult action. And not by his force, as he said. By my own momentum. By my own style.[32]

The hero is accused by his wife of being two-faced; two-faced nowadays is halfway honest. 'He wears their uniform but fights his own war'. In another Ibsenist speech, Evans tells Redfern that his own generation is 'rotten with failure, all of us rotten' – not a personal but a historical failure; then one is contemptuously pushed aside, as Evans is, by his own son.

There is a hatred in this raw edge of Williams's dominant voices, an unguarded hatred of what has been made in and of Britain since the muffled optimisms of *The Long Revolution*. It surely explains his late-come Welshness, as he moved towards that little group of cheerfully self-mocking Welsh historians led by Gwyn Williams and Dai Smith, and their sometimes comic, always serious politics in Plaid Cymru.

Dafydd Elis-Thomas

I was a tutor at Coleg Harlech. We found the source of Raymond's appeal was his absolute insistence on *culture* as being at the heart of Left politics, but particularly our kind. When he moved our way he learned enough Welsh to read it. He gave us the idea of the Welsh European, a regionalist Plaid Cymru in active pursuit of Raymond's version of an intellectualised politics.

I had a postcard from him – that's all his correspondence ever was, you know, postcards in his awful handwriting – after the defeat in the referendum

257

on Welsh devolution and setting up a National Assembly. That defeat made him more of a cultural nationalist, but without a costume. After 1979 the Plaid project was to redefine a Welsh socialist project without Labour, to break with cultural nationalism of the old kind. Welsh nonconformism was as dead as Welsh Labourism – the University of Wales is the last bastion of the old Welsh Liberals, Clement Davies and nonconformism. Gwyn Williams had a fine parody of a Williams-style secular hymn – 'Here we go on our journey of hope'.

Wales is full of failed political endeavours, simmering like near-extinct volcanoes. Now there's a return of a holy old ghost on the Left, the pastor-intellectual berating the sinful masses. That wasn't Raymond's line. He and the Plaid converged out of immediate political experience. The new New Left in Wales is a mixture of the peace movement, the Greens, English socialists and Plaid. The Welsh language is *the* sign of culture, you know, like sexual preference or skin colour. Language for Raymond was the cultural sign embedded in a political economy. Sociolinguistics has to encompass all political-economic activity.

Raymond had drawn nearer to these men – to Gwyn Williams and Dafydd Elis-Thomas, to Dai Smith of BBC Wales and Kim Howells of the National Union of Mineworkers – as his visits to Craswall became more frequent. He wrote a pamphlet on 'Welsh culture' for the Plaid,[33] and on 10 April 1976 gave a fiftieth anniversary address on the General Strike to the NUM in the grim industrial town of Pontypridd, home of one of the doughtiest Welsh club rugby sides and of the then national Polytechnic, a little place driven like a wedge into the green mountain rearing above the terraces.[34]

Then, again, amongst the gleaming white spa buildings and tough palms on Llandudno Bay, he spoke to the Plaid summer school in July 1977 on the meaning of community.[35] In each of these talks he effected a simple triangulation of political forces, with his family and his railway now naturalised as full-blown Welsh at one corner, a generalised enemy situated in ruling-class England at another, and a rather gestured-at, never-quite-feasible ideal future at the third. Past: the railway; present: bloody old England; the future: socialism? Something complex but much better, in any case. And however it would be, Wales could now provide, as he put it, a culture he could breathe in.

Williams and I came close to a row over his return to Welshness (presaged in the names of his children). I said he was lucky to have a national definition to play off against the class enemy. Coming from Durham, finding my way leftwards by way of solid bourgeois family, posh school, regiment, university posher still, helped more than a little by a strong and loving mother's strong and loving liberalism, I still found all that Home Counties greed and arrogance contemptible. 'That's not my England,' I said – 'but I have to live somewhere. And I need a picture of some kind, of another England, to fight them with.' 'You're English,' he said, 'you talk like them. Can't you get through quicker?' 'So do you,' I said, 'so *are* you.' And then I asked, 'What's the matter with the picture of 1945, but carried right through, completed. Wouldn't that do?' But it was 1978, and he wouldn't hear me.

He had the argument out, however, but with the wrong people. After the articles about his work in *New Left Review*, Anthony Barnett, always faithful and maddeningly persistent, had pressed Perry Anderson as editor to make a full and proper assessment of Williams's work in the journal. Williams had been contributing regularly since the little hubbub over Eagleton's attack, and had moreover been drawn into the keen debate on the future of both Marxism and Euro-communism as a new generation wanted to call it on the mainland. Markovic and Stojanovic in Yugoslavia, still buoyant about their chances of making a kindly communism work outside the USSR, had asked Williams to speak to the self-styled Praxis group at the University of Belgrade in 1976. He had been back to Naples (same train, same year). Such a European efflorescence was the whole theme of the *Review*.

Anderson wanted to make amends, even though he knew that Williams never bore grudges. He proposed an interview-article of some twenty pages; Barnett heartily supported the idea; the result was half-a-million words, spoken to Anderson, Barnett and Francis Mulhern by then working for New Left Books, across ten full days in Jesus College during 1977 and early 1978.

Francis Mulhern

> I had written to Raymond from Ireland back in 1973 asking for supervision of a PhD on literature and ideology in the 1930s. When I got to Cambridge in 1974 they assigned me to Frank Kermode, who had just arrived. 'Professor Kermode is new and needs graduate students.' The graduate Left was Althusserian in stratospherically high mode, and I was a young rip of that stripe. There were some historians and philosophers, associated with an Australian journal called, inevitably, *Intervention*, and there was a series of Occasional seminars of a very self-conscious, critically fast-moving kind, with only two or three literary figures. Raymond was not a presence, so far as I could see – I only had two encounters with him then – he had very carefully protected priorities.
>
> I joined the editorial board of *New Left Review* in 1975. When the interviews were proposed in 1976, I was sent to make the arrangements ...
>
> By the end of the second day we knew we had a big book on our hands. Raymond spoke perfectly finished prose sentences, paragraphs, at times chapters – though not necessarily in definitive order.

If Williams did, it has to be added that he had a match in Francis Mulhern. The three editors recomposed their questions, rewrote them, even invented several in order to break up the extraordinary, even flow of Williams's monologues. Some reviewers – John Dunn for instance – heard the three voices as one: 'the *NLR* team present the format of their dialogue with magisterial confidence ... and with unflagging didactic zeal, sustain[ing] their views as an elaborate and comprehensive system.[36] In truth, it was a monumental act of literary collaboration. There was in fact no single *NLR* voice; sometimes there were two sides – two against two – and plenty of disagreement.

Francis Mulhern

Many questions were literary concoctions, edited from conversation into rather stiff print. (One review referred to our 'Dalek voice'.)

Perry Anderson led much of the questioning. The concluding section was a long letter, written by arrangement, which I then broke up into conversation. Perry did the first cut on the raw typescript while he was in Hungary in the summer of 1978. The final version was 170,000 words – one third of the original. There was a certain amount of structural editing – deciding where Orwell should go for instance. But every time Raymond just picked up where he left off. Some of his recollections were very intense. I particularly remember him speaking of his time as a tank commander, one late afternoon, as the light faded . . .

There were fierce disagreements, but it was always friendly and good-humoured even so, and we'd go off to the pub for lunch. But Raymond started to sleep very badly while we were doing the book; we were folding up his life.

A deep friendship among the three editors was confirmed by this extraordinary business; it took in Williams also, for all his genial distance, much further than he had been ready for, so far in, he did not know the place. The astonishing soliloquies turned and returned in his mind unstoppably, as he reviewed his work, his public self, his history. In all this, he kept as always an absolute guard upon his private and domestic lives; only the strictly usable parts were moved, as before, into the category of public, political and therefore visible significance.

But the experience touched an exceptional fastidiousness in his sensibility; the unbroken communion with his own life and its meaning led him into a ghastly and helpless kind of misery, as well it might. The sustained act of complete introspection drove onwards the sound of his own reflection and could neither stop itself nor fertilise his thought. A lifelong habit of monologue became circular, and approached a psychosis.

When the book was already printed and bound, he wrote about this to Anderson,[37] wrote with the striking candour and openness which constitute his signature, but this time of the space of his life scarcely ever shown to anybody.

Dear Perry,

I enclose a copy of a letter to Francis, partly because I don't know where you both are, and partly because I wanted to add something, to you, which may or may not modify your possible reaction that I'm being only a bloody nuisance. The point of correction is substantial and important, as I've explained, and you know I mean it when

I say I will bear the costs. But beyond that there are other things, and I tell you them, privately, in the hope you'll understand. Though if you find them embarrassing or intrusive, please discard this.

The fact is that for the last three or four months I've been in a state of mind which is quite new to me and which I really don't at all understand. The usual words don't help, but for what they're worth it's a condition of almost overwhelming anxiety, perpetually preoccupied – not only as a working habit but now as an almost paralysing state – with qualification and revision and redefinition and exactness and so on, and the relations between that and the actualities and modes of past and present have come through as extreme distress. I've tried to keep going through it, and I've managed my ordinary work. But centrally there's still this fight to get back to good ground and out of the obsessions. And then it struck so suddenly, at a time of a lot of achievement, though you'll remember *Manod* and my (prophetic) reply about that inexplicable kind of sadness, which I was then talking about mainly in others. I've even known, for the first time, some of the states out of which defeatist and reactionary ideologies have been so often built since the war (and before); I mean known them quite directly, though all those years of analysis enable me quite easily to reject the projections and conclusions; what they don't help in is getting rid of the states themselves. But I'm fighting, and every handhold – what may seem to anyone else a marginal detail – has become crucial. That's why this correction to the book means more than its immediately and locally important point. I can only fight this state by going beyond it, not back from it; perhaps that's been the submerged history of the years.

And then of course I ask, I am bound to ask, whether the book itself has been a factor in this precipitation. It seems wrong to say this to you, for I remain deeply grateful for your initiative in proposing it, your thoroughness and skill in executing it, and your consideration throughout. But more than I realised before or at the time – and more than the tough and stimulating intellectual re-examination – I see that the project stirred some very deep sediments, as well as the ordinarily heightened self-consciousness of that kind of work, and though there are doubtless other factors this one may be central. And so the sense of the book being right, down to the last minute fraction I can manage, has got bound up with the literal and arguable possibility of getting again on to good ground. About the only really productive thing I can now do is garden, and after thirty-odd years of production that's not only strange but worrying, I suspect, for others beside me; I have such clear work still to do.

Well, I've said more than enough. And what I've centrally said isn't answerable; I mean I don't need an answer, I only want you to

261

know how things are. And of course as background to this other-wise abominable difficulty I've raised. Do keep the personal matters to yourself, if you would; but keep the letter if you like – I hope it will be of some retrospective morbid interest when things are better. Let's keep the correction business very practical; it has to be done; it can be done; I'll bear the cost. And maybe this handhold will pull me up.

Yours
Raymond

At the same time he wrote to Mulhern asking for a quite minute change to be made in all 3,000 copies of a finished book, but asking with a finality and desperation which are their own token of his state of mind. All that was at issue was a minor point about his one-time friend and collaborator on *Politics and Letters*, Clifford Collins. Collins, the moving spirit behind the business of the magazine, passionate, articulate, chaotic in all his conduct, often drunk, had failed to deliver his contribution to *Reading and Criticism*.

Williams wrote to Mulhern:

The necessary correction is in the discussion of *Politics and Letters*, in my answer beginning 'No. The journal ended . . .' (I don't have page proofs, only an old one, so I can't give a more exact reference). As you know, in the interview I was speaking impromptu, and in this case about something that happened thirty years ago, which was itself complicated and which was only mentioned in passing as part of an answer to the question why the journal ended. It was my best recollection, and is still substantially so, but the way I described the dispute with Collins can, I now see, be misunderstood. What could be misleading is that word 'contracted', which I tried to change. We had indeed agreed to write the book together, but the publisher sent me the contract, in my name, and I formally signed it. If Collins had done his chapters, the book (then called *English for Adults*) would have come out as a joint production. The other word that could be misunderstood is 'deadline', where I must, in context, have been thinking of when he and I agreed to get the work done by, though of course it could be taken, with 'contracted', as the publisher's dead-line. It is now essential to remove these possible misunderstandings; both for the record, and because I feel increasingly the sadness of much that later happened to Collins, and would not wish unneces-sarily to distress him. I have been over this again and again, and my decision is now clear. It must be changed.

I have no idea how this could be technically done. I just know it must be done. Obviously it's best to alter it on the page in some way. I don't know whether as a last resort an erratum slip could be used, though it's obviously less satisfactory and is inelegant. We can discuss ways and means, but I've reached the point now where I'd rather the book never appeared than have this possibility of misconstruction.

Francis Mulhern

What we did was this. Raymond rewrote the passage in question, observing a strict character count. We reset that page and then reprinted the whole leaf on which it appeared. The original leaf was removed by scalpel copy by copy, and the replacement leaf was then 'tipped in', again manually.

Anderson wrote back from his home in NW1 with exemplary fineness and warmth:

Dear Raymond,

I was very shaken and distressed by your letter. To learn that the book has in any way caused or contributed to such misery and anxiety brings a heavy sense of responsibility. I can only say that I am terribly sorry if we unfeelingly intruded where we shouldn't have done, or oppressed you with such a siege of questions and arguments. The passage that most worried you can be changed – as I said on the phone – completely. I hope that will allay your most immediate misgivings. I also trust that the public response to the book when it is published will allay any more ultimate fears about it you may have. We intended it to be a form of tribute to you: but the nature and quality of your own responses throughout have made it a free-standing work that can only evoke the greatest admiration for you among socialists, quite independently. Re-reading it, I can see mistakes we made (the section on *Culture and Society* is too aggressive and one-sided on our part, which was my fault). But I have no doubts about the effect of the book as a whole, and I hope yours will dissolve when it comes out.

All of us on the Left have drawn such strength from you over the years that it seems ironic to be wishing that you should recover your own. But very many people depend on your work, and the importance of your future writing is now greater than ever, in a time of reaction. I am sure that you will get back to the good ground soon. If I or any of us can do anything to help in the meanwhile, please let me know.

We all of us think readily in terms of a personal self living behind the defences of a more public persona. It is a tired old cliché. Easier to say that we simply are the versions of ourselves which may be seen, by anybody, ourselves amongst the anybodies. If this is so, then this version of Williams, still fluent and precise, still abstract, still political, but badly wounded, halt in his being, stopped by his own reflection, is both startling and dismaying.

It was 1979. He was just 58. The daunting self-examination of the interviews brought him to feel with paralysing force the 'interfused depth of social and personal sadness' of which he spoke to his interviewers.[38] Ageing, disillusion, we say; but he fought all his life against the loss of energy and the weakening of allegiance which causes it, which causes reaction both political and personal to set in, to stain one's being, to become both habit and style. But sadness, now; who cannot be sad to the point of sobbing at what they have done to you, England, Scotland, Wales? 'Hardly anything bears watching', the poet said,[39] and Williams could hardly bear to go on watching.

He recovered himself, for sure; it would have seemed to him cowardly to do otherwise. He was in any case at the height of his powers and of a substantial public's recognition of these. *Keywords* sold 50,000 copies in its first two years, and even if John Dunn asked of *Politics and Letters*, 'How could *anyone* have the nerve?' he then gave Williams rightful precedence over the worthies of the cosmopolitan Left; and so did everyone else. Williams was looked to for so much; he wouldn't let people down.

One lovely day in Cambridge in 1978 he was chairing the annual Judith Wilson lecture given (at Williams's choice) by the well-known playwright of the Left, Trevor Griffiths, whose honest nature often led him to declare his debt of gratitude to Williams. Griffiths was giving his paper on 'Working with and against television' and was well into his stride in the big concourse of the lecture theatre in Cambridge, 350 people crammed in any old how. Smoking a cigarette was essential to Griffiths's flow and at a crucial moment in his delivery he groped for Raymond's lighter, which was of course the size of a car radiator. The flame roared up and cracklingly ignited Griffiths's shaggy black Tarzan mop so that he had to beat out the flames on his own head, while the audience rocked and cheered this unforgettable piece of theatre. Raymond twinkled in an immobile sort of way, Griffiths put out the blaze, and academic conventions were resumed.

Williams's authority and example were shared only in the general esteem and affection of all those dreaming of a nobler politics by Edward Thompson. Thompson, no doubt, wrote finer prose – was a great prose master – a difficult man with it: ardent, immediate; caustic, capricious. Williams kept his distance and his serenity alongside. They only wavered for a few weeks.

That wavering was a harbinger. In 1979 Britain elected a Tory government with the first woman prime minister in her history. In November of the same year the USA elected as President an elderly, amiable and second-rate film actor. The next month, the two countries agreed with several others that a new generation (as the homely phrase goes) of super-accurate nuclear missiles should be scattered across Southern England.

Williams spoke in *Politics and Letters* of his sense of a deepening spirit of reaction abroad. *The Volunteers* showed British soldiers firing at Welsh strikers. The anger of *Manod* was directed at political corruption, its sadness at people's complicity in it. But Williams could not foresee just how strong a tide was sweeping in with Mrs Thatcher and Ronald Reagan surfing on it. He did not foresee how much would be lost, the defeats, the ravages. If he had, he might have thought that his heart would break.

12

END OF AN EPOCH

In April 1978, when F.R. Leavis died at the age of 82, Williams wrote one of his most searching pieces of occasional journalism. He saluted his some-time master, and then placed Leavis's characteristic mode of thought, or rather, his mode of being-in-the-world with a striking empathy, as well as a necessary judiciousness. 'All I sensed ... was a man confronting – I would not say contemplating nor analysing – a very particular kind of mystery, of which the relation to Cambridge was only a grievous form.'[1] Williams is writing rapidly in the piece, and although it is clearly the product of long meditation, the writing is at times clotted and thick as he labours with saying something absolute about his own life, momentarily stopped by this death.

He notes the remarkably class-bound quality of Leavis's method, even as Leavis threw it in the face of his epoch.

> The connecting mode of the [Leavis] faction, serious, widely read and intelligent as they all were, was a basic preoccupation with who was in and who was out, and in this, of course, even in negation, they retained and even emphasised the manners of their class.[2]

Williams was utterly free of this taint. He had his lordliness, his 'ducal' way as Ricks said, and he enjoyed turning for applause from the right part of the audience. But he truly didn't care who was in, nor shun those who were out, and in this he was radically unlike many pious Leftists of the present day while remaining faithful to the very best manners of his class, and the open, hospitable politics of the signal box.

But a deeper trope held him and Leavis in a common figure. Williams blames the academy for making something merely academic of Leavis's life work.

> What this excludes and is meant to exclude, is what must, in Leavis's whole work, be seen as central: not a profession but a vocation; an overwhelming, often overwhelmed response to a sense of a major cultural crisis ... But I could never forget, and do not now forget, the intransigence, the integrity, the fierce courage of the man.[3]

'An overwhelming, often overwhelmed response . . .'? It was not Williams's way to be overwhelmed by his contemplation of the world; his intelligent resolution, his faith in the future remained steadfast. But if he wasn't overwhelmed in his writing and his thought, something certainly bore him down and bore him prematurely off, and it wasn't just a dozen pipes of tobacco a day.

In 1979 Raymond Williams had seen the minority Labour government depart with little compunction. The leaden and inevitable descent of the British economy into criticality was not, he thought, going to be so very much inflected from either side (as he had made Robert Lane say in *Manod*). If it got worse, then the likeliest outcome would be the sort of National Government – a 1930s reprise – imagined in *The Volunteers.*

Certainly, he had predicted to his interrogators in *Politics and Letters* a deepening of political reaction in Britain, a marked movement towards more right-wing feeling. But he had prepared nothing on behalf of the Left – and nor had anybody else – for the whirlwind which Mrs Thatcher and her helots were about to release. And as for Ronald Reagan, well even to the unsmiling Left, he was just a joke, a forgettable funster precipitated by the sunbelt pensioners.

If this negligence on the part of the intelligentsia was venal, it was very widespread. But Williams was coming to the end of a spell in public life, and as usual wanted to ward off its excessive demands, and return to his moist little room and its clumping typewriter in Hardwick. He had been a three year member of the Arts Council between 1976 and 1978, invited on to it by Hugh Jenkins, Labour's serious and cultivated Minister for the Arts. It was a good appointment, of course, for Williams was, in my experience, the best of committee members, and far and away the best Chair I have ever known.

It is not a term of approbation many people would seek, though I think Williams would have been pleased by it for himself. It was he, after all, who had named committee procedure as being one of the most praiseworthy as well as most distinguishing marks of British culture. (He greatly admired Walter Citrine's little primer *On Chairmanship*,[4] and it is naturally no accident that Citrine was a trade union leader as well as Labour peer.) James Curran, editing the Labour Party's new house magazine *New Socialist* described, as others had before him, Williams's extraordinary capaciousness in committee, by which he seemed to absorb, contain and reconcile the often violently conflicting emotions and opinions around the table, redirecting them towards a common end. It was this gift which would have made him a great politician, in my judgement, able to deal calmly with an inevitably quarrelsome and fissiparous Party.

Williams had nurtured a certain resentment against his exclusion from those several academics and intellectuals Labour governments invited into the power élite. He complained to Anderson and company that:

> throughout the entire six years of Labour government in the sixties,
> I never had one inquiry, formal or informal, private or public, one
> invitation to a committee or a conference, from anybody in the
> Labour government or Labour machine. Not one line.[5]

The indignation is rhetorical and sincere. This is Williams's ducal side. But anybody could have told him that his 'Labour machine' was wretchedly poor, overworked and clapped-out. The Party recruited the people its ministers happened to have heard of, mostly economists from Cambridge or social policy scholars from the LSE just up the road. That's all there was to it.

By 1976 he was somebody, all right, and did his stint on the Arts Council with his habitual searchingness as well as charm. The Arts Council, after all, was founded by the Labour Party in 1946 at the behest of Maynard Keynes. It was empowered to spend the people's money bringing the arts closer to the people, which by and large meant finding audiences for approved works by giving Shakespeare or Mozart a subsidy. Meanwhile the commercial market went out hunting for works to give their much bigger audiences, especially for television.

Williams put it to Kenneth Robinson, then the Labour Party's genial chair of the Arts Council that the whole business could and should be run by organisations specifically adjusted to the forms of particular arts and of particular regions. For instance, literature would be better served if its panel on the Arts Council were to be elected by members of the Society of Authors and of the Writers Guild.[6] Williams put a lifelong trust in the practice of voting, sometimes to an extravagant degree and, at the Arts Council, at the expense of the genteel system of mutually reassuring agreement by which such outfits work in Britain. In one much-quoted incident he even asked, against all precedent and to the astonishment of the chair, that his dissent be formally recorded. If this was a touch over-done, there was also his absolute commitment to a picture of democracy which, Neal Ascherson once said, one was as likely to get from the British State as milk from a vulture.

He finished at the Arts Council just before the dark age of Mrs Thatcher and Ronald Reagan began, as Edward Thompson summoned CND onto the street once more with his rousing pamphlet. Williams's work was much in the public eye, or at least that fraction of the public which still prac-tised a politics of culture, and kept up its heart with a dose of anti-Labour old labourism and an evening at the Institute for Contemporary Art.

There was a Williams, John Berger, and Eric Hobsbawm day at the ICA in 1979 after the Tory victory, with a big turn-out of the shaggy Left in its heavy hermaphrodite sweaters and jeans and with a surprisingly wide age range as well. A new generation of student intellectuals had found its teeth set on edge by the cast-iron Marxism of Althusser and the rigidly theoretic anti-theory of Michel Foucault; Williams spoke with a so much homelier voice, the sometime prophet of old abstraction was become a domesticated radical, and none the worse for it. In addition, in the face of hard, just criticism from the feminists, he had begun to see how completely he had left the women out of things. Juliet Mitchell had long ago turned his own most famous trope ironically against him; famously, she had called her book *Women: the longest revolution*.[7] Newer voices now carried the criticism into Williams's own work.

On 23 February 1979 the BBC broadcast the second television programme devoted to Williams's work. Mike Dibb had spent portions of the previous summer with Williams making a film version of *The Country and the City*, elated to discover that Williams had never visited any of the country houses he put to such exemplary effect in the book.

Mike Dibb

> I realised that Raymond had never *been* to most of the places he wrote about in the book. The only two places he really knew about were Pandy and Hardwick. So we had to find the ideal house with which to embody the argument, and chose Tatton Hall near Knutsford.
>
> He was a wonderful person to work with, genial, talkative, he *enjoyed* himself so. And Joy threw herself into the research task of connecting Tatton to slavery (which didn't work) and of putting Tatton down in Manchester's industrial revolution (which did). All the same, Tatton fitted the book's thesis perfectly – the curator picked up the point very quickly, and found the local maps and little pastoral paintings which illustrated the case. And there was Mrs Gaskell in Knutsford, the Agricultural Show ... it worked like a dream.
>
> Raymond and Joy loved the music I chose. I discovered that they knew very little about music or paintings. Raymond worked only from the *word*.

Raymond knew so little about music that when, at about the same time, BBC Radio 3 asked him to choose eight pieces of music for their academics' version of *Desert Island Discs* called, inappropriately, *Men of Action*, he got as far as four with Mendelssohn's Italian Symphony and 'Men of Harlech' and then gave up.

Dibb took the two of them out and about. Raymond had read Jane Austen and Gilbert White all his life, and Wordsworth, as everyone said, was his familiar. Yet he had never actually been to Chawton or Selborne or even Dove Cottage, until Dibb took them on the rounds. They enjoyed the visits heartily, and then they went home to Hardwick, and Raymond resumed his habitual mode of transport, 'I'll travel in my mind'.

He travelled in this mode to Eastern Europe in the company of Rudolf Bahro in order to write a long article for *New Left Review*. Bahro's bold new book, for parts of which he had done some time in an East German gaol, raised Williams's faithful socialist heart to new speculations on the future of the faith. *The Alternative in Eastern Europe*[8] took as its subject

269

the forms of 'actually existing socialism', and tried to see in them the immanent possibility of the good society. What most pulled Williams to Bahro's side was his rejection of the view that the point of actually existing socialism was to out-produce capitalism – 'they are seeking with all their might to make their own the evil that they planned to do away with: the rule of reification, of alienation, and the anarchic competition of special interests'.[9] Against this, Bahro urged as the condition for the free development of each and all, a cultural revolution as the means with which to dissolve the structure of capitalism.

Bahro couldn't say moral revolution because that would smack of voluntarism, but given Mao's repellent efforts under this other rubric, he might have done well to avoid it. Nothing daunted, however, Williams took him up eagerly, wincing a little at the People's Republic and their 'confused' attempt at cultural revolution,[10] repeating the old, accurate and irrefutable case that capitalism is of its nature predatory, sudden, cruel, and incapable of moral cure. Picking up Bahro's wildly idealistic notion of 'surplus consciousness', which is to say a surplus of political energy once problems of food and shelter have been solved, he strove to press the best part of such consciousness to emancipatory ends.

There is something in this of Habermas, though it is never as roundly theorised as in the German's model. There is something in it of Fabianism also, in Williams's emphasis on dual planning and the intelligent mobilisation of the principle of coalition. There is also a fearful fog of jargon, of 'diversities' and 'specificities', of 'conjunctures', 'appropriations' and 'practicalities', when nothing is specific and no practice ever described. But his generalities genuinely generalise. The circumstances of an information intelligentsia in Britain, the East and West Germanys, Japan and North America are aligned, and the fact of their common perspective insisted upon.

The danger is 'a potentially lethal combination of abstract desire and practical cynicism', which has of course gone a long way to destroy reform all over the world since Williams wrote it down. The strategic fantasy, as ever in the books of revolution, is for educated élites to find 'common cause with those most subject'[11] to oppression and cruelty.

Well, yes ... 'heroic absurdity'? 'Saying it as if [he] had only to say it'? Hopeful as he always was, hope-filled as his remarks were, there is a blankness, a political weariness, maybe, in these bromides. They limn the forms of historical mobility and progress but cannot fix the sources of their energy.

In truth, in 1980 there was no chance to connect energy to progress. All energy was needed simply to oppose the armies of reaction, and that energy didn't always come happily to the point. In Britain, after the Tory victory the Labour Party threw itself into one of its periodic bouts of self-mutilation. Following a natural law of parties always to surge away from the political centre when power has been lost, Labour wrestled in its bowels between a leftish spasm led by Tony Benn and a rightish spasm led by a sanctimonious quartet who had been mortally offended by the comrades' rudeness about the quartet's claim to stand for the nicer side of the Party's traditions.

The quartet and its camp lost a vote or two, in particular a Party conference motion to the effect that the conference itself was the seat of absolute reason in the Party. Anyone who has been to a political conference of any kind at all will know for certain that such are occasions only for the display of vanity, herd sentiment, conspiracy, and crude bullying. But the conference voted that Conference could indeed execute reason, and the notorious quartet swept out in a huff to start a new party all of their own which would do as they said, leaving the Labour Party deep in its lurch.

Meanwhile, Mrs Thatcher set herself to carry through her particular cultural revolution. She doubled value-added tax on the poor by way of lowering income tax for the rich; she enacted anti-trade union laws of positively Victorian class virulence; she began the drastic reduction of the state's manufacturing power and the dismissal of its workforce with which she proposed to regalvanise private capital; and she threw herself into the arms and arms-racing propensity of the US President.

Rattled slightly by all this, middle-aged socialists who had exquisitely withdrawn from the Labour Party during the 1970s decided, Raymond Williams among them, that Something Must Be Done. So once again the bewhiskered and bespectacled Left clumped into central London with their nowadays rather less repressible women-folk, and settled back into the raked seats in their new brutalist cathedral at the London Institute of Education in Bedford Way on 23 January 1982. Once more they were told how matters stood by Williams and by Stuart Hall. Raymond was as ever in neat rolltop jersey and thick tweeds, his new false teeth fitting him a dream – he had almost never been to the dentist and his own teeth had been in a grim state for years – but pleased to be back in what momentarily felt like active politics.

The old New Left and the new one as well came together with some sense that something huge was changing out there. But the active politics that was called for to oppose a novel kind of capitalist monster could not even be touched by the conceptual net cast over it from either wing. The usual malediction was spoken over the Labour Party, but with hardly any of the old zest; the *groupuscules* were very subdued. Raymond was listened to respectfully, declined the chair but went on the committee, and gave an impressively detailed seminar on electoral reform and representation comically irrelevant to the politics in hand and culpably supportive of the Labour militants then wrecking the party.

The Socialist Society which founded itself that Saturday in January was, as the *May Day Manifesto* movement before it, limited to London and

271

vanished in no time. Opposition to Mrs Thatcher concentrated itself in CND on single-issue politics of the old English variety. People committed to both politics and the happinesses of private life would pay for a seat on the bus to the CND march through Hyde Park to Trafalgar Square from every corner of Britain, travelling all night, tunelessly singing, tucking a flask and sandwiches behind the baby in the pushchair and ambling with slovenly dignity in their one, two, three hundred thousands through Victoria.

But they wouldn't come to a worthy debate on unfeasible socialism for a whole weekend. So the Socialist Society sank without trace a little after the Labour Party was humiliated by a Tory victory in which they barely scraped second place in the popular vote.

On 11 May 1983, a month before the election, Williams took the train from Cambridge to London to talk to the Socialist Society on 'an Epoch's End – problems of the Coming Period'.[12] As before, he spoke from skeletal notes and somebody tape-recorded the result as couched in his habitually polished and well-turned prose.

Since 1979 he and Stuart Hall, rarely seeing each other, had given themselves to trying to understand the deep cultural structure and formation of the new politics. Disarmed by the suddenness of the Government's class offensive, utterly caught out by its vigour and invective, they sought for its appeal and the sources of its momentum which translated so effortlessly into Mrs Thatcher's success. Hall found it, in his useful phrase, in her style of 'authoritarian populism'[13] and bent this concept to the analysis of a general and hateful mood in the country in which surges of violent feeling could be attached by brutal governments to arbitrary or floating 'signifiers', that is to targets of hatred and slogans of aspiration quite detached from rational understanding.

Williams, beginning, so to say, from the other end to Hall, came up with the analytic concept 'mobile privatisation' (which he acknowledged was 'one of the ugliest phrases I know'). It meant what it said. He sketched out a contemporary consciousness (determined by conditions of work and pay – by 'social being') in which genuine liberties of movement and satisfaction had been won by those people with a decent wage to be enjoyed, on the move as like as not, and in private. The car, the hypermarket, cheap, accessible fashion, portable music and video, worldwide holidays, DIY, casualised labour, endless retraining, had all made for a new kind of person living in new social relationships. Unless a new socialism could match itself to this fluid identity, and fill the blanks in its social space, blanks of civic sensibility, of mutuality and natural duties and responsibility, in a language it could grasp and feel, much more than socialism would be at risk.

Unless, that is, this new state of mind and feeling can be brought to understand the contingencies of its own formation, its previous extraordinary and exploitative good fortune, then there is no chance at all of confronting the national (or, come to that, international) crisis, and making a future even barely habitable for our grandchildren.

It was this negligence of the future by which, in spite of his level tone, Williams was most angered and astounded. His move Waleswards during the mid-1970s was in part as a local hero going home, and part as an intermittent exile from the metropolis where he worked but in which he couldn't find a permanent place to live. So he held his breath until he got back, often enough, to Craswall – 'a culture I can breathe in'. When he got there, he felt all through himself the heavy hawser from the city towing the country inexorably in a wake filthy with its poison waste. And he lived the contradictions honestly enough. The new road through Pandy was an earthquake. It split the village, school on one side, pubs and chapels the other. The colossal trucks hurtled down its chute, fifty tonnes at seventy miles an hour, and made the ordinary trips to other houses a ceaseless anxiety for the slow, the elderly, the small. But the new road went round Abergavenny and returned the high street to a state of pedestrian busy-ness, the market to a scale fit for cows, sheep and human beings, the new schools to an enclave of safety.

These are the contradictions of always uneven economic development. Thinking with the concepts of Labour's 1945 manifesto or Crosland's *The Future of Socialism* would plainly no longer do. But nor would the apocalyptic strains of celebrated essays on the death of the globe by comfortably-off economists paid by the Twentieth Century Fund or the Club of Rome.

Thus Williams renewed his struggle with theory. Honourable and self-assured as always, he addressed the future of nature (and nature-in-culture), no less, and turned himself to revise those concepts with which socialism has played upon such grand themes. Muffled and over-generalised also, he spoke and thought as if changes of heart were there for the negotiating.

So when the high-minded herbivores of the Socialist Environment and Resources Association asked him to become a Vice-President he gladly accepted, and in that amazingly adequate way he had, turned himself instantly into a historian of the small voice of the culture which spoke through SERA.

The Association was funded, as it would be, by that complex association of capital, empire, chocolate and Quakerdom institutionalised in the West End of London as the Rowntree Foundation. Williams had been around long enough and was in any case more than gregarious enough to deal gratefully with the Liberal peer, Pratap Chitnis, who was then key executive for the Foundation. So in the autumn of 1981 he addressed a hundred or so ecological socialists ('a bit of a mouthful') from bare notes, and the tape-recording was again made into a pamphlet.[14]

He handed the Association an intellectual history – Häckel, Engels, William Morris, Thomas More [sic] – and sounded the note he had struck in the television debate on advertising. He pointed out, as people were so much beginning to do by that date,[15] that there were fixed material limits to life on earth, and that the feckless abundance still promised by capitalism was a deadly illusion. He was as hopeful as ever, and as commonplace, and as right.

> we must do it in a kind of good faith which is in fact rare ... Yet none of it is going to be easy ... the case for this new kind of enlightened, materially-conscious, international socialism is potentially very strong ...[16]

(It is this kind of arm-waving which so exasperated some of his more huffing-and-puffing enemies[17] and embarrassed admirers like me.)

He was never strong on admitting to being wrong. At much the same moment Williams became uneasily, remotely aware that, as Jane Miller put it,[18] there was 'one great silent area' in his thought (let alone his life), and that was the position of women in the turn of the wheel of long revolution. The drivers of the traffic of 'mobile privatisation' were all men; the directors, investors and manufacturers in the vast nuclear weapons industry were ruling-class men, and predominantly, capitalists. When British feminists (Williams never read the French ones) followed Juliet Mitchell's early lead in this argument, but did so with a certain decorous shyness, they were right to find him both defensive and customary in his response. Joy had lived, to all appearances, happily in complete subordination; Merryn had written her doctorate on her father's favourite novelist; his mother had been completely invisible in all his books; the non-productive realm of domesticity was deserving of an egalitarian's respect but not his theory.

So Williams fumbled rather with his picture of the new and fearsome politics given its portage into Britain by the country's first woman prime minister. The second most arctic phase of cold war had been cheerfully and mindlessly initiated by Ronald Reagan's fanatic band of buccaneers; Britain was to sing along with them, Mrs Thatcher marching at the head of her military men.

She released, as she did so, the first surge of political hatred from a large minority of Britain's unpolitical polity since the 1930s. Edward and Dorothy Thompson took Bertrand Russell's place in the van of the counter-marchers, a clever Monsignor and a beautiful, articulate politician of the street fell in behind them, and the middle-class peace movement turned into the biggest of Williams's 'resources of hope'.

His own position in CND was characteristically contorted. Dorothy Thompson was caustic about the Williamses' failure to turn out for the marches of the 1980s, as they had done for the ten years of Easter

Mondays between 1959 and 1968. But not only had he pulled back a little way from public politics apart from his short sallies to London for the Socialist Society, Williams was seeking for a feasible nuclear weapons policy beyond the bald slogan of CND, 'no cruise missiles here'.

He put his name down[19] for the European possibility of denuclearised zones, and saw the best kind of concerted action to be found at the intersection of very different groups simply trying to prevent absurd and extravagant enlargement of British nuclear weapons, in trying to hold back needless and provocative deployments of American ones, and in bearing witness against the hysterical urging of political élites towards the mad brink of detonation.

Towards 2000 was Williams's attempt to write a coherent politics of this moment. He made it, as he would, a politics of feeling. For some years after 1980, it was obvious that a new generation, exasperated by the older one, had broken out of the 'structure of feeling' which found its self-shaping expression in the grand narrative of the cold war.[20] Open contempt towards the waste, cruelty and corruption of cold war became far more candid and broadcast; one day soon the epoch will come to seem a monstrous, aberrant and completely irrational nightmare.

In 1983, when *Towards 2000* came out, people were still living in the nightmare which, given the right events, enforced itself with all the authority and exitless horror nightmares have. In 1982, Mrs Thatcher dispatched a British military force of several thousand men to recapture a town the size of a small seaside resort and a few square miles of sodden sheep turf about the size of Nantucket. 'The Falklands War' they called it; such an action would have occupied a forgotten morning in Burma or Belgium in 1944. It threw Britain in a frenzy of jingoism, as television audiences of thirty million (the biggest ever recorded in Britain) watched the nightly bulletins about a bunch of boys pointlessly killing a thousand of their number 12,000 miles away. At this temporal distance, the war is a bloody waste, an expense of life, money, spirit. At that geographical one, as Williams said in a fine piece of journalism for Karl Miller in the *London Review of Books*,[21] it was, precisely, distance which turned bloodshed into spectacle, the television in the sitting room compressing lived experience into a small, vivid, remote picture whose realities of pain and savagery led other people, somewhere else, to grief.

The ambition of *Towards 2000* was to summarise and theorise such a politics, to catch local knowledges in one grand theory. It could hardly be done, and certainly not on the run, as Williams attempted it. He had written to Carmen Callil at Chatto proposing the new book in May 1982, and although she had her doubts, none the less she said in an internal memo, 'I really want to keep RW'. So with many misgivings they allowed Williams to reprint and review for the accuracy or otherwise of his analysis the section called 'Britain in the 60s' from *The Long Revolution*. It wasn't a happy idea, and it came out distinctly garbled. Alec Nove, sometime Treasury economist and author of *The Economics of Feasible Socialism*, damned it utterly in the *Guardian* for its vagueness, evasiveness, its high-principled incantations and its incoherent psephology.

Once again Williams had tried to work out the future of the world with no help except from his own life and his typewriter. He didn't read much of the contemporary debate on feasible democracy, let alone socialism (there are only six books cited in the index, three of them his own), and his economic theory was perfunctory in the extreme. Even where he mentions, for instance, problems of investment or the vertiginous decline of the smokestack industries, his analysis is not so much economic as literary. Where he speaks, with a gratifying bitterness and enmity of owner-ship monopolies in public communication, he is close to a half-comical despair: 'the godfathers are taking us to a point where it will seem cheaper to be steadily ruined or simply to give up' [22]. If he had made the book into a new statement of the politics of moral feeling, he might have done much. This is the argument hidden in a decidedly dashed-off, half-baked mixture.

As often in Williams's thought, the best part – the part you can really use and think with – is in a title, a phrase, a striking paragraph. When he describes his hated enemy of the millennium, the authors of 'Plan X', who could forebear to cheer?

> Plan X has read the future as the certainty of a decline in capitalist profitability unless the existing organisations and expectations of wage-earners are significantly reduced. Given this reading, Plan X operates not only by ordinary pressures but where necessary by the decimation of British industrial capital itself. This was a heavy and (in ordinary terms) unexpected price to pay, but one which had to be paid if the necessary edge of advantage was to be gained or regained. Again many sane people say that this policy is insane, but this is only an unfamiliarity with the nature of Plan X thinking. Its people have not only a familiar hard drive, but one which is genuinely combined with a rational analysis of the future of capitalism and of its unavoidable requirements.
>
> In this kind of combination, Plan X people resemble the hardest kinds of revolutionary, who drive through at any cost to their perceived objectives. But the difference of Plan X from revolution is that no transformed society, no new order, no lasting liberation seriously enters these new calculations, though their rhetoric may be retained. A phase at a time, a decade at a time, a generation at a time, the people who play by Plan X are calculating relative advan-tage, in what is accepted from the beginning as an unending and unavoidable struggle. For this is percentage politics, and within its

tough terms there is absolute contempt for those who believe that the present and the future can be managed in any other way, and especially for those who try to fudge or qualify the problems or who refuse the necessary costs. These wet old muddlers, like all old idealists, are simply irrelevant, unless they get in the way.[23]

'Conspiracy theory,' someone says; what are we faced with if not a conspiracy?

This is Williams's polemic at its best. Dramatic, generalised, applicable, anyone with a shred of civic sense can grasp the picture, feel its force, apply its edge. Against it, in another dramatic phrase, Williams ranges our 'resources of hope', the common people hanging on to their great residuals of decency, mutuality, courage, kindliness, and the old parabola of equality. The people, the peace, the green, and the women's movements; our hopeful legions.

He wrote it on the run, as he always had, but the book fatally lacked grip – grip on either readers or ideas. Maybe it was a measure of his own distance from the political actuality of the day; maybe he aspired too largely to a grand purview, situated nowhere, except above the fray. Certainly, he had his strong paternalism, and the best of fathers is not immune to patronising his patronage.

The political surges-into-movements turned always to him, or to Edward Thompson and Stuart Hall. On the other hand, his academic patronage was rarely final. At Cambridge, at the office, the authority he could take for granted in the civil sphere of symbolic politics, was hardly acknowledged by his colleagues. Their 'vainglorious brawling' went on quite untouched by the dark times of the historic day. Yet as Williams himself would have said, their clashes of principle and of personality were not unconnected to the spasms of the world order.

The Faculty of English at Cambridge has had since its inception a small but striking niche in the great arch of the English imperium. That, indeed, was exactly why Williams so conscientiously took office first as subject chairman in the Cambridge Examinations Board and then served a term – for a small honorarium – in the chair of the whole enterprise, exporting syllabuses and 'O' levels and exam papers and being paid in hard-won hard currency by the poor ex-colonial territories whose independent new bureaucracies qualified themselves with essays on *Macbeth* and the *Ode to Autumn*.

The imperialism of knowledge, as Williams saw, was replacing the older, more military kind. But it was itself changing in mass and motion. *Keywords*, whatever its faults, was a sign of the times. As old imperialism mutated into something new, the study of Cambridge's English literature changed as well. It gradually became the study of English wherever

English was written in the endeavour of cultural expression. At its simplest, that extended English not only to North America, which had had, after all, quite a lot of English written down as literature for quite a long time, but also to the new and old countries of Old Empire. It extended beyond books to films and television. And it joined hands with the study of language in action – the varied actions of language in recorded speech, in dictionaries, in the manifold documents of a vast commercial and military empire going well past the official stories in novels and plays to the narratives hidden in legislation, administration, education, politics.

Keywords was one version of a new kind of study of the way moral and political concepts twine meaning upon meaning, as Wittgenstein said, like the strands of a rope. William Empson had done something of the kind much earlier,[24] but Williams, Skinner (and Williams as indebted to Skinner, having silently amended his text in response to Skinner's strictures), Edward Said, Foucault[25] were all addressing linguistic history with a new political edge.

This was the implicit and large change of bearing in Williams's work in the mid-1970s. He wanted to invent a new materialism which would make language the foundation of a grand social theory. Hence the thick struggle with the language of values in *Marxism and Literature*, the effort to embed Leavis's passionate trinity 'thought, words, and creativity' in the stuff of real history. Hence also Williams's hand in the appointment of a new, young lecturer in the Faculty of whose business he was always an attentive, powerless custodian, to teach 'English language in relation to literature since 1500'.[26] The lecturer was a sunny, breezy, stout lad of open features and golden curls called Colin MacCabe.

Williams had spoken strongly for this specialism in the appointment, although the Faculty also urgently needed someone to teach American literature. Familiar as he was with the *mana*, or totemic principles of the Cambridge English Faculty, he could never have anticipated the colossal row which erupted when Colin MacCabe came up in the natural course of things for confirmation as a permanent lecturer.

Mana is Durkheim's word for 'a power or influence, not physical and in a way supernatural; but it shows itself in physical force, or in any kind of power or excellence which a man possesses'.[27] Durkheim would have identified the Faculty as ritual and implicit in its social forms, hence pre-industrial, entirely un-modern. The ancient colleges held enormous power: they admitted any number of students to read English whom it was then the Faculty's business to administer and examine. As Williams himself said, 'it is only when we get the examination entries that we know how many students we've got'.[28] The Faculty staff each held collegiate positions, and in neither role subscribed to any principle of collective responsibility nor possessed any constitution expressing such a thing.

Moreover, the sociology of the institution – its relations of production (as you might say) – enjoined and created not the usual professional account of Faculty business but a vocational realisation of its human significance in each member's life. Thus the ordinary manners of academic exchange became charged with an electric aura of ultimate allegiance. As I suggested earlier, those for whom the lived force of a writer's life was a guide to everyday conduct would not tolerate the methodical technicalities of a historical linguist who didn't mind if the object of study was a James Joyce novel, a Godard movie, or a 1930s periodical. By the same token, a vocationalist for whom the curve and ring of a sentence were *the* tokens of both intelligence and sensibility would fight without pity not to give a job for a life at Cambridge to a junior who split infinitives, mixed his metaphors, talked streetwise and mistook the nominative.

The MacCabe Affair broke noisily into the culture columns of the press. It bears heavily on this biography for two reasons. First, Williams himself played a key role in a battle to redefine the academic subject to and for which he gave his life. Second, the quarrel bespeaks much about the high-principled vindictiveness in which much intellectual life is lived, dedicated as it is to discovering the great sources of sweetness and light. If the university is the citadel of reason, and English the essential discipline of the spirit, no wonder that the good society is still some way off.

The moment MacCabe is appointed to an Assistant Lectureship in March 1976, one member of the appointments committee resigns in disapproval at the change of direction in the subject which the appointment indicated. When MacCabe is invited the next year to present a paper to the Faculty on historical language study in the university, a senior member moves that MacCabe be dismissed from the meeting and the paper discussed in his absence. In an ineffable sequence of entries and exits belonging to radio farce, MacCabe is appointed to the Degree Committee and accepts; Christopher Ricks, one of the professors, promptly resigns; pressed, MacCabe resigns; the secretary of the Board then writes to Ricks to say that now MacCabe is off the Committee again, Ricks can come back on; Ricks does so, with stern constitutionality, some while later.

Williams watched it all from his usual impassive, sardonic distance. He never despaired of teaching his colleagues a properly rational bureaucracy, and nor did his lieutenant Stephen Heath, although Heath himself, far and away the brightest of the 1970s generation of lecturers in English literature, taught much in French and about movies, and was denigrated for doing so. As Ricks said to the *Guardian*, both airily and austerely, 'obviously no one objects to the presence of structuralists and theorists of film and linguistics in the English Faculty. But there is a question of proportion. It is our job to teach and uphold the canon of English Literature.'[29]

The difference over MacCabe was represented in the posh newspapers as being between modernists and traditionalists. But Christopher Ricks has written – none better – on T.S. Eliot and on Samuel Beckett.[30] His professorial opponents were Williams and Frank Kermode, then the King Edward VII Professor. Williams, on the contrary, never wrote at length on modernism, and all his feelings pulled him towards a socialist conservatism. Kermode, enormously catholic in his tastes as well as turning himself with great aplomb into an exegete of the Gospel,[31] was and is certainly no structuralist, and forcefully opposed to speakers-in-the-tongues-of-Theory. If Ricks was MacCabe's most fluent, merciless and entertaining enemy, it wasn't because of a battle of the books as divided up into Ancient and Moderns. It was because MacCabe spoke for theory against principles; because, as Ricks heard him, he garbled his sentences and read woefully; because he was more a linguist than a *literatus*; above all, because he had his stalwart doggedness, wrote a jargon-heavy prose, and lacked any gift for Ricks's own musketeering swordplay, his flashing rapidity of allusion and estimate.

MacCabe's was the way the world was going, and plenty of people in the Faculty with Ricks as their leader didn't like it. Braced by Ricks's scathing tongue, they determined to stop it.

It is important to be as exact as possible about the procedures then launched both in their routine and their particular aspects. Promotion from an assistant lectureship now only obtains at the University of Cambridge. It is attaining tenure in the USA. The post cannot be advertised; once it is filled those resources are allocated for good. There is no question of competition from candidates outside the university. Consequently, the business of the review is exceptionally tense, and plenty of exceptional candidates now distinguished in other universities had failed in the past to make it, Patrick Parrinder among them, Eagleton not having got that far. The very post of Assistant Lectureship was itself opposed as an anomaly by many members of the Faculty Board, Christopher Ricks among *them*. None the less, what had to be done, had to be done according to the rules.

So along with the routine there came, inevitably, much vieing for place, a smell of patronage, and much also of that high-principled, high-tempered kind of debate at which Cambridge English excelled, and in which there coincided also its inimitable combination of personal spleen and laser-like scruples.

The sub-committee appointed to review the assistant lecturers and recommend upgradings met on 10 March 1980 and voted twice on whether or not Colin MacCabe is to be granted permanent appointment. The first time for it, the second time against it, Williams and Kermode being his advocates. The committee received the usual reports on the lecturing performance of the three candidates for upgrading, Williams's handwritten one being full of quiet praises for MacCabe: 'well controlled, coherent, and intellectually stimulating' adding, importantly, that it helped 'supply a central current need in the Faculty'.[32] Christopher Ricks was mildly approbatory in one report, flatly hostile in the other (he had visited four lectures in the year 1979–1980 to Williams's one). He animadverted upon the confusions of two of these lectures, upon the muddle on the lecturer's blackboard, his general air of affable and energetic provisionality, and what he thought was downright poor reading of the poetry in question. While it might have been the case that the unhappy MacCabe did not do himself justice, Ricks observed thinly, he certainly did none to his subject.

On 22 May the Faculty Board meets, as somebody said, in 'an atmosphere of hatred and anger'. Only Dickens could have rendered it. Extracts from MacCabe's book on Joyce are read out aloud and scoffed at by Mike Long. Ribald laughter from two stout parties. John Barrell later writes to the Chairman in protest. Much is made of the notion of 'distinction'. 'Does this work show distinction?' 'What kind of distinction?' 'Well, true distinction. Distinction of intelligence. Of scholarship. Originality of mind. Distinction in the quality of prose.' Laughter. Uproar. Several members say they don't know what criteria of judgement are being applied. Frank Kermode says that it is ludicrous to invoke distinction in this way for a young man at the start of his career, a Regius Professor (which is to say a Crown appointment as he is himself) could hardly live up to such standards. Heather Glen is confirmed in her appointment, which is then revoked because of the flagrant discrepancies of treatment, the animosity of the debate, the disputes over criteria. Stephen Heath, himself not all that longstanding in his full lectureship, is characteristically caustic and intense in his determination to wring a just and rational procedure out of this tribal blood-sacrifice.

There is to be a new meeting before which the Edward VII professor, Frank Kermode, is prompted by Heath (who provides a very full template) to write to all colleagues trying to straighten out the criteria of judgement, and replace rancour with something a bit more like judicious debate. Between them, Heath and Kermode voice a dignified appeal to such canons.

> In a Faculty such as ours, openness to and tolerance of ideas that conflict with our own are essential to the whole enterprise. Ideological differences, it should go without saying, must not enter into our judgements of fitness . . .; the argument at such times is not about the validity of a critical position but about the quality and competence of the officer under consideration. I well understand that in practice it may be difficult to distinguish the two; an intellectual disagreement may be felt, and expressed, as a judgement on the quality of the candidate. But if we remember that we have an over-riding responsibility to exercise a measured tolerance in respect of intellectual endeavours different from our own we ought to be able to make the necessary distinction.

Indeed, it is hardly too much to say that if we fail to do so we are, as a Faculty, in a fair way to abandon many positions which I think we should all admit that it is our duty to hold. Already somewhat given to faction, we should be approaching a situation in which that variety of interests, approaches and skills which in a Faculty of English promote fruitful critical debate gives way to a punitive condemnation of views opposed to one's own. Such are the general dangers of our present position. The immediate issue, however, is that our differences, and the effect they may have on the application of our criteria for upgrading, should not interfere with our professional judgment when the careers of University Assistant Lecturers are at issue.[33]

It is hopeless. The reconvened – extraordinary, indeed – meeting gathers on 5 June. Ricks replies vehemently and stringently ('Dr MacCabe's book is a bad book') to Kermode. Long speaks a twenty-minute malediction over MacCabe's book on Joyce, motion and counter-motion are put, and after a tense telling of the arms raised, MacCabe apparently wins his appointment by one vote, and Heather Glen is confirmed in hers. It has at some time been pleasantly reported back to the successful candidates that an enemy of the people has congratulated the Faculty on appointing 'a pedant, a fool and an au pair'.

This has to be ratified by the University's official appointments committee in October. Williams, who had sat tight and taciturn through the last hubbub, goes off with Kermode to settle things. No such luck. Conscientiously, the appointments committee overturns the Faculty's recommendation, four–three, Williams and Kermode sticking together.

Appeals are made vainly to the senior officers of the University who are much put about. A delirium of animus is abroad, gripping the cortex of harmlessly domestic scholars. Certain enemies of MacCabe – specifically *not* including Ricks, who walks by himself – form themselves into a conspiracy to clinch victory. They plot darkly. Williams goes off to Hardwick and tells Joy all about it, but while it never crosses his mind to counter-plot, others do so on MacCabe's part. The plotters lurk, squaring assorted members of the Faculty for their support on either side. Williams and Kermode are routed. The two senior professors fail to be renominated to the appointments committee; their lieutenants, Heath and Barrell, are voted off the Faculty Board. The University's officers feel obliged to rule for good liberal reasons that the superordinate Board cannot interfere with a Faculty's autonomy but it is a near thing. The MacCabe affair is over.

There is a grace-note. Two things have been at stake in this demeaning to-do, and only Heath kept his eye on them both. The first was that the forum for agreeing upon the careers and well-being of any young probationers was splenetic, whimsical, subject to bitter vendetta, unworthy of the University. The second was that the English Faculty itself was over-loaded with students and understaffed for its duties, directionless in its policy, incapable of rational decisiveness, wholly without a coherent picture of itself or centre of intellectual reference. As always with bitter personal quarrels, there were structural explanations.

To say so is not simply to act as MacCabe's partisan. There was after all a delicious comicality in the case. MacCabe was advocate of the now fashionable view that 'language speaks the individual'; rather than our language being our intentional utterance, intention is always murky, rarely recoverable, open to multiple interpretation. But when things got bumpy and tempers high, MacCabe was pressed by a wild and woolly friend to sue *The Times* for calling him a Marxist, and he did take legal action against his colleague John Harvey for libel as reported in the newspapers, an action which surely betrays a lingering trust in the idea that statements are deliberately intended actions for which their speakers may be held responsible. (MacCabe subsequently dropped the case.)[34]

Heath hung on to his two points, it must be said, heroically. The University was obliged to take notice of him after three other members of the faculty signed a letter, as statutes required, calling for public debate. On 3 February 1981, a special meeting of the University Senate was duly arranged to discuss 'the state of the English Faculty'.

Its members were put on their most self-consciously academic behaviour. The splendid classical interior of the Senate House was packed. The broadsheet newspapers had made much of the row, rather to their credit, moreover; they had relished the clash of academic gladiators, but they had named the intellectual issues – new theory versus old literature, at bottom. Williams and Kermode had been much photographed, and everyone in Cambridge had enjoyed the *frisson* of celebrity and being able to make cleverly malicious remarks about fame-hunters.

So there were journalists, students, lecturers, and a rich selection of interested spectators with the necessary MA to qualify for admission all gathered to hear English as an academic subject debate itself, forensic-ally rather than eirenically, as though it all really were the matter of life and death which English as both language and literature must be able to speak of in a human idiom. Seven and a half hours of it, across two days.

Christopher Ricks took no part. His hostility to MacCabe was person-ally impersonal and expressed with his unforgettably swift and stinging fluency. MacCabe stood for him as emblem of all that was going wrong with the study of English. He detested MacCabe's way of thinking and the imperfections of his prose as inextricable and lethal faults; what he saw as social and intellectual defects located for Ricks a moral failure. He recoiled utterly from the appeal to tolerance exactly because he could not tolerate these things and because, moreover, he was (and is) a fierce constitutionalist. Famous, but not a seeker after fame, he said no more in public other than his lecture, 'In Theory' at the end of the month.

The big guns spoke from the two camps:[35] Heath first and best, addressing both justice and competence; Barrell strictly on MacCabe; Kermode, hurt and bitter about his colleagues; Erskine-Hill mischievous on the other side; Long, vain, *ad hominem*, egregiously referring to 'my vile and timid person'; the Professor of Greek, Geoffrey Kirk, classicist *and* structuralist, clear and ecumenical; Williams at his most grand and resonant, talking as ever and not without self-referentiality beyond the conflict to a large tomorrow, finding also in the bitter quarrel past things to speak up for and nurture:

> it is my own conviction that it was the extent of its intervention in a wide range of intellectual matters, not solely literary, which involved Cambridge English from the twenties at once in its achievements and its extraordinary perils. It is believed that it can solve any of those issues without the closest collaboration with neighbouring Faculties; the difficulty of doing this within our present organisation of humanities and the perils are undoubted. We are at present experiencing some of their results. But I still think that it is an honourable record over sixty years because that enterprise was attempted. I am here not to attack the English Faculty but to find, and help to find, conditions for the renewal of that enterprise, and I believe that those who have called today's Discussion are centrally moved by that intention.[36]

He took up this imperial theme in his last lectures to English students at Cambridge, in the summer term of 1983, typically turning the local fireworks into astral explosions against the movement of the intellectual heavens. The 'MacCabe affair' became a significant measure of an astrophysical shift, one in which Leavis's once-radical opening of Cambridge English hardened into a mechanics until the spray of new quanta – from Russian formalism, from French sociology, from ideology-critique – forced things into different patterns, to be read by the instruments of a new science, Williams's kind of science, of cultural history.[37] But though he talks there of fighting, fighting the recrudescence of the Right in 1983 as it tries to capture for itself certain amenable versions of Cambridge English, the way of Williams's theory was not a fighting way, and never had been. Fighting Williams was a journalist and, at times, a novelist; theoretic Williams a bard, hymning his poem of his people's deeply felt metaphysics.

Faculty business was getting him down. That particular fight now only commanded part of his attention. He had packed up regular attendance at the Board. These last days had weighed most unhappily upon him. His faith in the canons of university life, his loyalty to them, had been badly shaken. He did not know who he trusted, not even Heath, and he pulled back into reclusiveness.

Heath had been joined in the college by Lisa Jardine, the first woman fellow of Jesus, appointed by a special statute to admit women (which was none of Williams's doing) in 1975. Lisa Jardine is now one of the most formidable women of letters in Britain. She is daughter of Jacob Bronowski, an early star of science-on-television and a Jewish intellectual of some standing. A vivid, strong, squarely built and squarely minded woman with a fine taste for savoury gossip, she was socialist doyenne of her subject in Cambridge as a student between 1964 and 1966 (having started in maths), and went back a year later for her doctorate.

Lisa Jardine

We were at dinner in Howard Erskine-Hill's rooms. Howard was dead against Colin MacCabe but it was he and Moses Finley who got me the Fellowship at Jesus, against a lot of opposition from the old men, and *no* help from Raymond.

Edward Thompson was there, just back from Indira Gandhi's state of emergency in India (this was 1978). He turned savagely on Raymond. 'How *can* you sit there in that donnish way? How can you entomb yourself in this place?' I was on his side. Raymond just shrugged and said, 'I do my best', in that maddening way of his.

The MacCabe affair was intellectually null, a piece of late twentieth-century decadence. Ricks wasn't interested in the politics, just in literary criticism. He was hostile, therefore, to Williams and Kermode so he went for MacCabe, who wasn't cut out to be an intellectual.

In later life Raymond liked the role of Elder Statesman. And he became collegial all right. There was the King's Group, men only, who used to dine together. But Raymond had lost interest by then, and the political students with it.

He has lost interest in the faculty, perhaps in his subject as well. With *Towards 2000* he drowned his books, or those kinds of books, and determined to try to take Henry James's fervent advice: 'Don't, I beseech you, *generalise* too much in these sympathies and tendernesses – remember that every life is a special problem which is not yours but another's and content yourself with the terrible algebra of your own.'[38] Prospero was going back to the very private life he only intermittently left. He arranged with the University, on the sufficiently handsome terms then available, to retire some five years before his official due date, and to upholster the difficult and lonely trade of writing down his 'terrible algebra' with a decent pension. He would finish at Cambridge at the end of the summer term of 1983.

At the last Faculty of English meeting he ever attended no one bade him official farewell, but Stephen Heath's ten-year struggle to bring reasonableness and the iron cage of bureaucracy to the crazy jungle stir of Faculty life, was formally carried. Then they all went off to Raymond's goodbye party at which he was surprisingly ill-assured and troubled-seeming. Christopher Ricks spoke a memorably witty valedictory, Lisa Jardine's little daughter Rachel presented Raymond with a toy telephone in recognition of the difficulty of ever speaking to him on one, and on 10 June 1983 he and Joy moved to number 4 Common Hill, Saffron Walden.

They left White Cottage without a pang and in quite a bad way. For some years, since their children had left home, Raymond and Joy had kept at times to separate bedrooms, Raymond's with a bathroom of its own in which he would soak for hot, steam-filled hours, and a shaggy carpet in the bedroom heavy with the smell of his tobacco. They hadn't looked to their sodden house, the garden was overgrown and neglected, the hedge at the front over six feet high and dense with ivy, brambles and briars. The family who bought it were quite taken aback and embarrassed: the dire yellow paint and wallpaper hadn't been renewed in years, the big window on the landing so wet it could be pushed out of its frame.

No. 4 Common Hill, fifteen or so miles down the road in the very pretty, very well-kept, Trumpton-like town of Saffron Walden looked out on the common on which the Parliamentary army had bivouacked during the civil war.[39] It was a plain flat-faced pleasant house with no garden – Raymond said freely that he was too tired nowadays to do the digging – and it had not long since been workshop to a monumental mason's. It was in spruce condition, smaller than the Hardwick house, and Joy turned it into the sunniest, most stylish home they'd ever made.

He quit college, though he was still a Fellow, proudly kept his rooms there, and turned up for a few college feasts. But the college didn't even have his phone number; Stephen Heath was sole intermediary. That autumn of 1983, Williams went to the Cheltenham Festival of Literature, an excellently provincial beano founded by the town's bibliophile book-seller Alan Hancox, and much attended by literary grandees and harmless star-spotters then and now. David Hare joined him on the platform on which he spoke up for writing and came down heavily on literary criticism.

> ... he said in his lecture, let's not endlessly complain about what's not being done. Indeed if we feel so strongly, let's do it ourselves. Let's not peddle all that tired stuff about standards. Let time make judgements as surely it will.[40]

And then, talking over cups of tea afterwards, he agreed with the David Hare of 1966 that the study of literature as then practised in Cambridge was worthless, hostile to literature itself, and the David Hare of 1983 companionably agreed with the Raymond Williams of then and now that a steady, sanguine socialism had more to be said for it than the noisy complacencies of denunciation.

From then on he was a writer, turning out his regular quota a day, still doing his punctual reviews, as well as lending a contributory hand to James Curran's exemplary new fortnightly *New Socialist*, a journal funded briefly by the Labour Party in an effort to stem the tidal, effluent advance of the Right over the ideological beaches. He joined in, with mild scepticism and at a distance, the sharp debate joined when his old ally Eric Hobsbawm, lifelong communist and Party member as long as there was a party, proposed[41] the heresy at a conference that the working class could no longer be designated the agent of historical emancipation, that the Left tendency of the Labour Party led by Tony Benn had completely lost touch with its supporters, and that the only hope for the urgent necessity to defeat the new Nobadaddy of the Right was by an alliance of all its enemies, of whatever party or persuasion.

Williams coughed discreetly from the back, and argued for keeping the socialist flame alight no matter where the coalitions camped, but his heart wasn't in it. He was truly looking only at his books, not at the world. Maurice Glasman, a pupil of his at the time, remembers his own fierce tirade at an unresponsive Williams when Mrs Thatcher's government was selling off municipal houses to their occupants at rock-bottom prices.

Maurice Glasman

I was reading history, having come from a Tottenham comprehensive, and Williams sought me out for his sessions on political philosophy of the seventeenth century (which he wasn't at all well read in). We had a row about the sale of council housing. I was really angry. I shouted at him. He seemed quite stunned. I said, 'Your parents would have wanted to own their own houses, *you* own your own house.' It was a prelude to a big set-to with him, when I said, 'I can't predict what you think about any issue except disarmament, and that's *the* middle-class movement.'

An 'authoritarian populist' lurked in Williams, you know. His idea of 'community' was utterly vague, and he always refused to *act* in concert with others. He was so evasive also – look at the 1984–1985 miners' strike . . . and so self-deluding, for example about his aristocratic manner and the phoniness about keeping up a working-class appearance. By 1982 he was only concerned to show correct political manners.

It was his writing which had all his attention. He still taught one or two research students – Morag Shiach reported being well looked after by him – but fifteen miles outside Cambridge and in solitude, he wrote with a Dickensian lavishness. As soon as his retirement began, he had been in touch with Chatto, describing his plans for two new novels. The first, which appeared as *Loyalties* in 1985, was to be a series of interlinked scenes from the key moments of Anglo-Welsh political life across the learned-by-heart dates of socialist advance and retreat: 1937, 1945, 1956, 1968, 1984. The second was to be the centrepiece of his life as a writer, a narrative of the people of Black Mountains, caught in a series of silhouetted actions at dozens of points of a history culminating in the present but going back to an opening episode set as the ice age began, in the year 23,000 BC!

The people at Chatto flinched a bit; *Manod* had only sold half of the hardback print-run of 3,500, but Carmen Callil wrote back saying that they would do the whole thing as a 600-page monolith, and delivered a handsome £5,000 advance which she must have known wouldn't be cleared by sales for years.

Loyalties, which Williams had dallied with for a while, was finished in September 1984, by which time *People of the Black Mountains* was also up to 50,000 words. But September 1984 marked a point halfway through the year-long miners' strike by means of which the Tory government finally destroyed any threat still outstanding to their power from the 'brigade of guards of the Labour movement'. The miners had twice defeated the Tories, in 1972 and 1974; this time, they were not just defeated themselves, but, as industrial workers, vengefully annihilated.

The Yorkshire miners had come out in early March 1984, when a big pit in the area at Cortonwood was closed by the National Coal Board in spite of previous promises ('guarantees' is the cant word) not to do so. Capital never keeps promises; of its nature it can't do so, and the men were innocent to believe the Board. But nobody could have kept them at work the day the news broke.

Two days later, the miners' leader Arthur Scargill, a self-righteous class-warrior of passionate feeling and few wits but who had got hold of the truth that the class enemy was always a ruthless liar, was summoned by the Board and told that the industry was to cut production by four million tons, with the loss of 20,000 jobs. Now the constitution of the National Union of Mineworkers requires that a ballot be held by the whole membership before any concerted action can be taken, a clause the Union ruled binding upon itself long before Tory legislation made it law. But the NUM was organised by county areas, and an area strike could be called by the local area's executive committee. Scargill wanted to avoid a ballot, but he also wanted to declare class war by a national strike. So the Yorkshiremen came out, and the area was declared on strike. So too the Scots and the Welsh, in instant solidarity.

The counties of Nottinghamshire and Derbyshire were more of a problem for Scargill. Mining was easier, the seams were richer, the pay was higher as a consequence. For the same sorts of reasons, the Nottinghamshire miners had broken away from the Federation, and gone back to work in 1926. They didn't rejoin until 1945 and the default was remembered in mining folk-history.

The Yorkshire pickets, brawny young tearaways drunk on lager and righteous anger, poured down the motorway to persuade the Nottingham-shire miners to stop work. They were helped by an unprecedented campaign of vilification and lies against Scargill and his deputies, some of it arranged by the British secret police[42] and all of it viciously orchestrated by the violence of the fighting between police bussed into the minefields in thousands and met by equal numbers of miners. Night after night, millions of British people, divided between horror and fascination, watched the battle of Orgreave Colliery and had it dramatised for them by Government as a crusade against 'the enemy within' which Britain must win for the sake of lawfulness and good order.

Scargill and his National Executive may have been traduced and cheated, but they marched their men voluntarily and unrepentantly over the edge of absolutely universal closure and redundancy. For a year, from March 1984 to March 1985, the Welsh, Scottish, Durham and Yorkshire miners stood out against all reason, against self-interest, against fellow-colliers who resumed work, against a government of class warriors determined to break not just their spirits and their bank, but their very existence as a social and productive force. The miners were crushed and humiliated also; when they went back to work behind their union banners and their local brass bands, they went back to the certain loss of everything: jobs, neighbourhood, union, culture, everything.

Raymond and Joy drove several times over the Black Mountains during those winter months to the pit towns on the further slopes. They went to Bedwellty, Bargoed, Penrhyceibr. Strike pay was low by then, life savings were gone, all over the divided country unmilitant people who felt obscurely that the miners were being most cruelly mistreated donated tinned food, baby clothes, cash to the improvised collecting points scattered all over the towns. The collections were driven to the pitheads and the clubs for distribution carefully calculated according to need, and Joy joined in as gladly as she always did with little children, as they waited hungry and fretful in the community centres while their parents queued with an ancient class patience for the food and clothing which would tide them over for another week.

For Williams, these stirring scenes, the life of the strike and the closeness of it provided an unexpected realisation of his best-loved values. The Welsh miners stuck together with antique solidarity, a bitter humour, and a strongly expressed 'anger and determination against those who [were] so clearly and exultantly their enemies'.[43] For the Welsh miners as for Williams, it was once again the bloody English in London, the ruling-class English, who were, in the haughty features of modern management masking the old grimace of capitalism, destroying their local livelihood, their inheritances, their grim, homely towns. He saw the swift, hard operation of each day, packing a thousand bags of necessities for the long queues, heard the hard jokes. He saw the men, so cheerful and strong and drawn it broke your heart, and the women, healthier by far than in the old days, better made-up too, still with their own teeth mostly, but so tired-looking and washed-out, drained by want and the hateful indifference of those whose duty was to rule over and to care for them. And he felt all through himself the struggle of loyalties, the rough-tongued bell which called him home, and the prosaic actuality of his good pension, his stout ashplant and well-cut cap, the unfinished chapter on the table at the cottage, tucked in beside the wide chimney breast, looking out through the little window on his beloved hills. *Loyalties* was published in 1985 and Andrew Motion at Chatto sent off advance copies to, among others, Neil Kinnock, Arthur Scargill, Christopher Ricks.

Norman Braose (the name of one of the oldest Anglo-Welsh baronies in the marches), a communist, has a child by Nesta, a beautiful Welsh girl who becomes a gifted painter. She marries Bert Lewis, a miner who fights in Spain and in the tanks in Normandy where he is wounded and disfigured. He brings up Gwyn as his own son while Braose and a communist friend become vital to the development of computer networks, secrets from which they pass to the USSR during and after the war. Helped by money from Braose's sister (Norman never sees Nesta again) Gwyn goes to Cambridge and becomes a government scientist working on the disposal of nuclear waste. By way of the crisis years of cold war – 1956, 1968 and so on – the shifting allegiances, the betrayals, the alliances with former enemies and the breaks with old friends turned the cultural decencies of a nation into its barbarism and corruption. The present pitiable state of, first, England, and then parts of Scotland and Wales, the decadence of its ruling-class tradition, the rotten state of its public morals, all bear witness to this historic consequence.

Loyalties is an essay of meditation on these matters. It is confused as well as confusing, because the history is so confused, and Williams wants to avoid the simple name-calling of cold warfare. It is melodramatic in that Williams attributes such calm omniscience to the secret state – the interrogation of Gwyn the hero by the state inquisitor Meele is a quintessence of Ibsenism hotted up with good old-fashioned class hatred. But it is also a threnody on idealism and patriotism. Loyalty is still straightforward and fine in the Welsh valleys and during the strike. Everywhere else it has been turned and viciously compromised by the hard gangsters of political manipulation – the killer-managers of 'Plan X' – who are the true victors of this over-political century.

The novel is vitiated by some Mills and Boon psychology: 'He is nothing. He is a name. The man and the father are entirely burned out'.[44] There is Blackadder camp: 'You are a master not a servant of anything. You turn your very weaknesses to an always convenient adjustment'.[45] There is the blank assumption that something called socialism entails something called loyalty. But in *Manod, The Volunteers* and then *Loyalties* Williams names and tries to grasp the condition of the governance of England for what it is, venal, poisoned, hateful and obtuse, while always searching for a counter-condition in which to live, in Wales, in a politics of opposition, in beleaguered nature.

These are his 'resources of hope' and it isn't surprising if they have their sentimental side. Once he had retired in 1983, he divided his life tidily into three parts: writing, travelling-with-a-bit-of-speechifying, and spending time in the cottage at Craswall. (The traitor in *Loyalties* gives his loyalty at the end to the new ecology, and to cherishing an experimental plantation of trees not so very unlike Williams's coppice in Craswall.) His always strong reluctance to allow new experience to shift and resettle the forms of its old resolutions in him became, as it would for a man in his sixties, more and more obdurate. He met with another aged grandee, the black, West Indian, Marxist historian C.L.R. James when both of them went to Canterbury for an honorary doctorate in 1984 (Bernard Sharratt had proposed both, and atheistical dissent was thus quietly canonised in England's oldest See.) Williams recognised in James his own determined fixity of seeing, his *authority*, given and taken by himself.

In these years, that same fixity authorised his two modes of being and thinking with great finality. In October 1985 he and Joy went off by train to Yugoslavia to spend his 53,000 dinars of royalties. Raymond spoke to the remnants of the Praxis group in Cavtat, and descanted on 'many socialisms', allowing his taste for formalism such loose rein that his socialism no longer had any content whatever other than to be anti-capitalist, or perhaps not-capitalist. It was to be the product of an indefinite 'new order' arising from the diverse play of human creativities. But his formal description of socialism got no purchase on the fact that the leading edge of world production is the making of weapons of destruction, and the socialist offer to humanise the means of production collapses ignominiously when so much production is aimed only at destruction.[46] Williams saw this, but could think of nothing to do about it except to say hopefully, hopelessly, that socialism and peacefulness cannot be simply made equivalent.

The formalist habit of Williams's mind had its richly comic side. In 1986, still a Fellow of Jesus though he hadn't been seen in college for months, the new King Edward VII Professor, Marilyn Butler was proposed for a professorial fellowship in the college. Her university appointment, Christopher Ricks having gone off to Boston, was quite a moment for the older Cambridge, and Williams had taken to heart some of the feminist criticisms of his work, even though he never saw their point.

The college required Marilyn Butler to submit to a little rite of passage, a dinner which was also an informal seminar. Williams would preside.

Marilyn Butler

Stephen Heath was civil and friendly, Lisa was cordial and welcoming. Raymond started off with a ten-minute statement of our similarities and unbridgeable differences. It was utter self-parody – 'in short, and not to put too fine a point on it, it could be said to be a question of *form*'. In desperation I had to ask him to rephrase the question. One person just clutched his brow at Williams going on so, and Lisa said briskly that there was no need to go into all that, just for me to talk about what interested me, such as the Gothic; so I lumbered off.

I have a tremendous hang-up about the Left. There's so much enmity and in-group competition. When prestigious men take an interest in a topic, they assim-ilate it and they look down on the methods of feminism – empathy, identification, and so on. But Theory with a capital T is also a way of feeling.

The Left has a cult of adoration, co-existing with a curiously chilly atmosphere, the leader lofty and inaccessible.

Williams the leader was damned uncomfortable on that occasion, which may explain his ascent into the clouds of formalism. Anyway, Professor Butler went elsewhere for her Fellowship. So Williams gave up on college business, and apart from going to Glasgow in 1986 to meet Jacques Derrida with Colin MacCabe as impresario, he wrote *People of the Black Mountains* until he died.

Carmen Callil's memorandum to her colleague (and writer) Jenny Uglow, on receiving the first manuscript early in 1987, is the best single evaluation of the book I can find.

it is extraordinary but it is also extremely difficult to read ... It has a lot going for it, but it also has a lot not going for it: he is no novelist; his didacticism is wearisome; he is not a man to whom comedy, or any comic leavening of life came at all easily; therefore it is a rather solemn but immensely impressive history of the zillion different kinds of Welsh people from 23,000 to 1415 ... I can see that this is an amazing piece of work, but, Jenny, it's not very good.[47]

Admiring reviewers later[48] read the novel as an anti-English and anti-'Englishness' tract and, for sure, that plot is there. There is also the pre-history present in all Marxism, present indeed in all pursuits of the millennium, in which a classless people turns hardship into a garden with enough work and food for all its families. Fondly as Eagleton reviewed it, there was plenty of scope for his parodic powers, too. Williams spoke at his best in the novel in the rhythms of the bards – 'Ruin seize thee, ruthless king!' – but he wasn't so far away from Excalibur scientology either, what with men with names like detergents and computer gram-mars, Idrisil, Anailos, Voratin and Nemat, and a good deal of paintwork about the cold Gwent rock and thorn, the whinberry, and the strange broad faces, the light tunics of the newcomers.

The 'immense impressiveness' of the two volumes comes surely from that accurate communication of the feeling by which Williams lived, that the actuality of this landscape, its past, present and future, moved physically through his body, was immediate to him as history.

So the novel is a record of ghosts and traces, but not in the least played under a Celtic twilight. The scenes of past pain and happiness, bloodshed and struggle, emerge briefly from the past like a memory materialising on a videotape which then fades, before the action is done, back into obscurity. We screw our eyes up and try to see how things came out, wanting urgently to know, and a different scene, a thousand years later, suddenly gains definition and becomes briefly watchable.

There is much of T.S. Eliot in this, to whom Williams was always so unjust.

> We die with the dying:
> See, they depart, and we go with them.
> We are born with the dead:
> See, they return, and bring us with them.[49]

Eliot's and Williams's theme alike was time and timelessness in holy places. In the plan for the unwritten third volume, a farmer ploughing in the 1930s was to uncover the skeletons of a young man and woman buried during the action of volume one back in Beaker Folk days; an American pilot crashed and killed on Black Mountain would wear on his identity disc a local family name, long since emigrated.

> See this layered sandstone in the short mountain grass. Place your right hand on it, palm downward. See where the summer sun rises and where it stands at noon. Direct your index finger midway' between them. Spread your fingers, not widely. You now hold this place in your hand.[50]

He began the three-decker in autumn 1983, and wrote it alongside *Loyalties*, Joy doing all the heavy legwork on place-names, parish records, archaeology, genealogy. By the end of 1986, Chatto had all of volume one, and volume two only lacked the local history which Joy was tirelessly compiling from the *Victoria County History* and the Records Office. Volume three was fully planned; the whole thing would be a thousand pages long, polished off by the beginning of 1989. He only needed one more year.

It makes painful sense to treat the novels as closing the form of his life. They spoke so tersely of his return, the gifted son coming home to speak to and for his people, to speak so against all that harmed and menaced them. But in truth he was as busy and active as ever. He turned up to public meetings in Saffron Walden, and was filmed doing so by Anglia TV. He spoke, a bit tiredly they said, at the well-named society 'Oxford English Limited' and its conference in St Cross Road.[51] In March 1987 he gave an endowed lecture at the university in Bristol, and made of his analysis of modernism and postmodernism a ringing rebuttal of its selective ideology of fragmentariness, exile, homeless migration, dislocation; out of the writing of his novel he once more declared himself on

293

behalf of us all for settlement, for continuity, for control of the storms of the day on behalf of the places which belong to us and to which we belong. He spoke of the paintings of places, which Mike Dibb had taught him to love late in life.[52] In the rich city of Cabot and Burke, of slavery and Wills's cigarettes, of the SS *Great Britain* and Concorde, he spoke again from his bare notes for the same things, the right things. 'Heroic absurdity' . . .

In July 1987 I went up to Craswall for a visit, not having seen him since the Bristol lecture and having been much moved by it. He enjoyed visitors more than when he was working in Cambridge, but I never liked to stay long.

It was very hot, the sun squeezing the hot sweet smell of hay out of the thick grasses through which Raymond had cut a few curving swathes with the electric scythe to serve as grassy paths. The drystone wall was warm and lumpy to sit on. There were no cars, a solitary tractor in the narrow lane under the wall was still. A 747 from across the Atlantic droned very distantly above us.

Raymond was animated and cheerful; he told me all about a portrait John Bratby had done of him, and Joy brought out mugs of tea. I always felt a bit over-awed, pleased I'd been, a bit relieved to go. The sky was a Mediterranean blue.

The next month, back again at Craswall, his prostate began to hurt, and he stopped writing. It had begun in late July, staying in the Black Mountains. A steady ache, deep in his fork, so deep and yet so ill-defined it seemed in a place where one didn't know that one was, somewhere about the root and the tight knot next to it where everything should be going to exit, but where the thumping ache beat abominably at his very base.

They drove home, Joy driving some of the way although it still made him a bit uneasy when she did. He couldn't teach her, Ederyn had done that. But driving himself hurt hellishly, and he shifted around constantly, trying to take the weight off his prostate, acutely inflamed and grossly swollen as it was.

The drive home was bloody. All the way across England, from one border almost to the further edge, none of the big roads really made for such a trip, all of them cutting hard across the East–West line, going South, always to London, so that the sheer weight of motorway road and its traffic thrust you like a tide southwards, Craswall down to Raglan and Monmouth, then the ancient London road eastwards until the car could tug its way upwards and follow the swirl north of Oxford; eastwards again along the wide neutral corridors of Milton Keynes, give a miss to a quick cup of tea with Merryn near Cranfield, second to last leg now, slow though, up the A428 to Cambridge, cut across the Great North, oldest road in

England, torrents of vehicles pouring down to London in the summer evening light, curve round Cambridge, always, always slow, and now with him sweating heavily and in dreadful pain, stuck at the roundabout across Midsummer Common for twenty minutes, and then into the quiet main street of Saffron Walden as the last light turned golden behind them, and the relief of coming home eased the pain and cooled the fever. Some 250-odd miles, but the better part of six hours, and every mile of it fastened, one way or another, to his life-story.

A fortnight, his doctor had said in August, frowning a bit. A nice young man though they'd not had to see so very much of him in their four years there. Or rather, the doctor corrected himself, a fortnight's antibiotics, and then a bit of time after that to clear up. But the pills did not work. The fierce bacteria fought off the antibiotic, and September turned to October before the fevers failed to recur. The pain continued, vaguely roaming the very bottom of his anatomy, but always hard and concentrated where he sat, where he had believed the organs ended.

Visitors came, with helpless, propitiatory gifts: flowers, grapes, books. Joy was always there, smiling, vigilant, silent. Stephen Heath came often, with good gossip from the college, and a bottle of Harveys; or he phoned. But for the first time for many years, not since the deep clouds which had twice gathered in the past, Raymond was unable to read, but sat or lay, with the pain as his companion, and waited for it to recede, or to be violently cut out.

And at last the big capsules began to tell. Still listless, only summoning his habitual courtesy to visitors with an effort of will which drew it up, as it seemed from deep inside him, he began to recover. It hurt less to move. He got up and walked slowly, a bit wadingly, to the paper shop. The doctor pronounced himself pleased. Merryn came over with the children before Christmas, Madawc just after. It was good to see them, and they left him tired, but better, much better as they said to each other, as one does. Joy dropped a relieved and reassuring note to Stephen; Raymond hadn't been up to doing his own correspondence for ages.

On the morning of 26 January, he woke feeling really ill again. Not the prostate, not that at all, but sick, a bit dizzy, hemmed in, his throat constricted, the pressure on his chest and shoulders coming and going in a heavy beat.

At a quarter to nine, pain hit him like a punch. In the great aorta, the artery which carries the blood away from the top of the heart to the upper organs and the brain, a veinous purple membrane which had been bulging and depressing under the systole and diastole of his heart all night, bulged again like the inner tube of a tyre, and split wide. The blood pumped copiously into his chest cavity. He fought gaspingly for breath, aware of nothing except the need for air. Then brain and vision darkened together, he stumbled a pace or two, and toppled face forwards into a chair.

There is a seal around the aorta which, in one attack out of five, contains the blood long enough for emergency surgery. But not in this case. The seal held for a brief time, and he recovered momentary consciousness. But a second, sudden rupture tore open flesh and muscle once again, and damaged the heart and brain of the 66-year-old victim beyond repair. Raymond Williams was dead.

13

FOR CONTINUITY

As soon as she knew that Raymond was dead, Joy, with her habitual steadiness in the observance of the proprieties, phoned Stephen Heath and asked him to tell the newspapers. Then she set herself to her duties, to the things that must be done, the funeral, the estate, the work left unfinished, the papers to be collected, to be straightened, to be published. Three years' work at least, and she was never afraid of work, still less of subordinating herself to her beloved husband's labours, to the careful cherishing of his good name and the handing on of his intellectual inheritance.

As sometimes happens, the numb shock of Raymond's death still at her centre, Joy discovered an unexpected freeing of her friendliness when she became a widow. Her oldest friend Annette Lees noticed it, her more recent acquaintance, Julia Swindells, was much struck by it, Stephen Heath pleased and touched by it.

She fell to greeting Bratby's portrait of Raymond cheerfully, and, knowing so few people socially after her husband's death, was taken by surprise by a sudden zest for sociability. It was a queer parallel with old Mrs Williams's flowering after Harry's sudden death. Stephen Heath drove her to the film première of Bruce Chatwin's novel *On the Black Hill*, and as they passed the London School of Economics on the corner of Kingsway she confessed that she hadn't been there since LSE was evacuated in 1939. She thought the movie was 'wonderful', was taken to dinner by Heath and Colin MacCabe at Groucho's, and got back home at 3 o'clock in the morning having loved every minute of it.

She took eagerly to her new friends calling in, happily knocking back the bottle from Oddbins with which Julia Swindells or Lisa Jardine would call. She would put passionate and urgent questions to the two of them about the hard, obscure and knotted issues on which for so many years she had followed Raymond's lead. Coleg Harlech, the Welsh Adult Education centre, put on a Williams day, and Joy confessed to Julia Swindells that she knew she'd always seen her political and intellectual role only through Raymond, but she declared herself dedicated to keeping

297

not only Raymond's memory alive, but also the content of the arguments to which he had given his life.

So she worked, she taught herself to use a word processor and worked at his papers. She saw the first volume of *People of the Black Mountains* through the press, filled in all the palaeographic detail for volume two, *The Eggs of the Eagle* and, though she told Stephen Heath 'I can't write anything', in 1990 she wrote a long epilogue to the novel describing the outline of volume three which ends, as it began, in the present. She turned to with a will on behalf of all those many bibliographers assembling the posthumous collections – Eagleton's, McIlroy's, O'Connor's, Pinkney's, Gable's, Mulhern's, several conceived before his death, all of them now in commemoration, intellectual wreaths signifying devotion.

It has been suggested that the abrupt, unexpected death of someone much loved and long familiar may cause the nerves and cells of vital organs in the bereaved to shrink away in such horror at the shock, so to waver and tremble in the normal, busy traffic of bodily renewal and discarding, that the vital message systems fuse and disrupt. When they resume, their communications have been violently distorted; they start to print out cancer cells.

Joy had decided to buy a house in Fosterville Crescent, Abergavenny, near Annette Lees and the Welsh part of her husband's ghost. Early in 1991 she found her speech arbitrarily lapsing, and could not control a pen. Aphasia followed, a brain tumour was diagnosed. She took it with quiet courage. The work was done. She died in August in the Cardiff Cancer Hospital, aged 72.

W.B. Yeats once wrote:

> The intellect of man is forced to choose
> Perfection of the life, or of the work ...[1]

The cost of living Williams's work was high: that lifelong, daily application to the typewriter, a list of publications including thirty-three books of theory, criticism, essays under his name, seven novels, ninety chapters contributed to other people's collections, four hundred or so newspaper reviews, three plays, and one poem.[2] Was it worth it? Did he bring this work to some kind of fulfilment? Did it put a dimple with his signature on it in the shape of the times? Did the work conduce to the good society, did it cause men and women to think differently, to be happy, to live better?

Happiness now, laughter, desire,[3] these great simples of a child's politics (all the better for that) don't find much of a place in Williams's house of theory. Indeed, with theory – *theoria* – herself he isn't always truly at home, so her place in his architecture is often crude and lumpy, however hard he worked to make it fit. Theory has been the heart of the matter for the intelligentsia these twenty-five years – the leisure pastime of the theory class, as has been much said – and never more so than on the Left. One way of distinguishing Left and Right used to be to group together the pro-theorists on the Left and the anti-theoretical pro-custom-and-traditionalists on the Right.

But of late years, the Right has gone whoring after theory and tied her to the tale of a rabid politics, while over here, our senior, pragmatic sort-of-Marxists bent themselves to squaring a homespun theory with the life-in-earnest which history really was only yesterday. Anticipating the grand dissolutions of postmodernism, Edward Thompson uttered a great roar of malediction in 1978 and called it *The Poverty of Theory*.[4] His comrade-leader of the Left, Raymond Williams kept his fences more carefully mended. But he placed an absolute trust in the truths of his own experience. He kept up his faith in the moral content of ordinary life. He believed that people learned of necessity, and took to heart the lessons of solidarity and kindliness, peacefulness and an ecological good conscience; they only lacked the political chance to express them. They knew in their best selves the way to the good life, if only they could find the will.

There may be something vivid and colourful missing from this picture of life, desire, and the happiness which opens at the centre of strong feelings fully lived. There is also some naivety, and some complacency as well. But no picture of the good life will ever be complete, and without some degree of naive faith and a confidence in life which might be accused of complacency it is hard to see how anybody could even have the character and integrity with which to imagine a better human future.

Williams's life and thought come together in that imaginative sociology fettled out of his best phrases and ideas. Those phrases can be turned into a personal narrative of everyday politics. It is this story which he bequeathed to his grieving students and admirers. This was his fable. He may not have lived it himself, but then, as he might have said in his deprecating way, nobody could live it with politics the way it is. And anyway, he set himself the ambition of a big fable out of which he fashioned his plot and its symbols.

He had to weave together the songs of the border country and the plots of Cambridge. He calmly abided the incommensurability between his passion to be a writer and the prosaic necessity of professing and teaching. The odd-jobbing of endless writing commissions and the algebra of his own life and times made an irregular match. His domesticity was too homely to light the day, and I bless it for that. It was also too private to imagine a society bright enough to live in. The politics to which he gave so much energy was too small and frenzied for the largeness and ecumenicism of his gifts. Yet from these bits and pieces, he fashioned a moral example as compelling as his day could find.

The fable into which the patterns of his ideas fall tells the story he wanted his society to live. Like all fables, it expresses a longing for how things ought to be. It takes the measure of the gap between actuality and desire. If the gap is too wide, the fable is a religious one. If the gap can be seen across to the other side, and the other side is still on earth, the fable is political, even theoretic. '"What then?" sang Plato's ghost ...' Why then, seize the fable, and the day; live them if you can.

Williams's political fable starts from his own old chestnut 'the structure of feeling'. By means of the phrase he attached the lived feeling of the great Romantics to the socialist politics of an epoch. The vital source of Williams's appeal is exactly that: he may wheel out the cumbrous jargon-words of theory, but he always speaks of feelings alongside them. Like Wordsworth, his dark familiar, he rewrote an old politics of the heart; this is the venture which stirs me so.

'Structure of feeling' connotes holism, totality as the philosophers said. It implies that to understand our moment of history we shall need the comprehension provided by as large a movement of sympathetic feeling as we are capable of. Only full feeling can grasp the good.[5] To have that capacity, Williams goes on to tell us, we shall need the help of that 'know-able community' hidden somewhere in the unplumb'd, salt, estranging sea of the modern city and its circumambient nation–state. If you know of such a community, its friendships, customs, and the poetics of its place in history and geography, you will be able to feel the feelings you will need in order to act rightly and live well.

Those feelings in turn will tremble with the contradictory and jarring rhythms of past, present and future. They will direct us to value what is past, or passing, or to come, and to do so unevenly. Our valuing, which is to say our deep movements of allegiance and identification, of love and cherishing, will be at odds as between the value put upon 'the residual, the dominant, and the emergent'. Residual socialism tussles with domi-nant hedonism, with the happy abandon of the consumer's life; both resist the challenge of an emergent austerity, the needful denials of a good ecological conscience. This is the contention of the self and its knowable community with all that may be promised to our children.

It is also a bitter struggle with old power itself, with its grim structures and with its new helots as they try to put through the abomination of 'Plan X'. All of us, living in our own bit of border country, have put ourselves at a distance, and been put at even greater distance from the scene of the action by the X-planners. *They* will do all they can, by way of breaking up the ordinariness of our culture, our temporary unions and solidarities, our provisional settlements, in order to prevent our coming together to stop the Plan, our marching in from the borders and the margins in order to claim again for ordinary people what is ours and what belongs where we belong.

300

To be awakened to this common endeavour is to make a draft on 'our resources of hope'. It is to learn what the tragic chroniclers of everyday life and its inevitable creativeness who constitute our literature have to teach about the naturalness of those resources. It is to trust D.H. Lawrence, Thomas Hardy, William Wordsworth, Charles Dickens, when they tell us about the sheer strength of ordinary people, especially the people of the British working class. Williams determinedly joined to them the best men of his own day (Dennis Potter, Trevor Griffiths) whom he could find.

Trust, John Locke counselled and David Hume confirmed, is the keystone value of a polity. Political leaders have together traduced trust in the politics of the world's rich states for a generation, until politics has become a magnet for the filings of contempt, derision, hatred and indifference in the conversation of those societies. Williams battled to keep clean and speakable a language of unyielding opposition to this stinking climate of mistrust, untrustworthiness, cynicism. This little tour of his big phrases indicates, I hope, what it is like to think with and see through his language. It is to agree upon his essential judgements as together constituting the form of life best able to take us forward for another generation, in peacefulness, and in decent recognition of our mutual dependence.

This is to moralise Williams's life with a vengeance; to turn his theory into morality, and to grind a political edge upon his common culture. It is also to do him great honour, to put him in a line stretching back to Mill as public moralist, and with Dickens as maker of culture. He had more than a touch of the sage and the patriarch about him. The Victorian calm and comprehensiveness with which he spoke of and to his times have few parallels in his day. Indeed, this largeness of manner and obscurity of content were exactly what provoked and exasperated occasional critics[6] to accuse him of vacuousness of gesture and evasiveness of argument. The same faults are connected with his powers of self-deception; his refusal to meet the facts of conflict and bitter disagreement (as with the miners' strike); his sentimentalising of history (the General Strike); his invocation of socialism long after that resonant chord had lost both its economics and its agency.

Historical agency is a deep problem in Williams's thought, at least as far as the protagonist is concerned. The antagonist is another matter. The buccaneers of Plan X are easy to blame for the action upon the world stage: Reagan's men, Murdoch's satellites, the drug lords, the gunsmith kings, the still-arrogant scions of the old English ruling class. He had no difficulties at all with the knowable community of his enemies, and ours.

But as Richard Hoggart pointed out about him, he could not bring himself to name a less knowable but still solid presence amongst his nominal allies which had become utterly antagonistic to his best hopes.

'Mobile privatisation' was the best he could do, with which to catch and curse that new structure of feeling intoxicating new working classes and old bourgeoisies alike. That structure of feeling had released a loose bacchanal of wastefulness and happy indulgence across his own country and continent, and even socialists had turned a little giddy with its libations. Indeed the selectively mendacious and self-serving reading of the present which Williams's allies of both the old new Left and the new new Left consistently brought off was an offence done to intellectual life he simply didn't notice. They jollied along with commercial popular culture and blamed everything that was wrong upon such elusive miscreants as élitism, a racist bourgeoisie, and that old stand-by, the Government. Williams, anxious not to blame but to praise ordinary life and its creativeness made the best he could out of private pleasures and their exhilarating mobility and kept up his comradeship.

He could safely ignore the mean-minded enmities and virulent status-competition which, with a few handsome exceptions, disfigure the intellectual community of the British Left. The value Williams himself put on solidarity, 'in the opposition there's only the opposition. That's why I can't be against him',[7] together with the reverence in which he was held ensured that he had rarely to face criticism and so lost the power of collaboration. It is a wonder that his wandering, protean and insatiable spirit did not become any more peculiar and eccentric than actually happened. He kept on writing as some of his contemporaries kept on drinking. That was one of the things that began to go wrong: too many rot-gut reviews and articles. He kept himself going, out of the old disciplined habit and through the tiredness which others now frequently noticed and which had always been an observable attribute of the characters in the novels. Bill Webb, with the ruthlessness of journalists, had seen him in 1986 and said to Mulhern, 'Raymond isn't looking too good; you'd better start thinking about an obituary.'

'Perfection of the life, or of the work'? The work could hardly serve as a perfect œuvre; but then nobody's could; but the life? What was the life? Williams had tried out a surprising number of roles by way of an answer. He took the question with an immense seriousness, the seriousness being part of the legacy; hence his confiding in *Politics and Letters* in 1978 and to David Hare in 1983 that what he was, or had most wanted to be was a writer. But as many admirers agreed, he wasn't very good as a writer of novels, and the protracted registration of his thought in such books as *Marxism and Literature* or *Towards 2000* were hardly the work of a writer as commonly understood. Still less the textbooks he still turned out at prodigious speed – he wrote *Culture* in a trice, and in pretty well the manner of such steady sellers of the Open University lists as his little book on television.

All this production hardly warranted the title of writer and even though heartbreaking effort went into *People of the Black Mountains*, the achievement itself is so effortfully joyless, and even when gripping, so repetitious.

So what is it that commands the love and reverence in which he is held by such a medley, including my own generation of the intellectual Left (and me), and then substantial numbers of the next generation; by the tiny, mocking, endearing, intelligentsia of his own Welsh people; by unexpected cadres of reforming radicals in places as far apart and unalike as Argentina, Singapore, Naples, Belgrade and Queensland; by such leading intellectuals of dissent in the USA as Chomsky, Said, Jameson, Howe . . .? It is an extraordinary, even a rainbow, covenant of stoicism and hopefulness in the face of the future, whatever our new, lavish and devastating capitalism will make of it. What is this one life to them?

His example as a teacher? I think he sincerely felt his teaching as a vocation when he first went to the Oxford Delegacy, and for fifteen years fired such students as Ruth Middlemiss with an ardent love of the poems and novels he taught. He fired up as well the first commando of his pupils at Cambridge, now doyens of their subject. Long before he had left Oxford, the habit of a shaped, uninterruptable monologue held him to his bewitching incantation, 'putting back his head and speaking', so that he felt blindly for paper and for the audience which would heed him, and give him his say. His pupils boast of his having been their teacher; they mimic him fondly; they vie with anecdotes, Raymond with his feet in a mustard bath, Raymond dozing off. There were disciples, sure; but his teaching, as you'd expect, was laconic, practical, rather than Socratic. Or it was in his lecture-sermons, always rousing, sometimes of a force to change your life. But teaching, he said, wasn't his vocation.

If he was not first and foremost a writer like, say, Kundera nor an avowed teacher like Leavis, maybe he was a lost political leader, one with neither party nor opportunity, but with the stare and pride of a Milovan Djilas or a Sakharov. If so, then the moments he chose to make a move towards movement and the issues upon which he struck his standard were not always well chosen. *May Day Manifesto* could never have been policy, had no chance of being taken up by any more than a tiny segment on the Left, was even mistaken about the amount of support it could count on as a contribution to symbolic politics, and was impossible as a body of economic proposals. The National Confederation was worse: mournful, acrimonious, badly organised. Yet with Williams there, people were anxiously turning up to such an unfestive festival, giving it their heartfelt energies and sleepless nights.

The obvious name to give Williams is that of intellectual; an honourable vocation, a rational profession, a public figure. It has much been pointed out, of course, that in philistine, class-bound Britain the very word 'intellectual' can cause either outrage (at its implied condescendingness) or open sneering (at the absurd pretension that the intellect is of as much moment as good, solid business sense).[8] Certainly the term doesn't come very readily to the keyboards of cultural journalism. There was no British Sartre, people say, still less a match for the Frankfurt Institute for Social Research. (After all, when the Frankfurt exiles asked to come to the London School of Economics after Hitler won power, the Lords Beveridge and Robbins passed them smoothly on to New York; no Jewish-Marxist-polyglot-elitist-egalitarian-intellectuals here, thank you very much.) None the less British philistinism was much rattled by Bertrand Russell's fifty years of conscientious objection to mass stupidity. Russell is a start.

Williams once said himself, after the noble Lord had crept out of an anti-Vietnam war meeting in order to send telegrams to Khrushchev, Lyndon Johnson and Harold Wilson, 'Russell wrote to people I didn't even know had a letter-box'. Yet Williams carried off something of Russell's high-mindedness and authority. He too pronounced calmly and commandingly on the great issues of the day – nuclear weapons, unemployment, ecological danger, economic freebooting, class warfare – without any hesitation. Such pronouncements – 'an epoch's end', 'the politics of CND', 'Distance' – took their social cue as precisely as Edward Thompson took his robustly. Someone needed to be saying these things, someone with an idiom and an erudition which could match the occasion, and Williams could and did. He had the self-assurance, the conviction and serenity without which power, cruelty and evil cannot even be insubordinately spoken to, let alone successfully opposed.

Successful opposition to such presences is always rare. The great tradition of a Left-inclined intelligentsia identifies itself as I have said, in feeling and commitment, as well as in modes of thought, with history's losers. (There is something intuitively repellent about intellectuals who, however sincerely, espouse the doctrines of the Right, and therefore of established power, custom, wealth.)

Identification with the losers demands oppositional forms of thought. Williams lived those all his life, and by so doing, as like as not, accelerated his death. Opposition to the class enemy meant for him living from those deep roots in the border country, endlessly pulled up and displayed for self-vindication as they were. Drawing the water from that deep well, he was replenished in his fight against the usual horriblenesses of human society, as turned into the tales of capitalism and cold war.

The happy accidents of class membership, local history, personal temperament and his stern domestic schooling gave him the confidence to fight this good fight, to speak in the right accents and on behalf of others – others, people like us and not like us, not like him either.

The intellectual does this. He – and until very recently it was only he – speaks for others, re-presents them, and a touchy business it has all become too. Williams, untouched by touchiness, spoke largely for ordinariness, against Them, the Thing, the bosses, capitalism, weaponry, human indifference, vulgar self-indulgence, global poisoning, family betrayal, class disloyalty. He kept faith with Kolakowski's magnificent definition of socialism:

> Democratic socialism requires, in addition to commitment to a number of basic values, hard knowledge and rational calculation ... It is an obstinate will to erode by inches the conditions which produce avoidable suffering, oppression, hunger, wars, racial and national hatred, insatiable greed and vindictive envy.[9]

I think he saw that the church of socialism must dissolve itself into Kolakowski's antinomianism. But he saw it veeringly, hanging on to the canker-corrupted tongues of Marxism, abusing the stolid old horse of Fabianism as well. He might have taken to heart John Berger's valedictory to him:

> I want to admit a personal conflict within myself. The artist within me – the story-teller, the poet – tolerates badly what he understands by 'intellectuals'. For him their use of words is (usually) so facile that it resembles lying. At the same time the intellectual within me – the polemicist, the art theoretician, the social analyst – considers that all artists run the risk of pathological egocentricity.[10]

Williams's artistry, lovingly as he cherished it, was not enough to make him fully up. His intellectualism was pulled between loyalty to his best past and to his professional writing, criticism, teaching. Hence his long meditation on loyalties and their proper home.

Perhaps this comes down to a commonplace. The intellectual speaks from a privileged position on behalf of those with no privileges. Doing so, if the intellectual is a Williams, he becomes a celebrity. This gives him his authority. Given his place in the university, and the university's self-definition as an anomaly in the capitalist body politic, his privileges entail the absolute duty to stand up for all those done down, to speak – well – to speak for Wales, and England too, and Britain, even to the world, of what has been so wrongly done, done to the harm of ordinary people, by Kolakowski's demons, 'insatiable greed and vindictive envy'.

Thinking and writing in this way, one cannot escape the anguish of internal exile, so vividly pictured in Williams's journeying back and forth between the Black Mountains and Cambridge. He needed the security and eminence of Cambridge, the familiarity and allegiances of the border, needed both places to do the work and to live the life the work expressed.

So Williams the intellectual was given his peculiar version of a traditional narrative both by his professional observation of his duties ('he was a pro' as Kermode said) and by his refusal of professionalism ('the hired mouth') and intellectualism. His celebrity was such that he was invited in the role of professional expert to speak to his subject on television; his other celebrity called him centre-stage wherever old Dissent set up its platform; his longing to be a writer, his drive to solitude and that clenched withdrawal pulled him away from both, turned him into his father's son, digging with his pen, harvesting with the flail of his antique typewriter, filling his room and his life with the countless odd jobs as well as big projects of the building contractor or market gardener of letters he became.

A countryman, Eagleton said. He laboured at the centre of his intellectual plot of land, giving himself to the production of letters. In his last years, people called to ask for help with their loving labours of literary production, and he gave it.[11] He sallied out to show people how to start off their new building, telling them what, at Oxford English Limited or SERA or Literature Teaching Politics, wherever small numbers of similar jobbing builders were gathered together.

Time transfigured him into an elder, archivist and counsellor of those who would make their avocation of politics into the profession of scholarship without losing hold on the passion of one and the respectability of the other. He guarded the records of necessary dissent, and kept the memory of his people's pieties. His mistakes and his evasions were gathered into this aura, and dissolved. His life became his memorial, unifying the mass of his varied, uneven, copious and rubble-strewn labours in a single, commemorative architecture.

Perhaps he finally becomes Matthew Price, but a much more likable, tough, cheerful and accessible Matthew Price, as well as one who wrote a great deal more, thank goodness. But like Matthew Price, loved, admired, followed, turned to by all those who cherished his work and the example of his life, who cherished his work as an example of how to live.

There is something important in all this about how in our times we use the celebrity as won and worn by those we admire. Fame magnifies, such that the traits and achievements of actuality swell and shimmer slightly, and the actual life behind them becomes blurred. But it can only magnify what is truly there; hero and heroine must be capable of being what is asked of them.

If you tot up Williams's errors and shortcomings, his abrupt withdrawals, his lack of generosity to others in the field, his over-optimism about the Left, they are trifles. If you add up all he did and was, look to his strength of mind and sheer stamina, his courtesy, his massive rectitude and unwaveringness, the ease and simplicity of his life, then the love and admiration he created and held in so many people is the best reason for fame I can think of. Admiration means wonder, and I wonder at him. Love, whatever else, is somewhere love of the good, and I cannot doubt that to love Williams, to trust his life, and to give him his desserts as that rare creature, a modern hero, is one way to turn that goodness into the common good. You cannot copy a man's life; but you can ask what he would have done in yours, and translate his words into your own.

Given these times and his gifts, I don't think he could have done more. I get restive at the sparseness of joy or laughter in his life's work, the work of his life. For someone whose whole attention was given to culture, he didn't show much himself; he hardly partook of the pleasures brought by humankind's long passion to make good food, wine, music, pictures, journeys. He ran a plain, matter-of-fact home (as unlike D.H. Lawrence's as it could be – 'poor bugger', Williams said thoughtfully). He looked out, as we all do, for his children to get on, and he left not wealth but an honest penny behind him.[12]

Contradictions, no doubt. Pretentiousness on occasions, jargon on others. Self-deception, but then you need some of that to keep going at all in the face of defeat, and the horror and boredom of contemporary politics. And he wrote too much, the colossal discipline wasn't worth all of it.

Individual lives cannot make a lot of difference to things, except in the rare cases of saints or tyrants. Williams's life took up a multiple tradition fashioned by his countrymen out of the history and narratives of the nineteenth century. He bent the virtues of his character as he found them in himself to living and extending that tradition. It is a trans-class tradition, incorporating the idealism of English philanthropic Fabians, Scottish dominie democrats, and Welsh working-class radicals. It put the problem of praxis, or how to turn theory into beneficent action, at the centre of thought. Like the great Russians, such a tradition found literature the readiest, most familiar and shareable form of social theory. Work, steady work was its life-defining activity. The value of work lay in the good it might do for others, and the fulfilment it should bring to the worker.

It is not a revolutionary tradition; but conversable, argumentative, polite. It reaffirms the long canon of humanism, as Williams always did, and of a scientific rationalism also, a proper respect for the facts. Madness of all kinds assails it just now, and without the example of Williams's life it would be in much worse case.

Turning away from the end of this life and this book, I salute him and say farewell. People take his lead as best they can. Without that leadership, certain continuities would have to be picked up from much further back, and would be the more attenuated as a result. My biography is an act of homage, for sure; it is also an act of practical judgement. It looks to his lessons, and asks how to live them in the inherited story of our lives after his death. It is therefore nothing if not teacherly, as he was, in spite of himself, a teacher. This was the way it came; that is the way to go.

307

NOTES

1 PROLOGUE: IN MEMORIAM

1 'Behind enemy lines', obituary by the author, *Times Higher Education Supplement*, 5 February 1988.
2 *Independent*, 28 January 1988.
3 *Chronicles: a magazine of American culture*, vol. 12, 7 July 1988, pp. 14–17. All the Watson quotations are taken from this article, provided by Patrick Parrinder.
4 I am grateful to Stephen Heath for the gift of the text of his speech.
5 *Border Country*, Chatto and Windus, 1960, p.327.
6 Eagleton's funeral oration was first reprinted in *New Left Review*, here taken from a collection he edited as *Raymond Williams: critical perspectives*, Polity Press, 1989, p.1.
7 Ibid., 1989, p.1.
8 Ibid., p.2.
9 'Preface' to *The Lyrical Ballads* (1800 edition), Oxford University Press, 1911, p.237.
10 Eagleton, op. cit., p.4.
11 See Ian MacKillop, *The British Ethical Societies*, Cambridge University Press, 1986.
12 *Morning Star*, 4 February 1988.
13 New York, *The Nation*, 5 March 1988.
14 Edward Said, *The Nation*, 5 March 1988, p.312.
15 Ibid.

2 UNDER THE MOUNTAIN: RAILWAY HOUSE

1 *Border Country*, pp.279–280.
2 William Wordsworth, *The Prelude*, Book I, ll. 322–325.
3 *Border Country*, p.279.
4 *The Fight for Manod*, p.98.
5 *Border Country*, p.55.
6 See David Crouch's and Colin Ward's classic history *The Allotment: its landscape and culture*, Faber, 1988.
7 *Border Country*, p.276.
8 Ibid., p.277.
9 Ibid., pp.303–4.
10 *Politics and Letters*, p.35.

11 *Border Country*, p.136.
12 The details of signal procedure are taken from personal observation as well as the *Absolute Block Regulations*, British Transport Commission, December 1959. I am grateful to David Hornbrook for the loan of this.
13 Joseph Conrad, *The Shadow Line* (1917), Dent Everyman, 1956, p.247.
14 In his famous pamphlets of 1919 and 1926, *The Economic Consequences of the Peace* and *The Economic Consequences of Mr. Churchill*.
15 *Border Country*, p.83.
16 Ibid., p.83.
17 I take this potted history from Keith Middlemas, *Politics in Industrial Society: the experience of the British system since 1911*, Andre Deutsch, 1979. See also J.E. Williams, *The Derbyshire Miners*, Allen and Unwin, 1962, Chapter XVIII.
18 Pandy School Log, 1925–1932.
19 *Abergavenny Chronicle*, 1 July 1932.

3 THE GOOD TOWN: ABERGAVENNY AND THE SCHOLARSHIP BOY

1 *Politics and Letters*, p.25.
2 See Rachel Bromwich's edition, *Selected Poems of Dafydd Ap Gwilym*, Penguin, 1985.
3 Wordsworth, *The Prelude*, Book VII, ll. 637–649.
4 *Politics and Letters*, p.28.
5 Letter to the author, 12 October 1993.
6 *Border Country*, p.192.
7 See also *Politics and Letters*, p.30. 'The most ambitious took the form of a detective play which uncovers a social villain.'
8 See Raymond Williams, 'An Epoch's End', *New Left Review* 140, July–August 1983.
9 Philip Larkin, 'Show Saturday', *Collected Poems*, Faber, 1988, p.201
10 See Mervyn Jones, *Michael Foot: a biography*, Victor Gollancz, 1994.
11 *Border Country*, p.216.
12 Ibid.
13 *Abergavenny Chronicle*, 10 April 1937.
14 Raymond Williams, 'Two Views of Geneva', *Gobannion* (King Henry's Old Boys Magazine), 10 January 1938, pp.26–28.
15 Peter Laycock, *Gobannion*, op. cit., p.29.
16 1974 was the date of the implementation of the Redcliffe-Maud commission, inventing the county of Gwent instead of Monmouthshire.
17 *Politics and Letters*, p.34.
18 e.g. the boyhoods of Frank and Edward Thompson. See Fred Inglis, *The Cruel Peace: everyday life and the cold war*, Basic Books, 1992.
19 *Abergavenny Chronicle*, 16 April 1938.
20 *Politics and Letters*, p.37.

4 HIS CAMBRIDGE: UNDERGRADUATE COMMUNIST

1 This is the general argument of Francis Mulhern's splendid book, *The Moment of 'Scrutiny'*, New Left Books, 1979.
2 Q.D. Leavis, 'Caterpillars of the Commonwealth, Unite!' *Scrutiny* VII, 2, 1938.
3 Orrom's film was broadcast by Channel 4 in 1984 under the title *Fragment of*

Memory.

4 Fox as quoted in a commemorative article in the *Left Review*, vol. III, 1, February 1937, p.6.

5 Randall Swingler, 'William Blake: The imputation of madness', *Left Review*, vol. III, 1, February 1937.

6 Alick West, *Crisis and Criticism*, Lawrence and Wishart, 1937, p.133.

7 *Politics and Letters*, p.45.

8 *Cambridge University Journal*, 3 February 1940.

9 *CUJ*, 10 March 1940.

10 *CUJ*, 1 June 1940.

11 *University Socialist Club Bulletin*, 11 October 1940 (price one penny).

12 *USC Bulletin*, 13 May 1941.

13 *Politics and Letters*, p.51.

14 *USC Bulletin*, 21 January 1941.

5 GUARDS OFFICER

1 Angus Calder, *The People's War*, Jonathan Cape, 1969.

2 Edward Thompson, *Writing by Candlelight*, Merlin Press, 1980, p.131.

3 Arnold Wesker, *Chips with Everything*, Jonathan Cape, 1962. p.17.

4 Henry Reed, 'Judging Distances', *Collected Poems*, revised and enlarged edition, Oxford University Press. 1991.

5 Peter Carrington, *Reflect on Things Past*, Collins, 1989, pp.39–40. See also my *The Cruel Peace*, Basic Books, 1992, pp.363–369 for a record of my interview with him.

6 *Politics and Letters*, p.57.

7 Ibid., p.57.

8 Leo Tolstoy, *War and Peace*, Maude translation, Macmillan, 1942, p.1338.

9 Public Records Office Kew, War Office 171, Files no. 914, 4765.

10 *Twentyone* (the newspaper of the 21st Anti-Tank Regiment), 1944.

11 *Politics and Letters*, p.58.

12 *Twentyone*, no.1, 29 June 1945.

13 Thompson, op. cit., p.132.

14 René Cutforth, *Order to View*, Faber, 1969, p.119.

15 *Politics and Letters*, p.62.

16 *Drama from Ibsen to Brecht*, p.26.

17 Ibid., p.63.

18 Ibid., p.38.

6 WORKERS' EDUCATION IN THE GARDEN OF ENGLAND

1 In 1961 Frank Jacques did the same for me, a young schoolteacher, giving me the Modern Drama course in Northampton where I found a sixth former called Jeremy Seabrook among my students, who was both much cleverer and much better informed about the subject than his tutor.

2 The appointment was initially for three years, starting at £400 p.a. with £25 annual increments up to £600 p.a.; see Oxford Delegacy file DES/F/1013, Bodleian Library.

3 *Politics and Letters*, p.67.

4 Admirably restored to its central position by A.H. Halsey and Norman Dennis

in their *English Ethical Socialism*, Clarendon Press, 1988.
5 Bellchambers to John McIlroy, 3 August 1990.
6 John McIlroy and Sallie Westwood, *Border Country* NIACE, 1993, pp.314–315.
7 In conversation with Roger Fieldhouse, to whom I am deeply indebted for a copy of the transcript. The long conversation took place in Hodgkin's house in Ilmington, 16–17 November 1979.
8 Oxford Delegacy of Extra-Mural Studies files, Bodleian Library; reference DES/F/10/3. Frank Jacques, 18 July 1946.
9 DES/F/10/3 R.M. Rattenbury, n.d.
10 There is a brief biography of Dorothy Hodgkin in my book *Cultural Studies*, Blackwell, 1993.
11 To Roger Fieldhouse, 16–17 November 1979.
12 Ibid.
13 Scrimgeour to McIlroy, 22 July 1990.
14 Oxford Delegacy of Extra-Mural Studies, *Report to Congregation*, for the year ending 30 September 1947 (Rewley House Library).
15 'Open letter to WEA tutors'; published by the WEA, 1961; reprinted in McIlroy and Westwood, op. cit., p.224.
16 *Politics and Letters*, p.78.
17 Quoted by McIlroy and Westwood, op. cit., p.276 from *Tutors' Bulletin of Adult Education*, April 1952, p.5.
18 This letter was generously loaned me by Nicolas Tredell, who originally solicited the late Ruth Middlemiss's recollections.
19 McIlroy and Westwood, op. cit., p.146.
20 *Rewley House Papers*, II, ix, p.15.
21 Ibid.
22 Williams, 'Notes on British Marxism since the war', *New Left Review* 100, November 1976 – January 1977, p.88.
23 Eric Bellchambers, letter to McIlroy, 3 August 1990.
24 John Levitt, letter to McIlroy, 24 January 1990.
25 Jack Woolford, letter to McIlroy, 9 February 1990.
26 Jack Woolford, letter to Joy Williams after Raymond's death, 3 February 1988.
27 Raymond Williams, *Reading and Criticism*, Frederick Muller, 1950. This was published in the 'Man and Society' series, edited by Thomas Hodgkin and intended for extra-mural classes.
28 See *Reading and Criticism*, pp.x, 46, 109.
29 Ibid., pp.123–132.
30 First published by Chatto and Windus in 1932.
31 Each treated by Leavis in his collection, *'Anna Karenina' and Other Essays*, Chatto and Windus, 1967.
32 Details in the Delegacy's *Report to Congregation* for the year ending 30 September 1948.
33 Raymond Williams, lecture in honour and memory of Tony McLean, 17 September 1983, WEA (South Eastern District), mimeo, 1983.
34 *The Common Muse: Popular British Ballad Poetry from the 15th to the 20th century*, edited by V. de Sola Pinto and A.E. Rodway, Penguin, 1965, p.593.
35 Eric Bellchambers, letter to McIlroy, 9 October 1990.
36 *Modern Tragedy*, Chatto and Windus, 1966, Acknowledgements.
37 Jim Fyrth, letter to McIlroy, 20 May 1990.
38 *Politics and Letters*, p.77.
39 Eric Bellchambers, letter to McIlroy, 6 May 1991.

7 OUTSIDE THE WALLS

1 Perry Anderson, 'Components of the National Culture', *New Left Review*, 50, July–August 1968, collected in his *English Questions*, Verso, 1992.
2 Kay Burton, Chatto and Windus files, University of Reading Library, 31 January 1953.
3 Chatto and Windus files, March 1953.
4 Chatto and Windus files, 14 April 1953.
5 See Roger Fieldhouse's short history, *Adult Education and the Cold War*, University of Leeds Press, 1985. One or two people who were members of the Delegacy at the time are of the view that Fieldhouse overstates the McCarthyism with which some tutors were treated. I am very grateful to Professor Fieldhouse also for the generous gift of the transcript of his long conversations with Thomas Hodgkin conducted in 1979.
6 Thomas Hodgkin in conversation with Roger Fieldhouse, 16–17 November 1976: transcript.
7 John Levitt to John McIlroy, 24 June 1990.
8 Williams to Pickstock, Oxford Delegacy of Extra-Mural Studies files, Bodleian Library, DES/F/10/3, 3 December 1952.
9 *Politics and Letters*, p.77.
10 *Ibid.*, p.86.
11 *Ibid.*, p.77.
12 'The Idea of Culture', *Essays on Criticism* 3, 3 July 1953. Reprinted in John McIlroy and Sallie Westwood (eds) *Border Country: Raymond Williams in adult education*, NIACE, 1993.
13 *Culture and Society 1780–1950*, Penguin edition, 1961, p.28.
14 *Ibid.*, pp.72–3.
15 *Ibid.*, pp.65–84. For the edition, see F.R. Leavis, edited and introduced, *Mill on Bentham and Coleridge*, Chatto and Windus, 1950.
16 *Ibid.*, p.81.
17 This is a paraphrase of David Wiggins, in his *Values, Needs, Truth*, Basil Blackwell, 1987, p.106.
18 *Culture and Society*, pp.231–232.
19 *Ibid.*, p.205.
20 'Cinema emotions', as Williams wrote on an essay by an undergraduate (David Hamilton-Eddy) in 1963.
21 Chatto and Windus files, 3 July 1955.
22 *The Use of English*, 1, 3, 1950.
23 A bromide commended by B.S. Braithwaite to his fellow English tutors in adult education. See his 'Adult Education in East Sussex 1940–1960', *Rewley House Papers* III, 8, 1959–1960.
24 *Drama in Performance*, Frederick Muller, 1954; revised edition, New Thinkers Library, C.A. Watts, 1968.
25 This bracing anecdote appears, along with a history of the Suez and Hungarian lessons in Fred Inglis, *The Cruel Peace: everyday life and the cold war*, Basic Books, 1992.
26 See Edward Thompson, *William Morris: romantic to revolutionary*, Merlin Press, 1955; revised edition, 1977.
27 Their story is told in Harvey Kaye's exemplary study, *The British Marxist Historians*, Polity Press 1984.
28 See Peter Sedgwick's florid memoir, 'The Two New Lefts' in David Widgery (ed.), *The Left in Britain 1956–1968*, Penguin, 1976.
29 Hoggart's review appears in *Essays in Criticism*, April 1959, pp.171–179.

30 Graham Martin in *Universities and Left Review*, Autumn 1958, pp.70–74, and p.79. The text on p.79 is long, laudatory and very good.
31 Hoggart, op. cit., p.175.
32 Graham Taylor to John McIlroy, 8 May 1991.
33 Jim Fyrth to John McIlroy, 20 June 1990.
34 Chatto and Windus files, 7 December 1959.
35 Norman Mackenzie (ed.) *Conviction*, MacGibbon and Kee, 1958.

8 MR RAYMOND WILLIAMS AND DR F. R. LEAVIS

1 Dennis Potter, 'Unknown Territory', *New Left Review*, 7, January-February 1961.
2 *The Long Revolution*, Chatto and Windus, 1961; references are to the Penguin edition of 1965, here from p.15.
3 Williams to Parsons, Chatto and Windus files, 12 January 1956.
4 In Peter Sedgwick, 'The Two New Lefts', *The Left in Britain 1956–1968*, David Widgery (ed.) Penguin, 1976; first published, however, in *International Socialism*, 17 August 1964.
5 E.P. Thompson, *New Reasoner*, 9, Summer 1959.
6 See Martin Jay, *Marxism and Totality: the adventures of a concept from Lukács to Habermas*, University of California Press, 1984.
7 *The Long Revolution*, p.64.
8 Reported by Webb in a letter to me, 4 February 1994.
9 *The Long Revolution*, p.316.
10 An argument I put in my *Radical Earnestness: English social theory 1880–1980*, Basil Blackwell, 1982, by way of trying to repair the thoughtless damage done to Fabianism by Williams.
11 *Politics and Letters*, p.133.
12 Richard Wollheim, 'The English Dream', *Spectator*, 10 March 1961. See also Asa Briggs (also from Adult Education) in *New Statesman*, 10 March 1961, and Andor Gomme (at that date in the University of Glasgow Extra-Mural Department) in *Universities Quarterly*, Summer 1961.
13 Richard Crossman, the *Guardian*, 9 March 1961.
14 E.P. Thompson, *New Left Review*, 9, May–June 1961, 10, July–August 1961.
15 Williams to Parsons, Chatto and Windus files, 8 December 1960.
16 Compare Williams's own remarks in *The Long Revolution* about comprehensive schools, 'the soup-kitchen word'.
17 Denys Thompson (ed.) *Discrimination and Popular Culture*, Penguin revised and enlarged edition, 1970.
18 Here, as acknowledged in the bibliography, I depend on Alan O'Connor's truly astonishing labour of love in compiling the complete Williams bibliography published in his *Raymond Williams: writing, culture, politics*, Basil Blackwell, 1989. O'Connor also cites reprints of Williams's reviews in the overseas *Manchester Guardian Weekly*, which sold and sells 30,000 copies per week in the USA alone.
19 Webb to me, 6 December 1993.
20 Oxford Delegacy of Extra-Mural Studies file, DES/F/10/3, Bodleian Library, 30 September 1961.
21 Delegacy file, Pickstock to W. Styler, 8 January 1962.
22 Maurice Cowling, 'Mr Raymond Williams', *The Cambridge Review*, 29 May 1961.
23 John Dunn, 'The Quest for Solidarity', *London Review of Books*, 9 January 1980.
24 Williams to Parsons, Chatto and Windus files, 20 July 1962.

25 *Times Higher Education Supplement,* 5 May 1978.
26 *Independent,* 28 January 1988.
27 'Seeing a Man Running', in Denys Thompson (ed.) *The Leavises: recollections and impressions,* Cambridge University Press, 1984, pp.116–118.
28 Perry Anderson, 'Origins of the Present Crisis', *New Left Review,* 23, January–February 1964.
29 Tom Nairn, 'The nature of the Labour Party', *New Left Review,* 27, September–October 1964; 28, November–December 1964.
30 Edward Thompson, 'The Peculiarities of the English', republished in his collection *The Poverty of Theory,* Merlin Press, 1978.
31 Perry Anderson, *Arguments within British Marxism,* Verso, 1980.
32 Empson's phrase; Christopher Ricks's judgement upon Williams (in a conversation with me).
33 *Communications,* revised edition, Penguin, 1966, p.147.
34 George Steiner, *The Death of Tragedy,* Weidenfeld and Nicolson, 1962.
35 David Hare, *Writing Left-Handed,* Faber and Faber, 1991, p.6.
36 *Second Generation,* Chatto and Windus, 1964, p.9.
37 *Second Generation,* p.170.
38 'Democracy and the Bomb', mimeograph 1965; reprinted in *Sanity,* April 1965.
39 Chatto and Windus files: Peter Calvocoressi to Columbia University Press, 28 May 1964.
40 *Modern Tragedy,* Chatto and Windus, 1966, p.13.
41 Frank Kermode in *Encounter,* August 1966, pp.83–85. See also Stuart Hampshire, 'Unhappy Families', *New Statesman,* 29 July 1966; Asa Briggs, *Spectator,* 10 June 1966.
42 Kermode, op. cit.

9 LEADER OF THE LEFT-IN-EXILE

1 *The Long Revolution,* p.108.
2 *Ibid.,* p.107.
3 Raymond Williams, Stuart Hall, Edward Thompson, *New Left May Day Manifesto,* 8 Elsworthy Terrace, NW3, 1967, p.20.
4 Paul Hirst and Grahame Thompson, 'The problem of globalisation: international economic relations, national economic management and the formation of trading blocs', *Economy and Society,* vol. 21, no. 4, November 1992, pp.357–395.
5 David Hare did; see his *Writing Left-Handed,* Faber, 1991, p.9. For more recent criticism, see Nick Tiratsoo's essay 'Labour and its crisis: the case of the May Day Manifesto group' in *The Wilson Governments 1964–1970,* N. Tiratsoo *et al.,* Pinter, 1993.
6 Draft statement, n.d. kindly provided by Bernard Sharratt, as was much of the documentation in this part of the story.
7 A question finely posed by Roger Poole in an essay on Merleau-Ponty meditating the answer. See his 'The Prose of the World', *New Universities Quarterly,* vol. 28, 4, Autumn 1974, pp.488–500.
8 Institute for Workers' Control was based on Bertrand Russell House, with help from the Russell Foundation, and published radical trade union pamphlets and proposals between 1966 and 1979 or so.
9 *May Day Manifesto Bulletin,* 5, May 1968, p.14.
10 Quoted by Alan O'Connor in *Raymond Williams: writing, culture, politics,* Blackwell, 1989, p.24, but no source given.

11 Michael Rustin, *May Day Manifesto Bulletin*, 14/15, June 1969, pp.3–8.
12 *Report to Conference 20 July 1969*, 24 January 1970, mimeograph.
13 Bernard Bergonzi, letter to me, 5 January 1994.
14 e.g. O'Connor, 1989, op. cit., p.24.
15 See *Politics and Letters*, p.375.
16 Williams to Parsons, Chatto and Windus files, 30 November 1966.
17 The first of which was, I believe, produced by John Eyre at Bedford School in 1962.
18 Text reprinted in the journal *Stand*, vol. 9, no. 1, 1967. I owe a copy of this to the kindness of Charles Swann. Quotation is from p.25.
19 Ibid.
20 *The Listener*, 10 February 1969.
21 John Bayley, *New York Review of Books*, 8 October 1970, *Cambridge Review*, 29 May 1970, pp.198–199.

10 WATCHING TELEVISION

1 Perry Anderson, 'Components of the National Culture', *New Left Review*, 50, July–August 1968, reprinted variously, and in his *English Questions*, Verso, 1992.
2 G.A. Cohen, *Karl Marx's Theory of History*, Oxford University Press, 1978.
3 Gerry Cohen: paper presented to the Free Communications Group, mimeo, January 1969.
4 *The Long Revolution*, Penguin edition, p.40.
5 Ludwig Wittgenstein, *Philosophical Investigations*, translated by G.E.M. Anscombe, Basil Blackwell, 1953, Part II, p.207.
6 *The Long Revolution*, p.146.
7 *Communications*, Penguin edition, 1966, p.32.
8 Carmen Callil, Chatto and Windus files, 7 December 1984.
9 cf. letter to Andrew Motion, Chatto and Windus files, 17 July 1986.
10 *Drama in the Dramatised Society*, Cambridge University Press, 1975, p.6. Reprinted in Alan O'Connor (ed.) *Raymond Williams on Television*, Routledge, 1989.
11 O'Connor (ed.) *Raymond Williams on Television*, p.157.
12 Ibid., p.61.
13 Ibid., p.47.
14 Ibid., p.152.
15 Ibid.
16 *Politics and Letters*, p.395.
17 In a statement to the National Council for Civil Liberties, at a public meeting in Central Hall, Westminster on 14 January 1971 (printed in *The Cambridge Review* 29 January 1971, pp.94–95).
18 Ibid., p.94.
19 O'Connor (ed.) op. cit., p.116.
20 Ibid., p.117.
21 Stuart Hall, 'The Great Moving Right Show', reprinted in S. Hall and M. Jacques (eds) *The Politics of Thatcherism*, Lawrence and Wishart, 1983.
22 The phrase is David Hare's, in a conversation with me.
23 *Politics and Letters*, p.384.
24 Michael Walzer, *The Company of Critics*, Basic Books, 1988, pp.132–133. See also Richard Rorty, *Contingency, Irony and Solidarity*, Cambridge University Press, 1989, especially chapter 8.

25 Raymond Williams, *Orwell*, Fontana Modern Masters, Collins, 1971, pp.78–86.
26 Ibid., pp.92–93.
27 Published in *New Left Review* 67, May–June 1971, reprinted in *Problems of Materialism and Culture*, Verso, 1980.
28 *Problems of Materialism and Culture*, p.29.
29 *Television: technology and cultural form*, Collins, 1974.
30 To Chatto and Windus, not dated, about July 1972.
31 Ian Parsons, Chatto and Windus files, 10 August 1972.
32 John Barrell, 'Real and Unreal History', BBC Radio 3 talk, 9 July 1973, repeated 31 September 1973.
33 John Bull, 'Raymond Williams, his country', *Delta 52*, n.d., pp.26–34.
34 Ibid., pp.27–28.
35 *The Country and the City*, Chatto and Windus, 1973, pp.7–8.

11 THEORY AND EXPERIENCE

1 *The Listener*, 6 May 1971.
2 *Drama in the Dramatised Society*, professorial address, Cambridge University Press, 1975, pp.20–21. Reprinted in his *Writing in Society*, Verso, 1983.
3 cf. Michael Oakeshott, 'The language of poetry in the conservation of mankind', in his *Rationalism in Politics*, Methuen, 1962.
4 cf. Jürgen Habermas, *The Theory of Communicative Action*, 2 vols, Beacon Press, 1984 and 1986.
5 Richard Rorty, in *Consequences of Pragmatism*, Harvester Press, 1982. Jacques Derrida, most famously, in *Margins of Philosophy*, Harvester Press, 1982.
6 'Base and superstructure in Marxist theory', published in *New Left Review*, 82, November–December 1973, reprinted in *Problems of Materialism and Culture*, Verso, 1980.
7 F.R. Leavis, 'Under which king, Bezonian?' *Scrutiny*, vol. I, no. 3, 1932.
8 Willard Quine, 'Two dogmas of empiricism', *From a Logical Point of View*, Harvard University Press, 1961.
9 'Timpanaro's materialism', *New Left Review*, 109, May–June 1978, reprinted in *Problems of Materialism and Culture*.
10 *New Left Review*, 109, p.12.
11 Ibid., p.17.
12 Ibid., p.15.
13 *Keywords: a vocabulary of culture and society*, Collins, 1976.
14 *Ibid., p.9.*
15 *Ibid., p.16.*
16 R.W. Burchfield, *'A case of mistaken identity'*, Encounter, June 1976, pp.51–64. I am most grateful to Valentine Cunningham for this reference. See also Cunningham's *In the Reading Gaol*, Blackwell, 1993, pp.179, 199.
17 Quentin Skinner, 'The idea of a cultural lexicon', *Essays in Criticism*, XXIX, 3, July 1979, pp.205–224.
18 *Keywords*, op. cit., p.126.
19 Ibid., pp.166–167.
20 John Dunn's formulation, in his fine review, *London Review of Books*, 24 January 1980.
21 Terry Eagleton, 'Raymond Williams – an appraisal', *New Left Review*, 95, January–February 1976, later part of *Criticism and Ideology*, Verso, 1977.
22 *New Left Review*, 95, p.23.

23 *Legal, Decent, Honest, Truthful*, BBC debate chaired by John Tusa. Transcription in *The Listener*, 6 September 1976.
24 Steven Lukes, *Marxism and Morality*, Oxford University Press, 1985.
25 Norah Smallwood, Chatto and Windus files, November 1971, n.d.
26 I owe this geographic identification to Peter Hall.
27 *The Fight for Manod*, Chatto and Windus, 1979, pp.193–194.
28 Ibid., p.181.
29 Ibid., p.187.
30 Ibid., p.202.
31 *The Volunteers*, Eyre-Methuen, 1978, p.64.
32 Ibid., p.179.
33 Broadcast by BBC Radio 3, 27 September 1975.
34 'The General Strike of 1925', reprinted in Robin Gable (ed.) *Resources of Hope*, Verso, 1989.
35 Also in *Resources of Hope* and in *Radical Wales*, 18, Summer 1988.
36 John Dunn, *London Review of Books*, 24 January 1980.
37 These letters, never published before, have been given to me with exceptional generosity by Perry Anderson.
38 *Politics and Letters*, p.295.
39 Mairi MacInnes, 'Hardly anything bears watching', reprinted in Fred Inglis (ed.) *The Scene*, Cambridge University Press, 1972.

12 END OF AN EPOCH

1 *Times Higher Education Supplement*, 5 May 1978.
2 Ibid.
3 Ibid.
4 Walter Citrine, *On Chairmanship*, Labour Party, 1951. I owe my introduction to it to Kingsley Williams.
5 *Politics and Letters*, p.371.
6 See Williams's essay on the Arts Council in Robin Gable (ed.) *Resources of Hope*, Verso 1989.
7 Juliet Mitchell, *Women: the longest revolution*, Virago, 1984 (title essay first published in 1966).
8 Rudolf Bahro, *The Alternative in Eastern Europe*, New Left Books, 1978 (published in German the previous year). Williams's article 'Reflections on Bahro' appeared in *New Left Review*, 120, March–April 1980.
9 Bahro, op. cit., pp.264–5.
10 *New Left Review*, 120, p.6.
11 Ibid., p.18.
12 Later published under that title in *New Left Review*, 140, July–August 1983.
13 See Stuart Hall's 'The Great Moving Right Show', first published in *Marxism Today*, then in S. Hall and M. Jacques (eds) *The Politics of Thatcherism*, Lawrence and Wishart, 1983.
14 *Ecology and Socialism*, Socialist Environment and Resources Association, for a copy of which I am grateful to Lesley Aers.
15 He refers elsewhere to Fred Hirsch's classic *The Social Limits to Growth*, Routledge and Kegan Paul, 1977.
16 *Ecology and Socialism*, p.20.
17 e.g. Noel Annan in *Our Age: English intellectuals between the world wars*, Random House, 1990, pp. 266, 268.
18 Jane Miller, *Seductions: essays in reading and culture*, Virago, 1990.

19 Raymond Williams, 'The rebirth of unilateralism' in *New Left Review*, 124, November–December 1980, reprinted in R. Bahro and F. Halliday, (eds) *Exterminism and Cold War*, Verso, 1982. Also in Williams' *Resources of Hope*.

20 My book *The Cruel Peace: everyday life and the cold war*, Basic Books, 1992, represents an effort at telling this whole story.

21 'Distance', *London Review of Books*, 17–30 June 1982, reprinted in O'Connor (ed.) *Raymond Williams on Television*.

22 *Towards 2000*, Chatto and Windus, 1983, p. 139.

23 Ibid. p. 245.

24 William Empson, *The Structure of Complex Words*, Chatto and Windus, 1951.

25 See variously, J. Tully (ed.) *Quentin Skinner and his Critics*, Polity Press 1989; Edward Said, *The World, the Text and the Critic*, Faber, 1984; Michel Foucault, *The Order of Things*, Tavistock Press, 1970.

26 The phrasing of the post as it appeared in the *Cambridge University Reporter*, 21 January 1974.

27 Emile Durkheim, *The Elementary Forms of Religious Life*, Allen and Unwin, 1915, p.194.

28 Quoted by Tony Gould in *New Society*, 29 January 1981, p.190.

29 *Guardian*, 17 January 1981.

30 Christopher Ricks, *T.S. Eliot and Prejudice*, Faber, 1990; *Beckett's Dying Words*, Faber 1993.

31 See Frank Kermode, *The Genesis of Secrecy*, Harvard University Press, 1979.

32 Letter to upgrading committee, 30 October 1979.

33 Letter dated 25 May 1980.

34 Letter to the author from John Harvey, 9 March 1995.

35 The full transcript was published in the *Cambridge University Reporter* for 10 February 1981, pp.1–35. There was a relevant report of the impending debate in the *Guardian*, 24 January 1981; Christopher Ricks made his written contribution as 'In Theory', *London Review of Books*, 16 April 1981, part of a lecture given on 27 February 1981. See also John Stevens, 'The state of the English Faculty', *Cambridge Review*, 1 June 1981, pp. 188–93. I am most grateful to Jill Mann for a copy of this, and to John Beer for a fine letter.

36 *Cambridge University Reporter*, p.18.

37 The lectures are reprinted in a collection of Williams's essays published by Verso in 1983 as *Writing in Society*.

38 Letter to Grace quoted by Leon Edel in *Henry James: the conquest of London*, Bodley Head, 1962, p.505.

39 I am most grateful to Martyn Everett, one of the town's librarians, for ample detail about the Williamses' life in Saffron Walden.

40 David Hare, *Writing Left-Handed*, Faber, 1991, pp.18–19.

41 Eric Hobsbawm *et al.*, *The Forward March of Labour Halted?*, Verso, 1981.

42 Claims documented by a programme made for the Channel 4 slot *Dispatches* by Callum Macrae, broadcast on 23 November 1994. See also Paul Routledge, *Scargill: the unauthorised biography*, Harper Collins, 1994.

43 Williams's words, in an essay on 'community', *What I Came to Say*, Hutchinson-Radius, 1989, p.61.

44 *Loyalties*, Chatto and Windus, 1985, p.325.

45 Ibid., p.364.

46 This case is put with great firmness by Anthony Giddens in *The Nation–State and Violence*, Polity Press. 1987.

47 Carmen Callil to Jenny Uglow, Chatto and Windus files, n.d.

48 Terry Eagleton, *Observer*, 17 September 1989; Terence Hawkes, *TLS*, 22 September 1989.

49 From 'Little Gidding' in T.S. Eliot, *Collected Poems*, Faber, 1969, p.197.
50 *People of the Black Mountains*, volume one, *Beginning*, Chatto and Windus, 1989, p.1. Joy Williams describes the plan for volume three at the end of volume two, *The Eggs of the Eagle*, Chatto, 1990.
51 Tony Pinkney was the moving spirit of OEL and reprinted Williams's contributions in the admirable OEL journal, *News from Nowhere*.
52 Particularly (to me) of the work of the great Welsh contemporary landscapist, Kiffyn Williams.

13 FOR CONTINUITY

1 W.B. Yeats, 'The Choice', *Collected Poems*, Macmillan, 1950.
2 The only one published, so far as I know, and a mistake to do so, too. See *Writing in Society*, Verso, 1983, p.257.
3 A topic very obliquely addressed in his review of Carolyn Steedman's *Landscape for a Good Woman*; reprinted in *What I Came to Say*, Hutchinson-Radius, 1989.
4 *The Poverty of Theory*, Merlin Press, 1978.
5 I am following Williams's old comrade Charles Taylor in his paper 'Self-interpreting animals', *Philosophical Papers* II, Cambridge University Press, 1985.
6 e.g. R.W. Johnson in his *Heroes and Villains*, Harvester Press, 1991.
7 *The Fight for Manod*, p.138.
8 I take much here from Bruce Robbins's admirable *Secular Vocations: intellectuals, professionalism, culture*, Verso, 1993.
9 Quoted by Denis Healey, *The Time of My Life*, Michael Joseph, 1989, p.472.
10 John Berger, 'For Raymond Williams', *New Statesman and Society*, 11 March 1988, pp.28–29.
11 As Phil Stevens testified to me of the help Williams gave to his PhD about Williams, compiled deep in Devon.
12 Probate declared at Ipswich. His estate was valued in two parts (on 13 July 1988 and 6 April 1989) of £88,698 and £20,398 net.

SELECT BIBLIOGRAPHY

PRIMARY SOURCES

Editions of the works by Williams cited in the body of the text are given in the notes. However, no bibliography of Williams's work is now possible without recourse to the fully comprehensive one, including all Williams's journalism, provided by Alan O'Connor in his *Raymond Williams: writing, culture, politics*, and to which I am gratefully indebted. I am also grateful to Phil Stevens for the use of the bibliography in his doctoral thesis on Williams's relevance to education, which he made freely available to me.

1 Books

Reading and Criticism, Man and Society Series, London, Frederick Muller, 1950.
Drama from Ibsen to Eliot, London, Chatto and Windus, 1952. Revised edition, London, Chatto and Windus, 1968.
Raymond Williams and Michael Orrom, *Preface to Film*, London, Film Drama, 1954.
Culture and Society 1780–1950, London, Chatto and Windus, 1958. New edition with a new introduction, New York, Columbia University Press, 1963. Translated into Italian, Japanese, Portuguese and German.
The Long Revolution, London, Chatto and Windus, 1961. Reissued with additional footnotes, Harmondsworth, Penguin, 1965.
Britain in the Sixties Series, Communications, Harmondsworth, Penguin Special, Baltimore, Penguin, 1962; revised edition, Harmondsworth, Penguin, 1966. Third edition, Harmondsworth, Penguin, 1976. Translated into Danish and Spanish.
Modern Tragedy, London, Chatto and Windus, 1966. New edition, without play *Koba* and with new Afterword, London, Verso, 1979.
S. Hall, R. Williams and E.P. Thompson (eds) *New Left May Day Manifesto*, London, May Day Manifesto Committee, 1967. R. Williams (ed.) *May Day Manifesto*, Harmondsworth, Penguin, 1968, 2nd edition.
Drama in Performance, revised edition, New Thinkers Library, C. A. Watts, 1954.
Drama from Ibsen to Brecht, London, Chatto and Windus, 1968. Reprinted, London, Hogarth Press, 1987.
The Pelican Book of English Prose, volume 2: *From 1780 to the present day*, R. Williams, (ed.) Harmondsworth and Baltimore, Penguin, 1969.
The English Novel from Dickens to Lawrence, London, Chatto and Windus, 1970. Reprinted, London, Hogarth Press, 1985.

Orwell, Fontana Modern Masters Series, Glasgow, Collins, 1971. 2nd edition, Glasgow, Collins, Flamingo Paperback Editions, Glasgow, Collins, 1984.

The Country and the City, London, Chatto and Windus, 1973. Reprinted, London, Hogarth Press, 1985.

J. Williams and R. Williams (eds) *D.H. Lawrence on Education*, Harmondsworth, Penguin Education, 1973.

R. Williams (ed.) *George Orwell: a collection of critical essays*, Twentieth Century Views, Englewood Cliffs, N.J., Prentice-Hall, 1974.

Television: technology and cultural form, Technosphere Series, London, Collins, 1974. Translated into Italian.

Keywords: a vocabulary of culture and society, Fontana Communications Series, London, Collins, 1976. New edition, New York, Oxford University Press, 1984.

M. Axton and R. Williams (eds) *English Drama: forms and development: essays in honour of Muriel Clara Bradbrook*, with an introduction by R. Williams, Cambridge and New York, Cambridge University Press, 1977.

Marxism and Literature, Marxist Introductions Series, London and New York, Oxford University Press, 1977. Translated into Italian.

Politics and Letters: interviews with New Left Review, London, New Left Books, 1979, Verso paperback edition, 1981.

Problems in Materialism and Culture: selected essays, London, Verso, 1980. New York, Schocken, 1981.

Culture, Fontana New Sociology Series, Glasgow, Collins, 1981. US edition, *The Sociology of Culture*, New York, Schocken, 1982.

R. and E. Williams (eds) *Contact: human communication and its history*, London and New York, Thames and Hudson, 1981.

Cobbett, Past Masters series, Oxford and New York, Oxford University Press, 1983.

Towards 2000, London, Chatto and Windus, 1983. US edition, *The Year 2000* with a Preface to the American edition, New York, Pantheon, 1984.

Writing in Society, London, Verso, 1983. US edition, New York, Verso, 1984.

M. Williams and R. Williams (eds) *John Clare: selected poetry and prose*, Methuen English Texts, London and New York, Methuen, 1986.

Raymond Williams on Television: selected writings, Preface by R. Williams, A. O'Connor, (ed.) London, Routledge, 1989.

Resources of Hope, R. Gable (ed.) London and New York, Verso, 1989.

What I Came to Say, London, Hutchinson-Radius, 1989.

The Politics of Modernism, T. Pinkney (ed.) London and New York, Verso, 1989.

2 Short Stories

Short story in *Cambridge Front*, no. 2 (1941), 'Red Earth'.

'Sack Labourer', in *English Short Story 1*, W. Wyatt (ed.) London, Collins, 1941.

'Sugar', in R. Williams, M. Orrom, M.J. Craig (eds) *Outlook a selection of Cambridge Writings*, Cambridge, 1941, pp.7–14.

'This Time', in *New Writing and Daylight*, no. 2, 1942–3, J. Lehmann (ed.) London, Collins, 1943, pp.158–64.

'A Fine Room to be Ill In', in *English Story 8*, W. Wyatt (ed.) London, 1948.

3 Novels

Border Country, London, Chatto and Windus, 1960. Reissued, Hogarth Press, 1987.

Second Generation, London, Chatto and Windus, 1964. Reissued, Hogarth Press, 1987.

The Volunteers, London, Eyre-Methuen, 1978. Paperback edition, London, Hogarth Press, 1985.
The Fight for Manod, London, Chatto and Windus, 1979. Reissued, Hogarth Press, 1987.
Loyalties, London, Chatto and Windus, 1985.
People of the Black Mountains, vol. 1: *The Beginning*, London, Chatto and Windus, 1989.
People of the Black Mountains, vol. 2: *The Eggs of the Eagle*, London, Chatto and Windus, 1990.

4 Plays

Koba, in *Modern Tragedy*, London, Chatto and Windus, 1966.
A Letter from the Country, BBC Television, April 1966, *Stand*, 12 (1971), pp.17–34.
Public Enquiry, BBC1 Television, 15 March 1967, *Stand*, 9 (1967), pp.15–53.

Secondary Sources

Anderson, P. *Arguments within British Marxism*, London, Verso, 1980.
Anderson, P. *English Questions*, London, Verso, 1992.
Annan, N. *Our Age: English intellectuals between the world wars*, New York, Random House, 1990.
Bahro, R. *The Alternative in Eastern Europe*. London, New Left Books, 1978.
Bromwich, R. (ed.) *Selected Poems of Dafydd Ap Gwilym*. Harmondsworth, Penguin, 1985.
Burchfield, R.W. 'A case of mistaken identiy', *Encounter*, June 1976, pp.51–64.
Calder, A. *The People's War*, London, Jonathan Cape, 1969.
Carrington, P. *Reflect on Things Past*, Glasgow, Collins, 1989.
Cohen, G.A. *Karl Marx's Theory of History*, Oxford, Oxford University Press, 1978.
Crouch, D. and Ward, C. *The Allotment: its landscape and culture*, London, Faber, 1988.
Cutforth, R. *Order to View*, London, Faber, 1969.
Derrida, J. *Margins of Philosophy*, Brighton, Harvester Press, 1982.
Durkheim, E. *The Elementary Forms of Religious Life*, London, Allen and Unwin, 1915.
Eagleton, T. *Criticism and Ideology*, London, Verso, 1977.
Eagleton, T. *Raymond Williams: critical perspectives*, Cambridge, Polity Press, 1989.
Empson, W. *The Structure of Complex Words*, London, Chatto and Windus, 1951.
Fieldhouse, R. *Adult Education and the Cold War*, Leeds, University of Leeds Press, 1985.
Foucault, M. *The Order of Things*, London, Tavistock Press, 1970.
Giddens, A. *The Nation–State and Violence*, Cambridge, Polity Press, 1987.
Habermas, J. *The Theory of Communicative Action*, 2 volumes, Boston, Beacon Press, 1984, 1986.
Hall, S. and Jacques, M. (eds) *The Politics of Thatcherism*, London, Lawrence and Wishart, 1983.
Halsey, A.H. and Dennis, N. *English Ethical Socialism*, Oxford, Clarendon Press, 1988.
Hare, D. *Writing Left-Handed*, London, Faber, 1991.
Healey, D. *The Time of my Life*, London, Michael Joseph, 1989.

Hirsch, F. *The Social Limits to Growth*, London, Routledge and Kegan Paul, 1977.

Hobsbawm, E. *et al. The Forward March of Labour Halted?*, London, Verso, 1981.

Hoggart, R. *The Uses of Literacy,* London, Chatto and Windus, 1957.

Hoggart, R. Review of *Culture and Society* in *Essays in Criticism*, April 1959, pp. 171–179.

Inglis, F. *Radical Earnestness: English social theory 1880–1980*, Oxford, Blackwell, 1982.

Inglis, F. *The Cruel Peace: everyday life and the cold war*, New York, Basic Books, 1992.

Inglis, F. *Cultural Studies*, Oxford, Blackwell, 1993.

Jay, M. *Marxism and Totality: the adventures of a concept from Lukács to Habermas*, Berkeley, University of California Press, 1984.

Johnson, R.W. *Heroes and Villains*, Hemel Hempstead, Harvester Press, 1991.

Jones, M. *Michael Foot: a biography*, London, Victor Gollancz, 1994.

Kaye, H. *The British Marxist Historians*, Cambridge, Polity Press, 1984.

Kermode, F. *The Genesis of Secrecy*, Cambridge (Mass), Harvard University Press, 1979.

Leavis, F.R. *Mill on Bentham and Coleridge*, London, Chatto and Windus, 1950.

Leavis, F.R. *'Anna Karenina' and Other Essays*, London, Chatto and Windus, 1967.

Leavis, F.R. and Thompson, D. *Culture and Environment*, London, Chatto and Windus, 1932.

Lukes, S. *Marxism and Morality*, Oxford, Oxford University Press, 1985.

McIlroy, J. and Westwood, S. (eds) *Border Country: Raymond Williams in Adult Education*, Leicester, National Institute of Adult Continuing Education, 1993.

Mackenzie, N. (ed.) *Conviction*, London, MacGibbon and Kee, 1958.

Mackillop, I. *The British Ethical Societies*, Cambridge, Cambridge University Press, 1986.

Martin, G. in *Universities and Left Review*, Autumn 1958, pp.70–74.

Middlemas, K. *Politics in Industrial Society: the experience of the British system since 1911*, London, Andre Deutsch, 1979.

Miller, J. *Seductions: essays in reading and culture*, London, Virago, 1990.

Mitchell, J. *Women: the longest revolution*, London, Virago, 1984.

Mulhern, F. *The Moment of 'Scrutiny'*, London, New Left Books, 1979.

Nove, A. *The Economics of Feasible Socialism*, London, Allen and Unwin, 1983.

Oakeshott, M. *Rationalism in Politics*, London, Methuen, 1962.

O'Connor, A. *Raymond Williams: writing, culture, politics*, Oxford, Blackwell, 1989.

Quine, W.V.O. *From a Logical Point of View*, Cambridge (Mass), Harvard University Press, 1961.

Reed, H. *Collected Poems*, Oxford, Oxford University Press, 1991.

Ricks, C. *T.S. Eliot and Prejudice*, London, Faber, 1990.

Ricks, C. *Beckett's Dying Words*, London, Faber, 1993.

Robbins, B. *Secular Vocations: intellectuals, professionalism, culture*, London, Verso, 1993.

Rorty, R. *Consequences of Pragmatism*, Brighton, Harvester Press, 1982.

Rorty, R. *Contingency, Irony and Solidarity*, Cambridge, Cambridge University Press, 1989.

Said, E. *The World, the Text, and the Critic*, London, Faber, 1984.

Steiner, G. *The Death of Tragedy*, London, Weidenfeld and Nicolson, 1962.

Taylor, C. *Philosophical Papers*, 2 volumes, Cambridge, Cambridge University Press, 1985.

Thompson, D. (ed.) *Discrimination and Popular Culture*, Harmondsworth, Penguin, revised edition, 1970.

Thompson, D. (ed.) *The Leavises: recollections and impressions*, Cambridge, Cambridge University Press, 1984.

Thompson, E.P. *William Morris: romantic to revolutionary*, London, Merlin Press, revised edition, 1977.

Thompson, E.P. *The Poverty of Theory*, London, Merlin Press, 1978.

Thompson, E.P. *Writing by Candlelight*, London, Merlin Press, 1980.

Tiratsoo, N. *et al.* (eds) *The Wilson Governments 1964–1970*, London, Pinter, 1993.

Tully, J. (ed.) *Quentin Skinner and his Critics*, Cambridge, Polity Press, 1989.

Walzer, M. *The Company of Critics*, New York, Basic Books, 1988.

Wesker, A. *Chips with Everything*, London, Jonathan Cape, 1962.

West, A. *Crisis and Criticism*, London, Lawrence and Wishart, 1937.

Widgery, D. *The Left in Britain 1956–1968*, Harmondsworth, Penguin, 1976.

Wiggins, D. *Values, Needs, Truth*, Oxford, Basil Blackwell, 1987.

Williams, J.E. *The Derbyshire Miners*, London, Allen and Unwin, 1962.

Wittgenstein, L. *Philosophical Investigations*, trans. G.E.M. Anscombe, Oxford, Basil Blackwell, 1953.

INDEX

Page numbers in **bold** refer to letters or personal accounts.